The Accidental
SUPERPOWER

The Accidental
SUPERPOWER

Ten Years On

by Peter Zeihan

12
TWELVE

NEW YORK BOSTON

Twelve
Hachette Book Group
1290 Avenue of the Americas, New York, NY 10104
twelvebooks.com
twitter.com/twelvebooks

Originally published in hardcover by Hachette Book Group, Inc.
Revised trade paperback edition: December 2023

Twelve is an imprint of Grand Central Publishing. The Twelve name and logo are
trademarks of Hachette Book Group, Inc.

The publisher is not responsible for websites (or their content)
that are not owned by the publisher.

The Hachette Speakers Bureau provides a wide range of authors for speaking
events. To find out more, go to hachettespeakersbureau.com or email
HachetteSpeakers@hbgusa.com. [delete if author doesn't participate]

Twelve books may be purchased in bulk for business, educational, or promotional
use. For information, please contact your local bookseller or the Hachette Book
Group Special Markets Department at special.markets@hbgusa.com.

Library of Congress Cataloging-in-Publication Data is available

ISBNs: 978-1-5387-6734-4 (trade paperback), 978-1-4555-8367-6 (ebook)

Printed in the United States of America

LSC-C

Printing 2, 2023

To Dad

For everything

Contents

Introduction

I've always loved maps. My mom tells a story of how when I was five I unfolded a map of my home state of Iowa and started tracing roads away from my hometown, building up to the thickest, brightest line I could find and then connecting it to the next thickest, brightest line I could find until I had traced myself off the map's edge. When I inquired what was on the other side of the Missouri River, my mom realized that I'd be leaving Iowa someday.

Map tracing turned into backpacking and route finding, which in time evolved into a mixed-discipline university experience involving everything from Korean land reclamation to Caucasus pipeline planning to German refugee policy to Australian irrigation systems and Brazilian port development. It was all about determining why development strategies that worked so well in one place were disasters in others.

Somewhat ironically, I was almost finished with grad school before I realized that I wasn't the only person to have had such thoughts. In fact, there was an entire discipline based on the concept:

Geopolitics is the study of how place impacts…everything: the clothes you wear, the food you eat, the size and serviceability of your mortgage, how long you live, how many children you have, the stability of your job, the shape and feel of your country's political system, what sorts of war your country wages or defends itself against, and ultimately whether your culture will withstand the test of time. The balance of rivers, mountains, oceans, plains, deserts, and jungles massively influences everything about both the human condition and national success.

Of course, you shouldn't treat geography as deterministic. The Nazis *loved* geopolitics, but instead of using the study of geography to shape their policies, they used it to justify their ideology. They were hardly alone. Throughout the eighteenth and nineteenth centuries Europeans of all stripes used the subdiscipline of geographic determinism to assert their cultural and intellectual superiority over the rest of humanity. At one point, geographers as a whole realized that such concepts were, well, hugely racist and the study of political geography in most forms—particularly in the United States—was largely abandoned.

There is definitely a baby/bathwater issue here. There are good solid reasons as to why nearly every major expansionary power of the past has been based in a temperate climate zone, and why all those that have lasted have been riverine-based. This doesn't make the people of these zones better or smarter. It simply means they have more and more sustainable resources, fewer barriers to economic development, and economic and military systems that allow for greater reach. The trick is to begin with geography and see where it takes you; don't start with a theory and use geography to justify it. It's a strategy that has served me well in my life as an analyst, and one that I have attempted to apply to everything I study.

This means that I often find myself drawing conclusions I find unsettling. My personal ideology is green and internationalist and libertarian, which means I'm an idealistic pragmatist who falls asleep during long meetings. Aside from a few snarky footnotes that bravely survived the editorial gauntlet, my ideology is not represented in this book. I have solar panels on my house, but I see a global future in which coal reigns supreme. I'm an unflinching supporter of free trade and the Western alliance network, seeing the pair as ushering in the greatest peace and prosperity this world has ever known. Yet geography tells me both will be abandoned. I prefer small government, believing that an unobtrusive system generates the broadest and fastest spread of wealth and liberty. But demography tells me an ever larger slice of my income will be taken to fund a system that is ever less dynamic and accountable. I am not required to savor my conclusions. This isn't a book of recommendations on what I think *should* happen. This is a book of predictions about what *will* happen.

At its core, *The Accidental Superpower* is about the advantages and disadvantages that geography imposes. How such characteristics interact to create the world we now know. How fluctuations in those interactions are about to turn that world on its ear. How the most powerful state of the ending era will evolve into something far greater in the new.

Without further ado, let's get to the heart of the matter.

Introduction: Ten Years On

Well, maybe not *quite* yet.

Welcome to the tenth anniversary edition of *The Accidental Superpower*!

We have all been on a remarkable journey since I first embarked on this book project. Over the past decade, the world has been through the wringer, experiencing a whirlwind of events that have shaped our lives and altered the course of history. A *lot* of crazy has gone down. The trends of deglobalization, depopulation, and American disinterest that were once on the horizon are now embedded firmly in the here and now. The theoretical hasn't simply become real; the conversation has shifted to the details: How fast will deglobalization proceed, how hard will depopulation hit us, and what will the Americans truly fight for?

Doesn't mean I got it all right, of course. There's no way you kick out a 350-page book that is three-quarters forecast and you get it *all* dead-on. The biggest bitch is always timing. Inevitable is not a synonym for imminent. History may care more about the order of events than the tactical blow-by-blow, but we mere humans live in the here and now and care very much. It is undeniable that China has not cracked (yet) and the European Union is still with us (for now).

I have two things here for you. The first is a very brief rundown of my writings since:

Two years after *Accidental* I published *The Absent Superpower*, a book that brought America's shale revolution into focus both in terms of its transformation of the American industrial experience and its impact upon the broader global geopolitic. As part of *Absent* I predicted that the 2020s would serve as the backdrop of three major international wars. The first of these, the Ukraine War, is now in full swing. Two to go.

Book number three, *Disunited Nations*, popped out in 2020. Where *Accidental* provided the big American theme and *Absent* looked at the globe through an energy lens, *Disunited* is the book for everyone else. Why the countries most believe will rule the future might not even exist in a few years, and who will very successfully rise to replace them? *Disunited* bruised a great many egos.

Calendar year 2022 saw my fourth child, *The End of the World Is Just the Beginning*, released upon an unsuspecting world. You want to comprehend why the world is the way it is? You read *Accidental*. Need to understand the battles for the future? Turn to *Absent*. Want to know who will be in charge and why? Peruse *Disunited*. But if you plan to *live* in a world going through rampant deglobalization and depopulation, then it is *The End of the World* that you need in your life. It is, to oversimplify, the "economics" book. It's one thing to talk about China this or Brazil that or Germany the other thing, but *EotW* dives into all the not-so-little things that make up our lives: finance, manufacturing, transport, agriculture. And it became a bestseller and the audio features seventeen hours of my silky-smooth baritone. So there's that.[1]

Roughly starting at the same time *The End of the World* was making its splash, I steadily expanded my newsletter publication to include what is now a strong majority of videologues. Topics within are as wide-ranging as those within the books, and I've gotten into the habit of recording several weekly. Best part? Sign-up is free and I'll never share your data with anyone. You can get all the deets at Zeihan.com/newsletter.

So that's the content that's out there now. The second item I have for you is, well, what you're about to dive into. So, you've popped for this *Ten Years On* edition. What are you getting for your money?

In a word, you're getting more.

While when I scan back over *Accidental*'s original text I'm broadly pleased with how well it has held up, there have been shifts. Some of my

---

1. For those of you reading the hardcover or electronic version, note that I *did* record the audio version of this project's original text way back when in a bygone era, as well as all the add-ons that are in this *Ten Years On* version.

anticipations have come early, some are only now cresting, and others I've been simply...off. I owe you explanations. On all of them. Those explanations—where I was right, wrong, and why—is the ultimate motivation for this project.

The first four chapters in *Accidental* are putting history into context, and while there is *always* more history I could share, history doesn't change. I believe that what I penned back in 2012 is sufficient for the task of this book. Inversely, chapters 8 and 9—"The Coming International Disorder" and "Partners"—are all about the breakdown of the globalized system, how it will reshape the human condition, and who will join the Americans in figuring out what comes next. This is very much an in-process trend; the Ukraine War, the American withdrawal from the Middle East, and the building U.S.-China trade war are all testament to that. Any update I were to provide now would be outdated in the time it takes to get this revised text to publication. These chapters I'll let speak for themselves.

Instead, I'm going to focus the discussions on the specifics. You'll get a bevy of fresh words from me on the formation chapters, providing updates on the shift away from the Bretton Woods order, the accelerating global demographic bust, how the American shale sectors fits into the changing world of energy, and how everything from the Global War on Terror to the Ukraine War has shaped the American calculus on strategy and trade and the rest. Then we'll dive into the status of the major players, as well as a full rundown on the five fat chapters in the book's third act that detail the crises of the future.

I would be remiss, and a bit of a prick, if I didn't end this beginning with some egregious thank-yous. I haven't done any of this alone. Thank you to the folks at my publisher, Hachette, for making this possible, with special credit to my editor, Sean Desmond, for coming up with the idea of *TAS10* in the first place. None of this or anything adjacent to it would have been possible without the never-ending work and support of my team: Michael Nayebi-Oskoui, Quinn Carter, Kyle Cartwright, Adam Smith, Susan Copeland, and Wayne Watters. Investigating and explaining the world is what I love, something made financially possible by my endlessly demanding clients. And of course it is readers (and listeners) like yourself whose interest in my work enables me to do my thing. So thank you. Everyone.

And finally, just so we are completely crystal, I *still LOVE* maps.

CHAPTER 1

·◦═══════◦·

The World We Think We Know

On July 1, 1944, 730 delegates from the forty-four Allied nations and their respective colonial outposts convened at the Mount Washington Hotel in the skiing village of Bretton Woods, New Hampshire, with a mission to do nothing less than decide the fate of the postwar world. The scores of luminaries included high-ranking bankers, economists, government ministers, and the future leaders of Canada, France, Greece, New Zealand, and Peru. They had trained in overnight from Atlantic City, New Jersey, and were greeted by a sprawling resort in disarray: Many of the rooms lacked running, potable water; there wasn't enough ice or Coca-Cola to go around; staffing was so thin that some nearby Boy Scouts had to be drafted; and the establishment's manager locked himself in his office with a case of whiskey and refused to come out. This couldn't have been how the conference's organizers and lead delegates—Harry Dexter White of the United States and Lord John Maynard Keynes of the United Kingdom, who'd been discussing and planning the conference for nearly three years—had imagined the opening days.

But despite this inauspicious beginning, the delegates set to work on the agenda White and Keynes had laid out and over the next three weeks engaged in multilateral negotiations that were responsible for creating the World Bank, the International Monetary Fund, and the International Bank for Reconstruction and Development: the institutions that helped knit devastated Europe back together and that hammered out the foundations of the free-trade-dominated global economic system that endures to this day.

At least that is how history records it.

The banks and the fund—really, the negotiations themselves—were sideshows. The attendees had arrived in Bretton Woods knowing that they had no real leverage to negotiate or bargain with the United States; they had mainly come to hear what White and the other Americans had to say. And what the Americans had to say shocked them all.

On the eve of the conference, White and the American delegation were fully aware that they had the upper hand going in. America was running the Allied side of the war. Everything from Sicily to Saipan was in essence an American effort fought with American equipment and American fuel. Even in terms of manpower the fronts were largely American affairs, with American troops tending to outnumber all other combatants, Allied and Axis combined, by a two-to-one margin. Only grand affairs such as the Normandy landings featured the sort of multinational resolve the propaganda lauded. In the Pacific, the Americans were carrying the war all by themselves. For the majority of the attendees at the conference, the Americans weren't simply saviors or urgently needed auxiliary forces for ongoing combat missions, they *were* the war effort.

Immensely popular in his third term as president and seen by many as a shoo-in for a fourth, Franklin Delano Roosevelt had indicated that the Americans wanted to discuss the shape the world would take once the war had ended. This in itself raised international eyebrows. Until that point there really hadn't been a "global system" in an economic sense. Instead, various European nations maintained separate trade networks stemming from their earlier imperial ventures, in which their colonies served as resource providers and captive markets while mother countries produced finished goods. What interempire trading that occurred was largely limited to goods, whether raw materials or specific manufactures, that could not be sourced within the respective "closed" systems. Most of this cross-empire trade flowed through enterprising peoples like the Dutch who excelled at brokering deals among imperial leaders. Protecting each empire's trade were its national naval forces, and the use of navies to guard national commerce and raid the commerce of competitors was as old an industry as the use of sail and oar.

It was the naval component that signaled to many of the Bretton Woods delegates that the past they'd known was over. Even if (thanks to American help) they were able to win their homes back from the Axis, they had no navies. Building a navy is one of the most expensive and time-consuming projects a nation can undertake in the best of times, and it wasn't something that a country emerging from rubble and occupation could even consider. The current and future lack of naval power meant that almost all of the delegates at the conference knew full well that their countries wouldn't be able to use trade to bootstrap themselves back to normality, as they usually might. They would, for decades to come, be at the mercy of whoever could offer them security or economic well-being or both.

Keynes and the other delegates knew they were on the verge of momentous and unforeseeable change. But at least one aspect of the brave new world to come seemed both inevitable and imminent: There was about to be only *one* navy. The Americans' late entry into the war meant that the Nazis had been able to destroy the navy of every country in the world except Britain, France, and Japan. Then, to deny the Germans control of French ships, the British had sunk the remnants of the French fleet while it was in port in Algeria. And no one had any doubt that when the Americans (to say nothing of the Russians) were finished with the Germans and Japanese, they'd be lucky to float merchant marines. As Keynes realized all too clearly, the British could still claim to have a potent navy, but it was a subsidiary force compared to the American fleet—and that was before considering that the Americans now had more troops on the ground in Great Britain than the British did. The obvious lopsidedness of the playing field may have led Keynes to write that his American counterparts "plainly intend to force their own conceptions through, regardless of the rest of us."

For French delegates such as Vincent Auriol, future president of France (1947–54), and Pierre Mendès France, future prime minister (1954–55), the sense of relief and gratitude they felt toward the Americans for loosening the German stranglehold on their country must've been mixed with equal measures of disbelief and apprehension. Although they were at the mercy of friends rather than enemies, Auriol and Mendès France would be "negotiating" from a position of abject weakness, and they must've been wondering if their eighteenth-century predecessors had not inadvertently helped to create the monster that would now devour them.

The tension in the Mount Washington Hotel was palpable, not simply because the temperature was high and cool beverages scarce. Auriol and Mendès France, along with the Canadians, Australians, Danes, Belgians, Indians, Mexicans, Brazilians, Bolivians, Colombians, Ecuadorians, Cubans, Peruvians, Dominicans, and others in attendance, most certainly expected White and the American team to take a well-worn page from history and unveil the details of a Pax Americana: how the United States would fold all the far-flung European imperial holdings—up to and including the territories of the European states themselves—into a global American imperial system. It was what the Soviets expected the Americans to do, and, given their pasts, likely what various European nations would have done had the roles been reversed.

Imperial designs or no, the very fact that the delegates were attending a conference in New Hampshire rather than somewhere outside Novosibirsk spoke volumes about where their hopes rested. White and the American team didn't let the others sweat it out for long, and they presented their two-part plan with all the kindness and amused patience that comes from a position of unassailable strength. The first part alone likely stunned the conference into baffled silence: The Americans had no intention of imposing a Pax. They didn't plan to occupy key transshipment or distribution nodes. There would be no imperial tariff on incomes or trade or property. There would be no governors-general stationed in each of the Americans' new imperial outposts. No clearinghouses. No customs restrictions. No quotas.

Instead, the Americans said that they would open their markets. Anyone who wanted to export goods into the United States could do so. The Americans acknowledged that devastated Europe was in no condition to compete with American industry, which hadn't been touched by the scourge of war, so this market openness would be largely one-way. The Americans suggested ideas about a new global system to reduce tariffs, but that was to be negotiated separately and later.

As startling and unexpected as part one of the plan was, part two must have rolled the Europeans in particular back on their heels. The Americans offered to use their navy to protect *all* maritime trade, regardless of who was buying or selling the cargoes. Even trade that had nothing to do with the United States would be guaranteed by the overwhelming strength of the American navy. Far from proposing a Pax that would fill their coffers to overflowing with trade duties, levies, and tariffs, the Americans were instituting the *opposite*: a global trading system in which they would provide full security for all maritime trade at their own cost, full access to the largest consumer market in human history, and at most a limited and hedged expectation that participants might open their markets to American goods. They were promising to do nothing less than indirectly subsidize the economy of every country represented at the conference.

Either believing the deal too good to be true or that the heat had softened the Americans' brains, the delegates quickly agreed, ratifying the terms via signature in the hotel's Gold Room on July 22, 1944. This, however, was exactly what White and the Americans wanted. For no matter how the plan was regarded by the delegates or the rest of the world, it was firmly rooted in the United States' unique strengths: a singular combination of geography, industry, and technological development that constituted the primary source of American power, and that in turn is the subject of this book.

The Deal with the Americans

Over the next year World War II reached its conclusion. Nazi Germany and Imperial Japan were crushed. American troops guarded Western Europe's borders with the Soviet Empire. While American aid helped get Western Europe back on its feet, it was American markets' absorption of every bolt, table, and car that the Western Europeans could produce that proved to be the determining factor in resuscitating their fortunes. The American economy, never touched by the bombs that devastated Europe, was larger than any that the Europeans had ever had entry to, and the ability to access that market allowed the Europeans to export their way back to affluence.

In the early years, the cost levied upon the Americans by the Bretton Woods system was easily managed. Europe was in shambles and America was economically robust. Accepting European exports without question was only a few notches above charity. But as Europe recovered, the price grew. And that was just the beginning. The Americans didn't limit the deals made at Bretton Woods solely to their allies. The terms of the agreements were steadily expanded to countries not at the conference, to former colonies that became independent, to the defeated Axis powers, and in time to countries that were once pernicious rivals.

As more countries signed on, the price of the system continued to grow. As the Cold War ended and entire swaths of the globe changed economic and political orientations, the price grew, and as years turned to decades, the system expanded ever outward, until nearly the entire world had acceded to this American-guaranteed network. In fact, the Bretton Woods agreements are the single most important factor behind the Japanese and Korean miracles, the European Economic Community and its successor the European Union, the rise of China...and the statistical monster that is the U.S. trade deficit.

But many questions remain. Why did the Americans buck history and offer this deal rather than take a more direct role in global leadership, as the major powers before them had done? How did the Americans get so... *huge* that they could offer such a deal in the first place? More to the point, why did the Americans put themselves at such an economic disadvantage in order to offer it? Given that economic disadvantage, why are the Americans *still* offering this deal, seven decades after the war ended? Finally, just how strong is American commitment to the economically disadvantageous system that makes the contemporary world possible?

These are the questions that frame the contemporary world. This book is about the answers to these questions and the future they lead to.

As unhinged and precarious as Keynes and the other delegates must have felt their world had become by July 1944, it is striking how little has changed in the international system in the decades since. At Bretton Woods the United States produced about one-quarter of global GDP, about the same proportion as it does in 2014. At Bretton Woods the United States was responsible for nearly half of global defense outlays, about the same proportion as in 2014. At Bretton Woods the American military controlled half of global naval tonnage, about the same proportion as it does in 2014. At Bretton Woods the United States was the only country that for the past eighty years had exited every decade with an economy larger than when it had entered, a record of the modern age that the Americans have since extended to 150 years. Courtesy of the devastation and disruption of World War II, the United States had been catapulted forward to constitute the world's second oldest continuous government, a title it still holds in 2014.[1] At the time of Bretton Woods, the Americans were the only country in the world that hadn't had foreign boots on its soil in over a century, a record it continues to hold to the present day.

Most readers are probably unaware of the robustness and stability of this record. Some may be wondering how this record meshes with the conventional contemporary wisdom that the United States' best days are behind it. The conventional contemporary wisdom isn't simply wrong, it's laughably so. In 2014, we're not witnessing the beginning of the end of American power, but the end of its beginning. In fact, we're on the cusp of a shift in the international order just as profound as those delegates back in 1944 experienced. The free trade era Bretton Woods created is winding toward an unceremonious end. But there is no grand plan, no great conspiracy. Impersonal factors beyond our control are not only tearing down the world we think we know, but also haphazardly putting a new one in its place.

I've divided this book into four parts. The first, chapters 2 through 4, deals with how geography shapes international interactions, primarily focusing on what makes some countries more powerful than others and ultimately what makes the United States more powerful than all. In the second section, chapters 5 through 7, we'll dive into the current moment of history and break down trends that are all—independently—coming to a head. We'll see how they are all far past critical mass, and are now irresistible, even accidental. We'll revisit Bretton Woods in a new context, as well as address the world's demographic time bombs and the emergence of the shale industry as a major international factor.

The remainder of the book is reserved for the future. In chapters 8 through 10 we'll peer forward through the years until 2030, exploring the new world about to emerge, complete with the shape of a greatly revised American alliance system and the major aggressive powers. Finally, we'll

---

1. Anglophiles will be pleased to know that the United Kingdom still far and away ranks number one.

close out with the five crises of the future, the major threats and challenges of a fundamentally new era.

For now let us focus on the *why* of the world as we know it. The premier tool in this regard is geopolitics, the study of how place matters. How rivers lead people to interact differently than mountains. How those differences lead to great variations in wealth, culture, and military strategy. Geopolitics strips away the ideological, the emotional, and the normative (what we want, what we feel, and what we seek), leaving only what is.

It all comes down to three geographically based factors.

The first I call the *balance of transport*. Successful countries find it easy to move people and goods within their territories: Egypt has the Nile, France has the Seine and Loire, the Roman and Inca Empires had their roads. Such easy movement promotes internal trade and development. Trade encourages specialization and moves an economy up the value-added scale, increasing local incomes and generating capital that can be used for everything from building schools and institutions to operating a navy. Such constant interconnections are the most important factors for knitting a people into a nation. Such commonality of interests forms the bedrock of political and cultural unity. With a very, very few exceptions, every successful culture in human history has been based on a culture of robust internal economic interactions, and that almost invariably comes from easy transport.

But note that I called it a *balance* of transport. Long-term success isn't simply based on economic dynamism. Countries also have to be able to protect themselves. Just as internal trade requires more than a little help from geography—well-rivered plains preferably—so too does defense. Successful countries also have borders that are easy to protect. It does no good to have a great internal trading network if the next country over can park its tanks on your lawn. Deserts or mountains are good for such border zones. Oceans are better. It is this balance—easy transport within, difficult transport beyond—that is the magic ingredient for success.

The second factor is the ability of a country to benefit from the package of technologies known as *deepwater navigation*, including everything from easily portable compasses to cannon. In many ways deepwater navigation is simply a (gross) extension of the balance of transport. It adds a series of technologies that allow sailors to know where they are when they lose sight of land, as well as ensuring sufficient engineering robustness so that cargoes and crews can make it safely to their destination despite challenges natural and man-made. Economically, deepwater navigation allows countries to extend their local economies to the global level, radically increasing wealth opportunities. Militarily, countries that can operate on the deep blue sea can keep security threats far from their shores.

Third, there is the package of technologies known as *industrialization*: assembly lines, interchangeable parts, steam power, and the like. If deepwater navigation extended the balance of transport to a global scale, then industrialization put it on steroids. Industrialization is about using machinery both to increase worker productivity and to marry production to higher-output forms of energy like coal and oil, as opposed to wind and water. These changes increase economic output by an order of magnitude (or more). Courtesy of industrialization, vast portions of the planet that had been chronically stuck in a technological dark age suddenly became capable of development. Such is the ultimate cause of the rise of countries like Brazil, Russia, and India.

In all three cases—the balance of transport, deepwater navigation, and industrialization—the United States enjoys the physical geography most favorable to their application. Two facts stand out. First, since the root of American power is geographic and not the result of any particular plan or ideology, American power is incidental. Even accidental.

Second, the United States wasn't the point of origin for any of the respective technologies that created the modern world. Consequently, we need to turn to other countries and other times to show how and why these three factors arose, took on importance, and came to dominate the human condition. Then we'll be ready to explore how and why these technologies favor the United States more than anyplace else in the world.

For the first concept—the balance of transport—we'll have to go back. Way back.

Way, *way* back.

———◦———

CHAPTER 2

Egypt: The Art of Getting from Here to There

Moving things around is hard. Really hard. Anyone who has ever rowed a boat or paddled a canoe in a place where he had to make a portage can (quite enthusiastically) tell you how much easier it is to move stuff around on water than on land, but have you ever thought about just *how much* easier it is? Let's put it into a context that East Coast Americans can relate to.

The Geography of Limitation

Meet Farmer Smith. In the early nineteenth century, Farmer Smith had a small but productive apple orchard in upstate New York. Every fall he loaded his horse, Tobias, with 250 pounds of apples for market, which was all that Tobias could carry over the paths that snaked through upstate New York's hilly terrain. Farmer Smith's apples were very popular; he did well, saved his money, and planted more apple trees. In a few years Farmer Smith had done well enough to afford a cart to transport his harvest, and with Tobias strapped in he could now take two thousand pounds of apples to market with each cartload. Years passed, the weather held, and Farmer Smith's apples continued to sell; with his proceeds he bought more acres of land and planted more apple trees. By the fall of 1825, Farmer Smith was in luck: The long-awaited Erie Canal was finally finished and open for business. Tobias had long since been put out to pasture, so Farmer Smith roped his new horse, Jedediah, to the barge he'd rented in Albany. Jedediah was able to pull *thirty tons* of apples all the way across the state to Buffalo, where the canal ended and Lake Erie began. And thanks to the waterways of Lake Erie, Farmer Smith could now sell his apples as far away as Detroit.

Almost two centuries later the proportions in the above example have barely budged. In fact, all that's changed is that "horse power" has been replaced with "horsepower." Modern container ships can transport goods for about net 17 cents per container-mile, compared to semi-trailer trucks that do it for net $2.40, including the cost of the locomotion mode as well as operating costs in both instances. But even this incredible disparity in cost assumes access to an American-style multilane highway, the sort that simply doesn't exist in some 95 percent of the planet. It also assumes that the road cargo is all transported by semi rather than less efficient vehicles, like those UPS trucks that probably brought you this book. It certainly ignores your family car. It also does not consider the cost and maintenance of the medium of transport itself. The U.S. interstate highway system, for example, responsible for "only" one-quarter of the United States' road traffic by miles driven, has an annual maintenance cost of $160 billion. By contrast, the Army Corps of Engineers' 2014 budget for *all* U.S. waterways maintenance is only $2.7 billion, while the oceans are flat-out free. Toss in associated costs—ranging from the $100 billion Americans spend annually on car insurance, to the $130 billion needed to build America's 110,000 service stations, to the global supply chain needed to manufacture and service road vehicles—and the practical ratio of road to water transport inflates to anywhere from 40:1 in populated flatlands to in excess of 70:1 in sparsely populated highlands.

Cheap, easy transport does two things for you. First, it makes you a lot of money. Cheap transport means you can send your goods farther away in search of more profitable markets. Historically that's been not only a primary means of capital generation, but also a method of making money wholly independent of government policy or whatever the new economic fad happens to be; it works with oil, grain, people, and widgets. In business terms, it's a reliable perennial. Second, if it is easy to shuttle goods and people around, goods and people will get shuttled around quite a bit. Cheap riverine transport grants loads of personal exposure to the concerns of others in the system, helping to ensure that everyone on the waterway network sees themselves as all in the same boat (often literally). That constant interaction helps a country solidify its identity and political unity in a way that no other geographic feature can.

Until modern times, any particular person's world was a pretty small place. This was a simple matter of physics. The wheel eased overland travel, but carting your stuff across endless stretches of land took a lot of energy—so much energy that it was nearly unheard of for people to get their food from more than a few miles away. Anyone who spent his day lugging food wasn't spending his day growing it. Nearly all the work had to be done with muscle power, so the excess food produced per farm was very low. In the era before refrigeration and preservatives, hauling foodstuffs more than a few miles would have been an exercise in futility. Even armies didn't have much in the way of self-managed supply chains right up into the eighteenth century. Instead militaries relied on the kindness—or lack of defenses—of strangers for provisions.

This kept cities small. Very small. In fact, up until the very beginning of the industrial era in the early 1600s, all of the global cities that we think of as epic—New York City, London, Paris, Berlin, Rome, Tokyo, Shanghai—took up less than eight square miles. That's a square less than three miles on a side, about the distance that someone carrying a heavy load can cover in two hours, far smaller than most modern airports. If the cities had been any bigger, people wouldn't have been able to get their food home and still have sufficient time to do anything else. The surrounding farms couldn't have generated enough surplus food to keep the city from starving, even in times of peace. The same goes for civil administration. If the tax man, policeman, and garbage man couldn't physically service the territory effectively, then there was no government, no services, and no ability to protect civilians from the dangers of the outside world. Those cultures that tried to grow their cities larger than this natural limit found that famine and cholera returned them to the eight-square-mile size with all the speed and delicacy of, well, famine and cholera.

This smallness is why it took humanity millennia to evolve into what we now think of as the modern world. Nearly all of the population had to be involved in agriculture simply to feed itself. The minority was nonsedentary peoples (history calls them barbarians), who discovered that one of the few ways to avoid needing to spend your entire day growing food was to spend your entire day stealing other people's. The only way for the farmers to survive was to have some of their own ranks become soldiers and guard against the barbarians, or become engineers to build defensive works. But those who were not farming still had to be fed. Hitting a balance that would grant both security and full bellies was difficult, if not impossible, in most locations. Urbanization—which, considering the era, typically meant a few families building their huts near each other—was rare and temporary, and the global population remained low for eons. Historians often debate what to call this age, with some form of "precivilized" normally winning out. I refer to this age much more directly: when life sucked.

Location, Location, Location

Approximately eight thousand years ago, however, things started to change. Around 6000 BC, a few tribes had relocated out of the savannah of contemporary Sudan into the floodplains of the Nile. This was not a decision to be made lightly. At the time all settlements that engaged in farming did so as a supplement to hunting and gathering, not the other way around. The savannah's wide-open ranges were game-rich and offered robust supplies of fruits, nuts, and roots. The lower Nile, in contrast, flowed through the desert. The maximum width of green lands was no more than the floodplain—at most single digits in miles—and seasonal floods stripped most of the floodplain free of the sorts of mature vegetation that could support animals in numbers, humans included. After the floods the result was a muddy, denuded moonscape, which quickly cooked into a cracked, baked plain. Turning the Nile into a breadbasket would require centuries of backbreaking labor to store water for the dry season, rebreak and retill fields that would wash away in every flood season.

Yet for the lower Nile's early inhabitants, all that work was worth it. The Nile provided two things nearly unique on earth. The first was perfect agricultural inputs like reliable water and high-fertility soil. It wasn't scant desert rainfall that gave rise to the mighty Nile, but instead the seasonal torrents from the Ethiopian highlands and overflow from the African Great Lakes. The seasonal floods washed down soil of fertility far higher than what could be obtained outside the river valley. The Nile was flush with water supplies every year in a cycle so reliable that true droughts were quite literally biblical events.

Perhaps more important was the second factor: The lower Nile was safe. One could stand on the ridges above the Nile floodplain at any point within a thousand miles of the sea, look east or west, and be met with the exact same view: an endless desert waste. With the technology of transport largely limited to what you could carry yourself, it was simply impossible for any hostile force to cross the desert. Which meant that it was nearly impossible for anyone—whether in the form of lions or barbarians—to reach the lower Nile. It was one of the few places in the world where there was enough water to survive, and enough security to thrive.

This combination of factors—high soil fertility, water supplies independent of (and therefore more reliable than) local rainfall, and physical security—not only provided food surpluses, but it also meant that even with a permanent guard there was still a surplus of labor. That surplus labor could be put to use in expanding irrigation networks (and generating yet more food surpluses), building an army (and taking over the neighboring city and its food production capacity), building walls (generating more security and freeing up yet more labor), or for general civilizational advancements in everything from metallurgy to writing. In short, this specific type of physical geography nearly guaranteed that the Egyptians would be on the road to civilization.

Over the next two millennia small tribal farming settlements consolidated into a series of city-states for mutual defense and to more efficiently apply labor to the problems of taming the Nile. The higher organization and greater labor specialization led to the copper breakthrough of 3600 BC. Copper sounds like a small thing, but once humans figured out how to smelt and cast it, they replaced their wood and stone implements with metal, generating staggering improvements in the productivity of each worker—and each farmer. The resulting population boom generated more and larger cities with bigger and more complex political systems. Allied city-states merged into kingdoms that then struggled for supremacy. By 3150 BC, a single government dominated all of the useful Nile territories between the Mediterranean coast and what is today the city of Aswan. The era of the mighty Egyptian pharaohs had begun.

The Nile was not the only terminal desert river valley to give birth to an ancient civilization; Lower Mesopotamia and the Indus River share similar geographies and spawned similar cultures for similar reasons. Yet the Nile was the only piece of the ancient world that advanced not just in terms of technical skill such as writing and road construction, but also in terms of political organization into larger and more complex governing structures. Egypt also proved to be the longest-lasting of the ancient civilizations, outliving its ancient contemporaries by two millennia.

What explains Egypt's success? Why did Egypt consolidate while its peers remained fractured? How did it so outlast the dozens of civilizations that evolved from it?

It comes back to the first principle of the balance of transport: Moving stuff is hard.

Egypt: The Hard Part Is Getting There

Externally, Egypt's buffer areas were far superior to those of Mesopotamia and the Indus. The Tigris is only rarely out of sight of the Zagros Mountains, while the Tigris and Euphrates both flow from Anatolia. It may be difficult to move things about in mountainous territory, but most mountains are sufficiently high to wring moisture out of the air. Where you have rain, you can have food—agriculture even. Both Anatolia and the Zagros have housed human populations as long as human history has been recorded. As for the Indus, its upper tributaries directly abut the Ganges valley, allowing for regular contact with that—far larger—river valley. Local deserts insulated both Mesopotamia and the Indus from multiple directions, but not *all* directions. Their geographies were secure enough to spawn civilizations, but outside forces were still able to reach them, and so they never had the time to consolidate as Egypt did.

In comparison, Egypt's borders are a class apart. To the west, it is six hundred miles from the western edge of the Nile delta to where rain falls regularly enough to support a non-nomadic population (contemporary Benghazi, Libya). Six hundred miles of dry, hot empty is a long thing to raid across. Land attack from the east was more likely, but that's not to say it was probable. The Sinai Peninsula is just as inhospitable as the Bible suggests, and the three hundred miles between the delta and the Jordan River valley have proven to be a formidable barrier right up to (and even into) contemporary times. A southerly approach seems better, and indeed following the Nile is certainly a less painful affair than trudging through desert. But as one moves upriver south, the Nile valley narrows—to a steep canyon in places, complete with the occasional rapids (locally known as cataracts)—and it is a long, winding nine-hundred-mile route before you reach a geography and climate that can support a meaningful population (contemporary Khartoum, Sudan). Establishing multiple defensive positions along this route is quite easy.

In other words, you *really* have to want to get to Egypt.

Within Egypt, however, things are very different.

Within Egypt the Nile does two things. First and most obviously, it makes mass food production possible. Every patch of land within sight of the river is under cultivation, generating the most consistent food surpluses of any land throughout the history of not just the ancient world, but also the classical, medieval, and even early industrial worlds. This food surplus created the world's densest population footprint for most of human history (the only exception being contemporary Bangladesh).

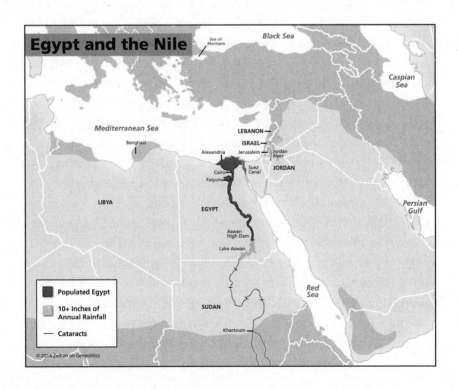

Combine that with the country's desert buffers, and any outside influence that was not an outright invasion would be so diluted in the sheer mass of the Egyptian population that the government would have little problem retaining control.

Second, by ancient standards the interior of Egypt was remarkably easy to get around in. From Aswan downriver, the valley is flat, in the dry season turning the river into a very slow-moving lake. The lack of elevation change results in a hazy, lazy downriver ride, while Egypt's prevailing north-to-south winds allow for fairly reliable upriver sailing. The Nile could support riverine traffic in a way that the Tigris, Euphrates, and Indus—cursed with faster currents, less reliable seasonal flows and winds, and omnipresent sandbars—never could.

The key is the *difference* between the ease of internal versus external transport. Just as the difficulty of external transport inhibited invasion for centuries, allowing the Egyptians to wallow in splendid isolation, the ease of transport within so facilitated governance that Egypt was able to consolidate into a single kingdom more than five thousand years ago. For the first millennia and a half of Egyptian history, outsiders simply could not penetrate into the Egyptian core. Yet within the Nile valley, the Egyptian government had very little trouble moving manpower, resources, the tools of governance, and even giant blocks of stone around within its riverine-based system.

The many braids of the Nile combined with the flatness of the terrain to allow the narrow stretch of Egyptian civilization to be seen from the river. The pharaoh could—and often did—take a boat cruise down the river and visually inspect nearly all of his kingdom without setting foot on land. The current and accurate assessments enabled by such easy travel helped governmental policy to match and respond to reality—a concept that might not seem a major deal in a world of smart phones, but was revolutionary in the world before paper. Tax collection could reach every part of the valley, and such activity ensured that the government maintained a firm grip on every aspect of society. Food stores could be distributed quickly and easily to mitigate local famine; the population crashes and rebellions that plagued cultures well into the modern era were far less common in Egypt. Revolts could be quelled quickly because troops could be summoned with speed; fast military transport enabled the government to nip problems in the bud. In their sequestered existence, the Egyptians thrived.

Sequestered, however, is precisely the word. Just as the invaders couldn't cross the desert gaps beyond the Nile valley, neither could the Egyptians. While everything about the river was core to the Egyptian identity, the Egyptians were never really able to expand beyond it. A grand canal dug from a western braid of the Nile allowed for the regulated flooding of the Faiyum Depression, bringing another five hundred square miles into Egypt's green zone, but that is the only significant expansion of Egypt's agricultural lands until the twentieth century, and even that expansion was only about twenty miles west of the riverbed itself.

Ventures farther abroad were almost unheard of. As the Nile flows through the desert, Egypt—ancient or otherwise—lacks trees. What few were available for boat construction were largely reserved for ego projects ranging from royal barges to monument construction. Reed boats were not just for biblical figures like Moses. Only once in the long reign of the Egyptian dynasties did Cairo make a serious effort to extend its power beyond the core Nile territories—in about 1500 BC Thutmose I conquered the Levant up to the Hatay—but even that effort was merely a fit of pique that didn't outlive the conquering pharaoh. The sheer isolation limited Egyptian knowledge of the world. It was so thin its leaders were shocked when confronted with the fact that some rivers flowed south.[1]

Yet while Egypt was safe on its side of the deserts, pharaonic power—and Egyptian identity—stopped where the irrigated land met the harshness of the desert, a line of demarcation between verdant fertility and arid sand so exact that it could be drawn with a pen. This simple dichotomy—easy transport within, difficult transport beyond—enabled Egypt to be home to not only the first ever national identity, and one of the world's largest well into the medieval period, but it also prevented it from playing a significant role on the regional stage.

This differential also shaped what type of people the Egyptians would become.

---

1. Don't be too hard on them. It was thirty-five hundred years ago and until their discovery of the Jordan and the Euphrates the Egyptians had never *seen* another river except the north-flowing Nile.

Every place that was within sight of the Nile was also a food-producing region, so there was never a pressing need to develop a nationwide food distribution system—that made the maritime transport system specifically, and transport in general, the province of the state. The military and the bureaucracy could move about (and did), but the common man could not (and did not), firmly entrenching the concept of central control. And as we well know from history, the term "common man" isn't particularly accurate. Deserts, even desert floodplains, do not magically produce foodstuffs. Harnessing the river to store water for the dry season is a year-round, labor-intensive chore that requires a high degree of top-level planning and organization. Failure in central planning and organization would without fail translate into famine within months. People were rooted to the towns of their birth and tightly, ahem, managed. Nor did they have options. Every town was an agricultural town, and for Egyptians to leave the Nile valley was as difficult as it was for invaders to reach it. Theirs was a geography destined not just to generate slavery, but slavery of the masses.

It was destined to generate a different sort of slavery as well.

. . . Must Come Down

Necessity is indeed the mother of invention, and for the first age of pharaonic history (roughly 3150–1650 BC) there was neither necessity nor even the ability to compare notes with a neighboring civilization. Developments in agriculture, transport, and education ended with unification. Instead of generating higher and higher food surpluses, or attempting either to advance their civilization or to expand it past the confines of the Nile, the Egyptians dedicated all spare labor to monument construction. They got really good at building really big piles of rocks, but technological innovation came to a screeching halt.[2]

---

2. The mind-set of eternal stability was so deeply entrenched that when ancient Egyptian scholars discovered that they had failed to account for the extra day in leap years, instead of adjusting their calendars they decided it would be less disruptive to wait until their calendar—too short by 0.25 days annually—simply cycled all the way around again, a process that took 1,461 years. When that day arrived, the Egyptian leadership declined to make the adjustment, since from their point of view the inaccurate

But only in Egypt.

Cultures elsewhere—even the ancient civilizations of Mesopotamia and the Indus—continued to exist in a crucible. For them existence was a struggle. A struggle against famine. Against nature. Against each other. New technologies developed to deal with problems that Egypt was blissfully unaffected by. Writing led to literacy. Copper led to bronze. Spears led to swords. Domesticated animals led to chariots. All of these technologies that most people associate with ancient Egypt were not actually developed there, because in Egypt there was no pressure for development past their original technologies of irrigated agriculture, basic engineering, small boats, and hieroglyphics. Even the word "pharaoh" was an import.

In time two of these "new" technologies—the domesticated camel and a sailing ship that could transport meaningful volumes of cargo—proved Egypt's undoing. Outsiders could use these techs to breach Egypt's desert buffers, and when they did they discovered the civilization that all had assumed was mighty and impregnable was in reality languid and backward. They also discovered that Egypt's slave-heavy population lacked motivation to fight for their country. Anyone who possessed the technical skills necessary to defeat the desert was also advanced enough to conquer Egypt with almost contemptuous ease.

Instead of being the greatest of the civilizations, Egypt became an easily conquerable breadbasket for anyone seeking to rule the Mediterranean basin. Once the Nile was secured, the conquering power could redirect the population from pyramid building to food production. The excess food output could be diverted out of the Nile region to fuel the conquering power's bid for Mediterranean control.[3]

The Egyptians first lost their independence in 1620 BC to the Hyksos (commonly known in the West as natives of Canaan), and then were independent only intermittently until the Roman conquest in the first century BC. From there the rule of Egypt is a who's who of the ancient, medieval, and industrial eras: Greek city-states, the Persian Empire, the Great Arab Jihad, the Sublime Porte of the Ottomans, the armies of Napoleon, or the

---

calendar had triggered no deleterious events in the past millennia and a half. It wasn't until the Greeks occupied Egypt that they forced the adoption of an accurate calendar.

3. At the Roman Empire's height, the capital sourced much of its wheat consumption from Egypt.

bureaucrats of the East India Company. The Egyptians never built another pyramid. And after the Roman conquest, they were not independent for a single day until the collapse of the European colonial era after World War II.

All of which came to pass because transport was easy for Egyptians within their own borders but almost impossible for them beyond.

CHAPTER 3

Technological Revolutions: Deepwater Navigation and Industrialization

There are many technologies that change the way people live, but only a rare few that change the way the world at large actually works. The reason is simple: Geography is static. Only a precious few technologies fundamentally alter how peoples interact with their geography. Either you have a river and can trade locally and cheaply and build your regional identity and capital base, or you don't and you remain unaffiliated and poor. Either you live in the mountains and are isolated from others culturally and militarily and have an independent streak, or you're part of the ebb and flow and rise and fall of empires. In the main, these are the ways that geography has shaped human experience.

But there are a few technological packages that have been so successful and far-reaching in their implementation that they have changed the rules of how peoples and nations interact. These few packages have come to define the age of the day.

As you may have guessed from the previous chapter, sedentary agriculture makes the short list of transformative technologies. Irrigation and crop differentiation took humans from the hunter-gatherer lifestyle to modifying the land itself in order to produce greater concentrations of what humans wanted, on time schedules that were sufficiently reliable to allow for settlement. Once crop cycles were hammered out, populations could grow and provide spare labor to build roads, walls, buildings, and everything else that makes civilization worthy of the name. Beginning around 6000 BC, the secrets of agriculture radiated outward from places like Egypt and Mesopotamia, and their adoption created the groundswell of civilizations, interactions, and competitions of the ancient world.

Many of the technologies developed over the course of the next five millennia allowed humans to improve upon agriculture, but none resulted in the fundamental shift in circumstance that agriculture did. Copper and iron increased productivity as compared to wood and stone. Cannon and muskets increased range and lethality and required changes in battle tactics. The details—*all* of the details—changed, but the core that stability and power came from a robust, secure, and sustainable food supply remained. It wasn't until the past half millennium that two packages of technologies, in sequence, radically altered the human condition. But before we launch into the first, it is critical to understand the shape of the world the day *before* the next transformative technology changed everything.

The Ottoman Empire: The Nearly Superpower

Keep in mind the balance of transport: Moving stuff is hard, and moving stuff by water is easier than moving stuff by land. Successful countries tend to be those that boast robust options for maritime transport, but that maritime transport has to be of a fairly specific type.

In the world before 1400, true ocean transport was a rare thing, being neither quick nor reliable nor safe. The problem was sight. Once line of sight to the land was lost, you had to more or less guess where you were and what heading might take you to where you needed to go and hope that you would make landfall before exhausting your supplies, or before the weather turned and the sea swallowed you up. The need to keep land in sight sharply limited long-range voyages, as coastal peoples often had opinions about who would be allowed to sail along their coasts.

In this era nearly all of the major, durable powers fell into one of two categories. The first were powers with navigable rivers that could easily extend their cultural reach up and down the river valley, enrich themselves with local trade, and use the resources of their larger footprint to protect themselves from—or force themselves upon—rivals. The second were powers that lived on seas sufficiently enclosed that they were difficult to get lost within. These seas didn't work quite as well as rivers, but they certainly blunted the dangers of the open ocean and allowed for regional transport and trade. France, Poland, Russia, and a few of the Chinese empires fell into the first category, while the Swedes, Danes, Phoenicians, and Japanese fell into the second.

In this pre-oceanic-shipping era, one country nearly emerged as the European hegemon, largely because it qualified for both baskets and did so in a way bigger than other powers. The Ottoman Empire originated on the shores of the Sea of Marmara, a nearly enclosed sea small enough that it functioned as a river in terms of facilitating cultural unification, but large enough that it allowed for a reasonable volume of regional trade. And Marmara didn't exist in isolation. To its northeast was the Black Sea, while to its southeast lay the Aegean and the eastern Mediterranean—all three enclosed bodies of water that the Ottomans were able to use their naval acumen to dominate. Emptying into the western Black Sea was the Danube, by far Europe's largest river, which allowed the Ottomans to expand as far north into Europe as Vienna. By the measures of the day, the Ottomans had within easy reach more useful land, river, and sea than any other power—and nearly more than all of their European rivals combined.

And then there was trade. From their home base at the supremely well-positioned Istanbul, the Ottomans dominated all land and sea trade between Europe and Asia and from the Black Sea to the Mediterranean.

The largest and most lucrative of those trade routes was the famous Silk Road, the source of all spices that made it to Europe. Pepper, ginger, cinnamon, cloves, nutmeg, mace, cumin, and saffron might seem like minor luxuries today, but their only sources were in South and Southeast Asia. Between the unreliable nature of ocean transport and the yet-to-be-mapped African continent, there was no reliable all-water route. The only way to access Asian spices was for the Silk Road to traverse China, Central Asia, Persia, and ultimately Ottoman-controlled lands. Between the hundreds of middlemen, the sheer distances involved, and the hefty tax the Islamic Ottomans placed on spice transfers to Christian Europe, upper-class Europeans often spent as much on spices as they did on food. In a manner somewhat similar to that of the contemporary Arab oil states, the spice trade perennially transferred massive volumes of wealth from Europe to the Turks.

Benefiting from the most strategic location on the planet, Europe's longest river, three manageable seas, and the most profitable trade routes of the time, the Ottomans came but one battle away from dominating all of mainland Europe. In 1529, they laid siege to Vienna at the head of the Danube valley. Had they won they would have been able to pour an empire's worth of resources through the gap between the Alps and Carpathians onto the North European Plain, a wide highway within which the Turks would have faced no barriers to conquest.

But they failed—because the world had changed.

Deepwater Navigation I: Expanding the Field

While the Turks were making their bid for hegemony in the fifteenth and sixteenth centuries, a technological revolution was altering how people and countries interacted not just with each other, but with their geography. Lands that languished in the old world began prospering in the new. The converse proved true as well: The new technologies transformed the Sea of Marmara from the richest and most secure topography on the planet to a backwater, condemning the Ottoman Empire to a slow-motion collapse.

Collectively the new technologies ended ocean shipping's likelihood of being a near-death (or worse) experience.

- **Compass (fourteenth century).** Never underestimate the importance of being able to know which direction you are going. Extensive cloud cover plagues much of Western Europe and its surrounding seas, particularly from October to March. Being bereft of sun or stars while plying the English Channel, the Bay of Biscay, and the Mediterranean was a risky business, and so naval shipping tended to be seasonal to avoid cloudy skies and the uncertainty they generated. The compass made sunny days less a requirement and extended shipping seasons, for example, allowing Italian merchants to make two annual convoy trips to the Levantine coast to pick up spices rather than one. The initial design of the compass probably dates back to eleventh-century China, but it was not until the fourteenth century that the Europeans were able to develop a "dry" compass. Earlier versions floated a magnetized metal filament on water, making them impractical in anything but the mildest of seas.

- **Cross-staff (fifteenth century).** Once you know what direction you are going, you need to know where you are. A cross-staff is a simple pole with a sliding crossbar that could be used to measure the angle between a known celestial object and the horizon, enabling its user to determine his latitude. A later version—the backstaff (1594)—allowed the same process without having to look at the object in question (which was often the eye-searing sun). In time the technology evolved into the mariner's astrolabe and the Davis quadrant. Combine the cross-/backstaff with the compass, and captains could consult the wind speed to estimate their locations out of sight of land.

- **Carvel technique (fifteenth century).** Dark Age vessels were constructed with a series of overlapping planks held together with pegs. The design was simple, but the ships were both heavy and difficult to repair, which drastically limited their speed, cargo capacity, and seaworthiness. The carvel process instead laid down a frame of wooden ribs to which exterior planks were attached, eliminating pegs completely. The result was a ship design that was lighter, faster, safer, and easier to scale up. The scaling up proved particularly important for trade vessels. Now not only could they transport far larger cargoes, but their sides would also be high enough that even the waves of raging Atlantic storms could not crash onto their decks and founder them. The only downside was that the new technique required far more skill than the traditional peg/clinker vessels to craft. This drastically slowed its adoption, allowing those few nations that commanded the appropriate skill sets to dominate global commerce for over a century.

- **Gunport (c. 1500).** Naval guns and supporting equipment are extremely heavy, and storing them on the deck not only created extreme safety hazards, but also often caused ships to founder. Consequently, it was rare for any vessel to have more than a handful of guns, which could only be stationed on the prow.

The gunport allowed the guns to be stored—and fired—from belowdecks. This lowered a ship's center of gravity considerably, making it far easier to avoid capsizing, while keeping the guns at a remove from potential boarders (you could just close the port). It also allowed guns to be mounted all along the side of the ship, increasing the potential firepower of a vessel by a factor of twenty and allowing a single ship to ruin almost anyone's day.

Nearly all of these technologies were developed, refined, and operationalized by two countries that had almost nothing to do with the Ottomans.

Europe's westernmost peninsula is Iberia. At the time of the Ottoman rise, the peoples of Iberia, the Portuguese and Spanish, had very little going for them. Nearly alone among the major European regions, Iberia has no rivers of meaningful length and only very narrow coastal strips, forcing most of its people to live in a series of elevated valleys. Unsurprisingly, in the 1300s Iberia was Europe's poorest region. It also didn't help that the two had borne the brunt of the Arab invasion, being occupied by the Moors for nearly seven centuries.

But it wasn't their poverty or history that induced them to turn the page of technological history. It was their location. Being at the far western end of the continent meant that the Iberians had to recruit additional middlemen—typically either the French government or Italian traders—to access the spice trade. The additional step pushed up the price even more, not to mention making their spice supplies beholden to the politics of often hostile powers.

They had a stark choice to make: Suffer on as Europe's laggards, or devise a means of changing the game. They needed to find a way to bypass the Ottomans. Bypass the Italians. Bypass the pirates. Bypass the known world in its entirety. Their solution was deepwater navigation.

The newfound reach allowed Spain to break across the Atlantic and dominate the Western Hemisphere without competition. American gold and silver played the central role in Spain's rise to become the most powerful of the Western European empires. Their application of that military power proved critical in undoing the Ottoman position. Spanish forays into the Apennine Peninsula (contemporary Italy) resulted not just in the occupation of the southern and western portions of the peninsula, breaking Ottoman control over the Mediterranean. Spain also put a portion of its long-arm navy permanently on station in the western Mediterranean. The Ottomans, still using pre-deepwater ships, had to downgrade their naval tactics to mere privateering. The Turks found themselves forced to divert massive resources from their Danube campaigns to an increasingly failed effort to defend their Mediterranean assets (most notably the Egyptian breadbasket).

But as potent as Spain was in challenging the Ottoman position, it was tiny Portugal that upended it. Until Portugal's arrival in South Asia, local oceanic shipping—including the maritime arms of the spice trade that the Ottomans controlled—was purely coastal, sailing with the monsoonal winds: east in May–June and west in August. Winds offshore may have blown year round, but they were erratic and local ships couldn't reliably navigate or survive the turbulence. The Portuguese deepwater craft, in contrast, found navigating the Indian Ocean to be child's play. Portuguese vessels were able to eviscerate the Ottoman connections to the Asian spice world, and then directly occupy key spice production locations, via its ships redirecting the trade in its entirety to Lisbon. Even with the

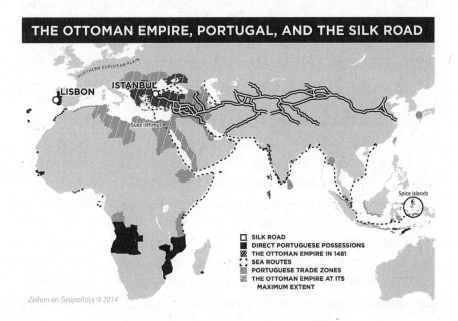

THE OTTOMAN EMPIRE, PORTUGAL, AND THE SILK ROAD

NORTHERN EUROPEAN PLAIN

LISBON   ISTANBUL

Suez Isthmus

Spice Islands

☐ SILK ROAD
■ DIRECT PORTUGUESE POSSESSIONS
▨ THE OTTOMAN EMPIRE IN 1481
┈ SEA ROUTES
▨ PORTUGUESE TRADE ZONES
▨ THE OTTOMAN EMPIRE AT ITS
   MAXIMUM EXTENT

Zeihan on Geopolitics © 2014

military cost of maintaining a transcontinental empire and the twenty-two-thousand-mile round trips factored in, the price of spices in Portugal dropped by 90 percent. The Silk Road and its Ottoman terminus lost cohesion, and the robust income stream that had helped make the Ottoman Empire the big kid on the block simply stopped, all because of the ambitions of a country less than one-twelfth its size.

In one brief century (the sixteenth), Iberia shot forward from being Europe's laggards to its leading economic and military powers. But like the Turks before them, the Iberians' very success set events into motion that would strip them of their empires and wealth. Unlike geography, technology *can* move, and it keeps moving until it settles in a geography that can make the best use of it. Just as agriculture didn't remain hidden in Egypt, the deepwater technologies that allowed the Iberians to overturn Ottoman power diffused out of far western Europe. It should come as no surprise that in time the deepwater technologies diffused from the previously landbound Iberians to a people who were already quite at home on the water.

Deepwater Navigation II: England's Rise

Since they were islanders, it shouldn't come as a major shock that a good portion of the English knew their way around a boat. But what truly set the English apart from Europe's (many) other maritime cultures was the body of water those boats had to deal with. The bulk of English life resides in the southeastern quadrant of Great Britain, in the general vicinity of the Thames River. The Thames provided all of the unification and local trade opportunities of Europe's other rivers, but it empties into the North Sea, one of the world's most dangerous bodies of water, frigid, tidal-extreme, and storm-wracked. There is no day where you dare bring your B game on the North Sea, as the Spanish discovered in 1588 when it wrecked over half their armada in their failed invasion of England. The severity of the North Sea is the quintessential example of why it took so long for humans to master the oceans, and it was in this crucible that the English naval tradition was forged.

Navies offer a flexibility that no land-bound powers can match, and their especially skilled and potent navy gave the English an unmatched advantage in the European competition for supremacy. England's maritime acumen enabled it to nimbly switch trade partners at will, keeping it an economic step ahead of all competitors. Its navy let it land forces at the times and places of its choosing, keeping it a military step ahead of all competitors. And its ability to easily relocate military and economic pressure made it the ally of choice for any European power that it was not currently in conflict with.

And that was *before* the English learned the Iberian secrets of deepwater navigation. *With* deepwater technologies, England leveraged its superior maritime acumen onto the global stage. Bit by bit, the better-skilled English navy reached out across the world and seized control of the Iberian trade network. Between 1600 and 1800, South Asia and the Far East were removed forcibly from the Portuguese sphere of influence. English colonies steadily supplanted their competitors at key locations in Gambia, Nigeria, South Africa, Diego Garcia, India, Singapore, and Hong Kong, relegating the time of Portuguese greatness to history.

The faster and more maneuverable vessels of the English allowed them to raid deep into the Caribbean while denying the Spanish treasure fleets the "safety" of the open seas, leaving the Spanish with no choice but to put their coastal colonies on security lockdown and to assign naval assets to protect convoys. It quickly became obvious that the only locations the Spanish would be able to derive long-term income from were those that they had directly colonized with populations sufficient to resist English attacks. In response, the English founded a series of their own colonies in the New World to start the ball rolling on a demographic overthrow of Spanish power in the Western Hemisphere.

The most lasting impact of the deepwater revolution, however, wasn't the shifting of the spice trade, the fall of the Ottomans, or even the rise of the English/British Empire. It was the transformation of the ocean from a death sentence to a sort of giant river. Deepwater navigation cracked the world open, launching the Age of Discovery, which in turn condensed the world both culturally and economically. Ships capable of making round-the-world voyages made every significant culture aware of the others. Those ships' cargo capacity enabled every previously sequestered river valley to trade with all of the others. Interaction, whether peaceful or hostile, trade or war, was no longer local but global.

It was an age custom built for a culture as maritime-oriented as the

English, and they crafted an empire greater in reach or wealth than any that preceded them. They emerged as the dominant global power, able to impose economic and military realities on cultures as varied as Northern Europe, southern China, the Indian subcontinent, and throughout the Arab world. Just as the Ottomans had done before them, the English seemed likely to extend their mastery of the seas and globe-spanning empire into something permanent.

But they failed too. Just as with sedentary agriculture and deepwater navigation, a new suite of technologies changed the rules of how the world worked. Ironically, the technologies that ended English dominance were homegrown.

As an island nation, the English didn't have need for as potent an army as the mainland empires, so the crown of England was not as absolute as the Iberian monarchies. There were many interests—political, economic, and even military—that coexisted with the government. When the time came for the English to start challenging the Iberian imperial systems, state assets alone were insufficient to the task. The crown had to mobilize not just its own forces, but the forces of its various aristocrats and businessmen as well. Royal dispensation was granted to a variety of private players—the most famous of which was the East India Company, launched in 1600—to pursue various interests for the greater good of the English nation.

When the profits from English successes started flooding home, they didn't just go to the royal coffers but also found their way into the pockets of any number of stakeholders, and each used the newfound financial resources in his own way. Unlike the Iberian monarchs, the English businessmen saw more in the wider world than just spices and precious metals. They also saw bottomless markets. The English system, therefore, didn't seek (just) simple plunder, but also to develop a global trade system with England at the center. Unlike deepwater navigation, which developed in response to the economic need, industrialization was an outgrowth of *opportunity*.

The diverse interests of the English system, the sudden and continuous onrush of wealth that came from the expanding empire, and the still-building shift from superstition and tradition to reasoning and scientific inquiry that began with the Renaissance led to a new sort of technological revolution: an industrial revolution.

Industrialization I: Manufacturing a New World

In the preindustrial world everything had to be powered by muscle, wind, or water. That is a trifecta of restrictions on the human condition. Work could only be done where there was muscle, wind, or water to be had, and then only to the degree that the muscle, wind, or water could support it. Most important, you couldn't just import muscle, wind, or water to a location that had none: A civilization wouldn't take root or flourish without being able to support a population of sufficient size. That largely eliminated desert, steppe, jungle, and mountain climates from approaching the degree of wealth and development that the Europeans had achieved. Deepwater navigation (vastly) reduced long-haul transport costs and allowed the European empires to nibble at the edges of this problem a bit, but at the end of the day it was still a contest between areas with easily navigable waterways. The world's marginal lands—which is to say, most of the rest of the planet—remained as undeveloped and untamed as ever.

Industrialization technologies brought with them the potential to change all that.

- **Steam and coal.** In fits and starts over the eighteenth century, steam began displacing muscle, wind, and water as the primary means of power. The first successful modern steam engine was introduced as early as 1712 by Thomas Savery to pump water out of coal mines, thus allowing for deeper excavation. In many ways, the first steam engine was a self-powering technology both literally and developmentally. The more powerful and reliable the steam pump was, the more coal could be produced, which lowered the cost of coal to power it. During the course of the century, the steam engine became more powerful, more reliable, and eventually smaller—and thus more mobile. Coal availability was key at every stage. Unlike wind and water, coal was a solid object that could produce useful energy far from its point of extraction. And unlike muscle, it wasn't particularly picky about the quality of lodgings or food during the trip. The increased accessibility of coal made it suited for developments in power, smelting, and ultimately transport. In all cases,

though, the magic year was 1805. Industry breakthroughs in
the 1780s had matured sufficiently that steel became available
in high enough volumes and strength to be used to build rail-
roads and steel ships. Steam engines became small and powerful enough to power steel vessels and railway locomotives.
Steamships made navigation—deepwater or riverine—faster,
more versatile, and more cost-efficient by breaking the link
between seasonal winds and shipping. Applying industrial
construction techniques to rivers themselves allowed bigger locks so that larger ships could reach deeper inland. Rail-
roads allowed the construction of a sort of artificial waterway
between fixed points. Places that didn't have the natural benefit of rivers or good port locations could now be inland/dry
ports. Constructing a mile of track is roughly the same cost as
constructing a mile of multilane road, but the combined oper-
ating/locomotion costs of rail systems are less than a quarter
those of roadways. That's still double the cost of maritime
operations, but unlike rivers, rail lines could be *built*, and thus
serve as powerful economic engines anywhere flat enough to
support rail traffic. Traffic times compressed from weeks and
months to hours and days.

- **Chemicals.** The two major breakthroughs in this area were
methods of mass-producing sulfuric acid (1746) and sodium
carbonate (1791), the precursor materials for everything from
glass, dyes, toothpaste, and washing detergent to steel, paper,
medications, and fertilizer. In the early decades of the Industrial Revolution, it was this last item that proved most critical.
Just as coal enabled energy to be applied far from a horse's ass,
fertilizers enabled farms to be more productive. If the farm was
on already productive land, this was nice to have. But if the
farm was on marginal lands, a true revolution occurred. Land
under cultivation expanded dramatically, even as the output
of the average acre increased. Between fertilizers and better
transport options, food could be produced in far greater quantities and be shipped far greater distances with only a fraction
of the labor previously required. The far higher per-acre out-

puts allowed many farmers to relocate to the cities, providing industry with an ever larger pool of labor. Another chemical breakthrough—the development of cheap, strong cements in the 1820s, reinforced with steel—allowed for the hallmarks of modernity that we are all familiar with today: multistory buildings, bridges, high-capacity roadways, and city-scale sewers. Between the new food supplies and new construction techniques, cities needed not be famine-ridden disease incubators. Their sizes exploded. By 1825, London was the world's largest city.

- **Interchangeable parts.** Until 1700, all of the pieces of any advanced manufacture such as a musket or watch were typically constructed by the same professional; such components were crafted and assembled one painstaking piece at a time by highly skilled labor, and had to be repaired in the same manner. During the eighteenth century, higher degrees of engineering precision developed interchangeable parts, and in the early nineteenth century the invention and manufacture of machine tools—everything from lathes to planers to millers—allowed that precision in engineering to be applied to almost every industry. These innovations *de*creased the need for skilled labor, and by the early 1800s the first assembly lines had appeared. The durability of finished goods drastically increased because anyone with a part could repair most items instead of having to put it in the hands of a skilled craftsman. Output, quality, and worker productivity all expanded by an order of magnitude in the production of everything from textiles to artillery.

Between deepwater navigation and industrialization, the tyranny of distance had been broken, and the impact on trade was dramatic. Output expanded well beyond the ability of the local populace to absorb it. Had the Industrial Revolution happened anywhere else on the planet, there would have been a market crash as the prices of goods would have cratered due to insufficient demand. But at the time the British (as the English became known after their union with Scotland in 1707) were masters of the oceans, ruling a vast military and commercial empire that spanned the globe. This allowed them to shove all of their (massive) excess production down the throats of any people that they could access via water, particularly within their own empire. The British were (easily) able to cover all of the administrative costs of their empire, the capital costs of their industry, and have huge additional streams left over to justify both a stronger navy and more industrial development.

Just as deepwater navigation guaranteed the Spanish a period of overwhelming superiority in the European power game, industrialization enhanced English prominence to the point of making it the clear European hegemon. But though Great Britain was a geography better suited to leverage deepwater navigation than Iberia, it was not the ultimate European geography for industrialization.

Industrialization requires large volumes of capital to build the industrial base and educate the labor, and then obviously large volumes of labor to work the industrial base. The English had the capital, but most of it was now imperially rather than locally sourced, and England still was at most a mid-sized population. English success was linked to their empire, and while it is sexy to say that the sun never set on that empire, the logistics and supply chains of a system that stretches around the world but is managed by less than 1.5 percent of its population were always going to be unwieldy and temporary.

Just as deepwater technologies migrated from Iberia to a geography that could utilize them better, so too did industrialization. By 1850, it was Germany's time to rise.

The German Pressure Cooker

Berlin is perhaps the best-located city on the planet from a purely economic point of view. It sits at the junction of the Spree and Havel Rivers, both navigable tributaries of the Elbe. Berlin is only sixty miles from the Oder, and the Havel reaches so far to the east as to almost connect the two river basins. This grants Berlin access to one of the world's very few maritime systems that taps into more than one river.

And those are just the rivers immediately proximate to Berlin. Close to the west is the Rhine, Northern Europe's financial-industrial powerhouse, navigable all the way south to the Swiss city of Basel, and possessing tributaries and distributaries that spiderweb through German, French, and Dutch lands. Close to the east is the Vistula—the last major navigable river before the Eurasian Hordelands. Close to the south is the Danube—the longest river in Europe as a whole, one of the very few that flows southward, and the only one mighty enough to punch through the Alps and Carpathians. Any economic hub centered at Berlin is uniquely situated to reach almost anywhere in Europe where wealth can be created. Berlin's waterways dictate that Germany emerge as the heart of a massive empire with economic links to the North, Baltic, and Black Seas, so long as Berlin is left to develop.

But Germany has almost never been left to develop.

Germany's location saddles it with three critical weaknesses that make it an insecure—and often poor—country, despite what ostensibly seems like the geography that most peoples could only dream of.

First, Germans don't live at the western end of the continent like the Spanish or on an island like the English; they are in the very middle of the North European Plain. While Germany's wealth potential is massive, German lands are inherently vulnerable. To the east is a nigh indefensible border with Poland, whose own eastern border is even less defensible. Germany's western border is similarly difficult: Opposite it is France, typically the most consolidated European power. Balkan upstarts often seethe on the other side of the Vienna Gap, while maritime powers can easily harass—and at times even hold portions of—the region's lengthy coastline.

Being in the middle of the North European Plain has made German lands the primary battleground for European dominance as long as the concept of Europe has existed. The Germans directly border six other nationalities: Poles, Czechs, Swiss, French, Dutch, and Danes. Nearby are the English, Norwegians, Swedes, Lithuanians, Russians, Hungarians, and Italians. In terms of proximity to and magnitude of their rivals, the Germans are in the most difficult strategic environment anywhere on earth.

Second, this man-in-the-middle position means that Germany has almost never been united. German rivers lead in different directions to different seas, making different cities look to different horizons for their economic well-being. The middle of Germany—the Harz Mountains region—is akin to having Appalachia between Boston and New York. The presence of not one but six major powers in immediate proximity long denied Berlin easy control not just of its borderlands, but large tracts of its interior as well, including most of the Rhine and Oder river systems. Unlike the English, who established a centralized government in the Thames valley as early as the tenth century, the initial German proto-state of Brandenburg didn't start stabilizing as a country in its own right until the fifteenth century.

Third, Brandenburg didn't even have the geographic characteristics that would suggest it would be able to build a successful state. Whether you are producing wheat, textiles, or cars, *distance* is key in determining your levels of income; the greater your commercial reach, the better you are at connecting your high supplies to someone else's high demands. Put another way, French wine is financially accessible in next-door Belgium, but in Chile it is for special occasions only.

The Germans lacked independent access to the ocean. Germany didn't control even one of its major rivers' delta cities until 1720, when it finally seized Stettin on the Oder from the Swedish Empire. Even then German ocean access was sharply circumscribed. The Danish island of Zealand is positioned perfectly to regulate traffic between the Baltic and North Seas. Germans only got their first full access to the ocean in 1871, when Berlin finally proved able to fold Hamburg, on the Elbe delta, into the German Empire. While the rest of Europe was enjoying an economic boom from the expansion in reach that deepwater navigation provided as early as 1700 (1600 for Iberia), the Germans remained dependent upon expensive roads for transport, keeping them locked into pre-deepwater levels of economic development.

Industrialization changed that.

For the Germans industrialization changed everything.

Industrialization II: The German Juggernaut

Geography does more than simply shape balance-of-power struggles and the flavor of the local economy, it influences cultures as well. Germany's geographic shortcomings molded German development in unique ways.

- **Local government.** If the patchwork nature of political borders and the nonunified nature of Central Europe's rivers kept Berlin from being readily reached for consultation, as was so often the case, then local authorities had to learn to act autonomously. They had no choice but to marshal their own resources—financial, labor, technical, and even military. In a world in which your country had perhaps one-fifth the strength of its competitors, and your city boasted perhaps one-hundredth the strength of an immediately neighboring empire like Austria, total talent capture was a prerequisite to survival. Local leaders and their staff developed excellent organizational skills, proving competent at mobilizing everyone from the intelligence apparatus to the bankers to the academics (and in contemporary times, the labor unions) in order to advance the interests of each particular major city. Unlike most cultures, in Germany *local* government is seen as a high calling, and it consistently attracts the best and brightest.
- **Infrastructure.** The plethora of regional rivers and the patchwork nature of political borders had the consequence that these hypercompetent cities often saw their destinies as lying beyond different horizons or even in concert with rival powers. The southern provinces of Bavaria, Württemberg, and Baden were all part of the Danubian system and as such treasured their close cultural and economic links with next-door Vienna. In the west, Alsace-Lorraine and the entire Rhineland had far more day-to-day contact with the French and Dutch. Despite being packed with ethnic Germans, Schleswig and Holstein were part of Denmark right up until the 1800s. Berlin had to find ways to link all Germans to a common destiny. The result was an incredibly advanced and forward-thinking infrastructure policy that would link all Germans into a region-wide artificial transport network. The Germans had a national rail network as early as 1840—fully three decades before Germany actually consolidated politically, and at a time when the Americans were debating whether to build a second road. The German rail network was expensive—crushingly so—but it was a requisite

for German coherence. As Brandenburg evolved and expanded under different ages and names—from Brandenburg to Prussia to the German Confederation and ultimately into Imperial Germany—this became more, not less important. New territorial acquisitions already had preexisting links to rival powers, links that had to be broken and rerouted to Berlin.

- **The quest for quality.** The omnipresence of competition, both external and internal, required a national government that was hypercompetent at forward-thinking national planning. Resources to knit together disparate populations and geographies do not magically materialize. Canals that link together different rivers do not miraculously dig themselves, and wishful thinking does not protect a small, exposed country from its much more powerful, richer, more mobile, and more numerous neighbors. So the Germans had to be better. By 1717, Prussia already had compulsory education—150 years before England. Germans pioneered the standing army, and by 1740 boasted Europe's fourth largest military, despite ranking twelfth in population. By 1860, Prussia had more kilometers of rail lines than France, despite being a laggard to the industrial era and holding less than one-third the land area. The need for technical advancement was reflected not simply in national infrastructure and Germany's military excellence but also in Germany's social pecking order. German territories were the first in the world to accord equal social status to industrialists and scientists as to military princes; corporate magnates regularly consulted and advised all levels of government up to and including the chancellor and, later, the emperor.

- **Capital capture.** All this national planning to overcome geographic complications required money—for standing armies, for infrastructure development, for education, for an industrial base. That money had to come from the population. Private savings were co-opted into government-linked banks, and those hypercompetent bureaucrats, whether at the local or national level, ensured that the money went where the state required it. This had a wide variety of effects. Most obviously, financing of government projects came first and foremost, enabling German governments to build all that expensive infrastructure and maintain a standing army in an era of peasant drafts. The national government urged the consolidation of local banks into powerful regional banks to better see to state needs, fusing the German financial world with the German industrial and governmental worlds.

Collectively, these innovations allowed the Germans to punch with all of their weight against whatever problem or foe arose, making them a force to be reckoned with even before Germany became one of Europe's major powers. They may have still been the half-pint of the neighborhood, but they were a half-pint with a gun and a doctorate in engineering.

The true power of those innovations, however, was how perfectly they had sculpted Germans to benefit from industrial technologies when they finally leaked into Central Europe.

Industrialization in Prussia started with pain. The British could, and did, shove their surplus production down the throats of anyone they could reach. In the American colonies, this led to revolution. It nearly did in Germany too. The endless quantities of cheap, high-quality goods decimated the Germans' painstakingly fostered cottage and guild industries. Economic depression triggered the revolutions of 1848. Prussia only held together because of its national planning mechanisms and the strength of its military class, which derailed the revolutions and ejected vast droves of dissatisfied citizens.

With their previous manufacturing base dead and gone, the Prussians did the only thing they could: apply the qualitative advantages of German culture to the technologies of the day and develop something extraordinary. As a result, industrialization was different in Germany than elsewhere by a variety of critical measures.

First, industrialization happened *everywhere*. Elsewhere in Europe, the various industrial revolutions launched from the respective capital cities. Money accrued in the capital and was spent from the capital, so road and rail networks radiated from it too, metabolizing whatever resources lay beyond in a system of diminishing returns. But the Germans, down to the most remote provincial city, were uniquely skilled in economic management and had already constructed the base road infrastructure that industrialization required to take root. Each and every one of the German cities was fertile ground for the seeds of industrialization. None were as powerful independently as London, but any ten of them surpassed the English core—and the Germans had *forty* regional cities. As industrialization proceeded, German cities each built their own local hub-and-spoke rail networks. The national government, needing to ensure that the various German regions remained knitted into a national whole, connected these hubs together into the world's first true national rail network. What few regional laggards remained were now surrounded and bolstered by ever-booming internal trade.

Second, industrialization happened *much* faster. Fractured fifteenth-century Brandenburg with no coastline or major port city was a very capital-poor country. Money had to be husbanded with ruthless efficiency. Imperial Germany of the 1870s, by contrast, controlled the bulk of Central Europe's river networks and was awash in war booty from its recent string of military victories against Denmark, Austria, and France. Germany's hypercompetent governments included industrialists on their cabinets, and the public-private pairing ensured that adequate funding reached each and every project that needed investment. Employment, growth, and output all exploded. The industrialization of England took nearly 150 years. The industrialization of Germany was carried out in less than forty.

Third, German industrialization had massive *military* applications. Most European countries' military application of industrial technologies focused on quantity: more guns, more uniforms, more transports. Only Germany truly embraced the fundamental newness of industrial technologies to remake how it waged war. This would have been impossible had Germany not entered the industrial age with the highest level of literacy in the world, largely due to its ongoing need to maintain a qualitative edge over its quantitatively superior competitors. The most important manifestation of this superior education system was the innovation of the General Staff, a sort of military middle management designed to disseminate information up and down the chain of command. A military commission required a college degree. Fusing the expertise of local governments with academia, industry, and finance, the General Staff achieved two things: It encouraged the development of ever larger cannons that the military thinkers redesigned their strategies around, and it pioneered new logistical methods to take advantage of the German rail system. The pair proved a crippling advantage. Europe's maritime powers regularly used the mobility of their navies to flit around each other and avoid paralyzing conflicts. That was hard to do when Germany's professionalized soldiers came hurtling down the rails in the thousands, backed by dozens of long-range cannons, switching not just between battle sites but between actual fronts in a matter of a few days. After three generations of fine-tuning, the world came to know the gentle German mix of technology, logistics, and force as blitzkrieg.

Finally, industrialization *unified* the Germans as a country and as a people to a degree unheard of elsewhere, before or since. All governments got a boost from industrialization. Industrialization brought per capita increases in wealth, health, and living standards so unprecedented that you have to go back to the domestication of animals to find a point in human history where the general populace experienced so rapid and sustained a period of improvement. With rising wealth came rising government legitimacy.[1] For the birthplace of industrialization, England, this was merely garnish; the English were already rich from the benefits of deepwater navigation and a globe-spanning empire. In Germany, however, the legitimacy gain wasn't so much radically different, but exponentially faster and larger. For the previous millennia, Germans had gotten the short end of the European stick, and only through centuries of hardship had managed to scrape together a few bits of identity, security, and dignity. In a single generation, industrialization took them from being some of the North European Plain's poorest people to some of its richest, and enabled them to impose decisive defeats in four significant conflicts with powers that had preyed upon them for centuries (Poland, Denmark, Austria, and France).

In the *next* generation all of the various German principalities were

---

1. The legitimacy gain was so pervasive that Lenin had no luck shopping communism around in industrial Europe. Even under World War I shortages, the Germans were much better off than they had been thirty years prior. He had to go somewhere where the Industrial Revolution hadn't yet happened to find people whose living standards were stagnant to falling, and therefore people who would be willing to try something revolutionary.

fused into a single empire courtesy of the diplomatic genius of Otto von Bismarck, and that empire became the colossus of Europe. Germanic cities that had been unassociated since the death of Charlemagne connected their rail networks together to discover a peer relationship, far different from when a sleepy country town became connected to mighty London. The effect, economically and culturally, was electric, and considering the era, that term is used both figuratively and literally. This was not simply a culture that had finally unified, this was a culture that was ecstatic with its identity and its government in a way that few other cultures have ever approached.

Germany quickly surpassed its competitors in economic, financial, industrial, demographic, and military strength. It was the first country in the world to have the majority of its population urbanized—a critical development to both foster and take advantage of skilled labor in the industrial era—and by 1900 its many regional centers had grown to the point that Germany had more major industrialized cities than the rest of Europe combined. It was the first country to develop mass universities and research labs, and then to link the two directly into local governments and corporations, giving German industry the ability to source everything from loans to staff to scientific research, and giving rise to the national economic champions model of corporate organization that pervades Europe even today. And the Germans methodically and assiduously applied every new breakthrough, whether scientific or industrial, to every aspect of their national strategy, culminating in everything from engines so efficient and small that they could propel individual vehicles (via Karl Benz, Rudolf Diesel, Gottlieb Daimler, and Emil Jellinek, whose daughter was the original Mercedes) and modern pharmaceuticals (Gregor Mendel, Robert Koch, Friedrich Bayer, and Paul Ehrlich), to cannons (Alfred Krupp) and blitzkrieg.

The sheer speed of Germany's rise so disrupted the European system that it almost enabled the Germans to overcome all other European powers simultaneously.

"Almost" being the operative word.

Germany's defeat in the world wars had nothing to do with luck, but rather with the same interaction of geography and technology that caused the German rise in the first place, the English rise before that, and the

Iberian rise before that. Simply put, neither deepwater navigation nor industrialization was done diffusing. England could make better use of deepwater navigation than Iberia, and Germany could make better use of industrialization than England, but there was another geography that could make better use of *both*.

CHAPTER 4

Enter the Accidental Superpower

Where to start when discussing the United States? With the fact that the Americans inherited the best lands in the world for a very low price in terms of blood, treasure, and time? The fact that within North America there are barriers that separated the early Americans from rival populations in Canada and Mexico? That the territory of the United States is better suited to deepwater navigation than even Great Britain and better suited to industrialization than even Germany? That throughout the nineteenth and early twentieth centuries the Europeans were so studiously building toward their wars of self-annihilation that they had little attention to spare for the young country that would so soon eclipse them?

These are all important points. So important in fact that each alone—much less in concert—probably would have been sufficient to create an American superpower, and so we will get to all of them over the course of this chapter. But while these advantages are indeed overwhelming from a global perspective, they are actually secondary. There is another factor in play that all but dictates the United States' global dominance: its waterway network.

The Mississippi is the world's longest navigable river,[1] some 2,100 miles long from its mouth at the Gulf of Mexico to its head of navigation at the Twin Cities in Minnesota. That's about one-third longer than the

---

1. From this point on the term "navigable river" refers to rivers that can handle drafts of nine feet for at least nine months of the year.

mighty Danube and triple the length of the Rhine. And the Mississippi is only one of twelve major navigable American rivers. Collectively, all of America's temperate-zone rivers are 14,650 miles long. China and Germany each have about 2,000 miles, France about 1,000. The entirety of the Arab world has but 120.

Yet there is more to America's waterways than just its rivers. The Americans benefit from a geographic feature that exists in few other places on the planet, and nowhere else in such useful arrangements: barrier islands. Chains of these low, flat, long islands parallel the American mainland for over three-quarters of the Gulf and East Coasts. The American barrier island chain turns three thousand miles of exposed coastline into dozens of connected, shielded bays. Tidal shifts are somewhat mitigated throughout the system, and the islands do an admirable job of blocking all but the most severe weather that the oceans can throw at the land, allowing for safe navigation from the Chesapeake to the Texas-Mexican border. The net effect of this Intracoastal Waterway is the equivalent of having a bonus three-thousand-mile-long river.

The most compelling feature of the American maritime system, however, is also nearly unique among the world's waterways—the American system is indeed a *network*. The Mississippi has six major navigable tributaries, most of which have several of their own. The greater Mississippi system empties into the Gulf of Mexico at a point where ships have direct access to the barrier island/Intracoastal system.

All told, this Mississippi and Intracoastal system accounts for 15,500 of the United States' 17,600 miles of internal waterways. Even leaving out the United States' (and North America's) other waterways, this is still a greater length of internal waterways than the rest of the planet combined. The result is that the United States has the greatest volume and concentration of capital-generation opportunities in the world by an absolutely massive margin, and that opportunity is very heavily concentrated in a single unified system.

The combination of size and interconnectedness of the system dictates a number of outcomes:

- First and most important, any culture based upon those waterways will be ridiculously capital-rich. When it comes to transport, distance is key. Low costs of transport allow goods to be shipped farther, and the more efficiently you can move goods from areas of high supply to areas of high demand, the greater the range at which your goods are competitive. In the American example this allows goods—whether Nebraska corn or Tennessee whiskey or Texas oil or New Jersey steel or Georgia peaches or Michigan cars—to reach anywhere in the river network at near-nominal costs *without having to even leave the country.* The sheer volume of those extra savings makes the United States the most capital-rich location on the planet, and that money can be used for whatever Americans (or their government) want, from iPhones to aircraft carrier battle groups.

- One of the things that the Americans have traditionally *not* needed to spend that money on is artificial infrastructure. In most countries the geopolitical necessity of infrastructure is a core motivator for government formation and expansion, with Germany being the quintessential example. Roads and rails do not come cheaply, so taxes need to be raised and government workforces formed. Not so in the United States. The rivers directly and indirectly eliminate many barriers to economic entry and keep development costs low. Even the early smallholders—pioneer families who owned and worked their own plots of land—found themselves able to export grain via America's waterways within a matter of months of breaking ground. It's a recipe for small government and high levels of entrepreneurship. It also means that as the United States developed, it was able to lay rail and road networks to supplement its preexisting river network, as well as open up new inland territories that lacked maritime transport options. These new artificial transport systems did somewhat displace riverine transport, but the constant competition that river transport provides for other modes keeps a lid on transport costs regardless of method.

- The American geography is also a recipe for a consumer base that is absolutely massive. If government is limited, then tax burdens are low, leaving more money in the citizenry's pockets.

If capital is readily available, then so is credit, enabling consumers and corporations alike the ability to expand with ease. If moving products from place to place is easy, food can reach areas that cannot provide enough themselves. It thus makes sense to specialize, and specialization steadily improves education, output, and income levels. The more people specialize, the larger, more sophisticated, and interlinked the economy becomes. The United States is far and away the world's largest consumer market and has been since shortly after the Civil War. As of 2014, that consumer base amounts to roughly $11.5 trillion. That's triple anyone else, larger than the consumer bases of the next six countries—Japan, Germany, the United Kingdom, France, China, and Italy—combined, and double that of the combined BRICs (Brazil, Russia, India, and China).

* Rivers promote unity, and an integrated maritime network promotes unity over a far larger swath of territory. Low-cost transport encourages economic and social interaction along the transport routes. The greater the level of specialization, the greater the need for that interaction (if your city produces cars, it probably needs to import steel, electronics, food, lumber, and so on). Such mutual dependence rapidly takes on characteristics that far surpass the purely economic. Deep, multifaceted economic linkages quickly generate deep, multifaceted cultural and political linkages. With the most robust, naturally occurring infrastructure, it should come as little surprise that the United States enjoys one of the strongest national identities of the major powers.[2]

---

2. In most cases international linkages don't achieve the same sort of cultural interaction because personal interaction doesn't occur very often. It's the combination of personal accessibility and economic interdependence that puts a riverine culture on the path to unification. It should come as little surprise that the portion of early America that was least integrated was the South. That region's rivers flow directly to the sea in a manner similar to Northern Europe, resulting in somewhat localized rather than federalized identities. Similarly, today it is notable that the Pacific coast states often seem culturally out of step with everyone east of the Rockies. That region is the one portion of the United States in which integration with foreign nations is of similar difficulty to integration internally. That, and next-door Vancouver is awesome.

America's waterways have created a legacy of extreme capital richness, remarkable political unity, and a powerful consumer-driven economy, all on a scale that makes the United States the outlier in a global context. And all that with a government that is relatively small, in personnel and resources, for a country of its size.

But that's just the beginning.

Land (and Water)

The first of the secondary factors is American lands. The majority of the Lower 48 is within the temperate climate zone—warm enough for people to live and crops to grow, cool enough to limit populations of deadly, disease-carrying insects. The Rockies are a very serious mountain chain, but unlike the world's other great mountains—the Alps, Himalayas, and Andes—they have six major passes with minimal avalanche dangers (so they can be kept open year round). Three of those passes are sufficiently wide to house major metropolitan regions—Salt Lake City, Las Vegas, and Phoenix—within them. East of the Rockies there is only one geographic zone that forms any sort of significant physical limitation to development—the Appalachian Mountains—and those mountains sport dozens of passes. The easiest and most famous of those openings, the Cumberland Narrows, was the location of the United States' first ever chunk of artificial infrastructure—the National Road, which linked the Potomac to the Ohio (and from there to the Mississippi) and is the home of eastern portions of the U.S. 40 corridor today. The two ends of the initial road, directly linking the two rivers, were only 130 miles apart. That was all it took to link the eastern seaboard of the original thirteen states to the Mississippi basin. Far from the thousands of miles of transport networks the Germans required to forcibly fashion a unified state, the early Americans only needed a short stretch of log planks. In all, roughly two-thirds (including nearly everything east of the Rocky Mountains) of the Lower 48 can be reached easily, with some 90 percent of it within 150 miles of some sort of navigable waterway.

Even better, most of that usable territory is in a single, easily digestible chunk. The greater Midwest is absolutely massive: With 139 million hectares under till, it is the largest contiguous stretch of high-quality farmland in the world. The central portions of the plain are humid yet temperate, making them perfect for corn and soybean production. The western sections are considerably drier as they lie in the rain shadow of the Rocky Mountains, making them ideal for several varietals of wheat. In bad years the Midwest produces a billion bushels of wheat, 2.5 billion bushels of soybeans, and an astounding 9 billion bushels of corn.

Like America's waterways, America's lands would make the United States a global superpower on their own. But the value and importance of those lands increase exponentially when one considers that they overlap America's world-best waterways almost perfectly.

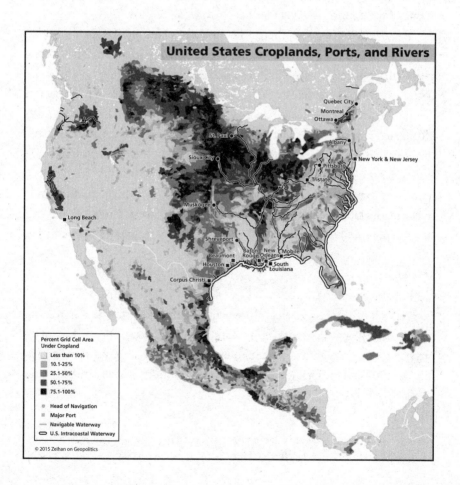

The world's greatest river network—that of the Mississippi and its six thousand miles of navigable tributaries—directly overlies the world's largest piece of arable land, the American Midwest. The Intra-coastal Waterway services the entirety of the Southeast as well as the plains of Texas. The Sacramento River and San Francisco Bay take care of California's Central Valley, and the Columbia and Snake service the agriculturally useful regions of Washington and Oregon. With the exception of the western fringe of the Great Plains that lies in the shadow of the Rockies, no American agricultural region is more than 150 miles from a navigable waterway. This allows the capital, agricultural, and transport bounty to reach the vast bulk of the American population. Of the United States' 314 million people, some 250 million of them live within 150 miles of one of the country's navigable waterways.

Thanks to this overlay, there are ample opportunities for local ("local" meaning local to the United States) economic development. The hostile geographies of most countries often make it cheaper to ship goods to the coast, and from there to other locations across the globe, than to engage in overland transport to service areas within one's own borders. The wealth of internal distribution options the United States enjoys means that for the bulk of its history American dependence upon the international trade system has been less than 15 percent of GDP.

There are portions of the global system that have high-quality lands in quantities that are in the same class as the United States, but almost all lack the potential to develop into a unified, internally focused system.[3]

Protecting the Core

As the luck of the geopolitical draw would have it, the United States' big chunk of high-productivity, high-capital land is also one of the most physically secure regions on the planet. Such security is best thought of in four layers: local buffers, local powers, ocean buffers, and potential global rivals.

---

3. We will address several of these lands—in particular Europe's northern plains, the Russian grain belt and the North China Plain—in later chapters.

Global Breadbaskets and Dust Bowls

Climate combined with terrain and elevation is an excellent predictor of what nations can potentially do. Elevations over five thousand feet typically mean mountains, which eliminate navigable rivers from possibility. Rail lines also quickly fall into uselessness in the highlands—a slope as little as 0.25 percent reduces the weight a locomotive can lug by half—and the separating nature of mountain ridges means that any infrastructure built in one area does not benefit another. Tropical climates similarly complicate infrastructure and introduce endemic disease into the strategic math. Deserts, tundra, and taiga simply cannot generate large populations or feed them from local sources. Such wastelands and highlands have never generated powers with a global reach. Tropical powers may support larger populations, but they too tend to be sharply circumscribed.

On the other end of the spectrum are the Goldilocks zones with warmth but not oppressive heat and water but not excessive wetness. All of the major powers of the past five hundred years have come from these easily developed, temperate lands. As pure happenstance would have it, the easily developed lands of the United States are not only the largest contiguous piece of such lands in the world, but they are also almost perfectly overlain by the American waterway network.

Between such zones of ruin and perfection lie the transitions lands that can be developed, but only if funded by a large and sustained supply of capital. Much of the economic and political activity of the past sixty years concerns these moderate-difficulty lands.

The map on page 54 illustrates the global land quality. The map on page 55 puts geographic theory into practice. Unsurprisingly, the vast majority of the world's farmland is located in lands where development is easy.

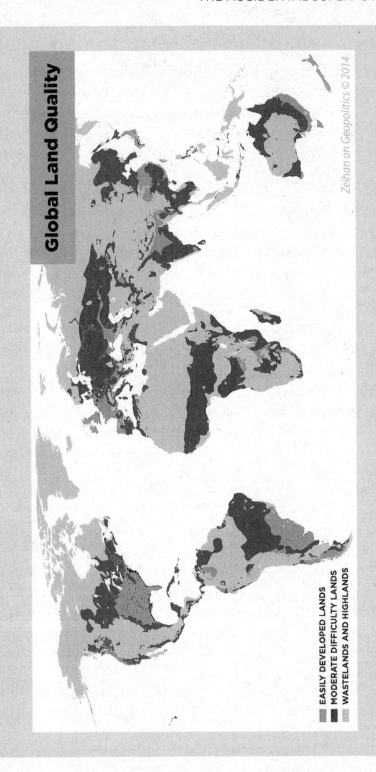

Global Land Quality

Zeihan on Geopolitics © 2014

EASILY DEVELOPED LANDS
MODERATE DIFFICULTY LANDS
WASTELANDS AND HIGHLANDS

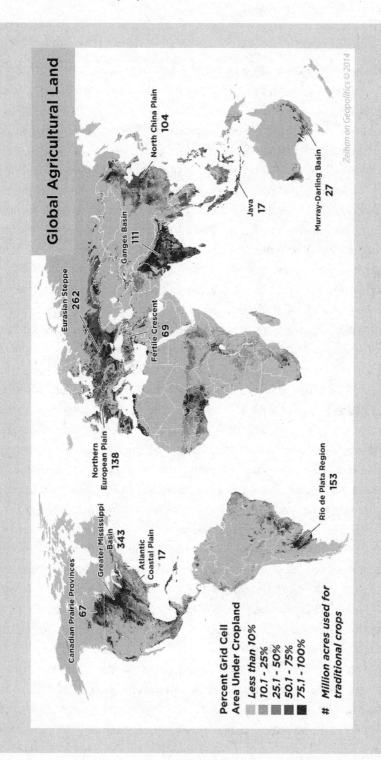

Global Agricultural Land

North China Plain 104

Murray-Darling Basin 27

Java 17

Ganges Basin 111

Eurasian Steppe 262

Fertile Crescent 69

Northern European Plain 138

Canadian Prairie Provinces 67

Greater Mississippi Basin 343

Atlantic Coastal Plain 17

Rio de Plata Region 153

Zeihan on Geopolitics © 2014

Percent Grid Cell
Area Under Cropland
Less than 10%
10.1 - 25%
25.1 - 50%
50.1 - 75%
75.1 - 100%

\# *Million acres used for traditional crops*

Local Buffers

As easy as it is to get around within the American section of North America, it is remarkably difficult to cross into the American core territories from either the Mexican or Canadian cores.

America's southern border region is all either desert or highland or both, relatively flat on the northern side of the border, but rugged on the southern side. Aside from the border communities themselves there are only two meaningful Mexican populations within five hundred miles of the border, Chihuahua and Monterrey, and even they are five hundred mountainous miles apart from one another. As Santa Anna discovered during the Texas Independence War, there is no good staging location in (contemporary) Mexican territory that could strike at American lands. In the Mexican-American War of 1846–48, the Americans took full advantage of that lack of staging areas, that thick buffer, and their superior transport to strategically outmaneuver the larger, slower, and exhausted Mexican forces—and this in an era before the Americans had battleships and jets. At the war's conclusion, the United States seized half of Mexico's territory (including California)—the half that was easier to get around in.

Canada's border with the United States is much longer, more varied, and even more successful at keeping the two countries separated. In the border's eastern reaches mountains and thick forests so snarl transport options that infrastructure even today is thin and vulnerable. In the far west the Rockies are a great border zone in that there is nothing for hundreds of miles on either side of the border that resembles a major staging area. The sole point of potential conflict is the Strait of Georgia, the body of water between Canada's Vancouver Island and the northwestern extremes of the U.S. state of Washington. A Canadian impingement upon the strait would block maritime access to Puget Sound, home of Seattle and Tacoma. Yet the region's population (im)balance is heavily in the Americans' favor: The three Pacific coast American states outpopulate British Columbia by ten to one.

In the middle portion of the border region—the Prairie provinces–Midwest border—connections are almost omnipresent. This is a bad deal not for the Americans, but rather for the Canadians. South of the border zone one encounters ever denser American populations with ever more developed land and ever better transport infrastructure, both artificial and natural. In contrast, moving north into Canada one hits an initial line of cities—Calgary, Regina, and Winnipeg—and then a whole lot of nothing. The Prairies have little choice but to be American in economic orientation and even somewhat midwestern culturally. Their physical links to both British Columbia and the core Canadian provinces of the east are weak at best and regularly disrupted every winter. Their links to the colossus to the south, however, are substantial, multimodal, multiply redundant, and almost always functional.

Local Powers

If the United States has one of the easiest geographies to develop, Mexico has one of the most difficult. The entirety of Mexico is in essence the southern extension of the Rocky Mountains, which is a kind way of saying that America's worst lands are strikingly similar to Mexico's best lands. As one would expect from a terrain that is mountain-dominated, there are no navigable rivers and no large cohesive pieces of arable land like the American Southeast or the Columbia valley, much less the Midwest. Each mountain valley is a sort of fastness where a small handful of oligarchs control local economic and political life. Mexico shouldn't be thought of as a unified state, but instead as a collage of dozens of little Mexicos where local power brokers constantly align with and against each other (and a national government seeking—often in vain—to stitch together something more cohesive). In its regional disconnectedness Mexico is a textbook case that countries with the greatest need for capital-intensive infrastructure are typically the countries with the lowest ability to generate the capital necessary to build that infrastructure. By the time the Mexicans completed their first rail line from their sole significant (preindustrial) port at Veracruz to Mexico City in 1873, the Americans already had over fifty thousand miles of operational track.

Canada has a similar unity problem, as geography splits the country into five pieces:

- The Canadian Rockies split British Columbia from the Prairies.
- The Canadian Shield, a region where repeated glaciation stripped the soil and shattered the bedrock, splits the Prairies

from Ontario. A single thousand-mile transport corridor
snakes through the shield to link the regions.

- That same shield keeps Ontario apart from Quebec. What
infrastructure links them hugs the Saint Lawrence River.
- The Gulf of Saint Lawrence separates Quebec from the Maritime provinces, again, linked by a single transport corridor
(well, the mainland Maritimes anyway—the island Maritimes
are obviously on their own). For most purposes each of these
zones functions as an independent country.

The one thing that Canada has going for it is that it does have a navigable waterway—the Saint Lawrence—but since that waterway merges with
the Great Lakes, the Saint Lawrence watercourse is shared with the United
States, making most Canadian waterborne commerce subject to American
proclivities. That, in fact, is the theme of Canada as a whole. It is far easier
for almost all of the Canadian provinces to integrate economically with
the United States than with each other.

Beyond Mexico and Canada, there are no other powers that could
even theoretically march on American territory. While technically North
America and South America are connected by the Panamanian isthmus,
the land is so swampy that even now—five hundred years after the region's
first European exploration—there is not a single road connecting the two
American continents.

Ocean Buffers

As hard as it is to conceive of a credible military threat to the United States
arising in North America, coming up with one from beyond the continent strains the imagination. The oceans serve as fantastic buffers, sharply
limiting unwanted interaction with the larger populations of Europe and
East Asia. As leaders like Napoleon and Hirohito learned, attacking over
water proves a bit of a logistical challenge. An amphibious assault requires
military infrastructure, equipment, and training that has little use in any
sort of military operation *except* an amphibious assault. For countries
like France or Germany or Russia that are perennially concerned about
the security of their land borders, simply having an amphibious assault

capacity—much less attempting an assault—is a luxury that they cannot typically afford. At the height of its power Nazi Germany abandoned plans to invade Great Britain due to the difficulty of crossing the English Channel, a body of water but twenty-one miles across at its narrowest point. The shortest distance from Europe to the United States is over three thousand.

Considering the distances involved, the outside world missed its best chance to disrupt America's development in the War of 1812, one of only two occasions when the Americans faced an extrahemispheric invasion (the other being the Revolutionary War). The critical battle was for Fort McHenry in September 1814.

The British had sacked and captured Washington, D.C., just three weeks before and were moving north by land and sea toward Baltimore. At the time, Baltimore was the largest city in the region and a notorious hub for the privateers who had been raiding British shipping lines. But it was also the sole meaningful land link between the northern and southern states: With the Allegheny Mountains to the west, all roads hugged the Chesapeake Bay, which in turn led to the bay's major city and port. As importantly, the *entirety* of inland America was dependent upon Baltimore. The Cumberland Narrows through the Appalachians lay just to the west, and only three years earlier the government had begun construction on a road to connect the Potomac River to the Ohio valley. Instead of a months-long sail down to New Orleans, then up the Mississippi to the Ohio, this new National Road would allow Baltimore to serve as an immediate outlet for Pittsburgh and lands beyond.

If the British could hold Baltimore, the war's other theaters would be rendered moot and the young America would be split into North, South, and interior. Luckily for the Americans, Major George Armistead's heroic defense of Fort McHenry convinced British commanders that the post could not be taken with available forces. While time has eroded the details from the American mind, all Americans instantly recognize the description of the battle and its outcome as recorded by an American who watched the battle from the deck of a British vessel where he was being held prisoner: Francis Scott Key's "Star-Spangled Banner."

The Americans got not just a catchy tune out of the event, but also a lesson in strategic vulnerability and sea approaches. The British attempt on Baltimore—indeed, the entire war effort—would have been impossible without launching grounds in Canada and the Caribbean.

The Americans took note of which territories were used and reshaped their foreign and military policies to ensure that those lands—and *any* like them—could never be used for such purposes again.

- After the War of 1812, the British were obsessed with reformulating Europe in the aftermath of Napoleon's fall. American diplomatic, economic, and military pressure succeeded in hiving Canada off from Britain and transitioning it to neutrality.
- In the latter half of the 1800s, the United States both purchased Alaska (1867) and annexed the Hawaiian Islands (1898). This did more than push back potential Asian hostiles twenty-six hundred miles. Beyond Hawaii the next meaningful speck of land is the 2.4-square-mile atoll of Midway, another thirteen hundred miles from either Hawaii or Alaska. The Americans militarily snagged Midway in 1903.
- In the Spanish-American War of 1898, the Americans seized direct control of Puerto Rico and de facto control of Cuba. This prevented any hostile power from potentially severing American access from the greater Mississippi basin to the outside world via the Florida and Yucatán Straits.
- The Americans usurped British control of the western Atlantic outright with the Lend-Lease program in the early part of World War II. By terms of the agreement the United Kingdom gave the United States rent-free control for ninety-nine years of nearly all of the serviceable British ports in the Western Hemisphere.

By the beginning of their participation in World War II, the Americans had already secured *all* of the potential approaches that could be used for an assault on North America.

Of course, approaches can go both ways. While the United States is largely immune to extrahemispheric invasion, there are any number of

ATLANTIC SEA APPROACHES TO NORTH AMERICA

GREENLAND: 1941
ICELAND: 1941
FAROES: 1949
ZEALAND: 1949
GREAT BRITAIN: 1941
CYPRUS: 1945
New Foundland*
SARDINIA: 1949
CRETE: 1952
SICILY: 1949
Lisbon - Boston: 3180 Miles
Bermuda*
BALEARICS: 1982
CUBA: 1898
AZORES: 1944
Jamaica*
PUERTO RICO: 1898
Antigua*
St. Lucia*
Trinidad*
Guyana*

*Lend-lease Locations, 1941

YEAR THE UNITED STATES
GAINED PHYSICAL OR TREATY
ACCESS TO THE TERRITORY

Zeihan on Geopolitics © 2014

potential routes that the Americans could—and during World War II did—use to invade Europe and Asia. By the end of the war the Americans had not only extensively used launching points such as Iceland, Sicily, and Great Britain, but the postwar NATO alliance brought islands like Zealand, the Azores, Cyprus, and the Faroes into the American defense network.

Asia's sea approaches are even more favorable to the Americans. Off the East Asian coast are not simply a series of archipelagoes, but a series of well-established, populous nations: Japan, Taiwan, the Philippines, Indonesia, Malaysia, and Singapore. All, like the United Kingdom, are full-on powers in their own right. What do they have in common? A fear that another regional power might one day be powerful enough to end them. In the past this has made them hostile to Japan (and friendly to the

PACIFIC SEA APPROACHES TO NORTH AMERICA

TAIWAN: 1945

SINGAPORE: 1965

JAPAN: 1945

PHILIPPINES: 1898

ALASKA: 1811

Tokyo - Seattle: 4750 miles

MARIANA ISLANDS: 1945

GUAM: 1898

MIDWAY: 1903

AUSTRALIA: 1941

MICRONESIA: 1945

HAWAII: 1898

YEAR THE UNITED STATES
GAINED PHYSICAL OR TREATY
ACCESS TO THE TERRITORY

Zeihan on Geopolitics © 2014

United States), and in the present this has made them hostile to China (and friendly to the United States). As of 2014 all—including Japan—are allies.

The net effect is that the United States now has a multilayered defense of the homeland before one even considers its alliance structure, its maritime prowess, or the general inability of Eurasian powers to assault it.

Which brings us to the final point about why the United States is nearly immune to rivals.

There is no one who is capable of trying.

A Lack of Eurasian Powers

Pulling off an invasion of North America would require three particularly onerous prerequisites. First and most obvious, it takes a huge population to duke it out with a country of over 300 million on its home territory. The only entities with the population that could even theoretically attempt such a task are China, India, the combined European Union, and Russia.

Second, there is (a lot) more to launching an extrahemispheric amphibious assault than a (whole) lot of troops. Also required is the industrial might and technological command required to construct the ships and sail halfway around the world into a region in which the defender would be able to bring land-based defenses—most notably aircraft—to bear. Currently, the world's second and third most powerful navies just happen to be the only two naval powers that the Americans have clashed with: Japan and the United Kingdom. Both are now allies. Beyond those two countries, there are none that have even moderate levels of military sealift capacity.

Third and finally, any would-be invader must have the strategic freedom to build an invasion fleet in the first place. For any country with land borders, an army to patrol and protect the state is an absolute necessity—but a navy is an expensive luxury, or at best a fringe armed services branch. It's the army that carries out the day-to-day mission of defending the frontier, while the navy's superior movement capacity makes it primarily an expeditionary arm. Expeditionary arms are handy when you have secure borders, and largely pointless when you do not. (What good is a small task force that can reach around the globe if a foe can simply roll across your frontier with his tanks?) It is this simple point—more than any others—that has sharply limited the number of significant naval powers in world history. Even at the height of their power, the Soviets never had free forces sufficient to contemplate an invasion of England, much less North America. Again, this limits the list to two American allies: Japan and the United Kingdom.

Pulling off an invasion that is continental in scope and extracontinental in reach requires a special constellation of factors and forces, and even with them in place it is just as hard as it sounds. In fact, it has only ever been done successfully once in human history, and it wasn't done against the Americans—it was done *by* the Americans.

Deepwater Navigation and the United States

In addition to the inestimable advantages discussed above, no geography on the planet is better suited than America's for the technologies of deepwater navigation, which in turn has made it the greatest maritime power the world has ever seen.

What made Britain the absolute master of the seas in the eighteenth and nineteenth centuries was pretty straightforward. An island was always going to be a better generator of sailors, captains, ships, and fleets than a mainland state. Resources didn't need to be dedicated to an army, so they were available to instead flow into a navy. And the same acumen that allowed for a powerful merchant marine (you can't trade by land when you're on an island) could also contribute to a robust military fleet.

Americans enjoy this same advantage, but increased by an order of magnitude. The United States isn't technically an island, but the inability of Canada or Mexico to threaten it by land makes it an island functionally. As an island-continent it simply has a greater quantitative ability to leverage deepwater technologies than anything the British on their mid-sized island could manage.

Then there is the absolutely dominating factor of how large and perfectly positioned America's waterways are. America's rivers transform cities deep in the interior such as Pittsburgh, St. Paul, Sioux City, and Tulsa into ocean ports. Having more internal waterways than everyone else combined has certainly got to make the United States the premier maritime power, right?

Correct. But the continental scope of the United States and its omnipresent waterways are only the *beginning* of why the United States is the ultimate home for deepwater navigation.

Ports

The United States has more port potential than the rest of the world combined.

Ports require a friendly coastline. Most ocean coastline is not suited to serving as ports. Tidal differences require the construction of expensive infrastructure—jetties have to be extended into deep water so that ships can dock safely regardless of the tidal cycle. Storms are an even bigger problem: Damage from winds—or worse yet, from hurricane-spawned storm surges—can wreck a territory miles inland. That's why most ports are located on bays, where the ocean can only punch in from one direction.[4] While bays are hardly rare, they are certainly not omnipresent and oftentimes very lengthy coastlines have but a few. The coast of Africa, for example, may be sixteen thousand miles long, but in reality it has only ten locations with bays of sufficient protective capacity to justify port construction, three of which are in South Africa.

Ports also require a sufficient hinterland to support them in the first place. In this, Northern Europe faced quite a few challenges in the centuries before European dominance, as much of the coastline was marsh and mud, as is northern China's. Brazil north of the 22nd parallel south— roughly the latitude of Rio de Janeiro—isn't much better. South of the 22nd parallel, Brazil's coast is all cliff, as is much of southern China's. Australia's coast may be accessible, but it is so arid it is almost devoid of people—as is North Africa's coast. Russia's coast—like most of Canada's—is (sub) arctic. What few African locations have a friendly coast are often backed up by swamp, desert, or jungle. The entire Sub-Saharan region really only has four coastal areas capable of supporting cities of significant size (two of which are *still* in South Africa).

The contrast to the United States could not be starker. When it comes to having ample coastal frontage, hinterlands for cities, and deep passages for shipping, Puget Sound, San Francisco Bay, and Chesapeake Bay are bar none the world's three largest and best natural harbors. Chesapeake Bay alone boasts longer stretches of prime port property than the entire continental coast of Asia from Vladivostok to Karachi. Additional areas such as New York Harbor and Mobile Bay are "merely" world-class.

And then there are America's barrier islands. They block the strongest of storm surges and mitigate tidal variations. Regular breaks in the barrier island chains allow for easy access to the open ocean, while the near omnipresence of the islands provides the Gulf and East Coasts with port opportunities that can best be described as egregious. Courtesy of those barrier islands, Texas alone has thirteen world-class deepwater ports,

---

4. Incidentally, these are also reasons why riverbanks are in general superior to seacoasts for capital generation. It takes a hell of a hurricane to make a river unnavigable, and rivers are typically immune to tidal surges. Additionally, rivers by definition have two banks, doubling the potential amount of port frontage real estate.

only half of which see significant use, and room for at least three times more. Why not expand port capacity? Because the United States has more port possibilities than it has ever needed, despite the fact that it has been the world's largest producer, importer, and exporter of agricultural and manufactured goods for most of its history.

Nearby Waterways

Beyond its superfluity of port potential, the United States actually has control of more waterways than even its river system would suggest.

The island of Cuba and the Yucatán and Florida peninsulas limit access to the Gulf of Mexico to two straits, creatively named the Yucatán and Florida Straits. These sharply limit the ability of extrahemispheric powers to play in the Gulf of Mexico.

Within the Gulf there is no contest. Of the score of active ports of note, only one, Veracruz, is not American. Mexico's lack of naval acumen allowed the Americans to capture Veracruz not once but twice in order to force its will on Mexico City. The inability of Mexico to challenge the United States by land, and the absolute ability of the United States to dominate Mexico by water, makes the Gulf of Mexico a de facto American lake. That means that since the Civil War the Americans have never had to worry about fortifying anything along the Gulf Coast, even when German U-boats were sinking shipping in the millions of tons off the East Coast.

To the north there is Canada's only waterway—the Saint Lawrence River—which too is in effect an American waterway.

In 1871, Canada first tried to solve the Saint Lawrence's winter ice and the Great Lakes' waterfalls problems[5] with a series of locks on the river and construction of the Welland Canal. By the 1890s, however, the Canadians had proposed a partnership with Washington for a more extensive, binational waterway that would link the Atlantic Ocean through the Saint Lawrence to the Great Lakes. The main selling point was that the Americans would actually benefit *more* than the Canadians from improving the

---

5. The Saint Lawrence's year-round head of navigation is at Quebec City, although when the river is ice-free ocean shipping can reach Montreal. After Montreal, however, extensive engineering is required to bypass shallows, rapids, and falls, the most famous of which is Niagara.

waterways on their common border. The Canadians were indeed correct: Bringing the Great Lakes online would turn places like Duluth, Milwaukee, Chicago, Cleveland, and Detroit into full-on ocean ports.

The American response to the proposal over the next few decades can best be summed up as a dismissive yawn. The American government knew that the Canadians were going to build the lock system anyway, because having some sort of transport system that allowed Quebec and Ontario to interact economically was a national imperative. To do otherwise risked hardening Canada's Anglophone-Francophone divide into something truly ugly. The Americans also knew they would be able to use the fruits of Canadian labor in an unrestricted manner regardless of whether Washington helped pay for it or not: The system would be right on the border and at least some of the canals would have to be on the American side of the line. The Canadians couldn't make the system operate without perennial American sign-off.

The American sign-off had a very clear price: *You* pay for it and *we* get unrestricted access to the entire thing. In the end, the Canadians had to foot over 70 percent of the bill, pay almost all of the maintenance, and the Saint Lawrence Seaway wasn't fully operational until 1959.

Premier Global Location

More broadly, the United States' global geographic position also serves it extremely well.

The United States is the only country with significant populations on both the Atlantic and Pacific coasts, with nearly 50 million people on the Pacific and twice that on the Atlantic. So only the Americans have broad-scale access to both of the world's great trading zones. This results in two outcomes.

First and most obviously, as the only country with easy access to both global trading basins, Americans are well positioned to reach all global markets and take advantage of the growth fad of the moment.

Second and less obvious is that this omnipresent exposure allows the Americans to shift their trade portfolio with a speed that belies their size. The Americans have sufficient infrastructure to enable their Pacific citizens to trade with Europe when Asia is in recession, or to allow their

Atlantic citizens to trade with Asia when Europe is in recession. Because they can easily switch dance partners, the Americans only suffer a recession caused by international factors when the *entire* world goes into recession. That's a polite way of saying that the world has not imposed a recession upon the Americans in the post–World War II era, but *every* recession the Americans have generated they have…exported.

Industrialization and the United States

Although I'm not exactly a fan of his work, Karl Marx made some solid points. Industrializing is most definitely *not* easy. First, it wipes out nearly all preexisting economic activity and radically changes how a people interacts with itself and the outside world. Second, thorough, widespread industrialization requires large concentrations of labor and financial resources, regular access to perennially hungry markets, and even when the process is successful, it triggers deep social pressures. Every country therefore adapts to the realities and rigors of industrialization in its own way, and because every geography is different, every industrialization is different. Two of the world's more *successful* industrializations gifted the world with Soviet Russia and Imperial Germany. Getting it right isn't easy.

Unless, perhaps, you are American.

America's industrialization experience was less stressful and more successful than that of the rest of the world largely because American geography stands apart from the rest of the world. The best way to illustrate the American command of industrialization—and just how *easy* it was for the Americans—is to view the United States in comparison to the characteristics that shaped the German experience.

Local Government

Germany had to have hypercompetent local governments because those local governments didn't have good physical connections to Berlin, and even the handful of communities that were physically close enough couldn't count on it for much help in the first place: Berlin's resources had to be spent on military defense. As the saying of the 1700s went, "Prussia is not a state with an army, but an army with a state." Each local government was its own organizational node that married all local assets in order to protect itself in a hostile Central European world.

The American developmental experience, on the other hand, took on an entirely different cast largely because American geography was a world apart from German geography. Germans needed always to be on their toes because they lived on disconnected pieces of smallish land and were duking it out with large and capable neighbors who were far more advanced culturally, economically, politically, and militarily. Not so with the Americans. American lands were at a more southerly latitude, providing longer growing seasons. Their soil was better, particularly in the Midwest. Their rivers were collectively eight times the length of the Germans' and drained more well-watered, fertile land than all of Europe combined—so much land that the early American government had to resort to giving it away. Most of it was even all in one conveniently contiguous piece, whereas smack dab in the middle of Germany, sandwiched between the Rhine and the Elbe, is an annoying knot of mountains that impedes Berlin's writ to this day.

In the United States barriers to entry were laughably small. A Conestoga wagon with six months of supplies could be purchased in inflation-indexed dollars for about the price of a modern-day Kia (about $11,000). For a modicum of start-up money an American could move out west and be exporting grain to earn hard currency in a single year.

Those lands were safer too. The War of 1812 drew a line that the Canadians would never cross, and the Mexican-American War established one of the world's largest buffer zones. Between the wealth of good lands and waterways that Germans could never match and a dearth of security threats of which Germans could only dream, there was never any pressure on the Americans to actually be well governed or, during the first several decades, to be governed at all. So while the Germans had to make the most of every worker and deutschmark, the Americans were so swimming in the land, labor, and capital that made the industrial age possible that they didn't need to worry...or plan. Germany became industrial and efficient because it had to. Private entrepreneurs and businessmen led the industrial charge in America because there were simply so many of the necessary inputs lying around in such vast quantities that ordinary citizens didn't need much by way of governmental assistance or organization to develop their little corners of the country on their own.

Infrastructure

Germany needed artificial infrastructure to weld its disparate regions into a single coherent state. Without a national effort to lash the Rhineland and the south into Berlin's influence, many German provinces would find more in common economically, politically, and even culturally with Germany's rivals. To a degree, the original thirteen colonies shared this concern: Their maritime nature meant that by design they were more linked into the British imperial system than into any "domestic American" economic system. The British took full advantage of this during the War of 1812, applying political calculus to their blockades of American ports, often selectively applying and relaxing their naval blockade to achieve political ends.

But so long as the British were not actively causing problems, the Americans faced no foreign cultural and economic beckonings. The mountains and forests of the Northeast blocked meaningful integration with Canada, while Mexico was on the other side of a highland desert. For the Americans, artificial infrastructure was a luxury that they could do without rather than an expensive prerequisite for national coherence. The river system of North America provided the early Americans with all the "infrastructure" they could ever want.

In fact, for the first half century of U.S. history the Americans built exactly one federal infrastructure project: the aforementioned National Road. From the road, the Ohio, Mississippi, and their sister rivers could take you anywhere you wanted to go without crossing meaningful boundaries. And that was that. With the same vessel you could travel from Pittsburgh to Sioux City and St. Paul, or down to Muskogee and Shreveport, or through New Orleans to the Intracoastal and over to Miami, Savannah, Hampton Roads, New York City, and Boston. These are some of the advantages that come with a *naturally* unified system.

Instead of the painstaking micromanagement of Germany, American development happened organically. Farmers in an area grew the same products and so had the same needs: tools they couldn't build themselves, docks and boats to ship their grain, schools to educate their children, banks to deposit their earnings. The farmers' mere presence spontaneously created small towns and agricultural entrepôt cities that popped up along the riverways. Larger towns (with larger banks) naturally formed at key points along the maritime system: where two rivers met, and at heads of navigation. Chicago, Pittsburgh, Louisville, Charleston, St. Louis, Shreveport, Albany, Minneapolis, Independence (better known today as Kansas City), and Memphis are some examples. Smallholders quite inadvertently created an educational and financial system that was national in scope but local in origin and with only moderate commitments from Washington.

By the time the industrial technologies percolated from Europe to the United States the United States already had fifty urban centers with their own organically generated education and financial systems able to apply the new technologies. Infrastructure expanded as required by the local population centers, and local solutions responded to local economic concerns rather than national solutions to strategic concerns, as was the case in Germany. When the need for faster transport options on a national scale started arising just before the Civil War, the resulting binge of construction was not government-managed. A few land concessions to the (aptly named) robber barons and in under five decades the Americans had stitched together their constellations of small towns and river cities. It may not have happened (quite) as fast as it did in Germany, but the result was the world's largest artificial transport network, with 164,000 miles of track by 1890—all with minimal government involvement... or money.

Capital Capture

Everything needed to be coordinated in Germany because the Germans were always racing Armageddon. Always behind. Always outnumbered. Always under threat. Addressing all of these issues required not just hyper-competent organization, but also money. Money for education. Money for roads. Money for rail lines. Money for industrial plants. Money for the army. Money for technological development. All that money had to come from somewhere. Berlin forced German banks to be part of the organizational networks that make Germany function at the state level. Financiers sat right along with generals and politicians and industrialists in making and implementing the decisions about how Germany would deal with this or that problem. Every scrap of cash was funneled to those banks, and the government leaned on them to make sure that any program in the national interest, whether public or private, received financing before anything else. On the downside, it is really hard to get a mortgage in Germany.[6] On the upside, the German state is better able to allocate its scarce resources to deal with whatever the crisis of the day happens to be.

If the German and American approaches to government and infrastructure are a world apart, their approach to capital is a galaxy apart. The United States' sixteen thousand-plus miles of integrated waterways and their position atop the world's best farmland absolutely swamp the country with capital. Far lower development costs and a complete lack of local strategic threats put drastically lower pressure upon that capital. Simply put, the Americans have the world's highest capital base, yet among the lowest need for that capital.

Since no organization and relatively small amounts of capital were needed, the American government felt little impetus to regulate how that capital was collected, managed, invested, lent, borrowed, or repaid. Instead the Americans allowed the market to take the capital to wherever it wanted.

One result was the world's first truly integrated financial system. With money unrestricted, there was never a need to establish regional financial regulators. In contemporary times the strength of this unity shined brightly during the 2007 financial crisis. In a matter of a few hours the Federal Reserve chairman, the FDIC chairwoman, and the Treasury secretary were able to squeeze around a two-top and hammer out emergency policies, fully fund them to the tune of $700 billion within days, and then tweak them repeatedly over the next several weeks without leaving town. The Germans, with their regional banking system and tradition of multi-tiered government, took months simply to come to grips with the scope of the problems their nation faced in the European financial crisis, plus four *years* of negotiations including eight summits with their EU partners to hammer out a European policy—a policy that is still under negotiation and won't actually be fully funded to its planned 55 billion euros until 2025.

------

6. Applicants have to open an account with the bank they intend to get a loan from, and then deposit the equivalent of their would-be mortgage payment monthly for several years before the bank will fund the mortgage.

Quest for Quality

The heated international competition and near-constant state of threat that Germany had to endure for centuries of its history is something that the Americans have only rarely had to worry about. From the Louisiana Purchase onward, the Americans have boasted the world's most capital-rich geography. By 1850, the Americans outnumbered the Mexicans and Canadians *combined* by three to one, and there haven't been any credible threats to U.S. territories for two hundred years. The Americans can afford to be—and often are—laggards.

But more to the point, America's "problem" is that it is the land of plenty. It is the world's largest agricultural, technological, financial, and, based on how you collate the data, industrial power—and has been all of those things for fifteen *decades*. Its availability of land, labor, and capital is unprecedented in human history, and all those cheap inputs mean that the United States does not have to be at its best to be better than everyone else. Why get better when you can simply get *bigger*?

- Upon independence the Americans gained the unsettled Ohio valley, doubling the amount of useful land the young country had access to.
- The acquisition of the Louisiana Territory doubled that again just a generation later.
- A deal with the British for the territory around the Columbia River increased American lands by an area similar to that of the original thirteen.
- The Texas annexation and Mexican-American War increased American lands by another (cumulative) third.

And even in contemporary times, the Americans still have loads of room to grow. Even if you ignore the portions of American territory that are less than ideal, population density in the United States is only 180 people per square mile, one-third that of Italy or Germany, one-quarter that of the United Kingdom, and one-fifth that of Japan.

Dawn of a Superpower

The characteristics of North American topography grant the Americans nearly endless capital, bottomless markets, low defense costs, and easy routes of power projection. But no matter how favorable a geography might be, everyone still needs time to grow up. At the beginning of the Revolutionary War, the American population (some 2.5 million) was less than one-tenth of the French population. Even in the most aggressive estimate, it was perfectly reasonable to expect the Americans to need a few generations to install the base infrastructure of farms, ports, towns, and industry that form the bedrock of all powers, great or otherwise. And every time the young country's borders expanded, the timetable was pushed back even more.

Serious industrialization didn't even begin until 1850, and was unceremoniously halted—or more accurately, skewed in decidedly military directions—during the United States' 1861–65 Civil War. *After* 1865, however, the Americans' security environment returned to its charmed nature. The Americans were able to once again forgo the cost of maintaining armed forces and pour all of their resources into development. For the thirty years of Reconstruction, the Americans didn't simply politically reunify North and South, but also applied all of the technologies that the Europeans had developed over the past two centuries to the entirety of the American lands. From 1860 to 1890 American railways had quintupled, creating a multimodal web of steel that lashed North to South to Midwest to—via two transcontinental lines—the West Coast. The trip from New York to San Francisco shrank from months in 1840[7] to eight days in 1870. Similar advances in telegraphy allowed instantaneous communication anywhere touched by urbanization or rail corridors. By the end of Reconstruction the United States had reemerged as the world's largest economy, its largest market, its largest grower of wheat and corn, its largest producer of steel. With their country finally secured, developed, and unified, the Americans traded in their "manifest destiny" for something greater.

---

7. Six months by wagon, or a little over three months by sea by sailing around South America.

All maritime powers are by their very nature offensive powers. They use their superior mobility to choose the time and place of conflicts. They use their superior transport capacity to ensure that their forces have a quantitative advantage when those conflicts erupt. And their superior capital position means that their forces typically enjoy qualitative advantages as well: longer reach, greater speed, better durability, more concentrated firepower, and so on. In this the United States is similar to the great maritime powers of the past.

But the United States is different from its maritime predecessors in two critical ways: insulation and size. All previous maritime powers have either bordered land-bound competitors or been very close to the mainland. The English Channel, the Korea Strait, and the La Pérouse Strait[8] are minuscule in size compared to the vast swaths of the Atlantic and Pacific. England and Japan can be—and have been—invaded from the mainland. So while British and Japanese military strategies throughout history have usually been offensive, those nations have always had to keep an eye out for countries or coalitions that might be able to challenge their position. That doesn't exactly make them defensive, but it certainly makes them somewhat thoughtful. In contrast, no one has attempted even a partial invasion of American territories since 1815. Even the global geopolitics at the time of the 1890s American emergence was benign. The world of British supremacy had passed. With the rise of Germany, the Royal Navy was forced to spend more time in European waters. There simply was no navy that could so much as harass American shores.

And then there is size. Most maritime powers are countries that possess relatively modest territories, like the islands of Great Britain or Honshu, chunks of land slightly smaller than the U.S. state of Michigan. From small lands come limited resources, particularly when you consider that roughly half of Great Britain and Honshu are useless highlands. For them to become truly powerful countries, they need more resources, whether in personnel or markets or raw materials—they have no choice but to expand into empire. In contrast, the United States has the better part of a continent to draw upon. Self-sufficient in everything that matters

---

8. The two straits that separate Japan from the Asian mainland.

from energy to markets, they ventured out as a peer power without peer exposures.

Combined, these factors make American power different from anything that came before: offensively relentless and strategically insensitive to defeat. Even catastrophic losses abroad would never actually harm the base of American power, rooted as it was in the charmed nature of American geography. If Britain lost its empire, it was reduced to secondary-power status. If the Maginot Line were breached, France would fall. If the Americans lost every scrap of land they held internationally, they would still be the most powerful country in human history. It didn't matter that the Germans were better industrialists or that the English were better sailors, the sheer mass and insulation of the United States veritably guaranteed that the Americans would surpass them both.

With their geopolitical position completely unhampered by international developments, upon their reemergence the Americans immediately became the ultimate arbiter of global affairs.

- In 1898, the Americans seized nearly all of Spain's remaining overseas empire, including the Philippines, Cuba, and Puerto Rico. By war's end, the Americans had 160 vessels, 114 of which were steel, placing it in the world's top five naval forces.
- In 1899, the Americans adopted the Open Door policy, ostensibly to allow trade with China. The policy was expressly designed to limit Japanese options and was certain in time to provoke a Japanese military response. While Europeans held most of the trade concessions in China, none of the European powers had the ability to project sufficient power into East Asia to protect them in the presence of Japanese action. The Americans, however, could. Open Door set the stage for the elimination of the European presence in Asia.
- In 1904, President Theodore Roosevelt announced his corollary to the Monroe Doctrine, indicating that the United States would proactively intervene in Latin American affairs expressly to minimize any and all European influence there; over the next twenty years the United States dispatched troops

to the region thirty-two times. Not once were they opposed by an extrahemispheric power.

- In 1905, the Roosevelt administration arbitrated an end to the Russo-Japanese War, splitting the disputed territories so that the Russians and Japanese not only had hopelessly entangled economic interests, but also something that Russia and Japan had never had before: a *land* border. The peace deal guaranteed future military conflict.
- The Americans completed the Panama Canal in 1914. As if the American territories were insufficient to sustain American power, they had now permanently locked Mexico, Central America, and the northern third of South America into the American economic orbit. The canal also sliced nearly a month off the time it would take for their naval vessels to switch between Atlantic and Pacific theaters, adding strategic flexibility that no preceding naval power had ever possessed.
- In 1917, the Americans became the last major belligerent to join World War I, where they turned a German near victory into capitulation. The Americans helped to implement a peace deal that resurrected Russia and humiliated Germany, but ensured that Germany would be able to rebuild and rearm. A second conflict was guaranteed to ignite, and ignite a good long distance from American territory.

From 1917 on—just twenty years after the Americans had reinserted themselves into the world with the Spanish-American War—the United States became the determining factor in European affairs rather than the other way around. It was neither pretty nor nice, but neither was it unique. Every naval power in history has tried to keep its land-based rivals bottled up with each other rather than floating navies that could challenge them. What set the Americans apart was that their home territories were so rich and so removed that they could keep the disruption, conflict, and bloodshed in a different hemisphere.

Rebooting the World

That's the nuts and bolts of what makes the countries that rule the world the countries that rule the world. The balance of transport determines wealth and security. Deepwater navigation determines reach. Industrialization determines economic muscle tone. And the three combined shape everything from exposure to durability to economic cycles to outlook. The Americans have been remarkably fortunate in that their geography is the best in the world for all three factors, and beginning in 1890 they finally started leveraging that geography to become the world's superpower.

The first time that the Americans fully brought their awesome power to bear was in the Second World War. In doing so the Americans did more than determine the course of a global military conflict; they shaped the entirety of the world in which we now live. That reshaping did the oddest thing.

It turned geopolitics *off.*

CHAPTER 5

◦———————◦

Buying Off Geopolitics

For most countries geopolitics are unforgiving. If you exist in harsh terrain or among harsh neighbors you just don't have many options for managing your affairs, assuming circumstances allow any options at all. The Turks surged up the Danube, as their home territories were not nearly large or secure enough to guarantee their safety and there were no other reasonable directions to go. The Iberians developed new transport technologies to open trade, as otherwise they would've been trapped in Europe's poor backwaters. The British had to have a navy because they lived on an island; had they done otherwise they would've fallen prey to any other naval power that could reach their shores.

The United States is in many ways the exception that proves the rule. America's physical place in the world is not just benign, but empowering. With no hostile nations on its borders, no hostile entities capable of bringing mass invasion to its shores, and an economy without peer, the American margin for error is absolutely massive. Only the United States could engage in a war as dubious as Iraq or roll out a social policy as byzantine as Obamacare and walk away largely unscathed. In most countries, suspect leadership is often rewarded with national destruction. By contrast, the United States is so huge and so far removed from the world and has such deep reserves of national power that highly questionable or even failed policies can lead to a second term.

But just because the Americans don't *need* a plan and accidentally stumbled into superpowerhood, doesn't mean that they have never *had* a plan. And when they do have a plan—good or bad—the world is remade. One of these plans not only radically reshaped the world, but is solely responsible for the world we are living in today.

To understand just how fundamental America's reshaping of the global system is, we need to take a look at the most destructive war ever fought.

The Limits of Superpowerhood

World War II was the most significant conflict in human history for any number of reasons, but two stand out above the others. To start, it was the first truly industrial conflict in that all of the players had fully internalized the whole host of industrial technologies. The Germans had introduced industrialization to land warfare in the mid-1800s, but from their speedy success in defeating Denmark, Austria, and France, it was obvious that their foes hadn't yet figured the technologies out for themselves. By the beginning of World War II, all the major combatants were fully industrialized, from the manufacture of machine guns and uniforms to the logistics of food distribution. Just as industrialization improves productivity and output by an order of magnitude, so too does it improve the capacity for destruction. Death was regularly dealt at ranges and in volumes on an entirely new scale. Even the low-end assessments for the war estimate 50 million dead.

The war's most enduring legacy, however, wasn't its reach or destructive capacity or the number of players involved, but the fact that one of those players had finally come of age. Because of American participation the war's outcome was never in doubt.

Not only could the United States put a number of men into the field that dwarfed Western European capabilities, but it could also equip them *and* provide matériel for its British and Soviet allies *and* overcome the German U-boat strategy by sheer mass *while* fighting *another* war in another theater. Making matters even worse for the Axis, America's core territories were never under direct threat, so the Americans did not need to focus resources on defense. By mid-1943, the Americans were on the offensive in almost every single battle of every single theater. Those infrequent occasions when the Axis was actually able to seize the initiative and attack were so rare that they've gone down in the American annals as landmark confrontations: places like the Battle of the Bulge[1] and Kasserine Pass. The surprise is not that the Allies won, but that the Axis held on for three years after raising America's ire.

But as awesome as the sheer magnitude of the American war effort was in absolute terms, it paled in comparison to the United States' strategic position when the dust settled.

- The Germans and the Soviets had lost 7 million and 26 million people, or about 11 and 15 percent of their total populations, respectively. The Americans had lost "only" 420,000 people, in relative terms one-thirty-fifth the German losses and one-forty-fifth the Soviet losses.
- At war's end the Americans had forces—on friendly terms—in the United Kingdom, West Germany, France, Italy, Japan, the Netherlands, Belgium, Denmark, Austria, and Norway. The European geographical advantage over the non-American world remained so huge that even in the ashes of the postwar devastation the occupied Western European states still collectively represented one-quarter of global economic power.
- There was little industrial capacity outside of the United States. The United Kingdom was running at full throttle, but running at full throttle on matériel and capital provided almost exclusively by the Americans. Only the Soviets had an independent system—a system that had depended upon U.S. matériel for the past three years. And even with that assistance it was still less than one-third of American economic output.
- Not only had most of the world's industrial and consumption capacity been destroyed, but the war had been so destructive that it had taken as well the bulk of the imperial militaries.

---

1. It should come as no surprise that one of the few battles in which the Americans did not enjoy such a numerical advantage was also one in which American naval power was useless: the Battle of the Bulge. That battle also holds the distinction of being the World War II battle in which the Americans suffered both the most casualties (eighty-one thousand) and the most deaths (ten thousand).

Only the Soviets still had an army, but bereft of naval transport it was an army that was not deployable in a global sense.

- The Americans controlled the oceans. In mid-1939, the Americans had 178 surface combatants and 58 submarines in the water out of a total fleet of less than 400 vessels. On the war's final day only six years later the Americans had a 6,800-vessel navy with over 1,000 major surface and submarine combatants. As important, the navies of every major naval combatant of every significant prewar power had been relocated to the seabed. The United Kingdom was the sole exception, and it could no longer operate without assistance beyond European waters. For the first time since the onset of the blue-water era in the early sixteenth century, there was only one navy on the oceans.

It was the single greatest concentration of power that the world had ever seen.

The question was what to do with the war gains. One obvious option was to absorb the Axis and Western European empires into itself and establish a Pax Americana over the global system. That's certainly what the occupied Europeans and the opposing Soviets expected. After all, it was what they had been doing to each other and all parts of the world within their reach for the entirety of the deepwater era.

But direct global control just wasn't the Americans' style. It wasn't so much a moral distinction as a practical one.

Despite America's numerical superiority vis-à-vis every foe it had battled to date, occupation doesn't play to American strengths. A Pax requires long-term occupation of key distribution and gathering nodes, large-scale urban pacification, and in general making the occupied populations offer up a sizable chunk of their wealth and income to their occupiers. Put another way, it means fighting a wide-ranging, manpower-heavy, low-intensity war of occupation. Forever. The Americans may have been numerous, but they were still maritime. Maritime powers favor highly mobile units that zip about, bringing superior firepower to discrete conflict zones, smashing foes and then flitting off before their adversaries can reposition their land-based forces. A long-term occupation would have parked U.S. detachments across the length and breadth of its new territories and compelled them to police local populations. Their mobility advantages would be surrendered.[2]

The tactics of occupation aside, the strategic picture a Pax presented wasn't very promising either. As of 1946, it was obvious that a cold war with the Soviets was already under way. The Soviet military was not only numerically larger, but clear and extremely present across the bulk of northern Eurasia. In a Pax arrangement the Americans would be draining money and resources from their occupied territories, so expecting Pax subjects to fight to maintain an American empire would have been a tough sell. That meant that the Americans wouldn't just need a few million men to keep the British and French and Italians and Germans and Dutch and Arabs and Persians and Indians and Indonesians and Taiwanese and Japanese and Chinese and Koreans and Filipinos in line, but that Washington would also need additional American forces in the millions to hold the defensive lines against the numerically superior Russian and Red Chinese forces. The Americans were powerful, but they just didn't have the numbers to occupy the bulk of the globe. With a Pax, the American "peacetime" army would have had to exceed wartime force levels.

In contrast, the Soviet/Russian military was built expressly *for* occupation. Russia has no geographic barriers at its borders. Gaining security comes from a simple, two-pronged strategy: occupying everyone nearby to secure strategic buffers, and establishing an intrusive intelligence service to infiltrate the occupied populations in order to keep them docile. The same techniques used to occupy Ukraine and Armenia and Central Asia were already being applied with brutal success in 1946 to occupy Czechoslovakia and Bulgaria and Latvia. As of the late 1940s, it was apparent that while the Americans had come in first in the war, they simply lacked the staying power to hold on to their gains in the face of strident Russian challenges backed by more men, simpler supply chains, a higher tolerance for casualties, and a practiced, casual willingness to apply massive violence to civilian populations to achieve political ends.

A direct American-soldier-for-Soviet-soldier face-off couldn't be won.

---

2. As the Americans painfully learned in Vietnam twenty years later and then painfully relearned in Iraq forty years after that.

What the Americans needed were not just allies to help carry the defense burden, but allies who were so eager that they would be *willing* to stand up against the awesome force of the Red Army, a Red Army that was still roused by the fact that it had single-handedly decimated the Nazi Wehrmacht at Stalingrad. *That* requires a special kind of motivation.

Specifically, it requires a hell of a bribe. And what the Americans came up with was one of the great strategic gambits in history. They assembled a plan, and then assembled their wartime allies on July 1, 1944, for a conference in New Hampshire to lay out their vision for the new world. Which returns us to Bretton Woods.

Waging Peace: Free Trade as a Weapon

The three-point American plan was nothing short of revolutionary. They called it "free trade":

- **Access to the American market.** Access to the home market was the holy grail of the global system to that point. If you found yourself forced to give up the ability to control imports, it typically meant that you had been defeated in a major war (as the French had been in 1871) or your entire regime was on the verge of collapse (as the Turks were in the early twentieth century). A key responsibility of diplomats and admirals alike was to secure market access for their country's businesses. The American market was the *only* consumer market of size that had even a ghost of a chance of surviving the war, making it the *only* market worth seeking.
- **Protection for all shipping.** Previously, control of trade lanes was critical. A not insubstantial proportion of a government's military forces had to be dedicated to protecting its merchants and their cargoes, particularly on the high seas, because you could count on your rivals to use *their* militaries to raid your commerce. As the British Empire expanded around the globe in the eighteenth and nineteenth centuries, they found themselves having constantly to reinvent their naval strategies in order to fend off the fleets of commerce raiders that the Dutch,

French, Turks, and others kept putting into play. The Americans provided their navy—the only one with global reach—to protect all maritime shipping. No one *needed* a navy any longer.

- **A strategic umbrella.** As a final sweetener, the Americans promised to protect all members of the network from the Soviets. This included everything right up to the nuclear umbrella. The only catch was that participants had to allow the Americans to fight the Cold War the way they wanted to.

Accepting the deal was a no-brainer. None of the Allies had any hope of economic recovery or maintaining their independence from the Soviets without massive American assistance. There really was no choice: Partner with the only possible consumer market, the only possible capital source, and the only possible guarantor of security—or disappear behind the Iron Curtain.

As the strategic competition of the Cold War took firmer shape, the Americans were able to identify critical locations in the geopolitical contest and invite key countries to join their trading system. Among the first postwar expansions, the Americans approached none other than the defeated Axis powers.

If America's Western allies thought the deal was a boon, the Germans and Japanese perceived it as too good to be true. The primary reason Germany and Japan had launched World War II in the first place was to gain greater access to resources and markets. Germany wanted the agricultural output of Poland, the capital of the Low Countries, the coal of Central Europe, and the markets of France. Japan coveted the manpower and markets of China and the resources of Southeast Asia. Now that they had been thoroughly defeated, the Americans were offering them economic access far beyond their wildest prewar longings: risk-free access to ample resources and bottomless markets a half a world away. And "all" it would cost them was accepting a security guarantee that was better than anything they could ever have achieved by themselves.

Bretton Woods expanded swiftly:

- India joined shortly after independence, which at a minimum complicated any Soviet efforts to gain a toehold in South Asia.

- Sweden, which controls the bulk of the Baltic coastline and boasts a potent regional navy and air force, joined in the 1950s, denying the Soviets the ability to use the Baltic safely.
- Argentina's membership in the 1960s limited Soviet influence in Latin America by putting the most advanced South American power in the other camp.
- After the failure of the 1973 Yom Kippur War, Egypt jumped into the Bretton Woods pool, robbing the Soviets of their largest client state in both the Middle East and the Mediterranean basin.
- Indonesian (1950), Singaporean (1973), and Thai (1982) membership both curtailed meaningful Soviet penetration into the most valuable portions of Southeast Asia and eliminated any hope of the Soviets exercising naval power in South or Southeast Asia.

The lure of Bretton Woods proved to be the critical component that made the Sino-Soviet split of the 1960s a reality. The unlikely partnership between America and China of course helped rework the strategic math of Southeast Asia in the age of Vietnam, but that was only a small piece of a much larger puzzle. The Soviets had plenty of Pacific coastline, but the only good ports they had access to were Chinese locales like Tianjin and Hainan Island. Once China joined Bretton Woods, the Soviet Union's only remaining deepwater, ice-free port was Petropavlovsk on the Kamchatka Peninsula, a base so removed from Russian population centers that it could only be supplied by air.

For their part, the Chinese were desperate. In the Korean War, superior American technology resulted in a four-to-one casualty ratio. The Chinese knew that as a maritime power the Americans would eventually lose interest and go home, but in 1969 the Chinese had skirmished with their Soviet "allies" along the Ussuri River. Soviet military technology was nearly as good as American military technology, but Soviet troops didn't come by boat: They were already on the ground and there to stay. Chinese human-wave tactics would be met by Soviet human-wave tactics—only the Soviet waves would also have tanks and aircraft. Unless the Chinese could also change the strategic math, they faced a war on their northern border that they could not hope to win.

The Chinese had to industrialize. But that required money. Raw materials. Technology. Markets. Sea-lane access. And *that* required the Americans.

But both countries also needed to change the public perception of the other. Luck intervened in 1971 at the Ping-Pong world championships in Nagoya, Japan, when U.S. team member Glen Cowan mistakenly got on the Chinese team's bus, where he was approached by Chinese champion Zhuang Zedong. After a brief translator-assisted conversation, the two exchanged gifts and found themselves plastered across first Japanese and later global media. *Time* magazine called it "the ping heard round the world."

Very quickly thereafter their friendly chat segued into big-time politics. China invited the U.S. team to play a series of exhibition matches in China later that year (making the team the first Americans to visit China since the 1949 revolution). Washington's reciprocation was accompanied by an end to the trade embargo. And in February 1972, Richard Milhous Nixon up and went to China to talk about, among other things, Bretton Woods.

The collective result of the American scheme was not simply a firm break with the imperial era, but the active and enthusiastic co-option of every meaningful non-Soviet power on the planet. Without firing a shot or engaging in any more than the mildest of arm-twisting, the Americans founded the greatest alliance in history while surrounding the Soviets with a thick hedge of hostile countries who were willing—even eager—to serve as the Americans' first line of defense against the Red Army.

The Soviets didn't stand a chance against the American-backed coalition. On one side stood an American-dominated maritime-and-trade alliance of states comprising North America, Western Europe, Japan, Korea, Taiwan, Australasia, and a double handful of key countries elsewhere—such as China—that the Americans flat-out bribed to join them. Facing off against this unprecedently potent alliance was the Soviet Empire, complete with its occupied satellite states in Central Europe and an eclectic variety of extraordinarily poor allies, such as Cuba, Yemen, Mozambique, North Korea, and Syria, scattered around the world and whose loyalty the Soviets had to secure with occupying forces or purchase with subsidies. One side controlled the money, the markets, and the ability to move across the oceans; the other didn't. The Americans started the Cold War with an economy far larger than the *entire* Soviet world, and by the end of the Cold

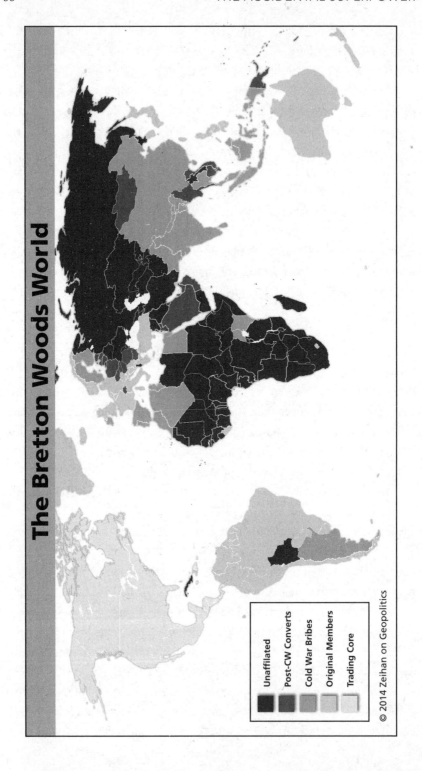

The Bretton Woods World

Unaffiliated
Post-CW Converts
Cold War Bribes
Original Members
Trading Core

© 2014 Zeihan on Geopolitics

War a lengthy list of states—including the once crushingly impoverished South Korea—had leveraged American economic offerings with such success that they themselves surpassed Soviet living standards.

Of course every plan has its complications. First, not every country had the same interpretation of signing over its security policy as the Americans did. Many of the European states assumed that the Americans had of course intended for the European *empires* to continue on, now simply under the American aegis. Such was not the American intent, and convincing some of the Europeans otherwise took a little doing. As the premier prewar maritime powers, the British and French proved the most in need of attitude adjustments. The Suez Canal Crisis of 1956, which concluded with the Americans intentionally and publicly humiliating the English and French by withdrawing post–World War II recovery aid and spearheading international opposition, was the most visible manifestation of the Americans driving home just who was in charge. Over the next generation every significant European colony got its independence. The Americans didn't take any of them over, because it didn't need them. Its goal was to break the European hold over the world and make the European powers dependent upon the Bretton Woods system.

The mass independence of the now-former imperial territories did that very well indeed, as it both forced resource supply chain responsibility into the hands of the U.S. Navy and removed a primary logic for the European states even having navies in the first place.

Second, as the security guarantor of their alliance network, the Americans had to, well, guarantee the security of the alliance network. It wouldn't do to tell your allies that *they* didn't need a navy or expeditionary forces if you didn't use *your* navy and *your* expeditionary forces to protect their core interests. That meant that the Americans had to abandon many of the strategic advantages of being a maritime power, the biggest of which is the ability to choose the time and place of combat.

The Americans could still initiate conflict wherever and whenever they liked, but the need to maintain their new alliance network meant that their foes could *force* combat upon the Americans at times and places of *their* choosing. Should the Americans decline to defend a Bretton Woods participant, the entire alliance structure would shiver. For if the Americans proved unwilling to engage the Chinese in Korea, then was their security guarantee for the Germans against the Soviets really worth what they said it was? Korea and Vietnam were wars the Americans had to fight not because they wanted to fight them or even because local strategic considerations were worth a war, but rather because failure to rise to battle would have generated a crisis of confidence that risked bringing the entire alliance structure down. The Americans' new grand strategy transformed them from a nimble, offensive power into a reactionary power forced to make large, static deployments in a manner of land powers. American military bases in places like Germany, Turkey, and Korea made little sense except to directly contain Soviet power. They certainly didn't help with traditional maritime power projection.

The third complication was one of perspective. Throughout the Cold War, the grand geopolitic between the Americans and the Soviets raged as sharply as ever. But as little as one tier down, things could not have been more different. Quite intentionally, the American system suspended local geopolitical competitions, relieving Bretton Woods members from needing to seek out markets or protect their trade flows. That freed America's allies from the need to defend against age-old rivals, many of whom were now allies. A few examples:

- France and Germany didn't have to arm to protect themselves from each other; instead they collaboratively formed the supragovernmental institution of the European Union, something that would have been laughable prewar.
- Mid-tier European states such as Sweden and the Netherlands were able to focus on their trade and brokering strong points with a minimum of effort to defense.
- With global trade lanes guaranteed, the need to occupy this or that location dissolved. The world's oldest wheat producer—Egypt—breathed free for the first time in two millennia.
- European colonies around the world were freed. The Southeast Asian states formed the Association of Southeast Asian Nations (ASEAN) and with it their own—also American-guaranteed—free trade network.
- Japan no longer had need to prey upon the East Asian rim. With American security guarantees, South Korea, Taiwan, and

Singapore emerged as three of the world's most dynamic economies. China, for the first time in its history, existed in a security environment that allowed it to consolidate free of outside interference.

After eons of struggling for economic growth and physical security, both were now guaranteed. Instead of wealth and security being the goal, they became the starting point. What we now think of as the developed world forgot what it meant to be in want, and broad swaths of territories that had never been able to incorporate into modern states were able to do so once the threat of European and Japanese imperialism disappeared. The deficits of geography and antagonisms of the past were put on hiatus.

Which brings us to the final—and what is about to prove the most problematic—complication. Many players—Germany, Korea, the two Chinas, Ireland, and Singapore, to name a few—did more than use Bretton Woods to simply export their way to stability. They redesigned their economic systems to take full advantage of a world of risk-free international shipping and easy American market access. These places, and many more, are now dependent upon the continuation of the current system for their economic wherewithal. And even those that expanded their international footprint more modestly lack the military capacity to protect their overseas trade networks. Most lack the ability to patrol much more than their own coastlines, if even that.

Scared New World: An Expensive Antique

However, one very important country doesn't need the economic benefits of Bretton Woods. It is the country that designed, imposed, and now sustains that system.

For the Americans, Bretton Woods is a strategic tool, not an economic strategy. As such, they plan and deploy their military efforts around it; American forces have global reach, and the American navy patrols the sea lanes to keep them open. But the Americans never redesigned their economic system around Bretton Woods, and even now, seventy years after the inception of Bretton Woods, only 11 percent of U.S. GDP comes from exports. That places the United States on the same list with some odd companions that are similarly economically isolated from the world: Ethiopia, Afghanistan, Rwanda, and Sudan. But unlike those poor countries, which have minimal international connections due to war and/ or their landlocked nature, the American isolation is due to the extreme opportunities it enjoys at home. Its internal size and local connectivity are simply unparalleled.

Consequently, for the Americans international trade has typically been a sideshow. And now, as throughout the past seventy years, the global system persists only because the Americans continue to pay the full price of sustaining it. The commitment to that system has been steadily falling for some time. The efforts of three post–Cold War American presidents—Bill Clinton, George W. Bush, and Barack Obama—highlight an ever-so-steady shift away from support for expanding the free trade network:

- Clinton inherited negotiations and completed ratification and implementation for the formation of the World Trade Organization and NAFTA, the two most significant trading systems with which the Americans are involved.
- Bush initiated—but failed to finish—talks for the next effort to deepen WTO commitments. The new free trade areas he initiated and completed were either with close neighbors such as the Central American states, or with allies like Australia, Colombia, and Korea.
- Obama has initiated no new free trade agreements with *any* countries, only implementing or continuing with talks launched by his predecessors.

Free trade isn't cheap from a military point of view. U.S. defense spending throughout the Cold War regularly topped 5 percent of GDP—typically over twice the ratio of its allies. The American navy costs a cool $150 billion annually (with another $30 billion for the Marines). And most of all, the countries that have chosen to specialize in exports turned the American trade deficit into a $700 billion monster at the peak of the last economic boom.

Such costs were easily justified in the context of superpower competition, but as you may have noticed, the Cold War ended in 1989 and the Soviet Union collapsed just three years later. The Russians may have emerged from the corpse of the Soviet Union, but they are a pale shadow in terms of their capability, ambition, and threat. Containing contemporary Russia requires no global network.

The looming crisis of the contemporary system is actually pretty straightforward. Everything that makes the global economy tick—from reliable access to global energy supplies to the ability to sell into the American market to the free movement of capital—is a direct outcome of the ongoing American commitment to Bretton Woods. But the Americans are no longer gaining a strategic benefit from that network, even as the economic cost continues. At some point—maybe next week, maybe ten years from now—the Americans are going to reprioritize, and the tenets of Bretton Woods, the foundation of the free trade order, will simply end.

That will hit hard enough, but it is only the first of three imminent convulsions that will tear the global order asunder.

Buying Off Geopolitics: Ten Years On

There's nothing quite like reality rudely interjecting itself into a meticulously crafted piece of analysis, especially when it's one of your own conclusions that blunders sideways into another conclusion.

On February 22, 2022, the Russian Army surged over one hundred thousand troops across the Ukrainian border, launching what the world has since labeled the Ukraine War. I have called it something a bit more flowery: Russia's Twilight War.

Russia's actions didn't surprise me at all. I've been anticipating a military conflict since before I wrote *The Accidental Superpower* ten years ago, and I outline a possible route to and through the war in book number two, *The Absent Superpower*. For reasons geographic and demographic this war was always going to happen, and it was always going to happen about when it did (you'll get a lot more on *that* once you get to the original text of this book's "Players" chapter).

No, I was not surprised by the war, but something *did* surprise me: the utter incompetence of Russian forces. Russia's economy dwarfs that of Ukraine, arguably the worst off of all the post-Soviet republics. The bulk of the old Soviet industrial plant lies within Russia, as does nearly all of the USSR's seven *decades* of military stockpiling. The Ukrainian Air Force is so small, its pilots so untrained, and its jets so old that at war's beginning even calling it a "force" was a misnomer. Fully a third of the prewar Ukrainian population either spoke Russian as their first language or identified as ethnically *Russian*. In the 2014 war the Ukrainian military was such a joke and local populations so pro-Russian that the Russians captured the Crimean Peninsula without firing a single shot. And yet and yet and yet, at the time of this writing sixteen months after the war's commencement, Ukraine not only still stands, it is *advancing* against Russian forces.

One more development surprised me: deep actions by the United States to support Ukraine militarily.

It would have been easy to consign Ukraine to its fate. Had the 2020 presidential election gone another way, I've little doubt that is precisely what would have happened. One of the Trump administration's (many) open secrets was that Trump unofficially indicated he planned to withdraw the United States from the NATO security alliance on the first day of his second term. Such a gathering of national marbles and going home was precisely the sort of bad-hair-day shift into retrenched isolationism I identified as a strategic probability in the 2012 release of this book—and have been quietly dreading ever since.

Instead, the Biden administration has bellied up to the bar with the most robust security assistance—weapons, ammunition, training, and targeting—of any ally since World War II itself. I've never been more thrilled to be wrong, but that doesn't mean I'm thrilled with the "why" of the Biden administration's decision.

The decisive moment came in the war's first week. A forty-mile convoy of Russian military vehicles proceeded south from Russia's mini-me, Belarus, making a beeline for the Ukrainian capital of Kyiv. It was more than enough firepower to—all by itself—obliterate the entirety of the Ukrainian military. Many—me included—were prepared to call the war for the Russians just a few days in.

And then reality shoved its thumb into the eye of conventional wisdom. The convoy...stopped.

It wasn't because of Ukrainian partisan resistance (although there was some of that), but instead because the Russians had neglected to bring... fuel trucks. The convoy then just sat there. For days. Then bit by bit Russian soldiers dismounted from their equipment and *walked* back to Belarus. Because the vaunted Russian military, heir to one of the greatest military forces in history, had also forgotten to bring...food.[3]

It was this blazing ineptitude that not only gave Ukraine a chance in what should have been a walk-over, it also altered Europe's and North America's assessment of the nature of the Russian threat.

The reassessment helped no one sleep better.

Russia's territory is absolutely indefensible. It is flat. It is wide open. And it is above all else plagued by weather so poor and so fickle that it can never generate the volume of population density or capital or infrastructure required to competently look after its own security. The only solution is expansion. Expansion beyond the flats until Russian forces can reach a series of mountains and seas and deserts that serve as strategic blocking

---

3. Many of them robbed, raped, and murdered along the way. Such is the story of the atrocities of Bucha.

points. Russian forces can then crowd into the gaps between those barriers, barring access to the vast wide opens of the Eurasian interior. Ukraine occupies the unfortunate position of not sitting in those gaps but being on the way to the two most important: the Polish Gap, and the Bessarabian Gap in northeastern Romania. This war was *always* going to happen.

And Russia was *always* going to be in it to the end. At the time of this *Ten Years On* writing, Russia has paid much of the price for a major war, while gleaning none of the benefits. Its one-foot-in approach to mobilization has left it in a weaker strategic position than when the war began, its hideous war crimes have made any sort of meaningful peace negotiation laughable, and its utter dependence upon foreign capital and skilled labor means Russia's place as a major food, energy, minerals, and fertilizer exporter is not long for this world. All that is left is the hope of security from victory.

The Russians will not stop. The Russians dare not stop.

Which means from the Western world's point of view, the conflict is far more dangerous than simply the ego-driven, neo-imperial conquering that is often portrayed in the media. The Russians *will* push until they have all of Ukraine, and then they *will* cross additional borders into Romania, Poland, Lithuania, Latvia, and Estonia, and then there *will* be a direct confrontation between Russian and NATO forces.

And the Russian forces—not capable of doing particularly well against underarmed, undertrained Ukrainian forces—will be obliterated. And since the Russians—rightly—see this war as a battle for their existence, and since they know a conventional victory is impossible, the Russians *will* use nuclear weapons.

Russia's failings at the Battle of Kyiv put the stakes of the war in stark relief. The Biden administration felt it had no recourse but to act. To train the Ukrainians as quickly as possible. To provide the Ukrainians with whatever weapons systems they could prove themselves competent on. To supply real-time targeting information to strike Russian forces anywhere in occupied territories. There are limits, of course. No American military personnel on Ukrainian soil (a direct NATO-Russian clash is precisely what needs to be avoided). No American weapons to be used on the other side of the Ukrainian-Russian border (which might trigger a defensive use of nukes). But with those two simple (and important!) caveats in mind, everything else is on the table.

On the Europe side of things, we've seen more American-European strategic engagement since February 2002 than in the entirety of the post–Berlin Wall era. A renewed Russian threat that was not merely calloused to mass casualties, but that was all but certain to go nuclear when the war reached NATO. It felt a *lot* like 1945. For a brief, shining moment, I was hopeful that the Americans would renew their original Bretton Woods pact with their allies, but this time with a heavier emphasis on improving the human condition. Maybe we would finally get an international version of the Thousand Points of Light mooted by George H. W. Bush three decades previous.

But the United States lending its weight to the Ukrainians has proven insufficient to salvage, much less reboot, globalization.

By the summer of 2022 it was clear that everything on offer from Washington was military, not economic, and that nearly all of the new agreements were bilateral, not multilateral. That granted the Americans what they want in the post–Cold War era—control—but at the cost of abandoning any dreams of a better world. If anything, the economics of global structures are breaking down even faster, for the Biden administration has ended precious few of his predecessors' trade embargos or tariffs, instead enshrining most of them into U.S. law. And so, the spinning apart of the American-led globalized trading Order continues apace.

Two emblematic examples.

First, the U.S. government adopted the Inflation Reduction Act, in essence the Biden administration's failed green legislation with a new marketing campaign. The IRA stipulates a series of strict (and rising) national sourcing requirements from everything used in transitioning from a fossil fuel–fueled system to one powered by green-generated electricity. At $1.2 trillion, the money available is the most robust industrial policy the Americans have adopted since World War II. Countries with preexisting free trade agreements with the United States can potentially secure participation. So far, the Canadians, Mexicans, and Australians are in, while the Japanese and Koreans are hammering out the details. Anyone else—for example, Europe, which is struggling through the economic impacts of a major war on its eastern border—is shit out of luck.

Second, maritime security. With Russia having displaced Iran as history's most sanctioned country, American financial sanctions have become far more regularized and effective. Not just against Russia, but against the country many of these types of sanctions were prototyped on: Iran. The

Iranians are, understandably, cheesed off. And so during the early months of 2023 they started seizing oil tankers—at the time of this writing, six so far. Had this happened in the 2000s, 1990s, or 1980s, the Americans would have launched an amphibious assault to free the ships and their crews, and undoubtedly used explosives to melon-scoop away significant bits of the Iranians' naval and energy infrastructure. Instead, the Navy issued a sternly worded press release, and went back to more important matters. And this in an environment when the very real threat of losing Russia as the world's second largest oil exporter looms over a jittery market.

Unless the mainland is threatened, Americans just don't care very much these days. I'm beyond thrilled that the Ukrainians are standing up to their foes. I'm beyond thrilled that the Americans and Europeans are doing their part to help. And I'm terrified that the American view of economic and strategic policy being utterly unrelated has become so deeply entrenched.

We may well be getting what—for most countries—is the worst of all worlds: an America utterly disinterested in maintaining global trading structures and commercial maritime security, while also pursuing an ever more nationalistic economic policy set, *while simultaneously* demonstrating a willingness to put its finger on the security scales. Populist, isolationist economic policy, married to activist, indirect military interventions.

Buckle up.

CHAPTER 6

The Demographic Roller Coaster

Individual persons tend to act pretty randomly and only rarely can anyone anticipate what a particular individual will do. But put those individual persons into large groups and individual randomness gives way to group patterns. Young people raise children. Old people retire. Babies scream. The experts in the study of population data, demographers, make their livelihoods out of predicting what entire *populations* will do. In that their study has a fair amount in common with geopolitics, where the base unit of a population is the nation.

Demographics leaves very little room for interpretation. For example, as a group, twenty-year-old Generation Yers behave in ways that are demonstrably different from forty-year-old Generation Xers and a world apart from sixty-year-old Baby Boomers. Similarly, the population of any age group is more or less solid, and thanks to mortality rates, we know that an age group will become a slightly smaller age group every few years. Put another way, there is a fixed number of Yers alive today. From that simple number we have a very good idea of how many thirty-five-year-olds we'll have in a decade, how many forty-five-year-olds in two, and so on.

Why the certainty? It's a simple matter of data and inevitability. Data in that once you know death and birth rates—information that any marginally competent tax office can provide—the math of figuring out the population structure is straightforward. Inevitability in that you cannot manufacture twenty-year-olds—that opportunity ended twenty years ago and their numbers can only decrease from here on out. There will be no more Boomers or Gen Xers or even Gen Yers. We can only manufacture Generation Z babies: Their generation is still being formed, and it will continue to be until about 2019, when the rolls of their ranks close for good and the next generation begins.

Marry demographics with geopolitics and you have a series of powerful tools for predicting everything from political instability to economic outcomes. Considering how complex and ever-shifting the "politics" part of geopolitics can be, demography's solidity and high levels of certainty can be incredibly refreshing.

That is, until you look at demographic data closely and it sucks the optimism out of the room. Just as geopolitics tells us that the free trade era is closing, demography tells us that the era of consumption-driven growth that has been the economic norm for seventy years is coming to an unceremonious end.

Demographics, Capital, and Technology

Industrialization has changed many things in human history, but one of the most important is birth rates.

Before industrialization, most people farmed. Preindustrial agriculture is backbreaking work. Land has to be tilled, planted, weeded, irrigated, and harvested. Animals have to be fed, tended, guarded, and slaughtered. Grain has to be gathered, threshed, bagged, dragged, stored, and sold. There is always something to be done and never enough time or workers. No wonder that for most of human history oxen and horses were indicators of wealth, because their labor could be used to produce it. And for those who were not wealthy, there were children. Children are free labor. Luckily for farmers, they know the secret of how to make children, and so they made a lot of them.

Industrialized agriculture, however, operates at higher levels of productivity—it takes (far) fewer man-hours to bring a bushel of produce in than before. The higher productivity creates a surplus labor force that gravitates to industrial centers—cities—in search of higher-paying manufacturing and industrial jobs. Over time, mass urbanization results, and as the population density of cities increases, the demand for living space outstrips the supply and rents go up. Children are no longer a necessary pool of free labor in the cramped, expensive confines of the city, but rather a luxury reserved for those who can afford them.

Put more simply, industrialization leads to plummeting birth rates. The depth and speed of this shift varies greatly based on any number of factors—the ability of agriculture to mechanize, the ability of locally supplied capital to support local industrialized development, the ability of people from the countryside to easily integrate to urban areas, and so on. As such, hyperorganized, hypercapitalized, webwork-infrastructured, small-footprint Germany became the first country to majority urbanize in 1890, and today what is left of the German countryside feels like an open-air museum being preserved for posterity. The sprawled-out Americans didn't hit majority urbanization until about 1920, and even today the United States remains the least urbanized of the major nations.

The (post)industrial map of finance doesn't so much follow river systems as it did in the preindustrial past (although to this day most major cities remain on excellent transport nodes, the most excellent of which remain rivers) as it follows the demography of workers. While workers' spending determines economic growth, and workers' savings determine financial strength, not all workers are created equal. Once your country industrializes, the difference that matters isn't race or ethnicity or (gasp) even geography, but rather *age*.

From a financial perspective the population can be split into four groups. The first are the children. They're not working but they are eating, wearing clothes, requiring shelter, and needing education. They are expensive and they give nothing back whatsoever. They are an absolute drain on both the system and maybe their parents' sanity. They have but one redeeming feature: In time they will grow up to be the workers and taxpayers of the future.

In the second group are young workers. This age group—roughly from eighteen to forty-five—are massive consumers. They are buying homes and cars for the first time. They are raising children, with all of the attendant—and rising—expenses that come from keeping growing kids fed, clothed, housed, and educated. Sometimes they are going to school themselves. They don't have that many years of expertise under their collective belts and they have the (lack of) paycheck to prove it. They are at the nadir of their earning potential but they are saddled with more expenses than they are likely to know at any time in their lives. They carry balances on their credit cards. They have home loans, car loans, college loans—both theirs and their children's. They are massive consumers, massive borrowers, and anemic savers. As a society, most of our economic growth comes from their debt-driven consumption.

The third group are the mature workers. For this group the hard stuff is behind them. The kids have moved out. The house is largely paid for. They are far more likely to own their vehicles outright. They have bills— who doesn't?—but those debts and bills tend to occupy a far lower percentage of their income than is the case for their kids. That's not simply because their debts are relatively lower, but also because their incomes are relatively higher. People in their fifties and sixties are at the height of their earning potential as well as the low end of their borrowing needs. Low debts and high incomes also mean they are at the height of their taxpaying existence. Governments *love* their mature workers.

These mature workers are as capital-rich as the younger generation are capital-poor. A very large chunk of this extra capital ends up being invested for various purposes, most notably to prepare for retirement. They are attempting to grow their money, so their investments tend to go into a wide range of stocks, bonds, and mutual funds, both domestic and foreign. Volatility is fine because they are taking the long view, and their continual savings mean that most market crashes are simply opportunities to buy up cheap assets that will later rise in value. They are massive providers of capital to the system at large, the government included, and their choice of investments is heavily skewed toward vehicles that promote rapid economic growth since those are the investments that tend to generate higher returns.

The fourth and final group within any population are the retirees. For them, large-scale participation in the financial world looks radically different from the young-worker borrowers or the mature-worker savers. These people are *done*. They have saved all they are going to save, and are whittling away at their accrued wealth. They live off the interest if they can get away with it, but typically the principal gets knifed far too soon.

While these retirees enjoy a strongly positive capital position, they operate radically differently from their preretirement selves. They cannot stomach reductions in principal value because they cannot make up for any losses with new income. Nearly, if not all, of their assets are domestically held. Volatility is not just the enemy of the day, but the enemy for the rest of their lives. It doesn't matter if that volatility is in the form of currency risk, stock market gyrations, or the sex, lies, and videotapes of corporate politics. Stocks and dynamism are out. Government bonds and CDs are in.

Consequently, it isn't simply the case that retirees don't put new investments into the system, or that the nature of their investments aren't the sort that generate much economic growth, but that their accrued investments also *shrink* as time goes on. And of course most of them will be drawing pensions as well. Unlike young workers who generate demand and growth, or mature workers who generate capital and investment, retirees as a population cohort are a net drag on the system, and that drag increases as their nest egg shrinks.

In a "normal" population there is a very straightforward distribution among these groups. Many infants followed by slightly fewer young children followed by slightly fewer children followed by slightly fewer teenagers and so on. Simple mortality steadily whittles away at the population until there are very few remaining retirees. Stack the data up in five-year blocks with young children on the bottom and the elderly at the top and you get one of demographers' more insightful inventions: a population pyramid. Below is India's pyramid at the time of this

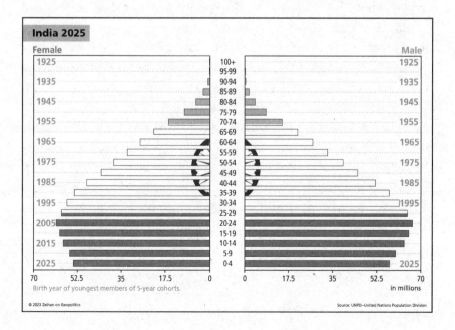

India 2025

writing. It is a textbook example of what a normal demographic pattern looks like.

In such a system capital is somewhat hard to come by. There aren't all that many mature workers generating capital, while a large volume of younger workers are demanding it. The result is a relatively strict capital system in which the cost of credit is fairly high, whether that credit be sought for a car loan or stealth bomber. In such systems there are constant restrictions on growth, but nearly all of them can be traced back to insufficient capital, which in turn is rooted in the demographic structure. Investments—whether financial, industrial, technological, or labor—just are not made unless a strong rate of return is expected. While this is a gross oversimplification, money is treated like, well, money. It is something that has a great deal of value and so is only doled out when the risks are deemed reasonable. In systems that have such demographic characteristics, banks and investors ask hard questions before committing funds.

Add industrialization to the mix, however, and decades of dropping birth rates generate a wildly different demographic result. The idea that children are no longer an economic necessity takes some time to sink in, and the average family size doesn't so much shrink across the years as across the generations. In time young adults become the dominant population cohort. Individually they are spending just as much as they did before, but they are spending more on themselves and less on their children (because they have fewer of them). That means not just fewer diapers and scooters, but also lower government outlays on education—the top line item for each and every state budget in the United States.

Across most of the developed world, this bulge in the young-worker demographic hit just as the Cold War ended. As one would expect, the mass of young workers generated unprecedented levels of growth across the rich world. In the United States this group is known as the Baby Boomers;[1] they are the largest ever American generation as a proportion of the total population. This demographic structure *should* have pushed

---

1. Everyone has his or her own start/stop years for the various generational breaks. Here are mine: Baby Boomers, 1946–64; Gen X, 1965–79; Gen Y (a.k.a. Millennials), 1980–99; Gen Z (a.k.a. Post-Millennials), 2000–2019.

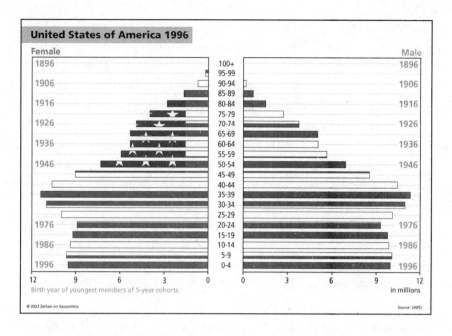

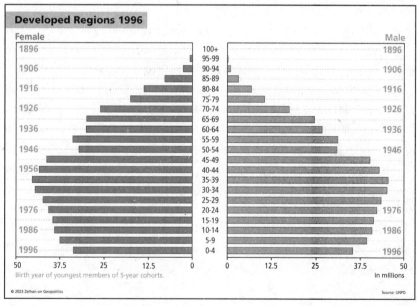

capital costs through the roof. But it didn't. Geopolitics intervened and the results—for the West—were magical.

First, there was the "peace dividend." Defense cutbacks allowed for many Western budgets to move into the black for the first time in two generations, freeing up capital for more economically productive means. Gone were the days of the Reagan budget deficits that often absorbed what free capital was on order. Instead all that credit was available for the private sector. In the United States alone the net defense savings built up to over $150 billion annually (in then-current dollars) by the end of the decade.

Second, the U.S. dollar emerged supreme among global currencies. In February 1992, the Europeans signed the Maastricht Treaty, which created the common European currency. The euro would not be introduced to the world at large until 1999, but the mere commitment to terminate all those different currencies radically decreased their attractiveness as stores of wealth. Few wanted to risk their money on Europe's unprecedented experiment in pan-government planning. Everyone who had cash on hand, from the Japanese central bank to Samsung to the Italian mob, switched en masse from deutschmarks and francs and lire to dollars. There is no good data as to how much cash flooded into American financial markets (as a rule cocaine smugglers don't have the best of reporting relationships with the U.S. Federal Reserve Board), but it is pretty easy to measure what the Fed needed to do to accommodate the influx. From 1994 (when the Fed realized that there was a storm surge of demand for the dollar) to 2002 (when the euro finally got some traction and the surge dialed back) the Fed had to more than double the U.S. money supply—a $2 trillion increase—to accommodate the surge in demand. Normally such a massive monetary expansion is the province of banana republics, with all the inflationary impacts one would expect from printing vast amounts of currency. But because real money was flowing into—instead of out from—the United States, the country actually enjoyed its lowest inflation rates since the 1960s.

Third, Soviet money fled to the United States. The average Russian found their savings made worthless overnight, while corrupt officials and a new breed of Russian businessmen who came to be known as the oligarchs looked for ways to profit from rapidly changing geopolitical alignments. With the demise of European currencies already announced, the U.S. dollar was the only refuge for all. Ordinary Russians took to storing dollars in their mattresses, while Russian statesmen and oligarchs alike held their gains—ill and not—in U.S. banks. The actual amount that fled remains a very hot topic in Russian circles even today, but whether it was tens of billions or hundreds of billions of dollars, the simple point is that it all flowed to the Western countries. On top of that, the Russian industrial base simply went away, but Russian commodities output did not. The excess didn't so much creep as hurl itself upon international markets to the tune of 500,000 bpd (barrels per day) of new crude supply per year for *nine straight years*. Similar dumping occurred in every mineral industry in which the Russians were players.

Russian Oil Production, Consumption and Exports

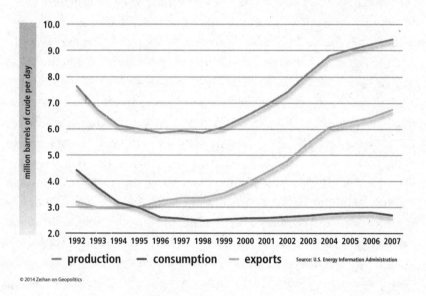

— production   — consumption   — exports   Source: U.S. Energy Information Administration

© 2014 Zeihan on Geopolitics

Collectively this geopolitical change overwhelmed the normal rule that lots of twenty- and thirty-somethings makes for an expensive-capital environment. Instead, the cost of capital plunged, allowing consumption-driven growth not simply to soar, but to explode. Somewhat restrained government spending during the Clinton administration combined with rising Boomer incomes (and therefore tax payments) steadily whittled the U.S. budget deficit away, with the federal government moving into the black in the 1998–99 fiscal year, freeing up even more capital for the private sector. And just as the post-Soviet windfall was about to wind down, the East Asian financial crisis kicked in, gutting raw materials demand— oil briefly dropped below $10 a barrel—and flooding the United States with capital fleeing from the entire East Asian rim. The amount spent on energy in the United States dropped from 4 percent of GDP to under 1 percent, and at least another $1 trillion of capital flight from East Asia sought American refuge. All told (a very conservative) $5 trillion in foreign cash—foreign cash that cared nothing for a good return, only seeking safety—inundated the American system in the 1990s.

And then things got *insanely* good; the American capital flood turned into a global capital tsunami. This time it wasn't geopolitics that was responsible, but instead demography. Recall that while young workers are the world's spenders and so generate economic growth, it is mature workers who are the world's savers and so generate credit. As the 1990s gave way to the 2000s, the American and European demographic pictures evolved.

The Boomers had grown up. Most of their kids had left home. Most of their houses were paid for. Most Boomers were saving up for retirement. Their consumption slimmed and their net assets ballooned. If the 1990s were the decade of growth, the 2000s were the decade of investment. Traditional demography finally pushed through the (admittedly happy) geopolitical noise and flooded the system with credit anew. This time, however, the credit wasn't the result of a bunch of spurious, one-time events, but was core to the population structure of the entire Western world. The average American 401(k) balance in 2014 hit $90,000. That might not sound like enough to fund your retirement, but that single source of retirement money amounts to over $4 trillion. Without even beginning to count the country's various pension plans (which have nothing to do with Social Security) or other personal assets like homes, you get a nest egg worth some $17 trillion, making the heady 1990s seem a mere warm-up.[2]

The Americans (and Northern Europeans, who had a similar demography) simply couldn't metabolize all this money. Not only were the Boomers no longer at the height of their spending, but their successors—Generation X—couldn't hold a candle to Boomer consumption. While the Boomers were the largest generation in American history as a proportion of the population, Gen X was the smallest. Consumption and growth—

---

2. None of this is meant to say that the Americans (and others) are not facing a pension shortfall. They are. They *all* are. But this is still the largest single class of financial assets that the world has ever seen, both in absolute and relative terms, and its mere existence has skewed not just national politics, but international economics as well.

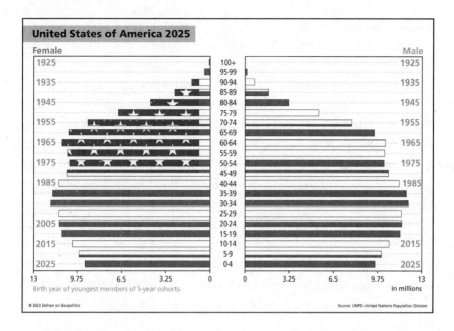

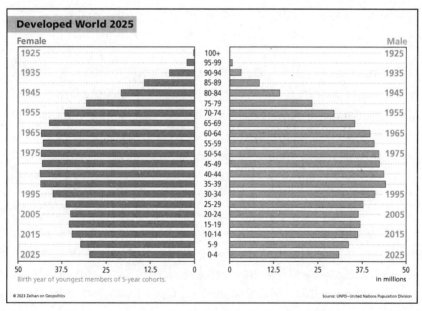

obviously—slowed. Credit—obviously—soared. The cost of credit plummeted to levels never before experienced. If you were ever going to purchase a house or have a credit card, the 2000s were *the* time to do it. But even then the Americans and Northern Europeans just couldn't absorb all of the credit windfall, and their surplus money spilled out everywhere. To Southern Europe. To Latin America. To undeveloped Asia. To the former Soviet Union. Everywhere.

But it was temporary. And soon, *very* soon, it will all be over.

In a few short years the mass of mature workers—first and foremost the American Baby Boomers—will shift from the "mature worker" into the "retired" category. As that happens, instead of having new infusions into their savings every month that go into a mix of high-growth credit instruments like stocks and corporate bonds, they soon will be withdrawing money from a static investment pool populated with low-risk assets that include a lot of cash. The party will be over. It will then be up to Gen X to fund the massive geriatric social programs that the Baby Boomers' superior voting numbers ensured for themselves *while they at the same time* replace the Baby Boomers as the world's primary source of capital. As there are one-quarter more Boomers than Xers, there just won't be enough capital to go around.

There are any number of outcomes from this demographic and financial wibble-wobble that will haunt us for quite some time:

- The Boomer-driven capital bonanza inflated bubbles in dozens of sectors. As in any system in which something exists in extreme excess, inefficient use becomes the order of the day. Too much oil in Venezuela? Gasoline sells for pennies a liter and you don't see many hybrids on the road. Too much labor in Bangladesh? The minimum wage is pennies per hour and the population lives in de facto slavery. Remember the 2000 dot-com bust? Same basic concept. Too many people thought the opportunity was too good and put too many resources behind the Internet explosion. Depending upon how big bubbles get and how they pop, the sector can take months to years to recover. Financial bubbles, however, are a class apart. When there is too much money, the financial world shoves that money *everywhere*, and *any* investment fad can get funding and the entire economy gets decidedly frothy. The dot-com bubble didn't spread much beyond the world of the Internet and so the ensuing recession was the country's second shortest and second shallowest. But the financial bubble caused by the Boomers' investment savings has flooded the system—hell, the world—with excess cash. One outcome of this was of course the 2007 subprime real estate bubble and crash. But there isn't a sector large or small, at home or abroad, that hasn't benefited from the wash of Boomer money. And so there won't be a sector large or small, at home or abroad, that will not be hurt when that money retreats.

- The developing world had a great surge of energy thanks to the money flow. Countries that could never generate their own excess capital—Brazil, Russia, and India come to mind—could access international markets to finance whatever they wanted. These countries exploded onto the scene. Chinese demand, fueled by absurdly cheap money abroad and at home, rose through and past ludicrously unsustainable levels. The resulting high commodity prices only further inflated the apparent success of developing states dependent upon raw commodity exports. Again, Brazil and Russia looked particularly good, and even Africa looked significantly less crappy than history had gotten used to recording. While many developing countries did use the credit more wisely than the Europeans—investing in infrastructure, for example—the same problem exists. When the credit tap is turned off the growth will stop. The portions of the world that are the developed world are the developed world because they can self-fund. The portions of the world that are not the developed world are not the developed world because they cannot. Every generation or four a constellation of factors—like the Boomers—allows these countries to surmount their geography for a time. But only for a time. That time is now. But it is also almost past.

- The fiscal cliff and budget battles of the past few years will be with us for at least the next *fifteen* years. As the numerically massive Boomers retire, the government will stagger under ever higher pension and health care costs. Yet as the numerically tiny Xers become the primary taxpayers, the ability of the population to support the current tax load will shrink. There are only two ways to go: sharply higher taxes or sharply lower benefits. Xers will certainly have a strong preference on this decision, but Xers will not have the political voice to get their way. United in their retirement, the Boomers will be the largest voting bloc this country has ever known. And they can probably count on at least some political support from their kids—a.k.a. Gen Y—who probably don't want Mom and Dad living with them. The Boomer/Gen Y solution will probably be simple: Suck Gen X dry.

- Perhaps the weirdest outcome is that despite a couple millennia of recorded history and twenty generations of global economic patterns, people became convinced that this brief twenty-year window of the Baby Boomers passing through the mature-adult stage had utterly changed how the world would work from now on. Most can be forgiven for that. It is just an issue of exposure. For Americans aged thirty-five to fifty-five—a group that includes nearly all of the U.S. Baby Boomers—the bulk of their formative experiences and professional careers were forged in the most distorted period of this extreme growth and capital richness: 1990–2005. The idea that extreme growth and extreme wealth and cheap credit is "normal" is a pretty easy trap to fall into.[3] But that demographic bulge was unprecedented and will not repeat on anything less than a historic time scale. Likewise, the post–Cold War financial flight was a once-in-a-generation event. The "good ol' days" of high growth and abundant and cheap capital should be more accurately thought of as a windfall. That magic mix will not return in our lifetimes. The soonest it *might* return would be around 2065 when Gen Z will be as old as today's Boomers, and even that will only happen if the generation that starts being born in 2020 happens to be considerably smaller than Gen Z.

The transition is already well under way.

---

3. I'm also counting upon the depth of that belief generating a lot of book sales.

As of 2014, the Boomers have already aged sufficiently that consumption-led high-growth levels are no longer possible from American demographics alone. By 2020, the youngest Boomers will be fifty-five, the majority of their cohort will have retired, and all of them will be reshuffling their money out of risky investments such as stocks and foreign interests into risk-averse investments such as annuities and domestic government debt. Within a few short years the entire financial sector will be turned on its head. Instead of a huge generation providing capital, we'll have a small one. Capital costs will skyrocket from the cheapest in history to something much closer to the most expensive in history, particularly once pension and health care costs for managing history's largest retiree class are figured into the calculus.

Most disturbingly, this is not a purely American phenomenon. Across the developed world unprecedented demographic bulges among mature workers are generating massive capital surpluses now, driving down the cost of capital and the likelihood of high returns on investment.[4] In every single developed country there is currently an American-style population inversion between the about-to-retire and the about-to-be-mature-workers age groups. Japan's Boomers bulge is a decade older than the American equivalent, while Spain's is roughly fifteen years younger. Everyone else falls somewhere in between. It dictates a period of chronically low growth and high credit costs, just not on precisely the same time frame.

Rage, Rage Against the Dying of the Light

So how does a country deal with aging populations? The short version is "badly."

Here's the longer version:

Some Boomers—and their international peers—may work longer to

---

4. In the financial world this is the infamous "chasing yield" problem. The idea is that there is *so* much investment capital out there that investors are willing to ignore warnings such as high debt levels, lack of collateral, poor credit histories, accounting malpractice, fraud, state intervention, default, theft (both white- and blue-collar), and some things that might even be considered serious in order to get a couple more percentage points of return.

supplement their savings, and that may well provide a few extra bits of capital to help the overall system adjust. More working years certainly help the financial calculus both from an individual and a government point of view. But there are limits. Worker productivity—and consequently, income—typically falls off after age sixty-four, and the American retirement age is already sixty-seven. Every bit helps, but most workers who choose (or are forced) to work longer are delving deeply into a world of diminishing returns.

What is needed is heavy research into technologies that improve the ability of the old to work, rather than the ability of the old to live. That in turn would require a fairly sharp policy adjustment not just in pension programs, but also in health programs like Medicare and Medicaid. The current setup aims to maximize years lived, and as such encourages (high-cost) convalescence rather than (high-income) productivity. These are certainly policy items worth exploring, but there is the simple issue of time. The oldest Baby Boomers started retiring in 2007 and the youngest Baby Boomers are turning fifty at the time of this writing. Even if America's various retirement and health programs were reformed today, and a mammoth research program into geriatric productivity were immediately funded and launched, it would be a decade before it could have a meaningful impact upon older worker productivity rates—just in time for there to be no Baby Boomers in the workforce to apply the results to. So should such efforts be considered? Absolutely. But they will have absolutely no impact on the unfolding problem until after that problem has fully manifested.

What about reversing the demographic decline? It is possible, but not very likely. Convincing young people to have kids when they don't want them is not easy. Raising a child is one of the most expensive things that a young adult can do. Children carry with them the ultimate opportunity costs: day care instead of cars, diapers instead of trips, heartache instead of job advancement. What few countries have peered ahead and realized the demographic disaster before them have come up with some interesting methods of addressing the imbalance, but all have atrocious side effects.

Back in 2006, Russia attempted to address the financial aspect directly, offering women cash to have children. The amount varied based on how many children a woman had, with the payouts distributed across the first few years of the child's life to help address expenses. Russia did indeed benefit from a reduction in its abortion rate—nearly the world's highest—as well as a bump in birth rates. A few months later, however, the government realized that abandonments had skyrocketed. Women were having children that they would normally have aborted, collecting their government check, and then dropping off their unwanted children at the steps of the closest orphanage. Considering the appalling nature of Russian orphanages—very few Russian orphans are ever adopted and at age fourteen the children are ejected onto the street to join Russia's million-strong population of street children—at best the Russian program was a wash.

What about in countries where the sense of societal well-being is stronger? Sweden is another illuminating case. In the Scandinavian heartland would-be mothers benefit from one of the most generous systems in the world: Parents can collectively take up to sixteen months of maternity leave, thirteen months of which are paid at 80 percent of their prebirth pay rate. These days don't need to be all used at once, but can be saved and used at any time until the child turns eight. Additionally, a woman can choose to reduce her hours by a quarter at any time until the child turns eight, although those are unpaid hours. The best part is that those benefits stack if the woman has additional children. So a woman who has three children in three years would gain four years of maternity leave that would not have to be used until her youngest child was eight, and could voluntarily reduce her hours by three-quarters until her oldest child turned eight. Additional benefits were added in 2008 to encourage dads to get in on the child-care action.

Because of this policy, Sweden boasts the highest birth rate and the healthiest demography in Europe. But there is a very dark lining. If a young woman applies for a job, the employer must expect that she will be taking years of time off. That employer will nevertheless be legally required to keep her job open *and* to pay for years of maternity leave. The expected happens. Young Swedish women suffer from the highest unemployment and underemployment rates among the advanced countries, and Swedish women overall are far less likely to advance into the top ranks in management, corporations, universities, or even government sectors than their Western peers.

As the Russian and Swedish cases suggest, adjusting a people's lifestyle is never easy, cheap, or free of unwanted side effects. But the need for

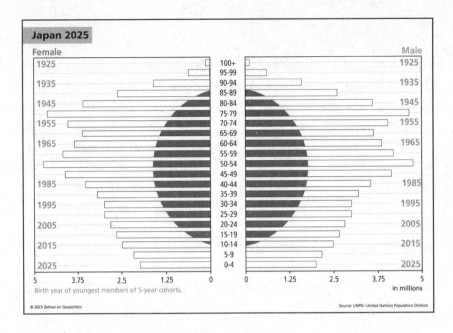

change remains. Take a look at the population pyramid above and you get a sense of what is possible—and impossible.

Japan is both the oldest and the fastest-aging society on the planet. Fully one-third of the population of 126 million is sixty and over. Since 1900 median life expectancy in Japan has increased from forty-four years to over eighty-three.

For more than a quarter of a million of Japan's elderly, there is a single, identifiable cause of their longevity: feeding tubes. The tubes are surgically inserted into the stomachs of primarily bedridden hospital or nursing home patients who average eighty-one years of age and stay on the tubes for roughly 2.3 years at a—largely state-subsidized—cost of about 5 million yen ($49,000) a year. The surgical insertion of feeding tubes has become so common in recent years that most families and patients aren't even consulted before it's done.

Feeding tubes are part of a phalanx of elder-care issues ranging from Alzheimer's to diabetes to government outlay policy: Every dollar spent on such procedures that keep treasured relatives alive is one less dollar that can be used for education or roads. In needing a better solution to this problem Japan is hardly alone. Globally the fastest-growing demographic are over-seventies.

Addressing this at a demographic level is largely impossible. Even if Japan dedicated itself to a nationwide breeding campaign today, it would not reap the financial benefits of a more normalized demography until *2075*.

Why would it take so long? Healing a demographic imbalance requires not just a lot of kids, but enough time to allow those kids to grow up and become mature workers so that they can generate capital. To actually regenerate a degraded demography you're talking about a sixty-year process (the amount of time it takes to grow a mature worker to the height of his/her income and investing capacity). And even that assumes that you can actually generate the kids who will one day become those sixty-year-olds in the first place.

A far more likely outcome is that forty-somethings will continue to act, well, their age. And they just keep aging. In just ten years the youngest edge of the Japanese population bulge will be fifty, a point at which demographic recovery is biologically impossible.

Most likely, things are as good in Japan as they are ever going to be. Japan will never have more young people than it has today, so economic growth is as high as it will ever be. Japan will only have more retirees, so pension outlays are as low as they will ever be. Combined, that means that the country's debt burden is as small as it will ever be and the ability to service that debt is as easy as it ever will be. And the Japanese are not alone. Europe and China, as we'll discuss in chapters 11 and 14, are only a few short years behind the Japanese.

Even if Japan and the rest are able to adapt to their rapidly aging demographics and maintain economic and political coherence, the world is still slipping away from them rapidly. In part because there is one country out there that is both aging more slowly and has a demographic that is already healing.

The American Exception: Youth, Immigration, and Regeneration

For Americans the demographic inversion is only a temporary development.

First, Americans are younger overall than nearly every other major culture. The United States was a latecomer to urbanization, and its vast tracts of land meant that the American urbanization experience was more suburban single-family homes rather than tight-quarter apartments. Consequently, the shift toward fewer children in the United States was both delayed and not as intense, resulting in a younger demographic more capable of reversing demographic decline (for example, it is *much* more feasible for American thirty-somethings to raise kids than Japanese or German fifty-somethings).

Second, it has been far easier for the Americans to assimilate immigrants than most cultures. As a settler society, the United States is one of very few countries where the concepts of nationality and government are not inextricably linked. Let me spell that out a bit. In most countries the dominant ethnic group originated in a specific geography, such as the Thames valley for the English. Early government was forged by the people of that ethnicity who lived in that geography, to deal with the concerns of that ethnicity and the problems and opportunities of that geography. The concepts of nationality and government fused right at the beginning. Even today, while the United Kingdom is technically a multiethnic society, the English are very clearly in charge.

Settler societies—a group of countries that includes Canada, Australia, and New Zealand—are different. Even in their initial waves of settlement they were not monoethnic, and they were settled across a variety of geographies rather than concentrated into one. National government was formed to deal with common problems of all of the ethnicities and all of the geographies rather than the discrete issues of one group in one place. In such places governments tend to naturally split into multiple levels of authority—national, regional, and local—to reflect the different ethnic, geographic, and historical legacies when compared to Old World governments. One outcome of this is that the national government of such settler societies is not beholden to any particular ethnicity, the opposite of the Old World systems.

Regarding immigration, the impact of these different approaches to managing geography is night-and-day. In a traditional state anyone from the outside is seen as, well, an outsider. Even when citizenship is attained, it does not necessarily confer membership in the ethnicity. Today there are millions of ethnic Arabs who are second-class French citizens living in French cities whom mainstream French culture continues to regard as not

French. As such, they live in ghettos—the infamous riot-torn *banlieues*—and have few paths to prosperity or acceptance, even though many of them are third-generation French citizens. In contrast, in settler societies no one ethnicity or geography controls the system, so it is fairly easy for an outsider to settle among the mélange. Just as the various groups who make up the system have chosen their nationality to be a pooled concept rather than an ethnic-based one, so can the newcomers. Actual citizenship isn't even always required. The result is that the United States and the other settler societies can partially rely upon a flow of new arrivals to help them out of a demographic crunch, while places like Sweden or Taiwan cannot.

Third and by far the most important is that the American generational tightening lasts for only one generation. Behind Gen X is Gen Y, the Boomers' kids. As you might expect from the kids of the country's largest ever generation, there are a lot of them—35 percent more than the Xers. Because of these factors, the United States' financial/demographic situation will repair itself with surprising speed (by demographic standards).

- In 2030, the oldest Boomer will be eighty-four. By then the Boomers will be passing on just as they retired: as a group. Dead people don't receive pension checks (outside of Chicago), and so their disappearance will lift a great weight from the system's financial commitments.
- In 2030, the oldest Gen Xer will be sixty-five, and the Xers will become the old fogies of American society. But just as there were not enough Xers to fund the country (much less the world) to the degree to which all have become accustomed, the financial load of the retired Xers will almost be comical in its smallness and manageability compared to the crushing omnipresence of aged Boomers.
- In 2030, the oldest members of Gen Y will be fifty, an age when they will start to seriously take over as large-scale contributors to the country's capital stock. Their numbers will allow them to do what the Xers could not: sufficiently fund the system.

Generation Y will not be able to repair the demographic balance overnight, but as they mature and step into their parents' current role as capital providers, the American demographic pyramid will eventually take a more "normal" shape. It will still be a fairly strict capital system, but no longer an inverted one. Given time, American capital costs will return to a more normal level. After 2030, the Americans will have moved through "painful" and be merely at "uncomfortable," and things will be improving by the year. By 2040, nearly all of the Boomers will have passed on, and all of Gen Y will be in the prime of their taxpaying lives. The Americans will have their financial feet firmly back under them.

But that will most certainly *not* be happening elsewhere. The United States is the only developed country to boast a widening generation like Gen Y. Throughout the rest of the developed world the Boomer equivalents simply didn't have many kids—not even enough to replace their own numbers. So while the American financial world will be past its period of maximum stress by 2030, for the rest of the world 2030 will simply be another year of an ever-deepening imbalance between retirees and taxpayers, with smaller and smaller generations coming up the ranks generating less and less growth. For the developed world beyond the United States—and even large portions of the developing world—chronic capital poverty and permanent recession will be the new normal from which there is no return.

Scared New World: Losing Interest

The demographic inversion will also have one additional impact on the international order: that of disconnecting the Americans. Economically, global trade is predicated on the ability to sell into growing markets. In the post–World War II era it has been the American market that has always been far and away the largest, and even in the most egregiously optimistic estimates for Europe and the BRICs it will remain so for at least the next twenty years.

Those egregious growth estimates, however, fail to take into account the chronic aging occurring throughout most of the world. Within a decade it isn't so much that the American market will be the largest one in the world, but that aging demographics will have capped—and in most cases reversed—consumer market growth in Japan, Germany, the United Kingdom, China, Italy, Canada, Spain, Russia, Korea, the Netherlands,

Switzerland, Belgium, South Africa, Austria, Greece, Norway, Denmark, Portugal, and Finland. That's not simply over half of the world's thirty largest economies, but it also includes most of the countries that the Americans created Bretton Woods for in the first place. If they are no longer consuming en masse, then much of what limited economic rationale exists for Bretton Woods disappears from the American point of view.

Couple that market degradation with America's Gen Y demographic regeneration, and as early as 2030 the United States will emerge as the only country that is capital-rich, the only country with a growing economy, and the only country with a growing market. And all this without any conscious demographic policy on the part of the Americans.

If that wasn't enough, the Americans have yet one more thing going for them that will magnify all of these advantages. We'll cover it in the next chapter.

The Demographic Roller Coaster: Ten Years On

With the benefit of a decade of hindsight, I'd argue that the biggest take-away from this chapter you just consumed is that we are at the beginning of a transition that is historically unprecedented.

Well, folks, we're now ten years into what's likely to be a thirty-year process. It isn't so much that we're now at the point of no return (we passed that point decades ago), but instead that the impacts of the demographic transition are now the determining factor in the defining economic trends of the here and now. Put simply, there is nothing theoretical about it any longer.

Allow me to break down a few once-theories that have blazed their way into obvious facts.

The Baby Boomers, a global phenomenon, have now reached retirement age, with the majority of them retiring by the end of calendar year 2022. This has far-reaching implications, but let's focus on three noteworthy factors:

1. Labor. The Boomers are both the largest generation of workers ever and the bulk of the skilled labor pool, and they are now over half retired. Worried about inflation in food or energy or housing? You should be. But all of them combined cannot stand up to the current and deepening impact of labor inflation. In the United States, this Boomer-instigated labor shortage will get progressively worse until at least the early 2040s.

2. Finance. During the period between the end of your biggest life expense (when your last kid leaves home and becomes someone else's problem) and your retirement (typically at age sixty-five), you generate substantial investment capital. This capital fuels easy financing for a range of endeavors, from government projects like building aircraft carriers to technological advancements in Silicon Valley to potheads using credit cards to re-up on Cheetos. However, retirees' income pales in comparison to that of older workers, and the financial assets they hold tend to be non-growth-driven. As a result, the return-seeking capital that fueled the tech and economic booms of the 2000s and 2010s has significantly

diminished. Low interest rates like 3 percent mortgages are a thing of the past. At the time of this writing in mid-2021, a standard thirty-year is already 7.7 percent. Brace yourself for 10 percent or higher rates.

3. Government spending. "Largest generation ever" and "largest workforce ever" are just another way of saying "largest group of taxpayers ever." The retirement of the Baby Boomers translates into a catastrophic decline in their contributions to government coffers, with instead the Boomers drawing upon Social Security and Medicare and Medicaid. This decade the Boomers will become the largest generation of tax beneficiaries ever. You think government budgets are broken now? Booooy howdy!

For the United States, all of this is long-lasting, but none of it is permanent. America's Millennials are now entering their midforties, and by 2035 enough will be reaching their capital-rich midfifties to lessen the financial crunch. The Millennials' kids are now being born en masse, and by the mid-2040s they will be entering the workforce, taking the sting out of what will by that point be a two-decade labor dearth.

But unlike Boomers, who are a phenomenon throughout the rich world, Millennials exist only in economically significant numbers in the United States, France, and New Zealand. By the time you ingest these words, the world will have already exited its last period of global, consumption-led growth. The Americans have a tight couple of decades ahead of them. The best the bulk of the rest can hope for is an economy that resembles a slowly leaking tire.

Beneath these bigger-than-big convulsions lies a seething cauldron of issues that are "merely" transformative. We'll deal with a whole mess of these topics as we hit the chapters ahead, but here are some teasers: Europe's ever-quickening slide, the now-imminent Chinese collapse, Canada's newfound lease on life, and the end of the U.S. Mexican border crisis.

Fun stuff, eh?

CHAPTER 7

The Rise of Shale

Americans have a love-hate relationship with the petroleum industry. They love having cars and air-conditioning, but hate pollution, global warming, and the environmental damage associated with exploding rigs or tanker spills. Yet no matter how Americans feel or how loudly they may complain, the simple fact remains that fossil fuels are their way of life. In terms of total American energy usage—whether it be from electricity production, chemical production, or transport fuels—by their own government's numbers, 34.7 percent originates from oil, 26.0 percent from natural gas, 17.4 percent from coal, 8.1 percent from nuclear, 5.5 percent from hydropower, and only 3.4 percent from nonhydro renewables like solar and wind. That's 80 percent of the total from fossil fuels. The same love-hate dichotomy applies to the shale industry.

I'm going to take us on a quick tour through the industry to help explain this disconnect. The point of doing so is not simply to show that shale is already a done deal—at the time of this writing the shale industry already produces a majority of American oil and natural gas output—but rather that public opposition to shale will soon crumble. When that happens, the full impact of shale will be realized, which in turn will unleash global trends that will underpin American power for the next several decades.

A Bit of Geology to Set the Mood

Let's start with the basics of petroleum[1] and shale.

Most petroleum formed as a result of life-forms—typically plankton—being trapped in layers of sedimentary rock. After millions of years of heat and pressure, these critter corpses cook into petroleum, which percolates up through the rock until it reaches a formation through which it cannot pass. These cap rocks allow the petroleum to collect into large pools. Most of the petroleum harvested around the world over the past couple of centuries has come from such "conventional" reservoirs.

But not all petroleum is located in large, easy-to-stick-a-straw-in pools. If the rock in which the oil and natural gas was formed is not porous, then the petroleum remains trapped where it was created rather than slowly collecting into an area where it can be easily harvested. In such rock formations the petroleum remains finely distributed, trapped between individual rock particles. The result isn't so much like chips in a cookie, but instead like the booze in a dry rum cake. The rum is there, suspended within a matrix of cooked batter. It is a devil of a task to coax it out. Data is far from complete, but most recent estimates project that some 90 percent of the world's petroleum is locked into such geologies. Even if such estimates are wrong by an order of magnitude, it suggests that the amount of petroleum in the wider world is *double* what we thought it was just a decade ago.

One of the major types of rock formations that trap petroleum in this way is called shales. Shales are sedimentary rocks, deposited hundreds of millions of years ago at the bottom of oceans. Because of their ocean-floor origins, they are typically found in long, thin horizontal layers covering up to tens of thousands of square miles. As with other unconventional petroleum basins, the ultra-fine distribution of shale petroleum makes the use of conventional energy production technologies largely useless.

So the energy industry had to get unconventional.

The integration of two unrelated technologies is what has brought us

---

1. "Petroleum" is a catchall term that includes all types of crude oil, natural gas, as well as associated liquids such as propane. When I use the term I'm referring to all types of petroleum. When discussing more specific products separately, such as oil or natural gas, I will use those terms specifically.

the shale era. The first technology is horizontal drilling. Your traditional petroleum well is a purely vertical affair. If you happen to miss in your downward drilling, tough. If you hit a particularly slanted formation on the way down that breaks your vertical descent, tough. If there is a particularly hard rock on the way down that you cannot drill through, tough. Horizontal drilling allows you not only to drill laterally but also at angles and around corners—even around multiple corners—to weave your way through complex formations to reach exactly where you want to go. A typical vertical well might only expose ten feet of petroleum-rich rock, but a typical horizontal well exposes up to a mile. As seismic detection techniques have improved in reach and precision, horizontal drilling has both made preexisting petroleum fields more productive and enabled energy firms to bring previously unreachable deposits online. In regions with less than stellar technology—Cuba comes to mind—horizontal drilling has allowed onshore producers to reach a few miles into offshore environments by drilling hard up on the coast but sending their drill shafts out under the seabed.

The second tech, hydraulic fracturing, uses water pressure to crack rock. In hydraulic fracturing, petroleum engineers inject a 90 percent water mixture down the well shaft and into the rock formation. Liquids, unlike gases, do not compress under pressure, and so the rock becomes spiderwebbed with billions of tiny cracks. Included in the liquid mixture is something called a proppant—typically some sort of sand—that wedges itself into those cracks. The rock itself absorbs some of the liquid and the rest is sucked back to the surface to be recycled. But most of the proppant stays behind, propping the cracks open. Those cracks provide pathways for the no longer trapped petroleum to flow to the well shaft.

In essence, hydraulic fracturing forces a nonporous rock to be partially porous. But not porous like the sort of rock formations that generate traditional petroleum deposits. Instead of allowing the bits of petroleum to slowly percolate upward over the millennia, fracturing enables them to travel *only* along the new specifically engineered fractures directly to the well shaft.

The use of these two technologies in tandem—colloquially if somewhat inaccurately known as fracking—is the basis of the shale energy boom.

The focused specificity of fracking technologies sets off a very predictable chain of events. Once the cracks reach the trapped petroleum it flows out (well, up) with considerable speed. At first. Remember that these techniques tap a reservoir, but one in which the petroleum is highly seques-tered and barely connected by fractures. Only those elements directly connected to the fractures can flow at all, and they can only flow to the borehole. The result is an initial burst of petroleum output, followed almost immediately by a quick drawdown. In most areas one-third of the total out-put of a well comes in the first year or two of its twenty-year life span.

The most obvious implication of this quick bleed-off is that if a shale energy industry is going to maintain—much less grow—its output, then a *lot* of wells need to be drilled every single year. In the United States that comes out to about fifty thousand fracked wells a year. That sounds like a lot. It *is* a lot. Since fracking took off less than a decade ago, the total num-ber of petroleum wells in the United States has doubled.

Sustainable Shale

Yet this is a pace that the Americans can keep up for a very long time. It is difficult to provide accurate data as to baseline information such as pro-duction rates or reserves, not because such data is unavailable, but instead because the newness of the industry means it is changing so quickly.

In August 2012, the Energy Information Agency, an office within the U.S. Department of Energy, released a comprehensive report on the then reality of shale energy. The EIA used the best data available at the time, which had been gathered by December 2011. They pegged American shale oil output at 2 million bpd, about the same as Norway's oil output. They also made projections as to how shale output would unfold over the next eight years. When this report came out it was the definitive work on the reality of shale.

A mere one year later that report was hideously out of date. With fifty thousand (or more) new wells coming online annually, keeping tabs on those wells across hundreds of legal jurisdictions is a logistical impossi-bility. And as is common in any high-value-added industry, innovations do not require government approval, registration, or even notification. Such innovations are, however, applied to every well the rig crew works from that point on. The result is an ever-building skill set that spreads

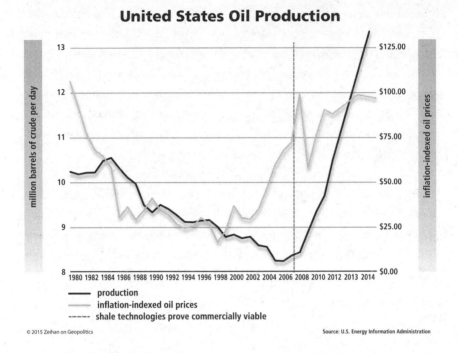

United States Oil Production

- —— production
- ····· inflation-indexed oil prices
- ----- shale technologies prove commercially viable

© 2015 Zeihan on Geopolitics   Source: U.S. Energy Information Administration

and compounds throughout the industry. In December 2013, only sixteen months after the EIA's exhaustive report, shale oil output had increased from 2 million bpd to 3.8 million bpd—that's not only more than Canada's oil output, but is about 50 percent more than the EIA's projection for U.S. shale oil output for 2020. At the time of this writing in mid-2014, even *that* data is now outdated. As of 2014 the United States is now the world's largest energy producer, bringing up more oil than Saudi Arabia and more natural gas than Russia.

What will U.S. shale output look like in the future? Details are murky: There are many shifting variables, there is no such thing as "average" when considering an industry that operates in wildly varied geologies and regulatory environments, and any estimate provided now likely will be overwhelmed in the time it takes this manuscript to make it into print.

But caveats aside, the learning curve is still extraordinarily steep, with huge gains being made at nearly every stage of the process. Deeper wells, longer horizontal shafts, more controlled and therefore more effective fracking, better fluids, more detailed imaging, more experience using recycled and subsurface water all add up to better reach, lower costs, and higher recovery rates. From 2012 to 2013 alone half as many rigs were able to generate the same output. "Overall" break-even prices for natural gas production have probably dropped from about $7 per 1,000 cubic feet in 2011 to under $5 in 2014. Similarly, the break-even price for shale oil production has dropped from over $100 per barrel a decade ago to $85 in 2011 to probably something closer to $70 in 2014, with many basins already nudging toward $50.

It is now a fairly conservative estimate to say that North America will be fully energy independent by 2020. We are not at the dawn of the shale era. We are already *in* the shale era.

(On the Verge of) Shale Acceptance

Yet Americans still do not trust the industry. In a September 2013 survey, Pew Research found that 49 percent of Americans oppose increased use of shale energy techniques. Specifically, Americans are concerned that fracking uses huge volumes of water, that frack fluid is toxic at best and carcinogenic at worst, and that the frack fluid leaks out of the well shafts and into the aquifers that supply drinking water. It is difficult to square the importance and growth of the shale industry with the circle of public concern. Luckily—for both—I expect that most of the public's distrust for the shale-related techs will evaporate within a few short years. There are three reasons for this.

First, the use of surface water is quickly being phased out in fracking operations. Surface water is full of algae and bacteria; such impurities must be removed to make water suitable for fracking. One of the more expensive portions of fracking fluids is the various chemicals required to purify the water. Add in the cost of trucking millions of gallons of water around (high-bulk cargo, high-cost transport), and surface water use is as much an economic issue for the shale industry as it is a quality-of-life issue for local communities. Luckily, subsurface drilling has discovered layers of mildly saline brackish water deep underground[2] in almost all regions. Energy

---

2. Such layers are typically in excess of two thousand feet below the surface. Also, note that brackish groundwater is not interchangeable with seawater. The many organisms that live in seawater make it unsuitable for fracking without extensive filtration.

firms have discovered that this lifeless, nonpotable water provides a better medium for frack fluids. And because a wellbore at the drilling site can
access this brackish water and the frack additives can be mixed with it on
site, all those trucks that needed to bring millions of gallons of water per
well[3] are suddenly not needed. By 2016, large-scale surface water use will
continue only in those few areas that do not have a brackish water layer.

Second, most aquifers that supply drinking water are within two hundred feet of the surface, and nearly all are within six hundred feet.[4] Some
90 percent of fracks occur at over a mile of depth, with only a handful
completed at less than four thousand feet. The longest frack cracks ever
completed are but six hundred feet long, with the vast majority being no
longer than two hundred feet;[5] with recent advances most fracks are often
as short as forty feet. That puts a minimum of a half mile of solid rock—
remember that by definition shale formations are impermeable—between
the frack cracks and the water supply. It adds up to a simple fact: There
has *never* been a case of fracking fluid subsoil contamination of drinking
water. But don't believe me. Believe the EPA under the Obama administration. Out of the roughly 1.2 million that have been fracked in the United
States since the Truman administration, the EPA has yet to issue a single
citation to any firm anywhere in the country for subsoil contamination
due to frack fluid.[6]

---

3. Just as there is no "average" for well depth, there is no average for water requirements. Various geological and technological factors—porosity, clays, chalks, number of
fracks, depth of wellbore, and more—can make wells need anywhere from 2 million to
12 million gallons of water. Liquid transport trucks normally carry 5,500–11,600 gallons of liquid, so being able to mix the frack fluid on site could potentially eliminate
90–180 truck trips *per well*.

4. At present the deepest water source for an American city is 1,700 feet for Rapid
City, South Dakota.

5. This improved concentration isn't just a safety issue. The more concentrated
the frack effort, the more impact it has on a very specific zone of high-petroleum-
concentration rock, rather than a less controlled frack effort that extends beyond the
densest concentrations of petroleum.

6. The EPA has been working on an overarching report on the status and safety of the
shale industry for several years. Its issuance has been delayed several times, ostensibly for
reasons of completeness. Odds are heavy that when it is finally released the EPA—and,
by extension, President Obama—will place a stamp of approval on the shale industry,
which will damage the administration's standing with the environmental community.

What citations the EPA *have* issued fall into two categories. The first, surface water contamination, makes up over 90 percent of the citations. It is largely an issue of drillers discharging recovered frack fluid into surface streams. (Such practices were actually legal in many states at the beginning of the shale era!) The second is various forms of methane (another term for natural gas) leakage, whether that occurs in the well shaft, the pad, or the transport system (more on that later). Methane leakage has been a regulatory and environmental concern for as long as there has been a natural gas industry. The biggest new challenge such leakage presents is that there are so many more wells in a shale field than in a conventional field that operators—and regulators—need to be scrupulous about well completion. Aside from that there is nothing that makes leakage from shale wells technologically different from any other well.

The third reason shale energy is going to become more publicly acceptable is that despite the public firestorm, frack fluid isn't all that dangerous and is edging toward becoming completely nontoxic. While there is considerable variation in ingredient proportions, the ingredients themselves are well known. All are approximately 90 percent water, 9.5 percent sand. For the remainder, the dominant ingredients are borates (a key component in laundry detergent), n-dimethylformamide (plastics), ethylene glycol (antifreeze), guar gum (ice cream), and isopropanol (glass cleaner). While it would be best to not drink the stuff, there is nothing in the components that isn't already cleared for presence in the average kitchen. Regardless, the industry has noted the public outcry and has been steadily removing all toxicity from the chemical mix. In 2011 Halliburton introduced a new frack fluid made entirely of components from the food industry, which Democratic Colorado governor John Hickenlooper made famous by taking a swig.[7] Other chemicals firms have followed suit, and disclosure of the various fluids' components is starting to be shared more readily in an effort to defuse the issue. The price difference is on average only 5–10 percent.

Once it is clear that surface water use has plummeted, that the Obama administration has signed off on the industry as a whole, and that the frack fluid itself goes reasonably well with tomatoes and mozzarella, the controversy surrounding shale will simmer down. In a few short years

---

7. He's fine, by the way.

opposition will be limited to two groups: environmentalists who are opposed to any petroleum developments on principle, and local groups who don't perceive any personal benefits. This is not an inconsequential slice of the American electorate, but it is probably only about 10 percent of the population.

Shale: An Industry That Speaks with an American Accent

So American shale is not only a done deal, but it is also about to accelerate considerably. What is even more notable about shale is that it will remain American for quite some time. It is extremely unlikely that the shale technologies will be applied en masse anywhere outside of North America before 2035. Why? Shale success reflects many features of the American system that we have already discussed. There are four factors that must exist simultaneously for a country to birth a shale industry in short order:

1. Huge, Deep Capital Markets

You have to throw a lot of money at a fracking project to get results. As with everything else about shale, there is no average, but costs can be extreme and typically everything—roads, pipes, drills, and labor sufficiently skilled to drill a mile beneath their feet—has to be paid up front. Rigs—whose rates include labor—rent at anywhere from $10,000 to $100,000 a day. An easy well might "only" take eight days, but difficult wells can be five times that. A low-end figure is usually in the range of $6 million per well.

Until costs are recovered, any investment that a firm puts into a shale project cannot be redeployed. Think of it like buying a house. Until you have paid your mortgage off it is difficult to gather the financial resources to get a second one. A good shale oil well only produces about seventy-five barrels a day across a span of twenty years. Even when you consider that a third of that output will be in the first year or three, it still takes at least a year (with oil prices at $100) to hit breakeven.

This financial factor puts an onerous limitation on where a shale industry can develop. The broader economy must boast a financial sector that is so rich, liquid, and stable that all those scores of billions of dollars of committed funds do not crimp credit availability for the rest of the economy. You think shale is somewhat controversial now, imagine if the American credit system were sufficiently constrained that a successful shale industry meant your mortgage payment increased by half.[8] If the local/national credit pool isn't absolutely huge, shale just isn't a viable industry. Luckily for the Americans, as the world's premier capital safe haven, they have the largest, deepest, and most liquid capital market in the world. Europe could have pulled it off until their financial crisis struck. With the exception of Japan (which has no shale), there just isn't enough money anywhere else in the world to generate a robust shale industry.

2. Highly Skilled Labor

Drilling a winding shaft into a complicated, variable-density geology several thousand feet underground in order to inject a pressurized fluid that will precision-crack a rock formation in real time so that the hydrocarbons trapped within are funneled up a well shaft is every bit as hard as it sounds. Moreover, every single well—even two wells on the same drilling pad—is different. This is not a job for the faint of heart or the faint of skill. Each well crew has to know precisely what they are doing and has to be in command of skills ranging from engineering to geology to chemicals[9] to fluid dynamics. This is not a task for a handful of state-owned oil thugs who got their jobs as part of a nationalization program, but for people with years of experience who benefit from the trust of their superiors to make adjustments as they go. Each well requires a crew of high-skilled petroleum engineers and support staff able to operate in a variety of environments with minimal supervision.

But there will never be shale gushers. A successful industry will be drilling thousands of wells a year. That means you need not one energy firm, or even dozens, but hundreds. And you also need thousands of extremely capable petroleum engineers.

Only the United States, with its tradition of small businesses, low barriers to entry, and an advanced educational system that specializes in outside-the-box thinking, can generate the necessary labor pool for a shale industry to thrive. Over the life of the global petroleum industry some

---

8. That's the net effect of an increase in rates from 5 percent to 9.5 percent.

9. Different types of frack fluid have to be used for different geologies.

5.5 million wells have been drilled, 4 million of which were completed within the United States. In the past five years 99 percent of the horizontal wells drilled globally are in the United States.[10] Every other country might have the required staff to tinker with shale, but no one at present can even attempt to make it an industry.

3. A Legal Structure That Rewards Landowners for Their Participation

Any attempt at a shale sector is manpower- and equipment-intensive. Across a shale basin that is many tens of thousands of square miles there will be significant pressure on local infrastructure—most notably roads—as well as chronic demand for all of the items ranging from foodstuffs to entertainment to lodging that come with any highly localized economic boom. The cost of everything from rents to groceries can be reliably counted upon to at least triple, and the traffic and noise from rig crews constantly coming, going, building, breaking, and commuting is far from insignificant. For a shale industry to be successful, local buy-in is absolutely critical, and the best way to make sure that this happens is to give the local community a say in the development process and a slice of the profits.

In the United States roughly two-thirds of all land is privately owned—a legacy of the country's origin as a settler state and the smallholder tradition of the pioneer era—so firms must contract directly with landowners in order to drill. This does more than simply make landowners millionaires—typical contracts give leaseholders a 12.5 percent revenue share—it also pours money directly into local government coffers because they can tax both the energy production and the landowners' income and land.

To Americans this might seem obvious, but it is far from normal. In every other country in the world, the national government holds the subsoil rights. Local governments and landowners will not get a dime of direct money (whether from taxes, development fees, or production royalties) from the actual shale production—only the national government gets that. It also means that national governments decide when and where

---

10. Source data for specific well counts is notoriously wobbly, as in many states reporting is voluntary and drillers do not necessarily have to disclose whether they are drilling for (or end up producing) oil or natural gas. The data in this paragraph is courtesy of GHK Companies, one of the major shale players in the United States.

energy production happens regardless of the wishes of the landowners, much less the local homeowners' association. In places like the Middle East and the former Soviet Union where desert and tundra drilling doesn't impact a local population, this isn't so critical a factor, but in China, Latin America, and Europe this factor alone dooms potential shale industries.

4. A Preexisting Natural Gas Collection, Transport, and Distribution Infrastructure

The final requirement has to do with the nature of the output. Shale wells produce not just oil, but oil and natural gas, and herein lies a problem. Oil is a liquid and so can be trucked, barged, railed, or piped anywhere you want. The multitude of transport options allow shale oil production to be very quickly monetized. And if you're not quite ready for it, you can simply pump it directly into a tanker truck until the pipe infrastructure gets up and running. Well over 90 percent of the active well work going on in the United States right now is looking for oil and associated petroleum liquids[11] that are nearly as easy to store and move.

Natural gas, however, is, well, a gas. It cannot be trucked, barged, or railed efficiently except under extreme pressure, which poses extreme costs for additional equipment and not insignificant safety issues for all involved. It also cannot easily be stored. At standard pressure it takes 1,400 cubic feet of natural gas to generate the power of one cubic foot of crude.

Unlike oil, which is omnipresent in usage, natural gas suffers from the chicken/egg conundrum so far as transport is concerned. A shale natural gas industry requires an infrastructure that links up preexisting pressurized pipeline networks to preexisting points of demand. If you do not have that, you not only have to build it from scratch but build the actual *demand* from scratch as well.

The same holds true for other types of infrastructure. Shale wells require hundreds of truck trips, and truck trips require, well, roads. Shale developments in virgin territory first require the development of a spiderweb of interconnected transport arteries. In the United States where energy production has been colocated with populated territories for over a century in places like Pennsylvania, Texas, and Oklahoma this is already

---

11. With ethane, propane, and butane being among the more recognizable.

in place. But in most of the rest of the world energy production has long been in remote, unpopulated areas like the North Sea, the Arabian Desert, or Siberia.

Europe and Argentina have solid systems nearly as good as the Americans' on both the infrastructure and preexisting use questions. Russia and Australia have the long-range transport pipes, but not the grid of roads. Few other locations have either. However you slice it, the answer to the infrastructure question is multitrillion and multidecade.

Put together these are exacting requirements. Few places in the world meet more than one of them, and only the United States has *all* of them.

The Benefits of Shale

Many of the benefits of shale energy are fairly obvious.

Like any new industry, its mere existence generates jobs. Back in 2010, the most recent year for which there is reliable data, the sector had generated 150,000 fresh jobs itself, plus another 200,000 jobs in related industries such as transport, mining, and steel. Additional induced jobs—those created by other sectors that take advantage of all the new local energy sources—probably added another 250,000.[12] Why so many? Since per-well production levels drop off so radically, maintaining output requires maintaining drilling. A large and growing shale industry, therefore, requires ever more engineers along with ever more of everything else associated with production.

Environmentally, natural gas is the cleanest fossil fuel from the point of view of emissions, whether those emissions be carbon dioxide, sulfur, or mercury. Because of shale, New York City was able to switch en masse from fuel oil—which is right up there with coal in terms of its pollution profile—to natural gas in less than a year. Specifically, burning natural gas releases about one-third less carbon into the atmosphere than oil and half that of coal—in addition to the fact that there is no attendant sulfur,

---

12. All jobs estimation data is courtesy of Citibank's Global Perspectives and Solutions Annual, 2011, pages 74–90. It is a source that is thorough without being wed to energy interests. At present the U.S. federal government has yet to generate any estimates of the impact of shale upon the job market.

nitrogen oxides, mercury, or other contaminants.[13] This is where the methane leakage issue becomes critical. Unburned methane is a powerful greenhouse gas, trapping twenty times more heat than carbon dioxide over a hundred-year time horizon. The EPA estimates that even with the massive increases in shale gas output, U.S. methane emissions are actually down about 5 percent since the onset of the shale era. That, of course, is not the same as saying that shale-related methane emissions are zero. For the argument that using natural gas is better for the environment than coal to stick, shale-related methane emissions need to be below about 3 percent of total production. Currently the EPA estimates that the industry is slightly below half that level. Driving that number down further is probably the best way the industry can not only claim to be green, but also gain the public trust. The way to do that is through better well completion—which will, among other things, prevent the natural gas from leaking into aquifers.

And even though shale seems water-intensive on the production side, shale natural gas is actually one of the least water-intensive energy sources over the entirety of its fuel cycle because it requires no water in its processing and transport. Total water usage as measured against the amount of energy generated comes out to about 1.1–1.6 gallons per million Btu. That's roughly one-fifth that of coal or nuclear, and one-sixth that of oil.[14]

There is also the price factor. Shale has produced so much oil in the American heartland that it has slashed oil prices by $10–$15 a barrel in the United States compared to the world as a whole. Even being very conservative with the math, that is saving the American consumer $100 million a *day.*

Then there is the security factor. If shale energy expands output in the Lower 48, then only events in the Lower 48 can disrupt Lower 48 energy production and consumption patterns. Rebelling Chechens, marching Russians, striking Norwegians, rioting Nigerians, exploding Palestinians,

---

13. This is an argument that the environmentalists know well, after all—they wrote it. Most U.S.-based environmental groups—most notably the Sierra Club, the Natural Resources Defense Council, and the Investor Environmental Health Network—quietly lobbied *for* shale development as recently as early 2012 because they were trying to force coal out of the American fuel mix. It was only when these groups realized that shale had been so successful that it was challenging wind and solar energy that they changed their tune.

14. Here's a fun fact: Despite shale's bad PR on the topic of water, all of the country's shale projects combined still use less water than golf courses.

and chest-thumping Iranians don't get as much of a vote in U.S. energy policy as they used to. And within a few short years they won't get a vote at all.

So those are some of the obvious benefits. Now let's turn to some of the less obvious ones.

Shale and Geography

Spatially, the most notable thing about shale energy is where it is (and will be) produced in comparison to traditional forms of energy. The map on page 140 highlights the world's major producing basins, both for oil and natural gas. It is a familiar map with concentrations in places like Siberia, the Persian Gulf, the northwestern Australian shelf, Nigeria, the North Sea, and the Gulf of Mexico—all places that are difficult to operate in, whether technically or politically. I've placed this information on the same map as the Earth at night. Why? Because the lights are where the people with money live. Much of the geopolitical angst of the past seventy years has been about getting the energy from where it is produced to where the lights are. Everything from the Arab oil embargo to the European-Russian squabbles over Ukraine to the Iran-Iraq War to all things Israeli are at a minimum heavily tinged with international energy politics.

Shale changes that, and it is very easy to see—and I mean literally *see*—how.

My personal shale eureka moment came a cold night in December 2012. My partner, Wayne, a pilot, had seen something out on one of his many airborne adventures that he insisted I needed to see for myself. So he loaded me into a Skyhawk 172R and off we flew. For an hour I watched the blazing I-35 corridor below our right wing while he chatted intermittently with various air traffic controls. At one point their discussion got decidedly lively, prompting us to plunge a few hundred feet just in time to dodge an aluminum whale barreling through at half the speed of sound. Wayne let fly a string of less than complimentary comments about a certain Dallas-headquartered airline.

As I finished relocating my stomach from the plane's ceiling to where God had intended it to be, Wayne directed my gaze outside. Apparently the descent—if not its rate—was part of the plan. We were now south of San Antonio, flying over some of the least populated parts of Texas. Aside from a thin, irregular spiderweb of roads and small towns, it should have been dark. Instead an array of lights like some incredibly lost aurora boiled up from the horizon. As we continued to the southwest the aurora did the damnedest thing. It stayed on the ground.

Wayne shouted an explanation over the engine roar: "It's natural gas flaring from the Eagle Ford shale." He pronounced it like a northerner, as two words. Not like the "Eagleferd" that I'd become used to hearing. "They'll break up into individual spots here in a minute."

And so they did. The diffuse, horizony glow coalesced into hundreds of dots of light, a bright yellow-orange clearly distinct from the whites and white-greens of the car headlights and streetlights that they shared the ground with. Constellations of constellations stretched to the horizon all around us, with hints of that misplaced aurora lingering beyond the ten miles of detail that we could see.

It is one thing to crunch the numbers and gain an academic appreciation for what shale means, or to visit a shale pad site and witness the sheer intellect required to make shale a local reality, but seeing it like this made it all just seem so . . . big. I may be from Iowa, but I've lived in Texas for over a decade. I'd like to think my appreciation for size has evolved.

Upon our return to Austin I pulled up some more recent maps. Shale development maps. Population density maps. It occurred to me that the Eagle Ford wasn't the only shale basin in Texas, much less the United States, which took me to more recent Earth-at-night satellite photographs. You can see them—the Barnett, the Permian, the Haynesville, the Woodford, the Fayetteville, the Niobrara, the Antrim, the Marcellus, the Bakken, all of them—from space, hundreds of thousands of well lights that are bit by bit remaking how the United States sees the world.

Which led me to make the map on page 141.

I've replaced the traditional energy basins with the known shale basins. There are two takeaways. First, there is very little overlap between the traditional basins and the shale basins, so any current energy producer who might due to geological blessings be able to try their hand at shale will still need a decade or three to build the infrastructure required. That, at a minimum, suggests a reshuffling of the global energy deck.

Second, and far more important, nearly all of the United States' "lights" are close to, if not on top of, shale basins. For the Americans, this means that the role of international energy supply chain guarantor is

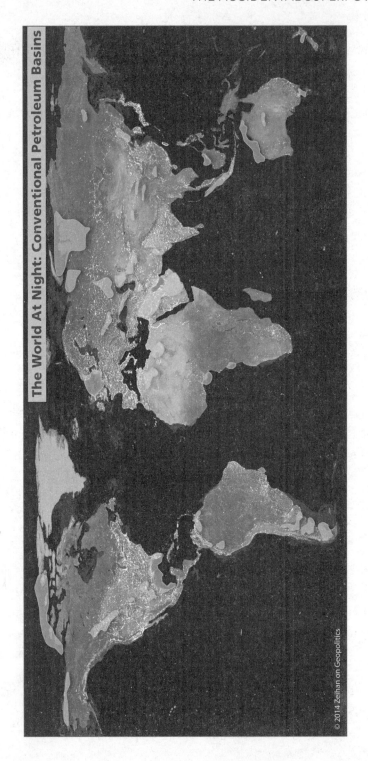

The World At Night: Conventional Petroleum Basins

© 2014 Zeihan on Geopolitics

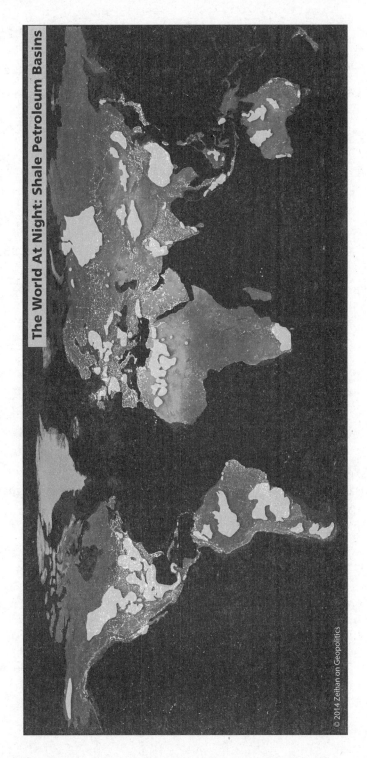

The World At Night: Shale Petroleum Basins

© 2014 Zeihan on Geopolitics

no longer something that they are doing for themselves at all—it is only something they are doing for their Bretton Woods allies. It also means that the Americans are one of a small handful of countries that has managed to colocate their production and consumption of energy. That has obvious security implications—if your city's energy comes from wells that are just outside the suburbs, it would take a particularly aggressive (para) military effort to impact energy prices, let alone knock the lights out. But less obvious is that it isn't cheap to move energy. It takes oil to move oil. In all it takes about 1 million bpd of crude oil—refined into various fuels, of course—to move the rest of the crude oil around the planet. Oil that the U.S. ships in from the Eastern Hemisphere travels on one of the longer shipping routes of the modern day. As shale output ticks ever upward, fewer long-haul trips need to be taken, meaning that the American shale revolution has already sliced about 50,000 bpd off of global energy demand simply from transport savings.[15]

Shale, Transport, and Electricity

Despite the radical difference in transport difficulty and market price between oil and natural gas, natural gas is being produced anyway because in shale the two petroleums are often found commingled; production of the oil inextricably results in production of natural gas. Even though many energy firms now see this associated natural gas as a waste product, it still makes economic sense to construct the necessary gathering infrastructure and link it into the national distribution system.[16] The result is regional price

---

15. And this is only one factor that is driving down U.S. oil demand. Demographics also plays a large role. A retiring population is, well, retired. Sitting at home or helping with the grandkids uses far less energy than the hustle and bustle of working and commuting. Oil prices have now been in the vicinity of $100 a barrel for seven years, encouraging everyone to adopt technologies that result in lower energy bills. Substituting out the Hummer for a hybrid, installing solar panels, swapping out old windows for double-paned, shifting to compact fluorescent light bulbs, putting radiant heating in your floors—these are all decisions that have had impacts that last for a decade or more. The technical term is "demand destruction," and it has already shaved more than 11 percent—some 2.5 million bpd—off of U.S. oil demand.

16. Even if you are selling your associated natural gas production at a loss, a couple dollars per 1,000 cubic feet is still better than zero.

crashes as shale gas supply overwhelms preexisting natural gas demand, or even overwhelms preexisting natural gas transport infrastructure.

Even leaving aside the other factors that argue for a bigger future shale boom, such price crashes are *not* a short-term development. First, the break-even price for shale natural gas production keeps going down, and lower break-even prices make more basins profitable. Second, while no other country is likely to experience its own shale boom, U.S. firms can work in Mexico and especially in Canada with limited restrictions, potentially adding vast volumes to "local" supplies with the commensurate downward pressure on prices.

Third, the cheapness of natural gas is inducing producers and developers to limit natural gas output where possible. In some cases this means that entire basins—like the Gulf of Mexico offshore—are shutting down. Such locations already boast all the infrastructure they need to produce, and so could be brought back online with a few months of work should prices rise. Shale basins are even better in that regard. Most shale developers are only developing oil-rich plays at present, but as part of that effort they must still install the road and legal infrastructure necessary for natural gas production. Drilling new shale gas wells in such areas would only take weeks to months—not years. And because shale well output rapidly drops over time, price crashes are somewhat self-correcting. Best of all, should prices spike, wells that have already been drilled can be refracked to bring up their output rates—a process that doesn't require new permitting, contracting, or infrastructure.

A good example is what happened in the natural gas markets during the vortex winter of 2013–2014. The system began the winter with near record-high storage levels, but repeated bouts of bitter weather depleted those stores to near record lows. In times past natural gas prices would have doubled (or more) and stayed high for years. Instead, prices rose by only 50 percent, and the price spike lasted for just two weeks.

The result? While natural gas prices are hardly guaranteed to remain below $6 per thousand cubic feet, any sustained move above $6 will lead to massive—and above all *rapid*—new output that will push prices back below $6. The United States is looking at decades of low natural gas prices—less than half what they are in Europe and one-third what they are in Japan.

The stickiness of natural gas's very low prices has a raft of implications.

The most direct impact of these price crashes is that utilities are switching wholesale to natural gas whenever and wherever they can. With the boom in cheap input fuels, electricity prices in shale-producing regions started going down in 2008 with such speed that U.S. average national electricity prices have flatlined and are now the cheapest in the developed world. High shale production regions like Texas have seen prices fall by one-fifth. Only regions that have chosen to not produce shale (the Pacific coast) or that lack the infrastructure to import shale gas from other parts of the country (the Southeast) are still seeing rising electricity prices.

Such cheap natural gas and cheap electricity is a massive boon for any industry, but certain ones will benefit more than most. Heavy chemicals, steel, aluminum, plastics, fertilizers, and manufacturing of all types—precisely the sort of jobs that shifted out of country during the 1990s and 2000s—are already returning to the United States, and the manufacturing sector alone has already added half a million jobs since 2008, in large part due to shale's impact.

One manufacturing subsector is particularly worthy of mention: 3-D printing (a.k.a. additive manufacturing). A 3-D printer sprays metal powder or plastic resin in a manner similar to how a laser printer sprays toner. But instead of spraying a single layer, it sprays thousands, one upon the other,

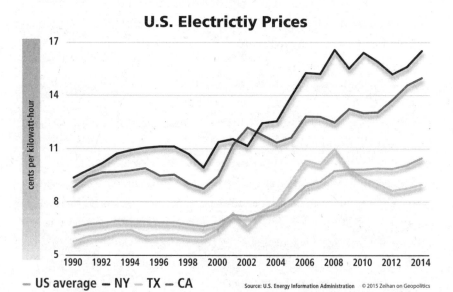

U.S. Electrictiy Prices

cents per kilowatt-hour

17
14
11
8
5

1990 1992 1994 1996 1998 2000 2002 2004 2006 2008 2010 2012 2014

— US average — NY — TX — CA   Source: U.S. Energy Information Administration   © 2015 Zeihan on Geopolitics

until a three-dimensional object emerges. These objects can contain moving parts, hinges, and even disconnections (like a Swiss Army knife, mechanical clock, necklace, or even a firearm), and be printed in all one run.

In most parts of the world 3-D printing is a fringe technology, but a number of characteristics make the merger of shale and 3-D printing particularly notable for the United States:

- Because it does not use molds, 3-D printing only makes one item at a time. This encourages customization and generates opportunities for design jobs in a highly educated country like the United States, but the lack of assembly lines (no mass production) also means that 3-D printing isn't very efficient from an electricity point of view. Cheap electricity—courtesy of shale—lets the United States have the best of both worlds.

- Whether for replacing a part or simply deciding you want *that* thing *now*, 3-D printing doesn't just cut out the middleman, it cuts out the Arab shipping company, the assembly facility in Vietnam, the component manufacturer in Korea, the steel foundry in Russia, and even the Mexican trucking company. Three-dimensional printing colocates manufacturing with consumption. The result is both a much slimmed-down supply chain and reduced need for transport fuels. If 3-D manufacturing captures but 1 percent of the market it will likely slice 50,000 bpd off of global oil consumption simply from transport savings.

- Since you only print what you need, you can create objects that would not be possible with standard molds or injection manufacturing methods. Objects can be of nonstandard shapes, hollow, or even have moving parts and gears right off the printer. This largely eliminates materials waste, reducing the materials used by roughly half, while making the resulting object roughly twice as strong.

- Specific industries that the United States already dominates in terms of supply and demand will benefit more from 3-D printing than other industries. Specifically I'm referring to industries in which production runs are in the dozens to thousands (rather than millions), where strength-to-weight ratios need to be as high as possible, where repairs are best carried out in hours rather than days, and where proprietary techniques need to be guarded behind a wall of intellectual property law and/or national security concerns. For aviation, automotive, medical, and defense industries, 3-D printing is the holy grail. Need to repair a piece of your Lexus or a jet engine? Don't wait overnight for a part to be air-freighted in, just click print and be on your way in an hour or two. Stuck with a new tank design suffering no end of glitches? Simply print out the intermittent development designs and reduce the development path from years to months. Have a patient with a shattered forearm? Just scan the undamaged forearm, invert the image, and print out a replacement bone.

The newness of 3-D printing as an industry makes it difficult to predict just how far and how fast it will spread. Constant innovation is a forecaster's biggest foe. But keep the following in mind: As of 2011, retail 3-D printers could only use plastics. As of 2013, some high-end retail printers could use metals, and printers that could use over two hundred different materials, running the gamut from paper to Teflon to crystal to stem cells, became available for machine shops and similar workplaces. In January 2014, the first multimaterial printers were released. At present they can "only" print out similar materials such as resins, plastics, and rubbers. But in a few years, materials like copper and silicon will be coming out of the same printer. At that point, you will be able to print your new computer at home. For American system designers, the sky will be the limit. For Asian computer-part manufacturers and everyone else in the supply chain that culminates with the American consumer, the floor will fall out.

Experimental prototypes are now creating everything from engine blocks for car enthusiasts to foodstuffs on the International Space Station. Unlike shale, however, 3-D printing technology will certainly diffuse out from the United States, but because of shale, it will be most intensive in its U.S. application for at least a decade.

The outstanding question is: How long can this last? We simply don't know. Shale is the source rock from which all petroleum originates, so when the shale is tapped out the petroleum era is flat-out *over*. But shale is a very new industry using a technological package that hasn't even been in the energy mainstream for a decade, and many of shale's breakthroughs can be applied to preexisting petroleum fields, extending "conventional" production as well. Every time a cost—whether for exploration, drilling, fracking, or transport—is nudged down, petroleum's sunset is delayed a bit more. Do we have centuries of additional supply? Probably not. What about decades? Probably so. We certainly have enough shale energy to deeply enhance the geopolitical and demographic trends that come to a head in the next few years.

Scared New World: The United States Moves On

The impacts of shale on the United States, American power, and therefore the wider world promise to be enormous. Most obviously, energy that is reliable, local, and—in the case of natural gas and electricity—remarkably affordable puts the United States in a category far above every other major developed power both economically and strategically. The Americans already enjoy a system only tenuously linked to the broader international system, and shale's rise alone is set to cut the current account deficit in *half*. And that's just from the energy import savings, to say nothing of shale's attendant benefits to a whole host of economic sectors.

As such, U.S. shale's many effects have the potential to be disastrous on the broader global system. The United States has been the world's largest energy importer for nearly all of the past thirty years. Now it will simply fall off the global energy map.

That will have far more than "simply" a massive market impact. Think back to chapter 5 where we discussed how the Americans refashioned the global trade system in order to build and maintain a global alliance. Since almost none of the American allies were energy exporters, protecting energy flows from the points of production to the points of consumption was part of the deal. The Americans guarded energy in order to enable trade, and enabled trade in order to have their alliance. America's shale revolution is separating the Americans from a supply system the rest of their allies remain dependent upon. There is no grand scheme at work here, just the Americans falling into events and trends that are quickly hiving it off from the rest of the global system.

But what is most disruptive is the timing. The Americans are backing away from Bretton Woods, the global demographic is inverting, and shale is paring back the single most energetic American connection to the wider world *all at the same time*. Any of these factors alone would shake the global system to its core. Together they will upend it completely.

In the next chapter we'll bring all of this together. It is nothing less than the end of the world we know and its replacement with something new...and chaotic.

The Rise of Shale: Ten Years On

Compared to the somewhat jarring updates in the previous couple chapters, bringing you up to speed on shale is pretty straightforward: We are *well* ahead of my forecast. Depending upon how one defines "energy," the United States became a net exporter of oil, natural gas, and refined oil products sometime between 2015 and 2019. After a brief COVID hiatus, these positions were all firmly reaffirmed in 2022.

Of course, there are a few updates worthy of exposition.

First, as the shale sector and its attendant technologies have matured, the industry has steadily consolidated into larger and larger players. While that absolutely encourages business practices to be more efficient as well as more financially and environmentally responsible, it comes at the cost of data transparency. We only know if a (largish) firm is concerned about how many resources remain on their plots of land if they tell us. So, yes, I was certain back in 2013 that the United States could maintain its output for a bare minimum of thirty years. Ten years on, any updated estimate would be pure guesswork. I don't overly enjoy guessing. The durability of American shale is probably fine for a good long time. But "probably" means precisely what you think it does.

Second, there is much more to the evolving American energy complex than just shale. Since 2013, the technologies of solar power have progressed moderately, while that of wind power have exploded. As of 2022 new green-tech installs surpassed that of natural gas, the fuel source that back in 2014 accounted for nearly as much electricity generation as all other fuel sources combined. Every clutch of electrons originating from solar or wind is a molecule of oil or natural gas that can either be exported or saved for another day. Oilmen and Greens will alternatively bitch and crow about each other's and their own efforts and preferred policies, but together they are building up a powerful, and powerfully redundant, energy complex that will entrench and extend American economic and strategic power for decades to come.

Third, we now know most of the shale technologies are *not* easily applicable to other parts of the world. The magic mix of deep capital markets to finance development, deep skilled labor markets to source the workers, preexisting connecting infrastructure to link wells and cities, relative proximity of those wells and cities, and above all else the private property rights to give landowners a vested interest in the sector's success simply do not exist anywhere else in the world. And that's *before* you consider that we now know that not only America's geography but also its *geology* is unique. Few places in the world have the sort of petroleum-rich shale geology of the Barnett or Niobrara, and none match the mighty Permian—a single, sprawling oil complex now producing more oil than all countries except Russia and Saudi Arabia. The Shale Revolution will *not* go global.

But its *impacts* still will. Surplus American oil and refining capacity is now fueling the Mexican expansion; U.S. fuel exports now supply *more* energy to Mexico than Mexico produces for itself. Farther afield, surplus American natural gas has given the Europeans the option of standing up to Russian expansionism. Even without policies expressly designed to link American resource power to external outcomes, America's shale sector is both adding fuel[17] to existing trends as well as pushing back other regions' use-by dates. For a technological suite with only two decades under its belt, shale is only beginning to reshape...everything.

---

17. Heh.

CHAPTER 8

⊷────────⊷

The Coming International Disorder

Technology, Development, and the Modern World

The current global system is downright bizarre by historical standards. For the first time, any country can access markets the world over without needing to guard any aspect of its supply chains—and in most cases, even its borders. What had been possible only for the major empires of the past can now be the core strategy for countries as diverse—and traditionally weak—as Uruguay, Korea, Honduras, Tunisia, and Cambodia. The Bretton Woods rules, and the American free trade strategy at its core, may be artificial and driven by strategic calculus, but they have resulted in the greatest era of peace and prosperity the world has ever known. Everyone can play the game of economic and social development, and play in relative safety.

It is easy for us to forget how very different the past has been.

Centuries of technological advances have created possibilities where few or none existed before. At their most basic, technologies allow people, if sufficiently armed with capital, to partially overcome their local geography and make it productive. The more difficult that geography—whether it be jungle, mountain, swamp, taiga, or desert—the more expensive it is to make it useful, and the more expensive to *keep* it useful.

Economic and social development, then, are about figuring out how to use technology and capital, to find out not only what is possible but also *feasible*. Economists call this opportunity costs. For example, you may be able to build a road to the top of the mountain to reach a remote chalet, build it strong enough to withstand spring floods, plow it to keep it open in the winter, and repair it and clear it of avalanche debris in the summer. But with those same resources you can build fifty times the length of road in flat lowlands and service several tens of thousands of people. Both tasks are possible, but only one is an efficient and productive use of resources and therefore the more feasible.

Feasibility comes down to money. If you don't have any spare cash, not a lot happens. If you are lucky enough to have access to credit, the question is how much does that access cost you? The lower the cost of the credit, the more options within your reach. It really isn't any more complicated than that. In 2012, the average U.S. home price was about $250,000. With a 4 percent mortgage rate, that's a monthly payment of $1,200. Increase the rate to 8 percent and the monthly payment is $1,800. Cheaper credit makes buying a home—or a larger home—a more feasible option. The same concept holds for economies writ large. If capital is available and affordable, there will be more activity: more consumption, more infrastructure, more development.

Every country has a set volume of indigenous or domestic capital that it can apply to its own development, but if additional monies can be brought in from the outside, then more development can occur. In the world before deepwater transport, what capital generation existed came from trade and taxes in individual river valleys. Money was tight. Credit—if it existed—was expensive. The world changed slowly. The development line—the point where an integrated economic and political system gives way to the frontier or, considering the Hobbesian nature of fifteenth-century Europe, the front lines—was pretty damn close to home. The concept of foreign investment normally involved a foreign army and was most certainly *not* sought out. Human development clung to the river valleys, with small archipelagoes of nearby choice bits of land being linked into the riverine systems with short spurs of road. Only lands with the lowest development costs and highest outputs—lands that made absolute economic or strategic sense—were developed. Cities that grew according to this logic are Paris, Osaka, Stockholm, London, Genoa, Istanbul, Copenhagen, and Amsterdam.

The dawn of deepwater technologies changed the world by allowing the European powers to reach out beyond their sequestered river systems and acquire empires. Borders in Europe remained (hotly) contested, but vast swaths of territories beyond Europe were brought into competing imperial systems. Money flowed back and forth between the seat of imperial power and these new provinces, each trading with and enriching the others. Additional money allowed for the digestion of additional lands, pushing back the development line on both sides of the relationship. Territories that may not have quite made the cut in the previous era could be added. Swamps along rivers were drained, rocks were removed from would-be farmland, walls were built to defend areas that were too exposed to justify development in the previous era of scarcer capital. Cities that sprang from this model are Buenos Aires, Sydney, New York City, Cape Town, Barcelona, Hamburg, Liverpool, Havana, and Guangzhou.

The industrialization technologies triggered another evolution, causing the land to bloom with crops and new constructions in ways impossible before. The development line wasn't so much pushed back (although it was) as redrawn. Instead of having isolated towns linked to a river valley by a single shoddy road, a rail line created a corridor of development between the two. The archipelagoes of lands merged—along with many of the lands between them—into far more integrated zones.

On the global scale, industrialization allowed potential city sites to import everything they needed—steel, timber, even people and transport infrastructure—to create metropolises from scratch. The old rules of what was possible could be suspended if you were willing to commit enough capital. Such insta-cities could be built to command a strategic position, to metabolize heretofore stranded resources, or to convert a dinky backwater outpost into something grand. As industrialization gained ground and the production and consumption of goods were augmented by the production and consumption of services (from cars, sneakers, and TVs to movies, overnight delivery, and the Internet), urban populations became not simply a source of labor, but also revenue streams in their own right, due to their ability to generate income and capital. While so much more was possible, feasibility still constrained development. Some projects were so problematic that they didn't justify investment—czarist Russia never industrialized, for example—and some places were quite literally a bridge too far. This is how the world worked right up until the end of World War II. Cities created or reinvented by these means include Moscow, São Paulo, Calgary, Manila, Singapore, and Denver.

At that point the Americans' tinkering with the structure of the global economy through Bretton Woods generated yet another evolution, pushing the development line still further out. With all of the advanced powers now in the same alliance, government outlays on defense plummeted, freeing up more resources for development. The advanced economies were now able to sell freely into the American market, resulting in vast inflows of capital creating yet more resources for development. Rivers were no longer required to generate economic growth because there was sufficient capital to develop transport systems from scratch. With such massive wealth flows, nearly all of the rich world's available territories became developed. It was inevitable that some of it would leak out into the wider world, reaching into the now-former empires' now-former colonies. The Cold War's end catalyzed the process. History seemed to be accelerating. Santiago, Port Harcourt, Dhaka, Mexico City, Beijing, and Seoul evolved into global points of growth.

A few short years later, history seemed to speed up again. The maturation of the Boomer generation flooded an already capital-rich world with a tsunami of money. The aging Boomer generation produced so much excess capital that the line of development drawn by the industrial age was pushed back still further. A *lot* further. Following the most basic law of economics—supply and demand—the huge volume of capital found it difficult to generate high returns and so surged into any investment opportunity it could find. In the United States, the money found a vast sink in real estate, what in time would become known as subprime. In Europe, the onset of the euro allowed for easy lending policies in the Southern European regions that lacked previous experience in managing large-scale financial access, fostering what would become known as the European financial crisis. In Brazil, Russia, India, and China, the flood of capital contributed to the rise of the BRICs (as well as what will soon be known as the BRIC bust). Elsewhere across the world, locations that were previously only known as part of the who's who of imperial overstretch became in-vogue investment destinations, cities like Lima, Dubai, Luanda, Wuhan, Bandar Abbas, Hanoi, and Mumbai.

The vast retirement preparation efforts of the Boomers have deluged the world with financial fertilizer. Territories that could never attract capital previously, even under global free trade rules, found themselves awash in it. Economic development kicked into high gear on a global scale. If the Bretton Woods era is atypical, then the Boomer boom is an aberration. Marry the atypical to the aberrant, and wealth and security have never been on offer for so many people at such a low economic and political cost. Marry the atypical to the aberrant, and we get the shape of the modern world.

It is a weird shape.

- The American dictum that its Bretton Woods partners get along suspended normal geopolitical patterns. Military conflicts among economic powers declined from the norm in the pre–Bretton Woods era to being unheard of once countries joined the network. Since 1946, the only participants who have engaged in direct, substantial conflict with each other are India and Pakistan, both countries that were very late to—and never fully embraced—the game of free trade. In fact, very few Bretton Woods participants have engaged in *any* sort of military action unless it was under the banner of an American military effort. This suspension of military activity has allowed for the existence and even thriving of many countries that would otherwise have been crushed under the heel of larger powers. Countries as varied as Slovakia, Macedonia, Korea, Bangladesh, Papua New Guinea, Latvia, and a host of Sub-Saharan African states had a chance to exist, despite their problematic geographies and often predatory neighbors.
- The removal of military tools from international competition turned most attention to economic development. The Germans and French and British could now not only avoid war, but also form a supranational economic alliance that in time evolved into the European Union. Cheap capital and large markets enabled the EU to expand beyond the more advanced Northern European powers to the weaker countries in Southern and Central Europe, and led to economic interactions with

those even farther removed. Countries and companies that would normally be starved for capital could suddenly access it, regardless of their physical location, track record, or business plan (or lack thereof). First-generation immigrants to Spain with no credit histories qualified for 100 percent mortgages. The Greek government gorged on euro guarantees to build out its welfare state. Russia, despite having sovereign defaults on its record and a history of defrauding *everyone*, discovered that its state firms could borrow at rates that a large, reputable borrower like Walmart couldn't have achieved just a few years earlier.

- Mass financing plus mass trade lowered the bar to entry for countries looking to manufacture goods for export. High global demand, leveraged by cheap capital, meant that any country that could muster a modicum of organization could sell vast volumes of manufactures to a hungry global market without having to strike political bargains to secure market access. Mass demand enabled mass supply, and the process helped a broad array of countries lift themselves out of poverty. Korea and Taiwan shot up the value-added scale, advancing from two of the world's poorest economies to two of its richest in a mere *five decades*. Bulgaria and Romania emerged from the Soviet wreckage to join the rich man's club that is the European Union despite having per capita GDPs of but one-third that of Mississippi.

- Industrializing and modernizing such a vast list of countries required raw materials in unprecedented volumes. Demand for everything from oil to tin became so high that commodities prices exploded over the past twenty years, with nearly all at least tripling. Because of the Boomers' financial boom, those purchases could be financed. Huge volumes of cash flowed to the commodities providers. Some of that income was spent locally, bringing political quietude to traditionally fractious cultures in places like Colombia and Oman. Copper revenue inflows single-handedly made the Chilean government's investments into education and infrastructure possible. Some of the funds were spent on aggressive foreign policies. Venezuela's government used its energy prowess to subsidize a wide array of ideological allies from Cuba to Bolivia to Argentina. Saudi Arabia used part of its $1 billion a *day* in oil revenues to fund its efforts to refashion Lebanon, Syria, Iraq, Pakistan, Afghanistan, and even southern Russia in its image. And a great deal of these funds were simply reinvested into the global system, augmenting the Boomers' already heady investment inflows, inflating the system at all levels. Not counting the far larger monies available to the royal families of the Arab oil states of the Persian Gulf, conservative estimates put the government-accrued nest eggs alone in those countries at over $3 trillion.

- Everything doubled down with the aging of the Boomers. Bretton Woods pushed international activity from the military to the economic field, and the Boomers' capital surplus lathered everything to a froth, vastly expanding the scope of what was possible, and the geographic reach of where it could be. There were pipelines across Kazakhstan, industrial development in Sichuan, ports in East Africa, economic nationalizations in Bolivia, banking empires in...Ireland and Iceland[1]—all floated by a developed-world credit boom. And of course any location that the free trade system had already unlocked waded in ever greater volumes of ever cheaper capital.

- Many of these imbalances have built upon themselves, creating houses of geopolitical cards. China's ability to tap global markets—for imports, exports, and capital—has allowed it to expand into a great industrial power. Its consumption is now sufficient[2] to move global markets all by itself. Part of that "movement" has spiked prices for commodities far higher than they would have otherwise, strengthening countries as varied as Oman, Vietnam, Venezuela, Zimbabwe, Norway,

---

1. Seriously. WTF?

2. China has been the largest importer of a variety of common industrial materials such as cement, copper, iron ore, tin, and lead for years, and in 2012 it surpassed the United States as the world's largest importer of oil.

Uzbekistan, Gabon, Angola, and Argentina. China's export income has also generated yet another mountain of capital that has allowed China to push back the development line from the economically questionable to the economically laughable. Feasibility has fallen to the wayside. Projects that would have been seen as folly before World War II, or even as too danger-ous as recently as the early 2000s, the Chinese boldly embraced: prospecting in war-torn Ethiopia; oil production in genocidal Sudan; copper mining in Zambia; soy production in interior Brazil. Many such projects made—at best—scant economic sense, but because capital was so cheap and demand was so strong, they were attacked with gusto.

The last seventy years have been incredible. But the trends we have both witnessed and enjoyed are nevertheless temporary. And they are nearly over.

Surfing the Peak

But not *quite* yet.

Most people think that October 16, 2007, was just another Tuesday. Taking the kids to school, picking up groceries, business trip, and so on. Me? I was most likely still in awe of the iPhone that I had just purchased two weeks prior. But one woman in New Jersey did something remarkable. Kathleen Casey-Kirschling applied for Social Security benefits for the first time. This wasn't remarkable because of what she did, but because of who she was. Born seconds after the apple fell in Times Square in 1946, Ms. Casey-Kirschling is America's oldest Baby Boomer. The aging of her gen-eration is the single biggest reason our world is holding together. And she and her cohort's retirement is the guarantee that it will fall apart.

While the current system is a highly atypical moment in history, things are actually going to get weirder before they shift back to something closer to historical norms. The reason is almost purely demographic. As workers age, they gain more experience, become more productive, and as such earn higher incomes, but as they approach retirement they tend to consume less. While a fifty-five-year-old might put a big chunk of her large income into savings, a sixty-one-year-old will sock away an even greater proportion of her even larger income because retirement has nearly arrived. This trend toward ever higher savings rates and volumes continues right up until the very day that a mature worker receives her final paycheck.

And then the inflows simply stop. In literally one day, a mature worker's financial contribution to the broader system shifts from the most she has ever contributed to nothing. Worse than nothing, in fact, because the day *after* she retires, she starts drawing money from her pensions—whether government or private—rather than paying into them. It is the financial equivalent of hiking up a mountain for weeks only to reach the top and leap off the cliff.

Timing is everything. The early wave of Boomer retirements doesn't signal capital scarcity, but rather its opposite: extreme capital richness. The world won't flip until the majority of the 200 million developed-world Boomers jump off the financial cliff into their Boca and Barcelona condos. The lemming-like charge has already begun, but the big plunge won't happen until around 2020.

Shifting from an incredibly capital-rich system to an insanely capital-rich system will make the future seem brighter—much brighter—than it actually is. Demand for everything from lead and platinum to wheat and rice and cars and tablets will actually *increase*, and in many cases increase sharply. Capital supply will be sufficient not simply to finance purchases but also to underwrite additional industrial production in everything from manufacturing to mining. The general rules of the past seventy years (that global market opening justifies nearly all development), as well as the aberrant rules of the past twenty years (that money is available for any purpose), will continue to hold true.

This is surfing the peak, and it is wonderful. It is a grand time to be alive. The view up here is unparalleled and the air exhilarating. With a pocket full of cheap money, humanity is truly achieving things beyond all precedent. The pace of technological change, buttressed by massive markets, a globalized system, and unprecedentedly deep supplies of capital, has never been faster.

But from such great and unprecedented heights, there is nowhere to go but down.

The Descent

The global financial wave will crest at some point between 2020 and 2024. Between now and 2019, Poland and Russia will join Japan in the ranks of the demographically impoverished. Between 2020 and 2024, thirteen of the world's top twenty-five economies[3] will be in the ranks of the financially distressed. The new arrivals will include Canada, Germany, the Netherlands, South Korea, Switzerland, the United Kingdom, and of course the United States. With over 90 percent of the developed world in that unfortunate basket, the availability of capital and credit for all will plummet.

Pair the coming demographic dearth with the end of the free trade era, and the future is as bleak as it is readily visible.

Aging demographies will sharply and suddenly contract credit availability to a level that has not been witnessed since the 1970s—in the best case. Interest and mortgage rates will climb into the teens in the developed world, and higher in the developing world. Consumer activity will plunge, due both to the lower volume of twenty- and thirty-somethings as well as sharply higher credit costs. But while economies will contract, government's role in them will increase. The unrelenting surge of people in their sixties will drastically increase government outlays on health care and pensions, even as the sudden dearth of people in their fifties will drastically lower governments' tax take. At the same time, the rising need of governments to borrow combined with the lesser supply of capital to lend will drive government financing rates ever higher.

The pace of technological change will screech to a halt. Boomer retirement means fewer researchers and above all less capital. Fewer and smaller markets mean less commercial impetus for technical advance. Higher

---

3. There are several developing states that will have considerably younger populations during this period, but they are not capital providers to the world. Having forty- and fifty-somethings who generate extra capital requires first reaching a level of industrialization that sports sufficiently high per capita incomes so that workers can start thinking of large-scale savings. None of the world's developing countries are at that point currently, and even if the average growth rates of the previous twenty years continue, none will reach that point by 2025. The one partial exception among the world's major economies is Saudi Arabia, but Saudi savings come from oil income rather than the retirement planning of their mature workers.

government outlays on retirees plus fewer young people mean fewer government dollars available for tertiary education. Everything from universities to corporate labs will slow.

Governments the world over will have to make ever more difficult decisions. One route is to placate the aged with the levels of income support and health care that they have been promised, but to do so by increasingly taxing an ever-shrinking pool of workers and therefore enervating the economy. The other is to dispossess retirees in an attempt to husband the economy's ever-shrinking size and strength, not a likely outcome considering that most of the world's democracies are aging into gerontocracies. Regardless of path, lower standards of living will be on deck for most segments of most societies.

The international economy will spasm and contract. The loss of the developed world's capital surplus as well as the developed world's consuming demographics will force harsh decisions on every economic entity, whether state or private, across the world.

Consumption of both raw commodities and finished goods will plummet. Countries dependent upon exports for their livelihood will suffer immeasurably. Lower demand for finished goods in the developed world will leave droves of firms and workers in both the developed and developing world destitute. But lower demand for the inputs that go into the infrastructure and industry that make global manufacturing possible will not necessarily reduce their price, just their sales volume. Without the rubric of the free trade order or the active management and protection of U.S. forces, the shipment of commodities will no longer be a risk-free venture. Between higher capital costs and higher insurance costs, only the lower-cost producers will have a relatively secure place in the market, and that assumes that either they or their clients are able to guarantee passage. The stage will be set for lower and more erratic supplies of industrial commodities, but not necessarily at lower price points. The one exception to the rule will be energy supplies sourced from shale in North America. The mix of local political stability, local supply, and local demand will prove the magic mix to uncouple North American oil prices from global pricing patterns, much in the way that the early years of the shale revolution did the same for natural gas prices.

Everywhere, American power will be overwhelming by its absence.

For countries like China, which are dependent upon exports to the American market, the pain will be direct and permanent. Others—Central Europe comes to mind—will suffer from the withdrawal of American military support. Others will have different sorts of dependencies, many of which will be overlapping.

Take America's role in global energy markets as but one example. One of the oddest conventional wisdoms is that the United States is heavily dependent upon the Middle East for crude oil supplies. In fact, the United States has only rarely sourced more than one-quarter of its imports from the Persian Gulf. In 2012, the figure was only 20 percent, with nearly half of that being supplies that the Saudis prepositioned in the Gulf of Mexico in order to prove their commitment to the American alliance. American involvement in the Persian Gulf has not been in order to secure energy supplies for the United States, but instead to supply energy for its energy-starved Bretton Woods partners in Europe and Asia. Put more directly, the Americans do not protect the Persian Gulf kingdoms and emirates so that the Americans can use Middle Eastern oil, but so that their Bretton Woods partners in Japan, Korea, China, Taiwan, Thailand, India, and Pakistan can.

In a world in which Bretton Woods is the linchpin of American global strategy, this is quite a cost-effective strategy. In a world in which the Americans reconsider Bretton Woods, however, it is a page from a strategic playbook that will itself be destined for the dustbin of history. American withdrawal from its guarantor role will simultaneously trigger economic and energy crises for Europe, East Asia, and South Asia and financial and security crises for the Persian Gulf states.

In many countries, positive economic growth will become a coveted dream of the past. With fewer jobs, lower incomes, higher costs, fewer services, and higher taxes will come diminished political legitimacy across both the developed and developing world. The dislocations and political disintegration of places like Greece and Syria in recent years are symptoms of the chaos to come.

And *that* is the positive scenario, because it assumes that everyone gets along. It is far more likely that they won't.

For seventy years the world has not had to worry about access to markets or commodity sources. Now it will. Countries far removed from supplies of food, energy, and/or the basic matrix of inputs that make the industrialized world possible will face the stark choice of either throwing themselves at the mercy of superior local powers or throwing what force they can muster at the resource providers. In their desperation, many will realize that American disinterest in the world means that American security guarantees are unlikely to be honored. Competitions held in check for the better part of a century will return. Wars of opportunism will come back into fashion. History will restart. Areas that we have come to think of as calm will seethe as countries struggle for resources, capital, and markets. For countries unable to secure supplies (regardless of means), there is a more than minor possibility that they will simply fall out of the modern world altogether.

This may sound harsh. It *is* harsh. But consider the degree of economic interdependence that globalized trade, cheap credit, and free security have generated. Of the thirty-odd European countries, all are industrialized, but only one—Norway—is self-sufficient in oil or natural gas. Germany, France, Spain, Turkey, and the Czech Republic import nearly all of their petroleum, as do such other varied countries as Chile, South Africa, Taiwan, Morocco, Japan, and South Korea. Europe won't be facing starvation, but the concept of affordable electricity for all—and cars on the road— will fade in more than a few places.

By contrast, much of the Middle East can produce its own energy, but nearly *all* of it risks famine: Of the twenty-odd Middle Eastern countries, none save Israel is industrialized, and *not one*, not even kibbutzy Israel, is remotely self-sufficient in foodstuffs. Each East Asian state has struggled mightily to retain self-sufficiency in rice—all save Malaysia have broadly succeeded—but few can support their other food needs. Along similar lines, Venezuela, Colombia, Singapore, Jordan, Saudi Arabia, Cuba, Iraq, Japan, and South Korea import two-thirds or more of their grain needs. All of these areas stand to be hard hit in the coming years, but East Asia— home to the greatest concentration of the world's manufacturing capacity but only a moderate amount of its agriculture and a starkly limited share of its raw materials or energy—will suffer on all fronts.

One of the few constants through human history is that when a resource—whether it be mineral, agricultural, labor, financial, or market—is in short supply, enterprising, capable, creative countries will go to great lengths to seize what they can for themselves. The Germans and Japanese were hardly the only countries that launched wars for regional domination to secure resources and markets. Africa's modern conflicts—even in the post–Cold War era of free trade—are consistently fought over oil, diamonds, mines, and agricultural land. Over the broad swath of the British Empire, it is difficult to find a corner of the world that the British did *not* launch their military against to seize something they thought they needed. Egyptian history up to the 1950s is about the Nile's agricultural capacity being harnessed by governments more capable than its own.

Making matters worse, the population footprint of the world has evolved radically during the past seven decades. The largest culprit for the shift is the green revolution (not to be confused with the environmental movement), the large-scale application of energy, botany, fertilizer, steel, concrete, and irrigation technologies to the developing world. Recall the land quality map from chapter 4: Much of the green revolution was about making marginal lands—the "moderate difficulty lands" category—bloom.

Collectively, these technologies—along with a massive application of capital—allowed vast regions of the world to become agriculturally productive. Bretton Woods enabled the industrial revolution's agricultural applications to spread to the developing world, allowing the global population to quadruple during the twentieth century. The Boomer credit bulge has taken those applications to some of the most technologically backwards parts of the planet with similar results.

But maintaining that population, to say nothing of growth, is impossible for most locations unless those inputs continue to be applied. The green revolution made deserts bloom and tropics productive, but those gains will only remain if the irrigation systems continue to irrigate and fertilizers remain on hand. Remove Bretton Woods, remove the Boomer capital surge, and everything about the green revolution and the populations it has created is cast into doubt.

The wars of the not too distant future won't so much be for glory or pepper, but in many cases for the ability to remain part of the modern world. Or simply to remain.

America in the New Disorder

The United States is immune to none of this, but it is heavily resistant to all of it. Its population is aging and so it too will face capital crunches, higher taxes, and higher calls on government resources. But America's population is aging far more slowly than that of its competitors. At the time of this writing, the average American is already younger than his Australian, Canadian, French, German, Italian, Japanese, British, Russian, Spanish, and Polish counterparts. By 2020—just five years after this book's publication—he will also be younger than the average Chinese.

The younger population also means it is likely that the American market will be the only significant market to grow year-over-year throughout the period. But even if the American market plateaus—or, God forbid, shrinks a little—it will still represent the largest market in the world by a factor of three. And it is a market that, courtesy of shale, does not require substantial access to the broader international system to maintain its size, growth, coherence, or structure. Or even to keep the lights on.

The United States is also the only country that still has prime lands that not only can be improved but are also likely to be. As the cost of capital increases in the aftermath of the Boomer tide going out, questions of feasibility will return to the fore. Those lower development costs of the Lower 48 territories east of the Rockies—and their colocation with large population centers—will prove a critical factor.

And land isn't the only thing that is both cheap and plentiful in the United States. Thanks to shale, American electricity will also be accessible, plentiful, and above all affordable. Cheap land and cheap power don't simply mean more development, more industry, and a larger and more stable consumption base, they are also the magic elixir that allows young families to thrive. Family formation rates the world over are highest when the basics of life—housing, food, and power—are affordable and reliable. They will be most affordable, most accessible, and most reliable in the United States.

As of 2008, only about 14 percent of U.S. GDP was wrapped up in imports. One-third of that, approximately 5 percent of GDP, was energy. In the past six years shale has already cut that segment by half, and will soon reduce it to zero. Another third of the total is trade with other countries in North America. That leaves under 5 percent of GDP for all other imports.

The export portfolio is similarly favorable to the United States. As of 2013 only 10 percent of GDP is sourced from exports. North America absorbs over one-third of the volume, while including the rest of the Western Hemisphere increases the proportion to half. Canada alone takes more than the entire European Union, and much of the extrahemispheric remainder is with stalwart allies like Australia, the Netherlands, Singapore, and the United Kingdom.

One of the secular trends that is driving down those remaining bits is colocation. During the Bretton Woods era, long and gangly supply chains were not a problem. The low-tariff world allowed manufacturing processes to use parts sourced from quite literally hundreds of different providers assembled at dozens of facilities. This is being undone at every level. Labor costs have increased by a factor of *six* in China in just ten years, sending manufacturers who used to see China as the promised land away in droves. Many are relocating much closer to their preferred American end market, with Mexico being a hot favorite. The high cost of transport fuels has similarly reduced not only China's manufacturing dominance, but also international supply chains with multiple steps, wherever those steps might be. And new technologies like 3-D printing allow for the fabrication in a single run of complex components that used to be made of a dozen or more simpler parts.[4] It all adds up to shorter supply chains, more focused on the high-value-added industries that the Americans already dominate, located closer to home, and in general less dependent upon other countries for everything from design to materials to replacements. Most hurt will be those economies less able to move up the value-added chain to justify their participation in such simpler—if technically more involved—processes: China, Cambodia, Peru, India, Bangladesh, Brazil, Ukraine, and Vietnam.

The United States won't just lose interest in global energy security, it

---

4. Think of a Swiss Army knife, the basic model of which has half a dozen tools (one of which is scissors), each held in place by a hinge, plus the lens for the magnifying glass, a key ring, and the two plastic covers. That's seventeen pieces. Current 3-D printing technology can print everything but the lens and the covers in a single run, and it comes out of the printer *assembled*.

will lose interest in global energy *altogether*. The United States won't just lose interest in global trade supply-chain security, it will lose interest in global trade in its *entirety*. The only pressing need for the Americans to go beyond their shores will be to guarantee their own shipping, and with evolving technologies like shale and 3-D printing, shipping is already accounting for a shrinking, not growing, percentage of American GDP.

Overall, Americans will be able to avoid the sort of Hobbesian, Darwinian environment that will develop, without the help of the rest of the world. Due to shale energy, Canadian energy, and Mexican energy, the United States will have all the petroleum and electricity it could need. The United States is the world's largest agricultural exporter by a sizable margin, and Canada is no slouch. Due to the Midwest and the Canadian Prairies, the United States has all the grains it could possibly need. Due to California's Central Valley, Florida, and Mexico, it will even be able to produce sufficient supplies for most noncritical foodstuffs like citrus and vegetables. So while a global free-for-all may endanger American imports of exotic products like out-of-season avocados, Americans will actually be fairly comfortable compared to everyone else.

As to what they will do with this relative security, wealth, and comfort...well, *that* is the question.

The near future will *not* be a hegemonic world. Hegemons are defined less by their power than by their needs. In a hegemony, the superpower has a goal in mind and so takes an interest in managing events, imposing an order upon the system. The Cold War, for example, was a bipolar system run by competing hegemonies. The Americans maintained the free trade order and its associated military alliances in order to combat the Soviet Union, which crafted and upheld its own economic/military imperial structure.

In the world to come, Americans won't have much need for the rest of the world. And what needs they do have will be largely divorced from what they perceived as important in the period of 1946 through 2014. Without global needs or global interests, there is no reason to impose a global order.

Disengagement will be the rule of the day. Trade links will wither. Global shipping will no longer be protected. Alliances will be allowed to atrophy. Countries long used to living under American protection will find themselves forced to act to keep the lights on, to keep their people employed, to keep their borders secure—and at best they will be out of practice. Other countries long used to being stymied by American security umbrellas will find themselves free to take action against their neighbors. Aside from a scant handful of strategic and economic allies that we'll discuss in the next chapter, America's primary means of interaction with the international community will be via its special forces and long-arm navy, which will use fast, discrete attacks to eliminate perceived threats or disrupt governments sufficiently unwise to attract the wrong kind of American attention.

In the scramble for resources and markets and money, countries of all stripes will jump back into the great game of geopolitics, plotting, scheming, and maneuvering against each other. But for the most part they will not be plotting, scheming, and maneuvering against the United States. Being the target of someone's ire or calculus requires that you have an interest that they can plot, scheme, or maneuver against. Since nearly everything that matters to the United States will be firmly anchored in North America, the Americans will return to the role that they played before World War II: a global power without global interests. No more guarding the Korean DMZ. No bases in Qatar. No Checkpoint Charlie. No patrolling the sea lanes. When it comes to the wider world, the Americans will just not care.

Most days.

Large-scale American disinterest in the broader world will be the rule of the day, yet the United States will remain the only country with substantial long-range military deployment options. It will have absolute dominance of the seas, but will only exercise that power when it sees fit. Unfortunately for anyone hoping to plan around American actions, the criteria for "when it sees fit" will not just be vague, but maddeningly mutable.

Scared New World: The American Scenario

This, all of this—the coming American divorce from the world at large, the demographic inversion and its impact on governments' stability, the end of easy access to global energy supplies, the ongoing ability of the Americans to brutally interrupt any portion of the planet without suffering or caring about the repercussions—is actually the *best*-case scenario because it assumes that American interest in the wider world will continue to wane at a slow pace. It assumes that most countries will have at least a few years to adjust to changing circumstances.

They might not get that. The reason is wrapped up in how geography shapes culture.

Every culture has a certain personality impressed upon it during the first century or two of its existence as geography and history inter-mingle to shape exactly who the people in question turn out to be. The formative period for American culture was the pioneer era. Consider the time frame:

While Napoleonic France was reintroducing Europe's peasant armies to the horrors of war, famine, and massed relocations, American freemen were happily pushing west to settle some of the world's best lands. Within a year of breaking ground, all could—via the world's best maritime trans-port system—sell grain on global markets for hard currency.

It is largely irrelevant that the Americans' ability to collectively capi-talize upon its advantages was due more to an unplanned confluence of unprecedented factors—the arrival of millions of Europeans anxious to escape Europe's wars, the largely completed genocide of the natives, the ease of accessing the Ohio valley, the presence of the world's best natu-ral waterway network, the availability of the world's largest contiguous piece of arable land—rather than some grand scheme. But such a phalanx of coincidences does not diminish one bit that the Americans' frontier period was the largest and fastest cultural and economic expansion in human history. And it held for five generations: The Americans found more and better lands, serviced by more and better waterways. It may have been accidental, but it held for so long and was so core to the lives of so many Americans that as a national culture Americans came to think of such an upward trajectory as normal. Ordained even. God shed his grace on thee indeed.

But what happens when things do not get better each and every year? What happens when the Americans suffer a stinging, public setback? What happens when the rest of the world reaches out and touches Americans on terms other than America's?

They panic. They panic with the desperation of a people who have no

sense of balance, no perspective, no understanding of context, no sense
that not everyone in the world wins every time. And then they fight back
with everything they have. Were the United States a small country such
overreactions would be odd, perhaps even comical. But the United States
is the global superpower and its overreactions typically reshape both itself
and the wider world.

- *Sputnik.* The Soviet Union's beeping aluminum grapefruit
  convinced the Americans that they had already lost the Cold
  War, despite the fact that they were ahead of the Soviets in
  electronics and metallurgy and led the greatest economic and
  military alliance in world history. The Americans revamped
  their scientific research and educational systems and retooled
  their industry on a mass scale. They created organizations like
  NASA and DARPA that sixty years on still rule the horizons of
  space.
- **Vietnam.** The Americans lost a postcolonial war to a rice producer, and fell into a national funk despite the fact that the
  United States was the world's largest rice exporter at the time, it
  wasn't their colony, and that not one American ally abandoned
  the alliance because of the defeat. The American reaction to
  Vietnam was the mass application of information technology
  to warfare, which landed them with everything from satellite
  communications to cellular phones to cruise missiles.
- **Japanophobia**. In the 1980s Americans became convinced
  that the Japanese had—not would, *had*—overtaken the United
  States as the global economic superpower. This belief perme-
  ated despite American naval forces still protecting global shipping, despite having an economy double the size of Japan's,
  despite Japan's total arable land being roughly the size of
  Massachusetts, and despite American forces *occupying Japan
  at the time.* America's reaction included the mass application
  of technology across industry to "catch up" to Japan, as well
  as Wall Street's at times brutal punishing of firms deemed too
  slow. The resultant capital formation funded, among other
  things, the Internet revolution of the 1990s.

- **September 11, 2001.** The attacks on New York and Washington, D.C., claimed some three thousand lives, making them the worst terror attack in history. A response—a very strong response—was warranted. But leaving aside the wars in Iraq and Afghanistan, few realize just how far the Americans pushed into the global system. As a side effect of American military actions in the Global War on Terrorism, the Americans now have solid defense cooperation, up to and including the ability to share local tactical intelligence, deploy special forces, and operate with minimal restrictions against militants, within Morocco, Algeria, Tunisia, Libya, Egypt, Jordan, Saudi Arabia, Oman, Bahrain, Iraq, Kuwait, Israel, the Philippines, Indonesia, Singapore, Kenya, Ethiopia, Djibouti, Kyrgyzstan, the United Kingdom, Italy, Spain, Portugal, Poland, Hungary, Romania, Bulgaria, and Turkey. That places, at a moment's notice, the sharp end of American power on either side of nearly all of the world's major trade and energy arteries.

America's geography grants it nearly endless riches, security, and opportunity. What it does not necessarily grant the Americans is the wisdom to appreciate what they have or make the most of what lies before them. Between the strategic and economic environment of the current day, America's insulation from the wider world, and above all the United States' trademark unpredictability, picking out precisely what will cause the Americans to pull the plug on the free trade era is an exercise in wild-eyed futility. Unfortunately for everyone else, it truly matters whether the American shift from Bretton Woods occurs slowly over a decade of neglect, or deliberately in a single day of panicked fury. The new world may well emerge just as the United States rose to power just over a century and a half ago.

By accident.

CHAPTER 9

·◁═════════▷·

Partners

Who's Who in the Disorder

In my speaking engagements, I essentially present the first eight chapters of this book in the first twenty minutes or so and then spend the rest of my time addressing the future from the point of view of my respective audiences. In the aftermath, the Q&A sessions can take us anywhere. What about Azerbaijan's efforts to resist Russia? What is the future of Dubai's financial sector? Will the Brazilian cotton industry survive? What parts of China's manufacturing base are most viable? Will wheat production in Saskatchewan be able to find new markets? What are Sweden's prospects in a post-euro world? What do you think of India? Will the aging state of U.S. infrastructure hobble American power? The list goes on. And on.

And on.[1]

In other words, I'm acutely aware that it's a great big mess of a world out there, filled to overflowing with complex interactions. One of the greatest challenges in crafting this book—not to mention trying to forecast out to 2030(!)—was not so much deciding who and what to cover, but instead who and what to leave out. Everyone has a story, and everyone's story impacts someone else's, but I couldn't tell them all. So in the remainder of this book I will endeavor to hit what I see as the key points of the future:

---

1. And on.

- The countries that will be most willing, whether due to opportunity or desperation, to put their mark on the world;

- The countries that will be lucky enough to find themselves in America's inner circle, and so will continue to benefit in some way from the American market access and physical protection that will be increasingly absent for everyone else;

- And, because this is ultimately a book about the reality, consequences, and use of American power, the major developments across the international system that are most likely to impact the lives of Americans. Note the diction: impact, not threaten. There are multiple pros and cons for the Americans within each of these developments, which we'll address in the final five chapters.

In this newly Darwinian, Hobbesian world there are any number of ways of classifying and evaluating countries. As a starting point, I think it is best to give you a map of the future so you can see for yourself what the rough contours will look like. I had considered spamming you with a variety of maps that presented the likelihood of demographic collapse versus growth, of famine versus plenty, or military disaster versus success. It would have been a *lot* of maps. Instead I'm going to start by giving you the result of my findings, and then in following chapters explore the dynamic factors and countries that make the conclusions possible.

On the following page, you'll find the global stability map of the future, circa 2020–30.

The world can be broken into six categories:

1. State failure: Syria, Greece, Libya, Turkmenistan, Kyrgyzstan, Yemen, etc. These countries do *not* have what they need to survive outside the parameters of the world as it has been for the past few years. Maybe the Cold War gave them protection. Maybe they are economically hopeless without Bretton Woods. Maybe their national identities never really coalesced, making them vulnerable under almost any circumstances. Maybe some regional power just hasn't gotten around to swallowing them up yet. Regardless of the cause, as modern states they won't be with us much longer.

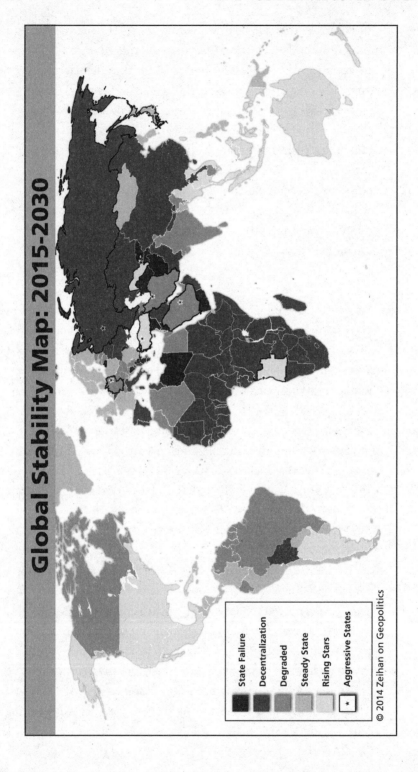

Global Stability Map: 2015-2030

State Failure
Decentralization
Degraded
Steady State
Rising Stars
Aggressive States

© 2014 Zeihan on Geopolitics

2. Decentralization: Russia, China, Bolivia, Nigeria, Cameroon, Sudan, Ethiopia, etc. Like the first category, these states do not have what they need to survive in the new era. Sufficient food, energy, raw materials, capital, markets, security—most lack at least three. Making matters worse, they won't have any allies, and they'll lack the capacity to even attempt to secure their needs in the long run. However, the pressures facing them are not *quite* state-destroying. Central government will hold, if only just. Life will be painful. But at least it will still be life.

3. Degraded: Brazil, India, Canada, Hungary, Saudi Arabia, Algeria, etc. These states are missing some of the basic building blocks of modern society: popular buy-in, government legitimacy, sufficient food or energy or markets. But what they do have is the capacity to partially address some of their challenges. They will fail at most of these attempts, but it won't all be bad. Most important, the pressures they are under—while multivectored and structural—will not hit them with critical force. Central authority in these countries will remain fairly strong, even as most everything else about the country weakens.

4. Steady state: United Kingdom, France, Denmark, Sweden, Peru, Philippines, etc. The countries in this group will *probably* be able to hold on to the level of stability they currently enjoy. But stability isn't the same thing as stasis; all of these countries are going to experience change and will have to find new ways to operate. What really sets this group apart from the earlier categories is that they will have the capacity not just to sustain themselves but also to secure what they need. Some will be able to muddle through on their own. Some will be able to keep or find some friends. Most will be able to reach what they need one way or another.

5. Rising stars: United States, Australia, Argentina, Angola, Turkey, Indonesia, Uzbekistan, etc. These are the masters of the chaos, the durable countries and systems that will be able to thrive under the harshest international circumstances the new world can throw at them. Most of these have exceptional geographies to begin with, and those that do not will fall in with a certain superpower that has more than enough to share.

6. Aggressive powers: Germany, Japan, Uzbekistan, Saudi Arabia, Russia, Turkey, Angola. Each country in this category also exists in one of the five previous. What makes the members of this overlapping category distinctive is that their attempts to grapple with the emerging disorder will lead them to make bold—or desperate—forays beyond their own borders. They will challenge their regional status quos. They will invade their neighbors. They will attempt to fashion new alliance structures, new political networks, new trading systems. Win or lose, these countries will be *loud*. They will be the newsmakers of the next twenty or so years. We'll address all of them in the next few chapters.

Partners: American Allies in the New Era

In the chaos to come, the United States will be *the* friend to have, for many reasons. Here are the top four:

- **Market.** In times of global stability, the United States already boasts a market larger than any other by a factor of three. As the global situation deteriorates, the U.S. market will tower above all others in its stability, size, and strength. It will also be among the few that not only boast the demographic and financial capabilities to grow, but also possess the security and stability necessary to grow continuously. The United States will be one of only a scant handful of developed countries with substantial populations of citizens in their twenties and thirties, making it *the* state to experience consumption-led growth.
- **Capital.** As the country with the greatest river network, the United States has a capital supply that is independent of its demographics. American capital, however, will not even be limited to its ample domestic sources. The relative stability of the American system will make it a magnet for capital fleeing less stable lands. In times of global strength like the 1990s, some $5 trillion—over 6 percent of American GDP over the decade—fled to the United States. Just imagine the sorts of vol-

umes that will flee to the United States in times of global mass disruption. In a world of rapidly shrinking volumes of capital, the Americans will hold the lion's share.

- **Security.** While other countries will be forced to reallocate scarce resources to secure their defensive interests at home and their economic interests abroad, the United States' geographic position and embedded, cordial relations with Canada and Mexico will spare the Americans that onerous cost. In fact, American defense spending may actually *decrease* while available American forces *increase*. Part of the Bretton Woods deal is that the Americans would patrol the seas for all and defend the territory of all. That will no longer hold. This raises the distinct possibility that the United States' military posture will return to the traditional role it played between 1898 and 1945: almost no foreign bases, but a posture of permanent offense. The United States will once again be a country with a global military, but one free of global interests. This will not only ensure that potentially hostile powers get nowhere near American shores, but will also enable the Americans to intervene where and when and how they wish.

- **Trade.** While the Americans are extraordinarily unlikely to provide freedom of the seas for the world at large, they will still have a navy that is triple the power of the combined world in terms of its ability to project power. That is actually more in favor of the Americans than it sounds: At the beginning of this age, the United States will have twelve fully deployable supercarriers against the combined fleet of the rest of the world's two, and those two will be British and French. Nearly every other navy on the planet is limited to coastal and support vessels. At the beginning of this age, only the Americans have aircraft that can be based at home and yet bomb any location on the planet. That means that only the Americans will have the capacity to guarantee—or more importantly, deny—shipments to or from any coast on the planet at any time. Any ocean-borne trade that is to be sustainable will require—at a minimum—American disinterest.

From almost any angle, the United States will be a one-stop shop for a country that wants to succeed in the newly Darwinian world, and the enmity of the Americans will be something to avoid at all costs. The process of securing American friendship in the new world will be radically different from the old. Instead of the Americans working assiduously and sacrificing to build a broad alliance network, countries will have to petition the Americans on a bilateral basis to get the market access, capital, technology, or protection that they will so desperately need. The trick for would-be allies will be to find something shiny that will catch American attention.

North America: The Inner Circle

In 2013 the United States exported roughly $1.6 trillion in goods and $680 billion in services, while importing $2.3 trillion in goods and $450 billion in services. That sounds like a lot—it *is* a lot—but it isn't as bad as it seems at first glance. The American economy settles in at a very non-dainty $16 trillion; its total trade exposure in absolute terms may be the world's largest, but in relative terms it is below that of everyone but Brazil and South Sudan—even Afghanistan is more internationally integrated. Additionally, what exposure the Americans have is remarkably local: The United States' top two trading partners for decades have been Canada and Mexico,[2] accounting for one-third—some $1.15 trillion—of the total U.S. trade portfolio. While NAFTA is by its very definition a free trade agreement, it was negotiated separately from the global free trade order, and is legally and administratively disconnected from the Bretton Woods system, complete with its own adjudication mechanism that exists solely for the NAFTA signatories. The United States doesn't even need to patrol the oceans to keep the trade open, since nearly all of it occurs either in territorial waters, the Gulf of Mexico, or via land routes. Bilateral American-Canadian trade on the Ambassador Bridge, which links Detroit, Michigan, and Windsor, Ontario, is by itself of greater volume than the total combined trade with all but four of America's other trading partners. NAFTA and its CAFTA extension, which brings in the Central American states of Honduras, Nica-

---

2. China recently edged ahead of Mexico for the number two spot in merchandise trade, but if services are included, Mexico and Canada remain the top two.

ragua, Guatemala, El Salvador, Costa Rica, and the Dominican Republic, are no-brainers for the Americans. All are already firmly integrated into the American economic system independently of Bretton Woods. In essence, they are America's backyard. The Americans can—easily—have their local trade without lifting a finger to support global trade.

Cuba: The Prodigal Returns

The notable outlier from the NAFTA/CAFTA system is of course **Cuba**. As a bastion of anti-Americanism since its revolution in 1959, Cuba has been the plank in the eye of the American strategic position in the Western Hemisphere for decades. This will not last, and not simply because Fidel Castro will (probably) not live much longer. Cuba's problem is primarily economic. It doesn't collaborate with the vibrant economic giant at its doorstep and so is dependent upon limited trade with the wider world. This is tolerable so long as the world as a whole lives by the rules of free trade. Remove that characteristic, however, and Cuba, which lacks even a merchant marine, is all on its own.

The Americans are certain to underscore that status, because Cuba's ability to vex the United States comes from its position at the mouth of the Gulf of Mexico. Capable military forces stationed on the island would be able to pinch closed the Florida and Yucatán Straits, blocking most trade that would have entered or exited the greater Mississippi system. However, "capable" military forces are not ones that could naturally originate on an island with as few resources as Cuba. The danger to the United States from Cuba isn't from Cuba, but from larger powers that would ally with Cuba. The Americans were willing to risk nuclear war during the 1962 Cuban Missile Crisis for just this reason. With the end of the Cold War there wasn't a hostile blue-water navy anywhere in the world, so Cuba fell into strategic irrelevance and Americans stopped paying it any attention. Fast-forward just a few years to a more mercantilist world, however, and the Americans are unlikely to tolerate a hostile country on such a strategically positioned chunk of land so close to their internal trade ways. Whether it is because Havana wants to avoid destitution or because the Americans force the issue, Cuba is about to be folded into the American system.

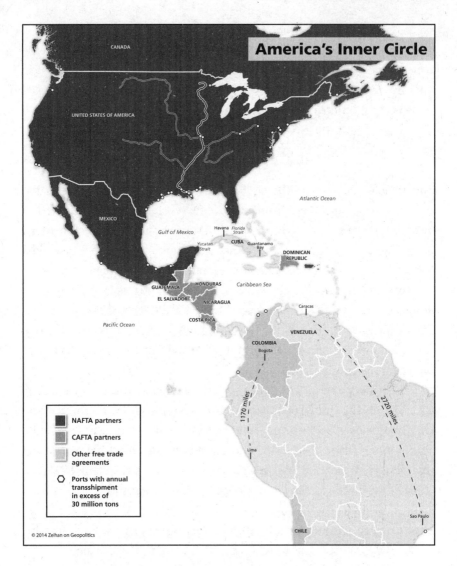

Colombia and Venezuela: Wealth or Ego?

Don't think of South America as a single entity, or even a single landmass. The combination of the mountains of the Andes and the tropics of the Amazon divides the continent into pieces. The northern tier of states— **Colombia** and **Venezuela**—are for all practical purposes in another world. Only the most remote and low-quality of roads link Colombia and Venezuela to their own tropical interiors, much less span the thousand-plus miles of the Amazon Basin to the developed portions of Brazil. The

Venezuelan rail network does not even connect to another country. Nearly all of the populated centers of both countries access the wider world by looking north to the Caribbean rather than south to Brazil or west/east to each other. Integration with each other would be difficult. Integration to the south is simply ludicrous. They are, in essence, part of the United States' extended backyard, and integration with the Americans is the only natural economic partnership they can hope for.

Colombia has accepted this fate—not a lightly made decision considering that under Teddy Roosevelt the Americans sponsored a revolution in Colombia, helping carve the country of Panama out of Colombian territory. Bogotá has partnered repeatedly with the Americans on issues of security importance to Washington, namely efforts to reduce cocaine and coca flows out of the Colombian highlands, and they have achieved a bilateral free trade agreement.

Venezuela has not. Ideological opposition has landed Caracas with one of the worst bilateral relationships with Washington of anywhere on earth. This need not be the case. But since Venezuela does not actually border the United States and it is not strategically located like Cuba, the Americans will not make the decision for the Venezuelans. If Venezuela is to be anything other than a dispossessed country with a crushingly impoverished population, it will need to start repairing relations with the United States before it is too late. It isn't a pretty choice, but unlike most countries in the coming era, at least Venezuela has the option of making a choice about its future. But time is running out, and it all comes down to shale.

Venezuelan crude is so viscous and thick with contaminants that only a handful of refineries anywhere in the world can process the stuff. Almost all of those refineries are on the Gulf Coast of the United States.

Hugo Chávez, who ruled as Venezuela's president from 1999 until his death in 2013, sought to reduce his country's economic connections to the United States in general and those refineries in specific. His solution was to sell his crude to China and subsidize the Chinese for the huge additional transport costs as well as compensate them for the lower volume of products their refineries could produce from crude grades they were not designed to handle. The Chinese happily accepted the subsidies, picked up the crude from the Venezuelans, sailed it north to the Gulf of Mexico, sold it to the Americans, and pocketed the difference.

This would be little more than an amusing anecdote about the opportunity costs of blind ideology, but then there is shale. Most shale oil isn't just sweet and light, it is ultra-sweet and ultra-light, and so is remarkably easy to refine into light distilled products, like gasoline. Unless Venezuela can find a means of repairing its relationship with Washington, soon America's Gulf Coast refineries will be retooled to run high-quality shale oil rather than low-quality Venezuelan oil and Venezuela will become the first energy producer in history to not have a market.

Europe: Cherry-Picking

To be blunt, from a strategic and economic point of view, the United States does not care much for mainland Europe. Leaving aside the American views of European distaste for American strategic policy and culture, Europe is a hard place to do business. It is overbureaucratized, burdened with heavy layers of regulation at the national and EU level, and should it—against all odds—coalesce into a truly unified entity, it would be a match for American power. But that doesn't mean that the Americans will ignore it completely. It comes down to simple size. Even in the ashes of World War II, the Europeans were collectively the world's second largest economy; so even in the coming economic shipwreck there will be any number of European markets of interest. The Americans just won't want to have to deal with those markets directly.

Luckily for the Americans, they don't have to. **Denmark** and the **Netherlands** are the quintessential middlemen of Europe. The Dutch own the lower reaches of the Rhine, Europe's richest river, and occupy a strategic spot midway between France, Germany, and the United Kingdom. As such, they have been consummate dealmakers of European history since the time of the Spanish Empire. For their part, the Danes command the opening to the Baltic Sea, and so quite literally can decide who within can access the outside world.

Both the Dutch and the Danes control access to massive trade arteries. Both the Dutch and the Danes occupy extraordinarily strategic locations. Both the Dutch and the Danes are distrustful (to put it mildly) that some singular power might arise from the North European Plain. Both the Dutch and the Danes are exceedingly pro-American. And both the Dutch and the Danes will be among the most attractive allies the Americans will have.

There is one broader lesson for the world that will emerge from the likely Danish-American partnership. Denmark's geopolitical expertise in managing the Baltic Sea's trade has been translated over the years into its nurturing of Maersk, one of the world's major shipping companies. In a world in which shipping volumes collapse along with world trade and supply chains, there may well be room for only one major player in that industry. If the Danes can keep themselves on America's short list of allies, that one major player certainly won't be Arab or Chinese.

The **United Kingdom** faces the best and worst of all worlds. On the upside, as the European Union's financial problems deepen, an ever-rising volume of enterprising Europeans are attempting to hide an ever-rising volume of capital from the claws of their governments' tax collectors. London's Square Mile—the greatest density of banking activity in the world—has accepted these monies with open arms, building the UK financial world into a global powerhouse and the kingdom's most dynamic economic sector. As the EU descends into depression and dissolution, that flow of capital—and London's fortunes—will only fatten.

Now for the downside. This huge inflow of capital already puts ever stronger upward pressure on the pound versus the euro. As the pound rises, every other economic sector in the United Kingdom—manufacturing, agriculture, shipping, steel, mining, everything—becomes ever less competitive. As the new world unfolds, the United Kingdom will be able to feast on Europe's bones, but its own nonfinancial economy will shrivel on the vine. Between a strong currency, an aging demography, and an ever more expensive social welfare state that is already well beyond the kingdom's economic means, the United Kingdom's very existence as a modern industrial economy is almost over. The entire country is becoming reduced to little more than a (admittedly huge) financial center.

Yet the Americans are still interested. There is no country in Europe more terrified by the concept of a united Europe than the United Kingdom, and no country with more expertise and experience in preventing a united Europe from coming about. This is something the Brits will apply their substantial energies to regardless of what the Americans do, and those energies now have a characteristic that cannot help but grab American attention: They're about to launch two supercarriers.

And never forget that Great Britain is an island. The cost of maintaining

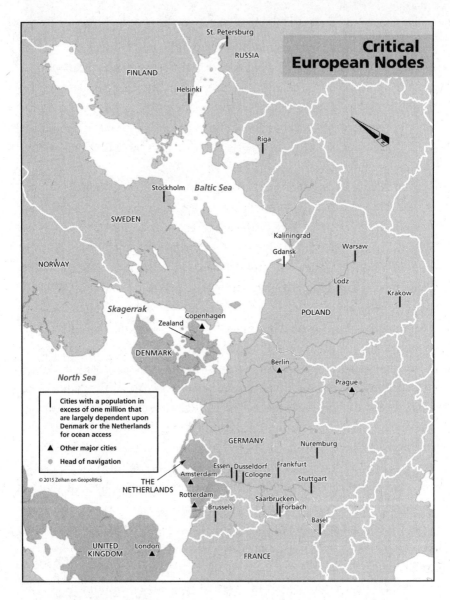

the United Kingdom's independence remains minimal, and London's ability to throw monkey wrenches of all sorts into Continental affairs remains legion.

Asia: Free Trade in Miniature

Thailand is in many ways America's favorite ally. The Thais occupy an interesting piece of real estate: a coastal bowl valley on a fantastically insu-

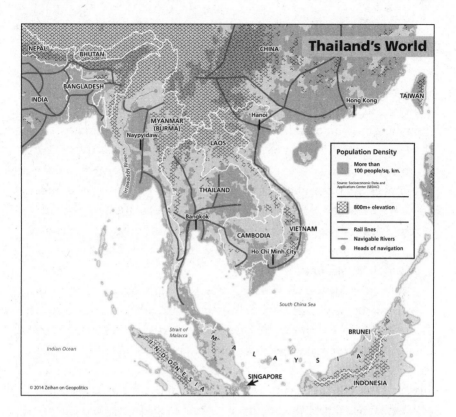

lated bay adjacent to an open plateau, all surrounded by jungle mountains so impregnable that even after seventy years of Bretton Woods only coastal rail corridors lead out of the country. That protection has allowed the Thais to develop with a minimum of interference from outside powers regardless of era, enabling them to hold on to their independence even at the height of the European imperial age. Thailand's mix of geographies grant it a capital-intensive, high-value-added industrial-technocratic society around its Bangkok core, but also a more agrarian highland interior that benefits from a modest amount of raw materials. It isn't simply mainland Asia's most secure state and best equipped to protect its own borders and interests, it is also the only one that can interface with the outside world on its own terms. Even better, perennial political discord between the Bangkok core and the inland plateau all but guarantees that Thailand will never pose a military threat to its neighbors. It is the perfect ally: It doesn't need U.S. troops stationed on its soil, it doesn't need much economic help, and it doesn't generate much heartburn. It is also a damnably useful friend due to its strategic position between India, China, and the Southeast Asian trade lanes. Additionally, Bangkok's extensive experience in dealing with its somewhat squirrelly neighborhood means it can even offer the Americans extensive security cooperation as a sweetener to any alliance deal.

One surprising potential partner is **Myanmar**, a country that has been on America's blacklist for the past generation. Myanmar has three things going for it. First, it has moderate volumes of a wide array of natural resources from oil and natural gas to zinc and copper to hydropower and timber. As it is right next door to Thailand, the synergies are many and obvious. Second, Myanmar's Irrawaddy River is the only river in the region that is navigable for any reasonable length. If there is a part of the region that cannot just rapidly develop, but start to bootstrap its own economy, it is Myanmar.

Third, the Myanmarese have a streak of paranoid mistrust of their more powerful neighbors. Throughout the 1990s and 2000s, this led to a de facto alliance with China in the face of Western disapproval of Myanmar's choice of political management system (i.e., military dictatorship). But in the early 2010s, the Chinese started treating Myanmar as a province, and such perceived intrusions into internal Myanmarese business resonated so poorly that as of 2014 the Myanmar-Chinese relationship has imploded. The result is a lurching democratization process in order to facilitate a strategic opening to the very Western countries that the government so distrusted for so long. You can count on the Myanmarese not to trust their larger neighbors. Those larger neighbors—India and China—are precisely the sort of would-be regional hegemons that the Americans would prefer to keep locked down. The mere continuing existence of Myanmar, regardless of the flavor of the local government, achieves that all by itself.

Taiwan and **South Korea** are not so clear-cut. Strategically, they are absolutely partners the Americans want. The two countries are smashed between the Japanese and Chinese spheres of influence, incredibly competent in managing their own defense, and could go nuclear over a long weekend if they were particularly stressed.[3] But keeping them in America's

---

3. The International Atomic Energy Agency has (repeatedly) censured South Korea for (repeatedly) creating small amounts of weapons-grade uranium in its labs. Either Seoul enjoys risking sanctions or it wants to keep sharp the appropriate skill sets for weaponization.

circle of allies will not come cheap. Both countries import nearly all of the energy and raw materials they use, and their markets are too small to support the world-class industrial base they have developed under the Bretton Woods regime. Keeping those economies alive and relevant would require the Americans to maintain on-land military footprints in East Asia, and to continue, at least in part, with the ocean-patrolling and trade-protecting activities that they would so like to get out of. For instance, just these two small countries require twenty supertankers of crude per month. That would force the Americans to convoy tankers from at least Southeast Asia, and maybe even the Persian Gulf, as well as maintain transpacific trade access so that Korean and Taiwanese goods can be sold into the American market. These two traditional allies will be the litmus test for just how far the Americans are willing to go to support allies in the new era.

Which brings us to **Singapore**. As Singapore sits upon the world's busiest trade and energy transport artery, it is difficult to imagine a country that gained more from the United States' forcing of free trade upon the world—or to imagine a country that will suffer more from its removal. Singapore has greater trade and energy throughput than any other location on the planet, the flows it manages form global benchmarks, and its considerable technocratic-industrial base is funded almost entirely from its trade facilitation profits. Simply put, Singapore *is* free trade in physical form. Without a global trade order, without the Americans protecting trade flows between East Asia and Europe and energy flows between East Asia and the Middle East, Singapore has nothing...except a damnably strategic piece of land. If there is to be *any* trade between East Asia and Europe, or *any* East Asian purchases of Middle Eastern energy, then Singapore is *the* place that would enable the Americans to short-circuit any East Asian rival at any time without firing a shot. But this makes Singapore a strategic ally, not an economic one. Bereft of American commitment to patrol much beyond the Strait of Malacca itself, Singapore's economic fortunes will need to be recast in a far narrower—and more local—net.

American involvement with Myanmar, Thailand, and Singapore raises potential solutions to the economic problem raised by America's possible interest in Taiwan and Korea. Those solutions are **Australia** and **New Zealand**. Between them they are low- to mid-cost reliable producers of nearly every significant industrial and agricultural commodity under the

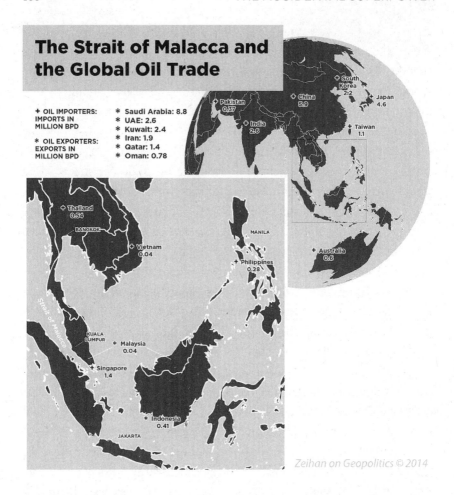

The Strait of Malacca and the Global Oil Trade

+ OIL IMPORTERS: IMPORTS IN MILLION BPD

* OIL EXPORTERS: EXPORTS IN MILLION BPD

* Saudi Arabia: 8.8
* UAE: 2.6
* Kuwait: 2.4
* Iran: 1.9
* Qatar: 1.4
* Oman: 0.78

+ South Korea 2.2
+ China 5.9
+ Japan 4.6
+ Pakistan 0.37
+ India 2.6
+ Taiwan 1.1
+ Thailand 0.54
+ Vietnam 0.04
+ Philippines 0.28
+ Australia 0.6
* Malaysia 0.04
+ Singapore 1.4
* Indonesia 0.41

BANGKOK
MANILA
KUALA LUMPUR
JAKARTA
Strait of Malacca

Zeihan on Geopolitics © 2014

sun: oil, natural gas, coal, uranium, aluminum, wheat, fruits, vegetables, dairy, beef, and lamb. There is no more perfect mating to the resource-poor and hungry states of Taiwan and Korea than the Anglos of Australasia.

While a commitment to keep trade lanes to the Middle East might be more than the Americans are interested in, commitment to keep the far shorter and less fraught lines to political and cultural mates in Australia and New Zealand would be comparatively simple. The pair are also so physically removed from the Asian mainland that the defense commitment required to maintain their sovereignty would be minimal. American involvement in Australasia would also solve—at least partly—Singapore's problem. A web of trade among the United States, Korea, Taiwan, Myanmar, Thailand, Australia, and New Zealand would put Singapore

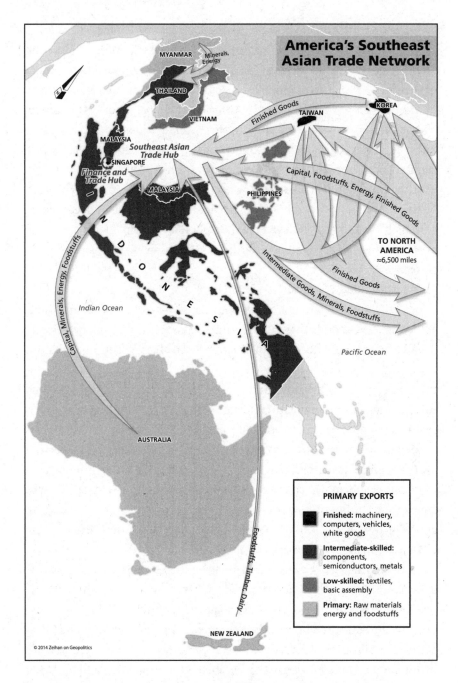

smack in the middle. In fact, in the middle along with Singapore would be its current economic partners: the **Philippines**, **Malaysia**, **Indonesia**, and **Vietnam**.

All four of those Southeast Asian countries will never be able to project meaningful amounts of power on the water. The first three are archipelagoes, but so disassociated across distance that they cannot develop into a powerful empire as Japan did, or even maintain a navy that might more than marginally threaten their neighbors. The fourth, Vietnam, has its northern and southern populations so separated by distance and geography that simply solidifying internal integrity is a century-long process that the Vietnamese are not even halfway through. These weaknesses also create a very peculiar demographic geography. All of the countries sport only lightly populated hinterlands, instead being extremely urbanized with very dense population centers packed with people trying to carve out a better life for themselves than is possible in tropical agriculture.

It is this odd characteristic that will make them so attractive to the Americans. First, all are perennial sources of low-cost, low- to medium-skilled labor. Second, that labor is already concentrated in the region's urban centers; the concentration of supply both eases recruiting and keeps labor and infrastructure costs down. Third, bracketed as these countries are by a mix of resource and energy providers, financial powers, and mid- to high-tech manufacturers, everything is perfectly positioned for a regional supply-chain network. All they need are sufficient food imports to feed their young, urbanized populations—something the American agricultural sector is eminently capable of doing for everything besides rice (and rice demand can be met from within Southeast Asia). Finally, collectively the Southeast Asian region represents a market for American goods of over a half billion people—that's one larger than the Chinese coast and far, *far* less politically complicated.

Convincing the Americans to treat Southeast Asia as a unit as the above implies may not be a simple sell, but likely American commitments will already ring the entire area, and no power within Southeast Asia could possibly mount a threat to American interests. In fact, a vibrant and interconnected Southeast Asia would help keep China and India apart, while involving the United States with a combined economy bigger than that of its NAFTA/CAFTA partners.

CHAPTER 10

Players

Those countries not fortunate enough to form partnerships with the United States in the stormy years to come will have to navigate the harsh seas of change on their own. Some of them will be forced, whether due to privation or opportunity, to strike out beyond their borders to secure what they need or take what they want. They will be the active—and often aggressive—players in the new age, out to put their stamp on the world.

Russia: Twilight Approaches

Populated Eurasia is a vast wedge, anchored in the west by the North European Plain; in the south by the Sea of Marmara region, the city-states of the Middle East, and the vast green of the Indian subcontinent; and in the east by the timeless civilizations of the Chinese. Traditionally, travel among these three great arcs of humanity has been limited. Middle Eastern deserts impede movement between Europe and South Asia, while jungles and mountains limit direct contact between South and East Asia.

What they all have access to, however—and what they all are threatened by—are the infinite flats of Central Eurasia. The North European Plain funnels open from only two hundred miles wide at the Polish Gap to over fifteen hundred by the time it reaches central Belarus and Ukraine. Moving west from coastal China, the arid interior gives way to a veritable sea of grass. Moving northwest out of the Indian subcontinent requires navigating a couple mountain passes and plateaus that ultimately give way to the steppes of Central Asia. Unlike every portion of the world we have discussed to this point, Central Eurasia has absolutely no meaningful geographical barriers, and from one end to the other it is over three thousand miles long.

It is a harsh land. Inland continental plains suffer from high winds, brutal winters, broiling summers, and fickle precipitation. Many of the lands are marginal for human habitation.

It is a place of poverty. The rivers are as hostile as the land, flowing *away* from the arable portions rather than through them, with the land's utter flatness and the weather's unpredictability generating constant challenges of flood and drought. Hunger often reigns. Yet it is a land of many. The central mass of somewhat usable land is over three thousand miles east to west and typically about five hundred miles north to south. It may not be a third as productive per acre as the American Midwest once droughts, floods, locusts, and transport and storage loss are factored in, but it is the greatest stretch of flatland on the planet, and possesses a combined population of a major power.

It is a place of insecurity. The lack of reliable weather combined with the lack of local barriers to movement make it easy for any piece of civilization to fall to forces natural or man-made. Any people who rise in this harsh landscape crave what bits of security they can find or wrestle out of the earth—or from each other. It is a land where governments are local, and where raiders of every epoch have swept fast and loose across the grasslands.

Combine that large population with low capital generation and the result is limited funds for infrastructure, education, and market formation, restraining everything from the productivity of the labor force to the effectiveness of the army. It is a land where only numbers matter. It is a land where only the hordes hold sway. And in those rare instances when some power is able to unite the lands under a single government, the civilized bastions on the Hordelands' periphery shiver in fear. This is the land of Attila the Hun. Of Genghis Khan. Of Tamerlane. Of Joseph Stalin.

Occupying most of that territory today is the Russian Federation, one of the most insecure countries of the contemporary world. While it is arguable that no Central Eurasian power can ever truly be "secure," there are two things that a power needs if it is to truly command the Hordelands.

The first requirement is that the power control *all* of the Hordelands. While Russia remains one of the largest geographic entities in human history, and holds the title of largest country in the contemporary world, it actually needs nearly 3 million additional square miles of territory if it is to be even reasonably secure. Just as any Hordelands power can push into any of Eurasia's three major civilized zones, any of Eurasia's three major civilized zones can push into the Hordelands. The Baltic coast, the Polish Gap, the Bessarabian Gap, the Black Sea, the coastal strips of the Caucasus, the Central Asian corridor, and the Tian-Altay Gap are all points where the Hordelands are vulnerable and where invasions have flowed in both directions. During the Soviet period the Russians commanded every mountain, water, and desert barrier at the Hordelands' extremes, giving them command over every single access point to their lands. They could anchor in those barriers and concentrate forces on the gaps, making them as secure as a Hordelands power could be. The day after the Soviet collapse the Russians controlled but two. With the capture of the Crimean Peninsula in February 2014, they now control three.

The second requirement is that a successful Hordelands power must have an actual *horde*. During the Soviet period, the Russians had 180-odd million Poles, Ukrainians, Romanians, East Germans, and other Central Europeans to use as cannon fodder to guard their western borders. They controlled all three of the Transcaucasian republics—Georgia, Armenia, and Azerbaijan—using them as a 16-million-strong series of highland speed bumps. They reached south across Central Eurasia's productive lands—the Russian wheat belt—and commanded the 50-million-strong Kazakhs, Uzbeks, Kyrgyz, Turkmen, and Tajiks to caulk up the southern frontier. All of these peoples and more have now broken away. In just a few years, the "Soviet" population was sliced by nearly two-thirds, with many of those peoples now in charge of their own countries that share the Hordelands with the Russians.

What's left over is disappearing. The Russian people—the actual ethnic Russians—are dying out. With the Soviet collapse, the bottom fell out of the Russian birth rate. What rebound has occurred can almost wholly be chalked up to the echo of the perestroika baby boom of the

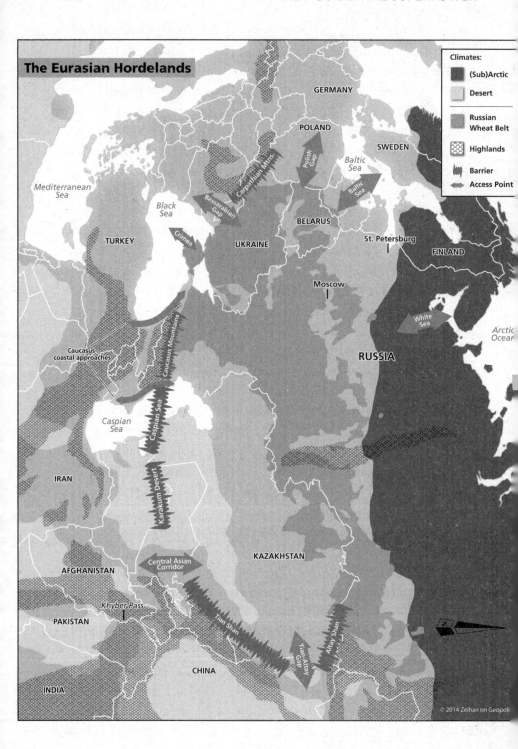

The Eurasian Hordelands

Climates:

(Sub)Arctic

Desert

Russian Wheat Belt

Highlands

Barrier

Access Point

GERMANY

POLAND

SWEDEN

Mediterranean Sea

Baltic Sea

Black Sea

BELARUS

TURKEY

UKRAINE

St. Petersburg

FINLAND

Polish Gap

Carpathian Mtns

Bessarabian Gap

Baltic Sea

Crimea

Moscow

White Sea

Arctic Ocean

Caucasus coastal approaches

Caucasus Mountains

RUSSIA

Caspian Sea

IRAN

Caspian Sea

Karakum Desert

KAZAKHSTAN

Central Asian Corridor

AFGHANISTAN

Khyber Pass

PAKISTAN

Tian Shan

Tian-Altay Gap

Altay Shan

CHINA

INDIA

© 2014 Zeihan on Geopoli

mid-1980s. Within five years it will be the far smaller generation of post–Cold War births who will be parents, and there simply are not enough of them to sustain a Russian population at even half its current size.

And this is the best-case scenario. HIV and multi-drug-resistant tuberculosis run rampant through the Russian population, with most of the cases concentrated in the fifteen-to-thirty-five age group: the age group most likely to have children. Even Russia's population pyramid is deceptively positive, as it contains the data for the Russian national population as a *whole*, not the Russian *ethnic* population. While many of Russia's conquered populations escaped the Russian yoke with the Soviet collapse, many others remain within contemporary Russia's borders. In particular Turkic Muslim populations like the Tatars, Bashkirs, and Chechens are young, vibrant, and growing. Their data are blended in with the ethnic Russians, who are rapidly aging, diseased, and not reproducing. By 2040, the Russian national population will almost certainly have shrunk below 120 million, with Russian ethnics but a thin majority within their own country.

Within that demographic catastrophe is yet another challenge. The Soviet/Russian educational system works on an apprenticeship program.

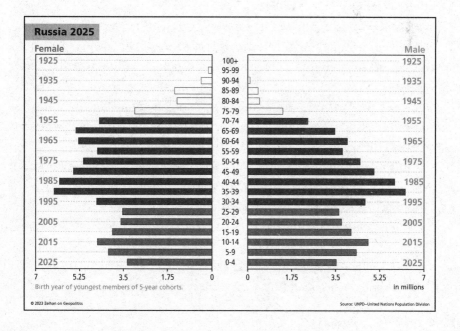

After finishing college/tertiary school, would-be professionals apprentice to a skilled engineer for a few years before entering the workforce. However, funding for Russian technical education collapsed in the late 1980s as the Soviet Union entered its terminal slide. It never recovered enough to maintain Russia's skilled labor force. As of 2015, the youngest population cohort that has experienced a full education is already fifty-one. The average age of male mortality in Russia is fifty-nine (or at least it was in the mid-2000s, which is when the last reliable demographic data escaped Russia's Federal State Statistics Service). Russia won't even be able to maintain what it has, much less reach for more, within a few short years.

Russia's challenge is straightforward, if not simple: Its demographic decline is so steep, so far advanced, and so multivectored that for demographic reasons alone Russia is unlikely to survive as a state, and Russians are unlikely to survive as a people over the next couple of generations. Yet within Russia's completely indefensible borders, it cannot possibly last even that long. Russia has at most eight years of relative strength to act. If it fails, it will have lost the capacity to man a military. To maintain a sizable missile fleet. To keep its roads and rail system in working order. To prevent its regional cities from collapsing. To monitor its frontier.

To delay its national twilight.

The most effective use of its time would be to attempt to reanchor in as many of Central Eurasia's border regions as possible, allowing Russia to concentrate forces in the Hordelands' access points. Success would doom Russia to a slow-motion demographic disintegration from within. Failure would leave Russia open to hostile forces along *all* of its borders *while* it is disintegrating from within. The first is a recipe for death over several decades. The second is a recipe for death over one or two.

It is extremely likely that Russia lacks the strength to plug all of the gaps in its frontier, so it will have to prioritize. Here is the order I see Russia acting to attempt to preserve its existence.

Russia's single largest concern is Ukraine.

- Ukraine occupies the single most productive portion of the Russian wheat belt (the area farthest south and with the most reliable rainfall). As Russia's manpower and capital shortages mount, maintaining a grip on the lowest-input, highest-output lands will become of increasing importance.

- Together with Moldova, Ukraine commands the Bessarabian Gap. Control of the gap would limit the ability of a resurgent Turkey (see below) to threaten Russia's core territories.

- Ukraine holds the largest population of ethnic Russians outside of Russia (true even if one considers the Crimea part of Russia and not part of Ukraine). Their numerical inclusion into the Russian system would delay twilight a few more years.

- Eastern Ukraine's industrial base is directly adjacent to Russia's. Combining them would assist all portions of the Russian economy to last a bit longer.

- Ukrainian infrastructure transports nearly half of Russia's oil and natural gas exports to Europe, making Ukraine an energy tool whose political leverage is nearly as valuable as its financial income.

- The Ukrainian border is only three hundred miles of wide-open flatlands from Moscow, making Ukraine—at a minimum— valuable as a buffer.

- The only truly navigable river of the former Soviet Union, the Dnieper, flows through Ukrainian territory, flows south, and allows Ukraine to integrate economically with the lands of the Black Sea, the Sea of Marmara, and the world beyond. The river not only makes Ukraine the most potentially capital-rich portion of the Hordelands, it also makes it the only portion that can perhaps seek a destiny independent of Moscow. Russia dare not let that happen.

- The Crimean Peninsula commands the mouth of the Dnieper and is home to Russia's only truly warm-water naval base, Sevastopol. As long as Crimea and Sevastopol are in Russian hands, Ukraine cannot make a true bid for economic independence, and naval powers—most notably Turkey—cannot dominate the Black Sea. Russia's efforts to reanchor started in the Crimea in early 2014. They will not end there.

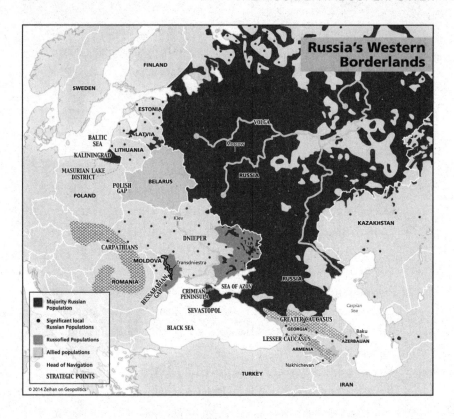

In any form an independent Ukraine is a threat to Russia. But it is only the first threat Russia must address before 2020.

The second most critical region is the Northern European frontier, home to Poland, Belarus, and the Baltic trio of Estonia, Latvia, and Lithuania. Collectively these five states command Russia's exposure to the North European Plain as well as the Baltic coastline and the fate of Russia's second city, Saint Petersburg. Russia must at a minimum neutralize this region, but in this faces extreme challenges. Poland and the Baltic trio are pathologically hostile to Russia, with extremely good reason: The Russians/Soviets occupied all of them for two generations. The four not only collaborate closely to resist Russian influence but are also increasingly partnering with two other countries historically famous for doing so with more success: Denmark and Sweden. In dealing with this frontier, Russia's key advantage is Belarus, which suffers from a culture cringe that is somewhat similar to Stockholm syndrome. Belarus suffered under Soviet times just as much as the other occupied peoples, but the Belarusians are the only former Soviet people who actually want to *be* Russian. They do not see partnership with—or occupation by—Russia as necessarily a negative. A Russian-Belarusian partnership/merger doesn't unilaterally solve Russia's North European Plain problem, but it is a great leap toward a solution.

The third target is lightly populated Kazakhstan. While large portions of the Russian wheat belt lie in Kazakhstan, Kazakhstan's role in Russia's future is primarily as a buffer region. It exists in a sort of no-man's-land between Russia's more densely populated European territories and the Turkic peoples of Central Asia to the south and the Chinese to the east. Moscow doesn't need Kazakhstan to be robust or even to be a successful state, it just needs it to continue existing. So long as there is an independent Kazakhstan, then there is no one breaking down Russia's back door.

Finally there is the Caucasus, perhaps the world's most unforgiving crucible of ethnic hostility. Imagine the pain of the Balkans, but inject it with the gentle mercies of the Huns, Persians, Mongols, and Russians and then let it fester for a few centuries. Even a brief overview of the region would take up at least a book,[1] so I won't dive into it here. Suffice it to say that Russia (rightly) fears that Turkish and Persian influence (or worse) will penetrate through the mountains and turn Russia's various Turkic/Muslim peoples against it. Sound far-fetched? Think again. This is in essence what happened with the Chechen wars in the 1990s.

The Caucasus is a fractured and fractious region, and maintaining control would require precisely the sort of manpower-heavy effort that Russia will find increasingly difficult. So, yes, Russian troops will certainly be used, but Moscow will use what money, technology, weapons, and intelligence it has to bolster multiple allied forces throughout the Caucasus region, the Armenians, the Abkhaz, and the Ossetians in particular. And as hostile influences and forces push into the region, the Russians will beat a fighting retreat behind the bodies of its falling allies.

The specific order in which Russia addresses these concerns will likely be determined by the level of European and American nondiplomatic opposition. At the time of this writing the Russians have already used their centuries-old propaganda tactic of "protecting minorities" to seize the Crimea and spark rebellions in the eastern Ukraine. While

---

1. Trust me. Helped write it.

ever-shifting economic, political, and military pressure pries the Ukrainian state apart, the Russians will begin work on the Caucasus, Belarus, and Kazakhstan—targets that generate far less concern in the West. Once those areas are pacified the Russians will return to Ukraine, "rescuing" those in the Russified east and south who "ask for help." In the western Ukraine invasion (accompanied by appropriate propaganda, of course) will be necessary. After that will come the true challenge: the EU/NATO members of Poland, Romania, and the Baltic States.

Turkey: An Ancient Power Awakes

For most of the past two millennia, the Sea of Marmara was the richest spot on the planet because it was *the* crossroads. Most land-borne trade between Europe and South Asia passed through the pair of double peninsulas that bracket the Sea of Marmara, while any waterborne trade between the Danube and Black Sea and the Mediterranean passed through the Sea of Marmara itself. For the many fortress cities of the Middle East, Istanbul was the fortress that managed to somehow be rich and cosmopolitan rather than starving and parochial. For the often overrun peoples of the eastern Balkans, Marmara was eternal—the epitome of secure civilization. Whether under the Romans, Byzantines, or Ottoman Turks, Marmara was the world's jewel.

But all ages end. The rise of deepwater navigation greatly diminished the land-borne trade routes by opening up cheaper, faster, and safer routes that bypassed Persia and the Hordelands. The opening of the Suez Canal in 1869 eliminated what land-borne trade remained. The death blow for waterborne commerce came shortly thereafter, courtesy of the Soviet rise. With the Soviet conquest of Eastern Europe in the final months of World War II, the great navigable rivers of the Black Sea, the Danube and Dnieper, became internal Soviet waterways. Trade linkages that dated to antiquity disappeared behind an iron wall of ideology, and the Sea of Marmara quite literally became a backwater.

The military defeats of the century leading up to the Soviet rise were in many ways just as painful for the Turks. They had lost control of every province of their once-sprawling empire that was worthy of the term. Egypt, Bulgaria, Romania, and Serbia had been stripped from them along with the Levant and the Muslim holy cities of Mecca and Medina. They still held Marmara itself—having fought bitterly and successfully for it at Gallipoli—but their only remaining territory was the rugged, arid mountain knot of Anatolia, a land that had been useful as little more than a buffer zone so long as there had been civilization in Marmara. In the short course of only three generations, the Turks had fallen from one of the great powers to little more than a regional satrapy.

Rather than attempt to play a great game in which they would be crushed, the Turks chose retreat. They fortified their borders—all of which were now uniformly hostile—walling their culture off from the world. After World War II, they fell under direct Soviet pressure, forcing them to stiffly accept membership in the rising Americans' security and economic systems in order to maintain independence.

Membership in Bretton Woods ended European preying upon what was left of Turkish lands and allowed them access, albeit with restrictions, to the European market. Between that income and the locally generated capital from Marmara, the Turks set about developing the near-useless lands of rump Anatolia. Over the decades, road and rail snaked into the highlands, turning villages into towns and towns into manufacturing centers. In many ways, life in Turkey between 1950 and 2000 was a preview of the developing world's experience of 2000–2010: capital from a rich area flooding into substandard lands because there were no other options.

Turkey didn't awaken from some ninety years of geopolitical slumber on its own. Once again, it was the Russians who forced a change of Turkish circumstances, only this time it was the Soviet collapse rather than the Soviet rise. In 1992, Soviet forces simply dissolved, and Turkey's entire eastern, northern, and northwestern horizons opened at once. History restarted, and the Turks, having been allowed to obsess about internal issues for three generations, were unprepared. Just as they are unprepared for the coming end of the free trade era.

All of the above leaves the Turks at the heart of one of the world's most mutable regions. Working clockwise from Turkey's southeast:

- Iraq will become the region's wild card. Either it will become a loose satellite under Iranian influence, or it will reconsolidate under a harsh, Saddam Hussein–style militarized dictatorship.

Either way, the southeast will be Turkey's most problematic border.

- To the south, Lebanon and Syria will collapse as modern states, devolving into a shatterbelt of poor and competing city-states. The only country in the region with the capacity to install order will be Turkey, but there will be little in the Levant of meaningful interest. Turkey will be able to pick and choose its friends, its enemies, and its issues.

- To the west, Greece will revert from being a country to being a geographic expression and cease being a drain on Turkish defense planning.

- To the northwest, the countries of Bulgaria and Romania were under Soviet occupation, then brought into NATO and the EU, and now face being cast out again as the free trade order breaks down. They are likely to see the Turks as a rare bastion of stability in an otherwise degrading Europe.

- To the north, Russian power will surge into Ukraine, opposed by an ad hoc coalition of Poland, Romania, and Sweden. As part of the Russian logic is to expressly limit Turkish options, Ankara will have little choice but to join the fluid competition.

- To the east, the culturally ancient but politically neophyte countries of Armenia and Georgia face collapse, both due to internal political and military weakness and to overwhelming pressure from Iran and Russia. And likely Turkey as well.

It is a lengthy, daunting list of changes and challenges, but unlike for most countries in the new era, there are many opportunities for Turkey as well. When countries have options, it is very easy to put them into the "successful" category, but harder to predict specifically what it is that they will do. The natural thing for the Turks to do would be to expand. Turkey has been experimenting in the past decade with extending its diplomatic and economic footprint in the Arab world, but has discovered that there is little there worth taking and what's there is a whole lot of trouble.

Still, some of Turkey's options (and challenges) seem more feasible (and more pressing). I see Turkey focusing its efforts in three primary directions.

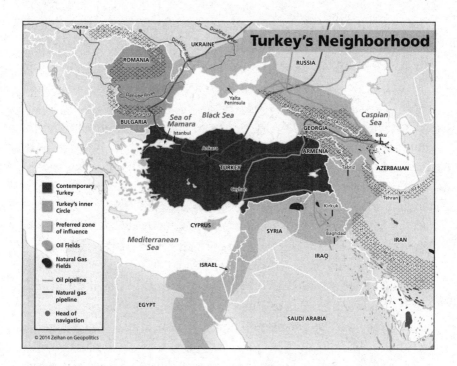

First, Bulgaria and Romania are a slam dunk. Whether outright conquering, an Ottoman-style suzerainty relationship, or a more traditional alliance, a formalized relationship with the two Danubian peoples would solidify Turkish control over both the western Black Sea and the lower Danube, end any possible chance of food shortages, and put a plug in Russia's ambitions.

Second, Turkey *must* secure some oil supplies. Luckily, Turkey's needs are moderate—it only requires about 700,000 bpd—and it has some options. Northern Iraq is home to the Kirkuk oil fields, which are capable of producing more than enough for Turkey as well as its Bulgarian and Romanian relations. Additionally, Kirkuk already has infrastructure linking it to Turkey, specifically a series of pipelines that terminate at Ceyhan, Turkey's southern energy hub and superport. Control of northern Iraq would also give Turkey direct overlordship over the largest Kurdish community not located in Turkey already, allowing the Turks to better smother Kurdish separatism.

Of course, control over northern Iraq will not come easily. Kurds aside, Turkey will be entering into direct and unrelenting competition with Iran. In terms of direct military competition, the Turks hold the clear advantage: Their army is better equipped, better trained, and actually skilled at military operations rather than domestic pacification. They also, unlike the Iranians, have an air force eminently worthy of the name. For their part, the Iranians have a far superior intelligence network and will delight in using it to spawn endless militant activity among Turkey's minority groups, first and most violently the Kurds—both the preexisting Turkish Kurds in Turkey and the new ones in northern Iraq.

Option two is equally viable from an economic point of view, but is far more strategically circumspect: Azerbaijan. Like Kirkuk, Azerbaijan's offshore energy complex is capable of seeing to Turkey's needs, and like Kirkuk there is already infrastructure bringing Azerbaijani crude to Ceyhan. Additionally, the Azerbaijanis are actually Turkish ethnically and so would be far more likely to welcome Turkish engagement than Iraq's Kurds. However, getting to Azerbaijan presents problems. Georgia, a country that is for all intents and purposes a failed state even before the free trade rubric dissolves, is in the way. It isn't so much that Georgia will resist meaningfully—based on how Turkey's efforts are packaged, it may even welcome outright occupation—but moving into Georgia in force will put Turkey at the very top of Russia's shit list.

Which brings us to the third theater that the Turks are likely to engage: Ukraine. This is *not* a must; Turkey can *choose* to play the imperial game in Ukraine. Turkey would vastly prefer that Russia remain an unanchored power in the Hordelands, without a purchase in the Carpathians. Such a vulnerable Russia will start breaking up from within a decade or two. In particular the Turks would like to reprise their strategy from the fifteenth to the eighteenth centuries and get a grip on the Crimean Peninsula, as it would put the Russians on the defensive without the Turks having to expose themselves to the dangers of the Hordelands themselves.

But rather than help shove the Russians into oblivion, the Turks may allow themselves to be bribed into neutrality.

Turkey doesn't need Ukrainian wheat, or really even Ukrainian trade. What it needs is natural gas. Ukraine doesn't have any, but it does control infrastructure that could bring it natural gas...from Russia. Russia may be able to offer the Turks recognition of Turkish supremacy in the lower Danube, in exchange for some good deals on natural gas exports. If the deals are exceedingly good, the Russians and Turks may even be able to find a means of working around each other's interests in the Caucasus as well.

Should the Russians fail to make an offer that is sufficiently lucrative *from the Turks' point of view*, then the Turks will be able to eject the Russians from the Caucasus wholesale and hugely complicate Russian efforts in Ukraine. The Turks are as young and vibrant as the Russians are old and sickly. Unlike most of the developing world, they boast a large and growing market that is not overly dependent upon external capital, or even external demand.

The Turks can draw upon many groups of similar ethnicities across the northern Caucasus region, most immediately the Ingush, Dagestanis, Kabards, Circassians, and Chechens, and farther abroad the Kazakhs and Uzbeks as well. Committed Turkish opposition would be more than enough to unravel Russia's entire southern rim. Which isn't to say that the Russians would take it lying down. Russia would repay the effort by using its world-class intelligence skills to destabilize Turkey from within, stirring up every minority the Turks control whether in territories new or old.

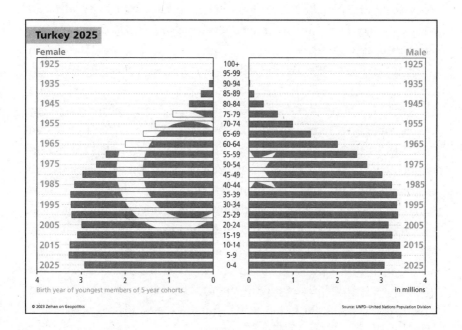

Turkey 2025

Uzbekistan: Survival of the Fittest

The Uzbeks are one of the oddities of the modern world. They didn't exist as a truly separate, self-defined ethnicity until the Soviet period when the Russians were busy bringing socialist ideology to the arid ranges and ancient Silk Road cities of Central Asia. Since then the post–Cold War government has done much to trump up the Uzbeks' "ancient cultural roots" by talking up historical "Uzbeks" such as Tamerlane in order to justify and solidify their rule. In reality, Uzbeks owe more to clan and village than country. Yet as weak as the Uzbek national identity might be, all of their fellow Central Asians suffer from even weaker identities. There are also a *lot* more Uzbeks than anyone else in their region—more, in fact, than all of the neighboring Kazakhs, Turkmen, Tajiks, and Kyrgyz combined.

If there is a truly independent and self-sufficient country in the world beyond the United States, it is Uzbekistan. Bretton Woods and the entire free trade architecture could burn, and it would cause but a ripple in the Uzbek pond. Uzbekistan is one of the few countries not just in its region but in the Eastern Hemisphere that is broadly self-sufficient in oil, natural gas, and grains. While Westerners keep Kazakh energy flowing and Russians manage the Kyrgyz hydropower system and guard the Tajik border, the Uzbeks are not dependent upon foreigners to operate key portions of their economy. Even Chinese influence is largely limited to the purchase of some natural gas.

But this does not make the Uzbeks a happy, secure people. The country faces three particularly ugly problems.

First, Russia sees the Central Asian region as a problem, specifically in that there is an access corridor from western Siberia to South Asia that passes through the Uzbek heartland. Since Uzbekistan boasts the densest population concentration in the broader region, the Russians are naturally suspicious both of the Uzbeks themselves and anyone they might partner with south of the corridor. The unsurprising result is a competition for the loyalties of Uzbekistan's many clans. The Russians favor the cloak, the Uzbeks the dagger.

Second, the Uzbek government is, well, horrid. Like any new government—Uzbekistan only became self-governing in 1992—it makes a *lot* of mistakes. But the Uzbek leadership was born and bred in the Soviet communist ranks, complete with the penchant for political oppression that the Soviets were known for. Add a training in tyranny to general incompetence and you get one of the world's most brutal and backward countries, with a standard of living less than one-tenth that of the United States. Anywhere else in the world it would have been torn down by its neighbors, but the most progressive neighbor Uzbekistan has is...China. No one local criticizes Tashkent when it boils its dissidents alive.[2]

Third, Uzbekistan is the quintessential example of a marginal state that geopolitics has pushed to the breaking point. The region's two major rivers, the Amu Darya and Syr Darya, flow through Uzbek lands, but they start in the mountains of next-door Kyrgyzstan and Tajikistan. Normally this would not be a major issue, but the 1973 Yom Kippur War set the Uzbeks on the path to ruin. In the war's aftermath, Egypt switched allegiance from the Soviet bloc to the West. Soviet industry thus lost access to Egyptian cotton. Moscow's solution was a massive hydrological project that rerouted much of the Amu's and Syr's waters to huge cotton plantations across the region, most of which were located in the then Soviet republic of Uzbek SSR, which in time became Uzbekistan.

Right from the beginning the system overdrew water from the rivers. Upon independence, the Uzbeks, now cut off from Soviet subsidies, doubled down on the cotton scheme. Leaks in the irrigation system are omnipresent, but the Uzbeks lack the technical skill to repair them and instead increased irrigation throughput to compensate. Water now only rarely reaches the rivers' terminus at the Aral Sea. As of 2014, 95 percent of the sea's volume has evaporated away.

Without the Aral to moderate the region's climate, Central Asia's deserts are rapidly expanding. This has raised temperatures throughout the region and quickened the rate at which the glaciers of Kyrgyzstan and Tajikistan are melting. By 2025 the glaciers will be but seasonal nubs. Those glaciers are the primary water sources for both the Amu and the Syr, and when those rivers dry up, so too will downstream Uzbekistan.

This will leave the entire region with a very interesting situation (if "interesting" is the correct word): There will only be enough water left for maybe half of the region's population. Uzbekistan has the food, energy,

2. Oh, how I wish that were hyperbole.

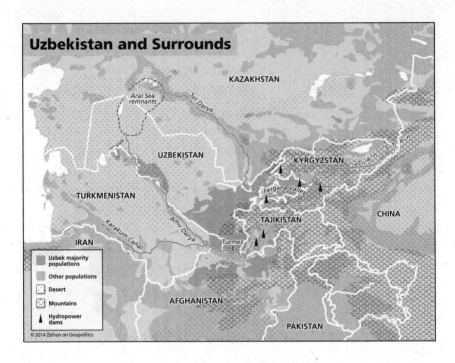

Uzbekistan and Surrounds

military, and above all the coherent state apparatus required to make sure it is the Uzbeks who get that water.

The competition isn't exactly stiff. Stalin drew all of this region's borders to ensure maximum conflict should any of the republics gain independence, ergo their spaghetti-like characteristics. He wielded his pen with skill.

- Tajikistan is not even a functioning state. The country's northern neck separates Uzbekistan proper from its Fergana territories, holds all of the connecting road and rail infrastructure, and is populated by Uzbeks. Additionally, the Amu's headwaters are all in Tajikistan, along with several hydroelectric dams that control its flow. The Uzbeks will take Tajikistan in its entirety.
- Kyrgyzstan controls nearly all of the slopes and highlands of the Fergana Valley, as well as all of the Syr's headwaters and several hydroelectric facilities that both control the water flow on the river and supply electricity to Uzbekistan. Uzbekistan will want the entire southern half of the country.

- Turkmenistan's defining characteristic is the Soviet-built Karakum Canal, which floods portions of the desert country to grow cotton. Nearly all of the 1 million Turkmen Uzbeks live in the Amu border zone, while nearly all the Turkmen live along the canal. It would be fairly simple for the Uzbek military to seize this Uzbek-heavy border region and shut off the flow to the Karakum. Turkmenistan will simply dry up and blow away.
- Kazakhstan is nearly as large as the continental United States, but with a population less than Florida's. Its population is also scattered in clusters hundreds of miles apart. The only portion of Kazakhstan the Uzbeks want is the bit hard on their border that houses the lower reaches of the Syr, home to nearly all of Kazakhstan's Uzbeks.
- That just leaves Afghanistan, but there is little there that threatens Tashkent. The only piece of infrastructure in the region happens to be the only bridge that crosses the Amu at Turmez, and it is already under Uzbek control. The Uzbeks can simply work through local Afghan Uzbeks—of which there are 2 million, concentrated in the border region—to make sure that nothing south of the border impinges upon Uzbek wishes.

The only regional power that will have the interest and proclivity to perhaps intervene is Russia—not for humanitarian reasons, but rather because Uzbek success in consolidating control of the region's water would make Uzbekistan a regional hegemon. While such a power would still be on the other side of the Central Asian steppe, the Russians have good reason to be worried.

First and most immediately, the Uzbeks are Turkic peoples and the governments of Uzbekistan and Turkey enjoy broadly positive—if currently distant—relations. Any strategic cooperation between the Turks of Turkey and the Uzbeks of Central Asia would present the Russians with an allied opposition on both their Caucasus and Tian Shan flanks.

Second, and ultimately of more concern to Russia, the Uzbeks are not the only Turkics in the former Soviet Union. Several of Russia's subject peoples originated from similar stock. All told some 17 million Russian citizens are of ethnic groups that feel kinship with the Turks and Uzbeks.

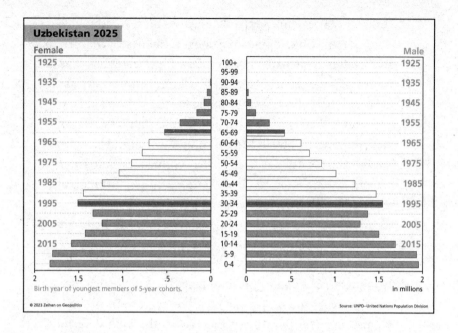

An Uzbek-Turk alliance could set fire to Russia's carefully policed ethnic balance.

Plenty of questions arise as to how much force the Russians will expend to hold off the Uzbeks. Kyrgyzstan, Turkmenistan, and Tajikistan lack the capacity to contribute to their own defense in any appreciable way. The region is over a thousand miles removed from the Russian border and two thousand miles removed from populated Russia. The only thing going for the Russians in this fight is that the Uzbek's drought-driven invasion *might* occur before Russia's own demographic-driven twilight. But if the Amu and Syr don't force the Uzbeks' hand before 2020, then Russia will have utterly lost its capacity to compete meaningfully in distant Central Asia. And a wave of young Uzbeks will wash asunder all foolish enough to stand in their way.

Saudi Arabia: Wrath of the Righteous

Saudi Arabia is a quintessential example of the sort of oddities that Bretton Woods encouraged to proliferate. Over 90 percent of the country is hard desert. Most of the region's agriculture is based on a series of oases on or near the country's western coast, generating a line of fortress cities, the most notable of which are Mecca and Medina. Even this western fringe—the Hejaz—is only heavily populated by the standards of the surrounding desert. Overall there is no capacity to support large populations, and insufficient capital to allow more than the most basic of infrastructure. There is no industry. No real educational system. The Saudi portion of the Arabian Peninsula simply lacks the features that allow a country to take root.

But there is oil. Anything is possible when you are willing to apply an unlimited amount of capital to your labors. Bretton Woods created a global market for Saudi oil, and the Americans guaranteed the security of both Saudi oil shipments and Saudi territory itself. The Saudis had all the money they needed to carve their magic kingdom out of the harsh desert landscape.

This transformation was—and remains—utterly dependent upon the current global setup. In the Bretton Woods world, the Americans guarantee Saudi security in order to protect energy flows, guarantee energy flows in order to enable trade, and guarantee trade in order to maintain their security alliances. But in a post–Bretton Woods shale era, the Americans have no need for the security alliances or the trade or the energy flows, which means they have no need for the Saudis. The no-questions-asked protection that the Americans have extended to Riyadh is about to be lifted wholesale.

Dealing with the aftermath will require admitting Saudi Arabia's fundamental weakness: It doesn't have an indigenous workforce.

Since the discovery of oil, the Saudis have been able to end their nomadic existence, hire outsiders to do all their work for them, massively expand their population under the aegis of a generous welfare state, and in general become impressively lazy and gloriously fat. The tendency to import labor has become so omnipresent that roughly one-third of their entire population—some 8 million people—are expatriates and guest workers. There are so many foreigners working in the kingdom that the twenty- and thirty-something bulge in the Saudi population pyramid is actually entirely made up of temporary foreign workers, particularly men.

Because of this quirk, the Saudis lack many of the advantages of a modern state, most notably an industrial base or a tax base. They have no navy to speak of, much less one that could guarantee the security of

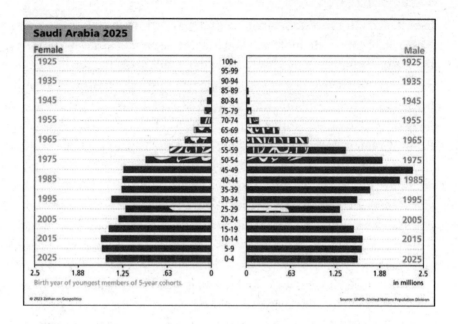

their exports and by extension their income. They also lack a (meaningful) army and so cannot guarantee the security of their state.[3]

Consequently, the Saudis' existential challenges fall into two categories: naval threats and local ones.

In terms of naval challenges, anyone who needs oil and has the ability to reach Saudi Arabia will be both a threat and an opportunity to the Saudis. The Saudis will want countries to come to them to *purchase* their oil, but they won't want countries to come to them to *take* their oil. Unfortunately for the Saudis, their oil complex is eminently seizable. Nearly all Saudi oil production is in the country's extreme east. The Ghawar superfield, which currently produces some 5 million bpd, is in fact less than a hundred miles from the country's major exporting infrastructure on the Persian Gulf. But nearly all of Saudi Arabia's population is in inland

---

3. The Saudis *have* spent billions on the best hardware the Americans are willing to sell, but they don't train on it. The equipment—complete with Abrams tanks and Apache helicopters—simply sits shrink-wrapped in air-conditioned warehouses, the Saudi strategic plan being that should they ever be directly threatened, the Americans will send troops to man Saudi Arabia's prepositioned equipment and defend the kingdom. In a Bretton Woods world, it is a fairly clever strategy. In a post–Bretton Woods world, all that equipment is really just a lot of very expensive paperweights.

Riyadh or the country's extreme west. Convincing any country that has the power to protect sea lanes *for* Saudi Arabia that it should not simply seize the relevant bits *of* Saudi Arabia may prove a hard sell. The Saudis cannot even count upon their own citizens to resist. The Saudis who live in the oil-producing eastern regions are predominately of the Shia minority rather than the Sunni majority.

As for local challenges, Saudi Arabia faces a single massive problem: Iran. Whether under the empires of old, the shah, or the ayatollahs, the Iranians have always desired to control the territory that is currently Saudi Arabia. In part this is due to the ideological split between the two branches of Islam: The Saudis are Sunni and the Iranians are Shia. In part it is due to the presence of the holy cities of Islam; the Persians covet the religious authority that flows from their control. In part it is economic; control of the Saudi oil fields is an end unto itself. And while the Saudis do not have a capable military, the Iranians certainly do. Without an external sponsor or an army, the Saudis' entire defense strategy relies upon the Arabian Desert being too harsh a barrier to cross. In the industrial age, that doesn't count for as much as it used to.

The core of Saudi Arabia's Iran problem is that there is no one to replace the Americans as the Saudi security guarantor, certainly not in the short term. Bretton Woods meant that no one needed a navy, so there is no alternative naval force with an interest in protecting Saudi interests. For nearly every country out there, it will take years to build the sort of navy that can handle even regional needs, which means that for at least a decade (or two) there will mostly be local navies. Any Saudi cargoes that sail will have to negotiate their way through endless local naval authorities. And as the Somali pirates have shown, it doesn't take much naval acumen to capture a slow-moving supertanker.

Options for new friends are so thin as to be nearly nonexistent:

- China might *want* to become Saudi Arabia's new protector—or new overlord—but it lacks the military capacity and geographic proximity to try.[4]

---

4. We'll cover China in depth in chapter 14.

- India is fairly close and might serve as a potential customer, but it lacks the military capacity to grant any sort of meaningful protection beyond perhaps convoys to India itself.
- Turkey is probably the best possibility for the Saudis, but it is not an automatic fit: Gaining a Turkish alliance would require that Turkey first control all of Iraq, otherwise it couldn't project military power into the Persian Gulf. A Turkey that pushed that far south not only would face a grinding war with Iran but would also have control of so much *Iraqi* oil that it wouldn't need *Saudi* oil at all. Saudi Arabia might be able to induce Turkish interest with a sufficiently attractive offer, but it would have to be huge.
- That just leaves the European powers, of which the United Kingdom and France are the logical candidates. Unfortunately, they are far more likely to source their energy needs from more proximate North Sea and North African sources—or, in a pinch, Central African locations like Nigeria, São Tomé and Príncipe, Equatorial Guinea, and Gabon—rather than make the long run to the Persian Gulf.

The bottom line is that the Saudis are most likely going to have to grope their way forward on their own. Preparations have already begun.

As the keepers of the holy sites, the Saudis hold considerable religious sway throughout the Islamic world, and they use the power of the pulpit to induce Islamic-minded fighters[5] to flock to this or that cause. You may have also noticed that the Saudis are absolutely loaded, and they can use the power of the checkbook to shape political forces at the local level far and wide. Since the Americans completed their withdrawal from Iraq in 2011, Saudi foreign policy has become substantially more aggressive and militant. In particular:

- The Iraqi government is sliding toward becoming a satellite of Iran, the country that the Saudis see as their nemesis. To

---

5. Depending on the international mood, you may have heard them called freedom fighters, mujahideen, or Islamic terrorists as well.

prevent that, the Saudis are using their paramilitary connections and financial muscle to empower the Sunnis of central Iraq who are resisting the Iranian encroachment. To date they have successfully spawned an insurgency that is already as bloody as the worst years of the American occupation.[6]

- The Syrian civil war is another place where Iranian power is under threat. Syria has long been an ally of Tehran, and the Saudis are using their one-two punch of militants and money to attack the Syrian government at every opportunity. Saudi support has become so omnipresent that they are now bigger backers of the rebels than all other foreign forces combined. The nature of the Saudi-aligned militants—extremely violent and extremely Islamic—has also reached such extremes that it has caused American, European, and Turkish support for the rebellion to become more circumspect.

- Pakistan has been at best a halfhearted partner in the United States' war in Afghanistan. As American interest in South Asia plunges to the level of "meh," the Americans are highly likely to completely cut the Pakistanis loose. Saudi Arabia is increasingly stepping in to be Pakistan's new partner. As the two states share a general antipathy to both Iran and India, there is considerable room for dovetailing. Pakistan needs less than a half million barrels of crude daily; Saudi Arabia has plenty. Pakistan desperately needs outside financing to compete with India; Saudi Arabia is well moneyed. Saudi Arabia's workforce needs huge volumes of skilled and unskilled labor; Pakistan has long been the largest source of foreign labor for the Saudis, in 2014 hitting 1.5 million workers. Pakistanis even serve in the Saudi military, in particular the air force, which would be the branch most likely to be able to protect Saudi oil installations or forestall an Iranian assault. There is even the possibility that under the right circumstances Pakistan might share its nuclear technology with Saudi Arabia, up to and including a functional nuclear weapon.

---

6. For full data on how bad things are, the best source remains Iraqbodycount.org.

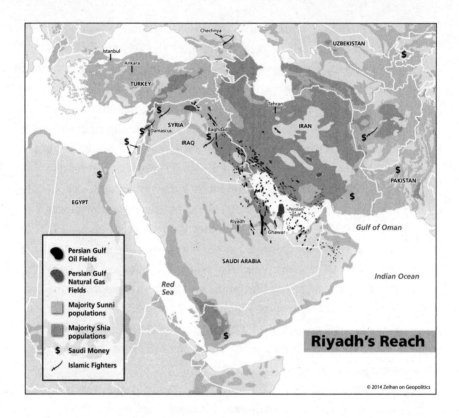

This strategy, however, generates its own risks. Arm enough men with weapons, fill them with righteous fury, send them to kill legions of apostates, and sooner or later some of them will start choosing their own targets. The last time the Saudis lost control of such men, the September 11, 2001, attacks occurred and the Saudis ended up fighting a brief civil war against their own militants. Managing a carefully metered flow of violence out of Pandora's box will prove a constant struggle.

Japan: Dusting Off Tojo

Japan is one of the great aggressive maritime empires of the not-so-distant past. Bereft of resources or markets at home, Japan ventured out from its home islands in search of both and in doing so built an imperial commercial empire stretching along all of the East Asian archipelagoes and continental coastline all the way to Myanmar.

That was then.

The Japan of today is not the aggressive empire of World War II or even the economically dynamic Japan of the 1980s. Japan today seems a listless, spent force. Demographically it is the world's oldest and fastest-aging society, and the ranks of its younger population are now so thin that a return to the heady era now past is simply unthinkable. Japan's role in global export markets has shrunk to one-third of its peak. Between high taxes and an aged demography, industry has steadily relocated out of Japan. Toyota, Honda, and the like now do their best work at facilities close to market, particularly in the United States, and simply ship the profits home to help service an ever more decrepit population. It may not be a cheery model, but in a world of free trade it is one that allows an ever-failing Japan to live out most of the rest of its national life in relative comfort.

Which means that when the free trade era ends, this approach to life is completely and utterly screwed.

More than most peoples, the Japanese will have some very rapid-fire decisions to make, but there is reason for optimism. Yes, their best industry is located out of country, and that earns key income. But income isn't the same as food or energy. It can be replaced or, in a pinch, lived without. In the post–Bretton Woods world, the ongoing functionality of these facilities will be up to bilateral relations, with a *very* heavy eye toward supply-chain feasibility. In most cases, the Japanese will bow toward inevitability and allow formal ownership to be sold at discounts to entities in the host countries. The key point is that these "export markets" are not actually employing Japanese citizens, so Japan's social structure would not be overly stressed by their loss.

Yes, Japan's remaining home-located industry is utterly dependent upon imported raw materials, but this too is not as bad as it seems. The offshoring of its export industries means that what remains of them at home is actually quite small: only about 15 percent of GDP. And Japan's refuse reclamation system is among the world's most efficient, with more than half of their residential and industrial trash being recycled, lowering their materials needs still further.

Japan would certainly prefer to remain internationally engaged in the Bretton Woods system, but it really doesn't need access to markets—or even raw materials—to the same degree it used to.

All this isn't to say that Japan won't need to be aggressive—*very* aggressive—at seizing what it needs, it just means that it can be a bit choosier about targets and tactics. The Japanese certainly won't need to go all banzai on the entire Pacific, just very specific parts of it. They have flexibility now that they didn't have in the early decades of the twentieth century.

Far and away Japan's biggest concerns will be oil, natural gas, and food, and those specific needs will shape the nature and reach of Japan's actions. It imports less than 10 percent of its rice needs, but nearly 90 percent of its wheat and all of its corn. All told, Japan imports nearly three-quarters of its basic cereals. Japan's oil and natural gas needs are even worse. Factoring out the 500,000 bpd of refined products that it exports and the 500,000 bpd of demand that will vanish by 2020 due to demographic aging, Japan will still need nearly 4 million bpd of oil to maintain its current system. It will also need at least 10 billion cubic feet of natural gas imports per day to keep the lights on, and even that figure assumes that the Japanese escape their post-Fukushima shell shock and restart their nuclear electricity system in a very big way.

In meeting its needs, Japan will become a textbook case of finding the right tools—diplomatic, economic, and military—for the right job.

North America will emerge as the world's most reliable source of foodstuffs and energy products, forcing Japan to seek as excellent relations as possible with the Americans. Some Japanese nationalists may call for a direct military approach, but only the inane will have forgotten the lessons of 1945—or that the Americans' military position in the Pacific would dictate a replay of the Japanese defeat in World War II in a matter of weeks. Japan simply purchasing what they need would actually put U.S. naval power in the indirect service of Japanese needs, a far more pleasant arrangement. This isn't a one-stop shop, however. North America can easily meet Japan's caloric needs, but not necessarily its *rice* needs. Additionally, North America may be able to spare Japan 1 million bpd of crude oil and fuels. Maybe even 2 million. But not 4 million. The Americans may also be able to share a few billion cubic feet a day of natural gas via LNG (liquefied natural gas) exports, but not 10 billion. Cutting a deal with the Americans is a good first step, a required one even. But it is no panacea.

Unfortunately, Japan's other current energy suppliers—Australia and the Persian Gulf—will disappear as options, either having been already spoken for, too far away, or both. Which will exhaust the nice side of Japan.

The first military target is likely to be Russia's Sakhalin Island. It is just off the coast of Japan's northernmost Hokkaido Island, putting it well within Japan's naval and air force power projection range. Its infrastructure was largely built by Japanese firms, that infrastructure terminates on the island's southern tip, the Japanese have the technical skill to keep all of Sakhalin's offshore energy production running, the Russians do not, and Japanese nationalists still fume that the Russians seized it from Japan in the wars of the first half of the twentieth century. Securing Sakhalin

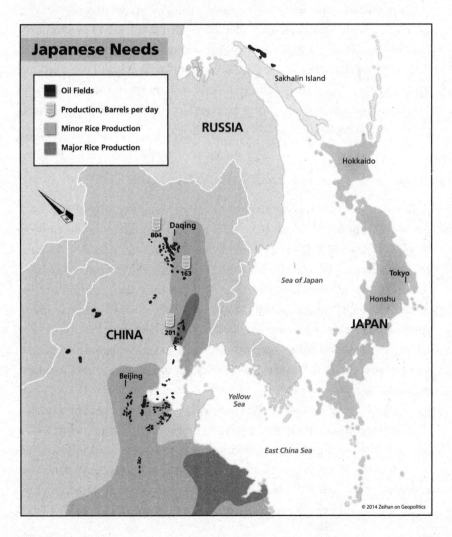

would place just under 300,000 bpd of crude production and 3 Bcf/d (billion cubic feet per day) of natural gas production into Japan's output column. Seizing Sakhalin will also permanently sever any chance of having positive relations with Moscow, but to be blunt, Moscow is five thousand miles away, so the consequences of breaking that relationship aren't very high. Cooperation with Moscow could never really be part of the Japanese solution, since the Russians don't have the labor or capital to contribute to developing their Far Eastern territories. Besides, Japan and Russia never actually signed an armistice after the end of World War II. Technically, they are *already* at war.

The second target will be Chinese Manchuria. Manchuria isn't known for its rice fields—the region's cold winters dictate the use of greenhouses to prepare spring plantings—but it has enough to satisfy Japan's needs. Just as importantly, the Daqing area's oil complex produces over 1 million bpd of crude. While that volume is likely to halve over the next decade, that gives Japan years to find new supplies elsewhere and/or slim down its consumption profile.

Angola: Managing Genocide

Africa is an incredibly difficult continent to live on if your goal is to hack out a piece of civilization. It is blanketed in swamps, jungles, mountains, and deserts, making even basic development an incredibly painful process. But the real deal killer is Africa's plateaus. At nearly every point of the continent, the interior juts up rapidly from the coast, forming a series of escarpments. Consequently, not one of Sub-Saharan Africa's many rivers is navigable, and what rail lines exist largely date to colonial-era efforts to extract specific commodities from specific sites rather than to service local economies. Infrastructure development of any sort is at best onerous.

In the coming disorder Africa's lot will be a difficult one. Lower materials demand will deny them the income to improve their lot, while lower capital supply will make it nearly impossible to source funding from the wider world. The continent's future will be one of deindustrialization and even worse infrastructure. Bereft of American trade protection, foreign powers will treat the region as a resource playground, grabbing what they need in a manner somewhat reminiscent of the nineteenth century's European competitions. The French and British will of course be involved, but so too may the Japanese, Koreans, Taiwanese, Singaporeans, and Australians. From time to time even the Americans are likely to realize that Africa holds supplies of this or that hard-to-source material.

But one country—one geography—stands out, and its story is the wave of Africa's future. That is *not* a good thing. Angola is a country born in war—both colonial and civil—that is trading the genocide of war for the genocide of consolidation.

Angola is one of the few spots on the continent that enjoys a nontropical climate, allowing for its government to extend its writ more effectively than most of its peers. The dominant Angolan ethnicity is the one that emerged victorious after two decades of civil war, the Mbundu. Their homeland lies along the Kwanza River. While the Kwanza isn't navigable by boats of oceangoing size, it does punch through the escarpment without too many rapids, making it the best transport corridor—and most capital-rich location—within a thousand miles. The Mbundu also had the advantage of possessing the national capital (and former Portuguese colonial capital) of Luanda, allowing them unrestricted access to the global system. In the era of Bretton Woods, that meant that they were not pillaged as the Portuguese had done to them for four centuries, but instead were able to collect Angola's offshore oil income and tap the international system for the guns, gasoline, and vehicles they needed to fight the war. It would be an overstatement to say that the Mbundu were destined to win the war, but their location meant that they entered the conflict with all of the right tools. After twenty-seven years, 800,000 dead, and 8 million refugees, the Mbundu proclaimed triumph.

With the war now over, the Mbundu now focus on consolidation: the long grind to destroy the other groups' identities, either by forcibly assimilating them into the Mbundu themselves or simply eliminating them. Unfortunately for the Mbundu, their targets outnumber them three to one. Angola's most numerous ethnicity are none other than the Mbundu's primary foes in the civil war, the Ovimbundu of the Angolan Planalto (plateau). A key tool in the Mbundu's genocide effort is the thousands-strong paramilitary group called the Ninjas who impose the Mbundu's will upon the other Angolans via terror and mass murder. It will take at least a century for the Mbundu to grind away the competing identities, and to achieve this they need to avoid outside interference.

The Mbundu fear—and what has put them on this list of in-play countries—is that they will not be left to their own devices. Angola's civil war was part and parcel of the Cold War and witnessed participation by groups as varied as the Cubans and Americans. But the Mbundu consider their true foe to be much closer to home, an African country that at times has deployed thousands of troops to fight them directly.

That country is South Africa.

Like Angola, South Africa is an exception to African geography. It isn't so much that the African escarpment is kinder in South Africa—it isn't—but instead that the tip of Africa is far enough south that the escarpment's elevation lifts the country out of the tropical zone, mitigating Sub-Saharan Africa's otherwise omnipresent disease exposures. Simply put, less disease means better health and longer life spans, and that allows for higher levels of worker skill and taxpaying. What truly sets the South Africans apart from their cocontinentals is not their (post)colonial past, but that their geography allows them a demography that enables them to *afford* to build infrastructure and have the indigenous skill base to build it *themselves*. South Africa's mining sector—it is a leading source of diamonds, gold, and platinum—doesn't hurt either.

The big chunk of highland that makes South Africa possible doesn't stop at its borders but extends north as a spine along the middle of the continent, a spine that the South Africans have constructed infrastructure along. This infrastructure is the only meaningful one in the region, and it leads to the only sizable ports in the region—which are of course in South Africa. That allows South Africa to tap a nearly bottomless source of cheap labor, while utterly dominating economic development throughout all of Lesotho, Swaziland, Botswana, Zimbabwe, Zambia, and southern Congo. If you want to transport anything in bulk—copper ore, bauxite, and wheat being the largest cargoes—you have to deal with the South Africans.

It is this network that gives the South Africans outsized influence throughout the region, and so it is this network the Angolans feel that they must disrupt. They are using their oil income to fund an infrastructure build-out for the first time...well, ever, and part of that effort includes the

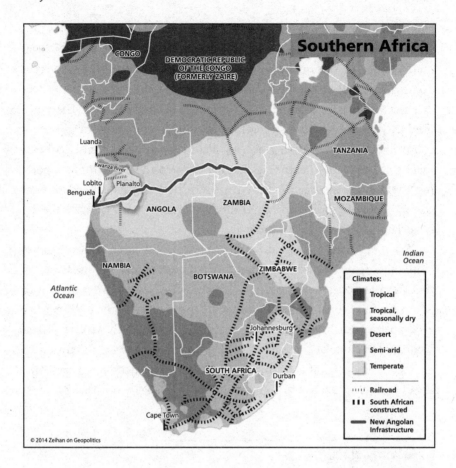

construction of a modern container port at Lobito and a spur rail line from the port into the African interior. Once it is completed, and at the time of this writing the project is already in the T-crossing stage, Angola will start siphoning off traffic that for a century had been destined to South Africa, and South Africa's chokehold on the region's economic and political life will end. At that point it will be up to South Africa to respond. It is poorly positioned to do so.

First, the South Africans are out of practice. South Africa used to have a highly capable special forces branch that efficiently pursued the nation's interests throughout the southern portion of the continent. With the end of apartheid, however, the military writ large fell into disarray and disrepair. It would take a dedicated multiyear effort to regenerate the country's expeditionary fortunes, and at present efforts in that direction are middling at best. They certainly will not be completed by 2015. Even maintenance of the infrastructure that ensures South Africa's current dominance is falling back to more typical African standards.

The Mbundu, in contrast, didn't stop at the end of their war. They have used their rising military strength to intimidate and sculpt neighboring countries, complete with engineering a coup to install a friendly government in Namibia and bombing Zambia to warn them off from supporting Ovimbundu insurgents. The Ninjas have been particularly effective at strengthening friendly regimes in Zimbabwe and Congo (Brazzaville) by terrorizing dissident groups there.

Second, it isn't clear that South Africa *can* put up a fight anymore. While their plateau certainly lifted them out of the tropical disease zone, that elevation does nothing for nontropical diseases. Some 80 percent of South Africans carry tuberculosis while 30 percent of pregnant women are HIV-positive. Such diseases have absolutely gutted South Africa's skilled labor and tax intakes, preventing the government from maintaining its apartheid-era levels of growth, security, and infrastructure—to say nothing of taking a proactive foreign policy. In contrast, Angola's lack of infra-

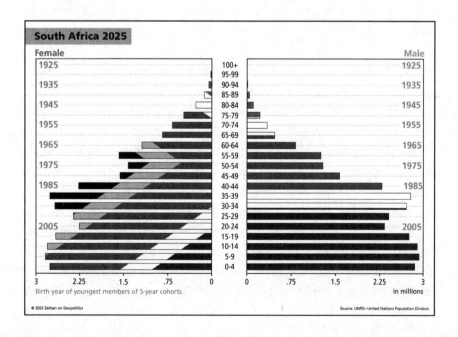

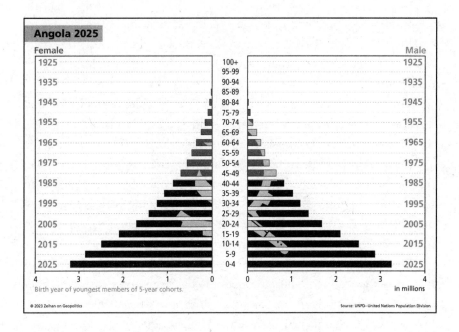

Angola 2025

Female / Male

4 3 2 1 0 | 0 1 2 3 4
Birth year of youngest members of 5-year cohorts. / in millions

© 2023 Zeihan on Geopolitics / Source: UNPD–United Nations Population Division

structure and the horrors of its civil war mean that it is the sole southern African country to have (so far) escaped the ravages of HIV. It has a demographic so young it is literally a throwback to the preindustrial age.

In short, Angola is clearly coming from (far) behind in the contest, but in the long game it seems almost certain to win.

Iran: From Enemy to Ally

Iran is not a typical power. In fact, from the criteria that we've been using, there is nothing about Iran that indicates that it should be successful.

The country certainly has a balance of transport, but it is balanced in the wrong way. Iran enjoys no big piece of flat land from which to generate a large community and food surpluses. It has no navigable river to speak of that could raise capital (and few rivers of any size or reliability). The country lies in the heart of the African-Asian aridity belt, starving it of water. Nearly all of its people live in the hundreds of mountain valleys that are high enough to wring some precipitation out of the air. Moving around within Persia is difficult and expensive at best, and there is no obvious nearby economic node to which Persia might connect to mitigate its poverty.

In contrast, *reaching* Iran is devilishly simple. Its entire south and southwest are abutted by the Persian Gulf, the world's calmest large body of water. To the east is the Indus valley, a dense population core going back to antiquity.

To the northeast are the steppes of Central Asia. Distance in that direction is a factor, but if one can handle the arid lands of the region, reaching the Persian border is a fairly simple matter. To the north is the Caucasus region. While certainly mountainous in many areas, the portion that borders Iran is actually the region's most open terrain. The eastern half of contemporary Azerbaijan is an excellent staging point for an attack on Iran. Both the Russians and the Mongols used the northern approaches in their successful conquests of Persia.

The final approach—from the west—is the one that normally keeps Iranian leaders up at night. Mesopotamia has been home to any number of grand civilizations in the past, and most have at one time or another taken a crack at conquering their Persian neighbors.

The merits of deepwater navigation are completely lost upon mountain peoples, and Iran is no exception. Very few Iranians live near the Persian Gulf coast and so the country has very few ports. Any naval power can easily prey upon the Iranian coast should it choose, and the Strait of Hormuz is a perfect blocking point to limit whatever vessels the Iranians manage to float. Bandar Abbas, Iran's largest and best port, is eminently vulnerable to a Hormuz blockade.

Industrialization passed Persia by rather completely until very recently. Only with the discovery of commercially exploitable quantities of oil in the early twentieth century did the Iranians have sufficient capital even to consider partially industrializing. But it was and remains a poorly managed industry. Iran lacks the common culture to have a mass education system or the common infrastructure to have a single market or the common wealth to have a mass market. What industry Iran has developed falls into two categories: servicing the capital of Tehran, or servicing the energy sector.

Yet Iran is still *there* and has been there in some form since antiquity. That requires an explanation. Iran's secret lies in how it has dealt with its difficult geography. Each of Persia's many mountain valleys is home to a different ethnicity, each of which has its own identity and history and language and customs. As was famously noted in the movie *300*, there

are a "thousand nations of Persia." Over the centuries, a cluster of mountain valleys managed to merge to become the people we now call Persian.
Add in another few millennia of ethnic cleansing and intermarriage and a
kaleidoscope of peoples have been painstakingly fused into a more coherent nationality. It has been a long road, and even today nearly half of the
people of Iran define themselves as *not* Persian.

One of the ways the Persians have historically managed their system
is to turn weakness into strength. Agriculture in mountains is difficult
because rainfall from year to year varies greatly, generating cycles of feast
and famine. In periods of feast, Persia's population explodes. In periods
of famine, it crashes. The Persian solution was to transform population
surges into military excursions. If Persian forces came back with booty
and food or managed to conquer another valley, that was wonderful. But
the real goal was to have fewer mouths to feed back home. Such feast-
driven expansions led the Persians on massive conquering campaigns
when their climate-driven demographics forced the issue. And when the
homeland starved, the tax burden upon the conquered territories sparked
revolts that forced the empire to contract back to core Persian lands.

This feast-expansion and famine-contraction cycle continued for two
full millennia. But with the development of deepwater navigation and
especially industrialization, the era of Persian empires faded into mem-
ory. While Persia was more than a match for any local power, deepwater
navigation and industrialization allowed powers with a more stable food
profile far removed from the Middle East to enter the regional power calculus at the times and places of their choosing. Against such qualitatively
superior and far more mobile forces, the Persian hordes simply couldn't
compete. As the two technological packages spread and extraregional
powers like the Turks, Russians, British, and French probed deeper and
deeper into Persia's Middle Eastern playground, the maximum limit of the
Persian feast-expansions shrank and their famine-collapses accelerated,
until by the sixteenth century Persian expansions were local and painfully
brief. By the eighteenth century, the Persians became locked up in their
mountain fastnesses in more or less the borders we know today.

Which brings us to U.S. foreign policy.

To say that there is bad blood between the two countries is an exercise
in understatement, but consider the strategic context. Iran's territory is

mostly useless desert, but in the Zagros and Elburz Mountains there are highland valleys that lift their populations to high enough altitudes to glean some moisture out of the dry air and thus have agriculture. These highlands are where nearly all of Iran's population resides. The rules of other mountain societies certainly apply here: People in one mountain valley do not necessarily identify with those in the next valley over, much less four over. Keeping all of these various groups under the same political authority requires a harsh system to induce cooperation, which is why modern Iran has a million-man army. Iran, in effect, occupies its own territory. The existence of a large army is not an option for Iran.

Of course this particular tool of state formation has other uses, and therein lies the rub. Any army large and coherent enough to hold Iran together is more than large and coherent enough to conquer almost any of Iran's neighbors, particularly the lightly populated and even more lightly defended Arab oil states of the Persian Gulf: Kuwait, Saudi Arabia, Qatar, Bahrain, the United Arab Emirates, and Oman.

That capability is the primary reason for the American-Iranian hostility of the past thirty-five years. Forget terrorism. Forget Israel. Forget the hostage crisis. In the Bretton Woods era, oil security is the foundation of everything from NATO to ANZUS; the United States uses energy to guarantee trade, and trade to guarantee its security alliance. If Iran were either to conquer the Arab oil states or close the Gulf, the free trade order would quite literally run out of fuel.

But oil and trade won't be central to the American strategic equation much longer, and that turns Iran from a perennial pain in the ass to perhaps the most valuable ally the United States could dream of—entirely because of where Iran is located.

Iran easily meets the most exacting criteria for American allies: In the post–Bretton Woods world, Iran can never be a strategic threat to the United States. American power ultimately flows from its nearly unassailable position in controlling the bulk of the North American continent. The only way that power could be meaningfully threatened is if a power on another continent proved able to float a navy of sufficient strength and size to launch an assault on North America. That power could *never* be Iran. Iran is a mountain country. That means, among other things, that it has no navigable rivers, no tradition of watercraft, and lacks the facilities, expertise, and capital needed to float a navy. If against all odds it some-how could, the Iranian navy—and the entirety of the Iranian economy—would be bottled up in the Persian Gulf. It would be child's play for U.S. naval forces to simply cap the Strait of Hormuz and destroy the entirety of the navy along with the Iranian economy. In the Bretton Woods era, Iran's position on the Persian Gulf empowers it. In a world in which oil isn't cen-tral to American planning, however, Iran's position on the wrong side of the Strait of Hormuz cripples it.

If anything, this is better (for the Americans) than it sounds. Some three-quarters of Iran's imports flow into a single port—Bandar Abbas—which happens to be at the mouth of the Persian Gulf, completely exposed to anyone with a ship. Within the Gulf, over 90 percent of its oil exports flow from another single point: Kharg Island. An American effort to remove Iran from play could be completed in a single afternoon, and since Kharg does not have a bridge or tunnel connecting it to the mainland, reentering energy markets would take years.

But these vulnerabilities are only vulnerabilities against the maritime superpower. For anyone else in Iran's broader neighborhood, Iran's posi-tion is a nightmare. While mountain states are typically neither rich nor naval, they are also damnably difficult to invade. Each mountain ridge is a new defensive bulwark that has to be ground through. But such mountains do little to inhibit the offensive capabilities of the locals. A large mountain state like Iran can in one critical way act like a naval power: It can bide its time, secure in its mountain fastness, until it makes sense to boil out. In past spurts of activity, Persia has conquered lands from Egypt to Greece to Tajikistan to India.

There are four regional power centers that would likely be the tar-gets of Iranian expansionism, one of which has been somewhat pacified already.

- The pacified target is directly to the west: ancient Mesopotamia, better known in contemporary times as Iraq. Iraq in any
  age is a riparian country that draws its strength from its ability
  to use the Tigris and Euphrates to generate massive, sustained
  agricultural surpluses and thus generate population booms as
  necessary. It has historically used those booms to extend its

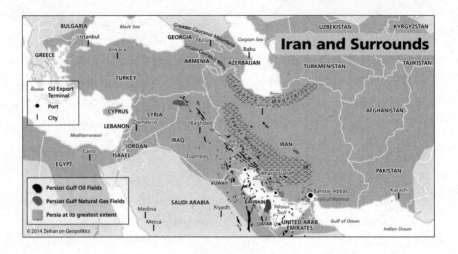

control not just up and down the river valleys, but south into Arabia, west into what is now Syria, and east into the Persian highlands. It has always been the geography that has generated the most difficulties and hardships for the Persians, and as such is typically the first territory that Persia absorbs in its own expansionary phases. At the time of this writing, the United States' war with Iraq is over, and Iran has taken advantage of the American withdrawal to install many of its allies into the Iraqi government, up to and including the prime minister. While it would be overly simplistic to say that Iran already controls Iraq, it is certainly more of a springboard for Iranian future ambitions than a sandbag.

- To the southwest lies Saudi Arabia, the largest of the Gulf oil states and the world's largest exporter of crude oil. Iran's goal is nothing less than the subordination of Saudi Arabia, and the two countries' religious differences—Saudi Arabia is the keeper of Sunni Islam while Iran is the protector of Shia Islam—only adds a layer of religious feuding to a contest that is already economic, political, and strategic. Iran is clearly the superior power, with nearly triple the population and a military that is actually used to shooting people while the Saudi military does not operate well outside of air-conditioning. But an Iranian victory would not be clean, easy, or quick. Saudi power comes from its oil money and its possession of the holy sites of Islam. Combined, these two features allow them to recruit Islamic fighters to do battle for them when and where they wish to project power, with the more (in)famous locations being Afghanistan, Russia (the northern Caucasus), Iraq, Libya, and Syria. They have nearly nudged Iraq back into civil war, and in the Syrian civil war these Saudi-backed militias now form the backbone of the revolutionary forces. Saudi initiatives in both theaters are merely the leading edge of Riyadh's efforts to bring battle to the Iranians. As it becomes more obvious that the American withdrawal from the region is not temporary, the gloves will come off, and the Saudis will work to unleash hell not just in Iraq, Syria, Afghanistan, and other places in which the Iranians have interests, but in Iran itself. Of particular importance will be Iran's Arab minority, concentrated in the southwestern border province of Khuzestan. That just happens to be where most of Iran's oil production takes place. In addition to more conventional tools (like an invasion), count on the Iranians to return the favor. Saudi Arabia's Shia minority is concentrated in its own eastern oil-producing region.

- To the north is the Caucasus, an excellent buffer between Iran and the lands of the Russians. Well, excellent for the Russians anyway. While the Russians no longer count the Caucasus as an internal region as it was during the Soviet period, they still have several thousand troops each in Armenia and Georgia,[7] while Azerbaijan realizes that its ongoing existence as an independent power requires it to collaborate with Moscow on a host of issues. Iran's problem is that 16 percent of its population is Azerbaijani. That places more Azerbaijanis in Iran than exist in the independent country of Azerbaijan. That makes the "buffer" not only directly adjacent to territories that house Russian troops, but introduces an irredentist threat hard up on

---

7. Russian forces in Armenia are there by mutual agreement, mostly to serve as a military tripwire against Azerbaijan and Turkey. Russian forces in Georgia, in contrast, help two secessionist regions—Abkhazia and South Ossetia—maintain independence from Georgian control.

Iran's northwestern border. The only way that Iran's northern flank can truly be secure would be if it occupied most of the Caucasus region itself. Unfortunately, the only way that Russia's southern flank can be secure would be for Russia to do the same. For both Iran and Russia—to say nothing of Georgia, Azerbaijan, and Armenia—the Caucasus is a zero-sum game. While Russia is far from a pushover and attacking the Caucasus would be expensive and difficult, time is on the Iranians' side. Iran has a young and rapidly growing population, while Armenia, Georgia, and Russia have three of the world's oldest and most rapidly contracting.

• Finally, to the northwest lies Turkey. Most of Turkey's economic and political interests lie in the Black Sea and Danubian basins, but that is in a world in which free trade thrives. Once the Americans stop guaranteeing global energy supplies, the Turks will have to secure their own. The closest energy lies in northern Iraq, an area populated by Kurds whom the Turks have always feared will stir up problems among Turkey's own Kurdish citizens. The only way to guarantee both the unity of the Turkish state and secure access to oil is to either conquer

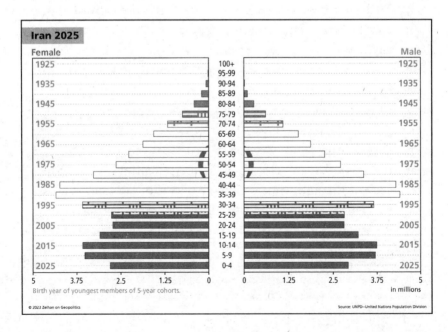

northern Iraq outright or to pack it so thoroughly with Turkish "advisers" that it would no longer be functionally independent. Either way, Iran will have an opinion on the issue. Iran also has a strong opinion on what unfolds in Syria. As long as the fighting there continues, the Turks must fret about developments along their entire southern periphery.

With America's gradual withdrawal from the Persian Gulf, the strategic logjam that has existed for the past half century is breaking up, but it is not the victory that the Iranians had hoped for. The American departure means that Iran is being released to engage not one but *four* regional powers in a general melee. That melee is the unspoken goal of American foreign policy: to ensure that all of the world's other major powers are preoccupied with each other rather than thinking of putting to sea. No matter what Iran prioritizes, no matter what Iran does, no matter if Iran wins or loses, its very existence keeps four other powers firmly nailed to local developments. And all the United States has to do is nothing.

And Now Things Get a Bit Complicated

Each of these countries, whether due to opportunity or desperation, will attempt to sculpt their neighborhood into something more to their liking. Their interactions will determine the specifics of the world of the future. But none of them will have a large-scale impact upon the top workings of the American government, much less upon how the Americans live their lives.

In their splendid isolation, the Americans will have a very high bar for noticing what is unfolding elsewhere on the planet, and an even higher bar for jumping into the fray. What follows, the remainder of this book, will detail the five situations that are most likely to pass that bar.

Players: Ten Years On

Most of this chapter is very much in progress, so I'll leave the vast bulk of it as is, but two countries do stand out.

I think the Japanese read this book. Hell, I know they did. There's a Japanese edition. Why am I sounding so smug? The Japanese have acted with an aggression that I wasn't sure they were still capable of in efforts to address many of the limitations I identified in the original text.

Changes to tax codes, health care systems, and labor laws have made it easier for young adults in Japan to form families and raise children. The country remains the world's most demographically advanced society, but no longer is it the world's fastest aging. South Korea, China, Thailand, Germany, and Italy are now all in worse shape.

But the biggest shift is the change in Japan's relationship with the United States.

During Donald Trump's tenure in the White House, the Japanese got spooked, and rightly so. They suspected the rising, erratic isolationism of the United States would cost them the good graces of their primary trading and security partner. So the Japanese prime minister headed to Washington and asked for a deal. The Trump administration wrote up one that addressed every single irritant in the bilateral relationship from the past generation in the Americans' favor. Positively humiliating. The Japanese signed the deal without comment or amendment.

And history turned.

Ten years ago, I feared that a retrenching United States and an insecure Japan might find themselves at odds, perhaps leering at one another across the expanse of Southeast Asia. No more. Japan has bought itself into the American inner circle of allies. Its two new *Izumo*-class carriers—two of the four most powerful military platforms in history not operated by the Americans—will soon be flying exclusively U.S. fixed-wing aircraft.[8] Add in an even more in-depth American security relationship with Australia, and the remainder of the twenty-first century will be one of an American-allied dominion over the Pacific. It cost the Japanese some ego, but in one fell swoop they have found a way to have their cake (and rice and oil and

---

8. The other two of those four platforms are the Brits' *Queen Elizabeth*–class carriers.

natural gas and iron ore and lithium and on and on and on) and eat it too. In essence, Japan is no longer simply a player, it is now also a partner.[9]

The biggest loser of this new American-Japanese partnership is *not* China, and not because the partnership very clearly has China in its sights. No, the United States and Japan have any number of independent reasons for opposing Beijing and would have cooperated on that topic regardless of the status of their alliance. Instead, trouble will be coming for the Koreans.

South Korea *is* everything that Japan *was* in the 1980s. A resource-intensive economy in a resource-poor geography. A demography that has very clearly turned. An intense dependence upon access to the wider world for resources and markets, but no military hope for securing any of it without the Americans doing all of the heavy lifting.

The best way to showcase the split in trajectories between the Japanese and Koreans is to compare policies from the American point of view.

- Japan has that pair of fully deepwater carriers—actively deployed since 2017—that now regularly operate hand in glove with U.S. fleets. Korea's navy is decidedly local in range and mission. Seoul regularly protests the very existence of the Japanese carriers.
- In 2022, Japan barely murmured discomfort when it signed up to U.S. tech sanctions to box in China's semiconductor industry. Korea has taken advantage of protracted negotiations with the United States on the topic to sell as many high-end semis to the Chinese as possible while sales are still legal.
- Japan immediately followed the U.S. lead in applying financial and economic sanctions against Moscow for its actions in the Ukraine War. Korea is not only still providing goods to the

---

9. Oh, a quick word on the Australians. That aforementioned security deal does indeed provide the Aussies with American nuclear-powered submarines, and yes, that is a very sexy piece of military technology. But the deal's real game-changer is the Australian acquisition of American mid-ranged air-launched cruise missiles. Australia, a country with but 26 million people, has now joined the rarefied ranks of countries that can easily close the Strait of Malacca, and thus utterly destroy the Chinese economy in a matter of weeks. (Japan was already among those ranks.)

Russians, some with dual uses, but at the time of this writing is still refusing to sell weapons or ammo to the Ukrainians.

One of these countries is a partner with its eye on the future. One is not. And now Japan, the Koreans' former colonial tormentor, commands the keys to Washington.

This is normally where I'd say something like, "There is no future for South Korea except what Tokyo allows." But if there's one thing I've learned from the Koreans in my professional career, it is that they are creative and tenacious on a scale most people cannot fathom. If any people can figure out a future that flies in the face of geopolitical and demographic dogma, it is the Koreans. I'll be watching.

One more country to add to the players list: Ukraine.

The Russians are in many ways a force of nature. Mammoth in size and population, not simply tolerant but embracing of tribulation, paranoid without peer, violent as both a means and an end, and above all else inured to casualties. Few have ever stood against them for long. This and more the Ukrainians know in their bones. After all, Russia conquered the land that comprises modern-day Ukraine back in the late 1700s and proceeded to hold and abuse it ever since…

…until the Soviet breakup in 1992. Ukraine's single-generation vacation from history wasn't particularly fun. The economy crashed in the 1990s and never recovered. An oligarchy formed that looted the state right up until the war wrecked most of what remained.

Numbers are against them. Russia sports over triple the population, an industrial base easily an order of magnitude larger, deep strategic buffers, and the better part of a century of materiel stockpiling. Russia has roughly 8 million men in their twenties. All else being equal, and that all-else includes a half million men fleeing Russia *every year* to avoid the draft, Russia can maintain its tempo of losses for a minimum of another five years.

Geography is against them. The border with Russia is nearly as featureless as it is flat. There are few places to hide, and in the great wide opens of the Eurasian Hordelands artillery is the ultimate weapon. The Russians *love* their artillery. Remove either the United States or China from the math, and Russia fields more artillery than the rest of the world combined.

And yet the Ukrainians have held. I would like to think that if I were in the Ukrainians' position back in February 2022 when the war started, I would have shown the same strength. The same resolve. The same willingness to suffer and sacrifice for my people. The same morbid defiance in the face of oblivion. I…I don't know. All I can say for sure is I feel extremely grateful that the plucky Ukrainian upstart is taking to task the country that has threatened me, my family, my friends, and my fellow countrymen with nuclear annihilation my entire life. Threats that incidentally have become far more shrill—and serious—of late.

Unfortunately, the Ukrainians' biggest enemy isn't Russia per se, but instead time. Win or lose this war, Ukraine will *not* survive.

The Ukrainian demographic structure is right up there with the world's worst. Before the war, Ukraine's experiences with economic dislocation landed it with a birth rate below 1.5 per woman. That's not simply a crippling figure, but instead one no country has ever recovered from. That's on top of the nearly 10 million Ukrainians—fully one-fifth of the

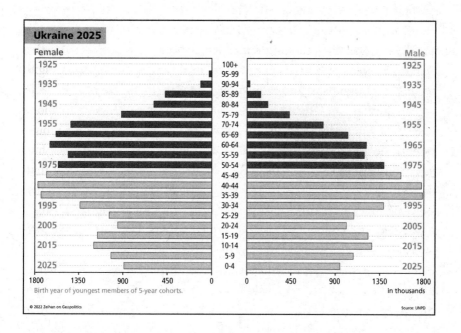

population—who emigrated *before* the war began. Most of the leavers were under forty years old. Data on this particular point is impossible to source, but between economic dislocation and outmigration, I suspect as many Ukrainian children have been born outside of Ukraine as within it for several years now.

Since the war's commencement, another 6 million have fled as refugees. According to UN data, fully 90 percent of the refugee adults are women, while 30 percent of the adult refugees self-identify as holding advanced degrees and/or technical skills. Worst of all, over 2 million of the refugees are minors. Prewar Ukraine only *had* 7 million people under age twenty. The refugees are *not* huddled in camps on the border. Europe, contrary to most folks' prewar conceptions—including my own, including *Europe's* own—has welcomed these refugees with open arms. Should Ukraine emerge victorious, some will undoubtedly return to their ancestral home. But many will not. And the more they establish lives for themselves in Poland and Germany and the rest, the more likely it is that more Ukrainians will join them rather than the other way around.

Nor did everyone who stayed truly "stay." Russia has a cabinet-level minister dedicated to the mass kidnapping of Ukrainian children in the occupied territories, and their forcible transfer to Russia's eastern territories, thousands of miles from their origin. The minister has proudly proclaimed that all of the children's documentation has been destroyed so that their forced de-patriation can never be reversed. The Russians admit to tens of thousands of such kidnappings (they prefer the term "rescues" or "rehabilitations" or "Russifications"), and at the time of this writing have been occupying territory with roughly one-quarter of Ukraine's prewar population for sixteen months. Considering the spectacle the Russians are making of the topic, "tens of thousands" is almost certainly a lowball figure.

And that's before one considers the more traditional demographic hits a war can inflict upon a people. Most of the Ukrainians battling the Russians are in their twenties and thirties. That's child-raising age. That's a demographic that was heavily depleted even before the war. That's whose efforts will be required for Ukraine to recover after the war. They cannot help if they are dead.

Taken together, the country of Ukraine faces utter demographic dissolution. Within three decades, there will not be enough workers even to maintain basic industrial-level infrastructure.

Worst of all, this bleakness is the *best*-case scenario because it assumes Ukraine *wins*. When the Ukrainians recovered some of their territory in counteroffensives in the summer and fall of 2022, they uncovered several dark omens; mass murders, torture chambers, and rape clinics in places like Bucha, Izyum, and Kherson hint at a far worse outcome than mere national oblivion.

Win or lose, we are in the final generation of the Ukrainian state, and probably no more than two from the end of the Ukrainian nationality itself. But for the rest of us, the Ukrainians are holding back the darkness. They may be doomed, but *damn* they are making a mark on the world.

CHAPTER 11

History Returns to Europe

As hopefully was made clear from last chapter's sections on Russia, Turkey, and Iran, few countries of the world exist in vacuums. Nearly all swim in large ponds, interacting constantly with other powers, smaller, larger, and peer. In that light the remaining country on the aggressives list gets a chapter all its own. Or perhaps more accurately, its crowded and busy pond gets a chapter all its own. The country is Germany. The pond is Europe. And what follows makes for a messy future indeed.

The European Geography

Europe is a land of contrasts. The majority of Europe's population lives on the aptly if not particularly creatively named North European Plain (NEP). The portion of the coastal plain in Europe proper is one of the world's narrowest, less than three hundred miles at its widest point in Germany, but it is also one of the world's longest, stretching over fifteen hundred miles from the Pyrenees in southern France to the Belarusian border. And it doesn't end there, but rather expands into the European Hordelands of Central Eurasia. A series of broken highlands and stark mountains back the entirety of the NEP's southern border, which generate sufficient rainfall to make the NEP a lush agricultural zone and fuel a score of rivers that transect the plain—the Seine, Meuse, Rhine, Weser, Elbe, Oder, and Vistula in particular—many of which are navigable for most of their lengths. Between ample local food production, high capital-generation possibilities, and ease of movement, the NEP has had one of the world's densest population footprints, densest local trade networks, and richest populations for nearly a millennium.

But there is a dark side. There are no barriers between the various river valleys. The easily crossed nature of the plain condemns the people of Northern Europe to be constantly in each other's faces. Every country's heartland is their neighbors' borderland. Civilization may come easily to Northern Europe, but so does competition. Success and security for one would mean want and instability for all others. The all-or-nothing nature of that simple fact has led to some of the world's most infamous wars being fought among the NEP powers in their efforts to carve out some security for themselves.

There is more to Europe, however, than just the NEP. Peninsulas and mountains riddle the lands around the plain. The Iberian Peninsula, home to Spain and Portugal, lies south and west of France across the Pyrenees. The Alps separate Germany and France from Italy's Apennine Peninsula, and the Balkan Peninsula is on the far side of the Carpathians from Austria and Poland. Most of Scandinavia is self-contained on its eponymous peninsula. In every case, the balance of transport proves true: Mountains inhibit movement and peninsulas limit lines of approach. The insulation that geography grants the peninsular states allows them to stay somewhat apart from the cultural, economic, and military crucible that is the NEP.

That's doubly true for Europe's islands, two of which merit specific attention. Denmark's island of Zealand has been home to half of the Danish population since its emergence as a force in the eighth century. The Danes are and always have been an island people who own a peninsula rather than the other way around. A more recognizable island people are of course the English who call Great Britain home. The peoples of both islands have long acted independently of the NEP. The strongest tie that binds the peninsulars and the islanders together is a fear that someone on the NEP might actually emerge victorious from their perennial competition. Should that ever happen, the richness and might and power of the plain would no longer be spent on local feuds, but instead be available to surmount the geographic barriers that have long protected the peninsular and island peoples.

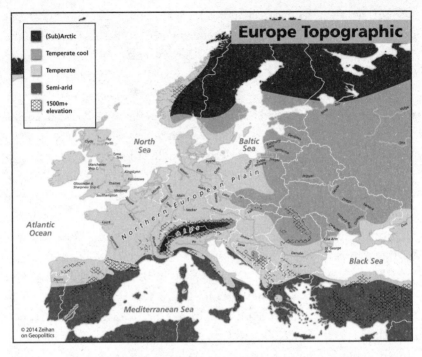

Europe Today

A continent riven by war is hardly how most of us think of Europe, but that is because the Europe we know has been transformed utterly by Bretton Woods.

With the imposition of Bretton Woods and the American alliance network, the Europeans no longer needed to struggle for iron ore or steel or oil or food or spices or markets or borders. Instead of battling to be the NEP colossus, France and (West) Germany could cooperate economically and focus on exporting to wider Europe and the wider world. Instead of being nervous about the NEP uniting, countries on the European periphery could, with some caution, participate in Bretton Woods' legion trade opportunities. The Europeans were not only able to take a vacation from geopolitics, but a vacation from their own brutal history. The result—as elsewhere in the world—was seventy years of peace and prosperity, although in Europe the emphasis was definitely on the "peace" part.

The end of the Cold War had any number of impacts on the world writ large, but in Europe it was absolutely wonderful. Europe was the primary Cold War battle line, so defense outlays were far higher there

than anywhere but in the United States, the Soviet Union, and the Koreas. With the Cold War's end, resources dedicated to defense could be redirected to investment. A belt of states from Estonia to Bulgaria ceased being Soviet property and started down the road to European Union membership, eventually providing an infusion of over 100 million new consumers and low- and mid-cost workers. But most of all, the Cold War's end made the French and Germans sufficiently confident in a future without war that they launched their most ambitious unification project yet: a currency union.

Which is where contemporary Europe's problems begin.

Problem One: Enter the Euro

In the United States, finance is somewhat nondenominational. There are so many rivers servicing such a substantial population that capital practically grows on trees. Everyone is in the same river network and so is in the same resultant financial system. It is considered perfectly normal for a Nebraska bank to fund a Vermont mortgage or a Georgia credit union to enable credit card use in Idaho.

Not so in Europe.

Europe's river systems are not integrated, and the differences that fact spawns do not end with different languages and identities. French trade travels on French rivers with French profits deposited in French banks where they are used to further French goals. Rivers, trade, and banks are all considered national assets. As one would expect from any such national asset, the banks' responsibilities are first and foremost to look out for the interests of the state. In 1992 the Europeans may have committed themselves to launching the euro era, but they never united their disparate financial and banking systems into a cohesive whole. That split is the root of the European financial crisis.

Once again, it comes down to the balance of transport, but this time from an economic rather than a strategic point of view. The balance of transport isn't easily swayed by political agreements—even ones as potent and far reaching as Bretton Woods. The NEP remained the economic hub of the European wheel, but not everyone in Europe had rivers and so not everyone in Europe could generate the surplus capital that made everything from infrastructure to education possible. Geographically less-endowed areas like Iberia, southern Italy, and Greece were perennial laggards. European "structural adjustment" monies poured into these areas to help close the gap, funding everything from highways to olive groves, but the capacity created by this assistance couldn't hope to keep up with what the richer portions of Europe invested into their home systems simply as a matter of course. On anything remotely resembling a level playing field, well-rivered, flat, and integrated Northern Europe would always be more thoroughly educated and more productive and richer than highland, arid, and disconnected Southern Europe.

But in a common monetary system, capital could flow nonetheless. Currency unity meant that the surplus capital generated in the north could be lent out to southern economies that had no experience using it wisely at rates normally reserved for countries like Germany. Currency unity meant that Northern European exporters had unrestricted access into southern economies that couldn't hope to compete with the northerners' superior infrastructure and workforces. The result was the buildup of mountains of debt among southern economies, consumers, and governments at the same time that the hollowing out of southern economies made it impossible for the debt to be paid back. Far from being the crowning achievement of united Europe, the euro was guaranteed from day one to destroy it.

The ensuing calamity was as harsh as it was predictable. Less than a decade after the euro's 1999 launch, all it took was a recession to crack the finances of many countries to pieces. The now-infamous bailouts of Greece and Ireland—and the less notorious bailouts of Latvia, Portugal, Hungary, Cyprus, Romania, and Spain—have (as of February 2014) collectively totaled over 600 billion euros in funds transfers and write-offs.

At the time of this writing, the Europeans are not (quite) to the point that they can admit to the inanity of the euro; most serious efforts are still focused on helping a broken system limp along. Unfortunately, Europe's corporate, government, and consumer debt crisis is only one of seven challenges that the Europeans face, and it is probably their most manageable.

Problem Two: Banking, the Sick Man of Europe

The European financial crisis has had many economic impacts, but the results have been worst in banking.

Because the Europeans see banking as a national prerogative, concerns such as national infrastructure needs, maximum employment, and government budgetary stability are tossed into the mix of bankers' concerns right along with concerns of collateral and profitability. This has encouraged—and oftentimes actually required—Europe's banks to put national directives above corporate decision making, particularly on topics like due diligence.

This enables European governments to use their banks as a means of speeding investment in this or that targeted sector, to construct or repair infrastructure sooner than if they had to raise capital from private sources or taxes, or to help maintain governmental budgets in times of stress by simply directing the banks to invest in government bonds. Unsurprisingly, many of Europe's banks are state-owned in majority or in part, and even those that are not are often used as slush funds for various political interests at the local, regional, and/or national level. In essence, the various governments see the financial sector as a tool of governance and use it as such.

An excellent example is that of Belgian-French bank Dexia. Many Belgian communities purchased shares in the bank to ensure that they would always have strong "private" demand for their local debt.[1] As the European financial crisis deepened in 2008, it became obvious that investors were shunning the bonds of highly indebted governments (such as Belgium, where the national debt was rapidly approaching the country's total GDP). Dexia did not join the exodus. Far from it. Its owners—Belgian government entities—directed Dexia to purchase even more Belgian debt. As the financial crisis proceeded, Dexia assets soured—especially its government debt—the bank ran out of operating capital, and in September 2008 it was forced to apply for bailout assistance. When all was said and done, the bank's assets were so overvalued and its operating capital so negative that it cost taxpayers 6 billion euros over two bailouts to close the thing down.

As regards geopolitics this has two inevitable outcomes. First, in Europe finance writ large is state-directed rather than market-directed. That maximizes the presence of the state-linked banks in the broader system, while minimizing the involvement of nongovernment financial sectors such as stock markets and corporate bonds. This is the opposite of the American system where finance is somewhat agnostic and government's involvement in the sector is normally limited to regulatory matters. Consequently, approximately 70 percent of all private credit in Europe is obtained from banks, while in the United States it is the faceless stock markets that generate fully half of all credit, with banks playing only a supporting role.

The second outcome of this bank-centric system is that when Europe suffers from a recession, its banks' highest priority is to keep governments functioning. That means that they must double down on financing government deficits. Couple a financial crisis with a recession, and banks

---

1. If a private corporation had done something similar it would have been illegal in Europe (and the United States) as an antitrust violation.

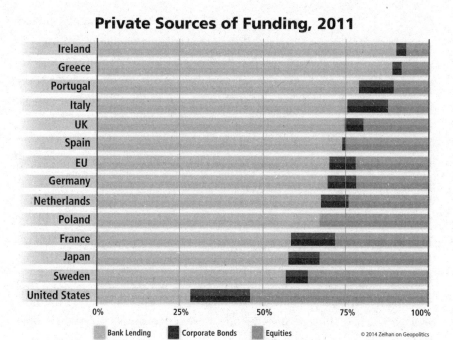

Private Sources of Funding, 2011

Bank Lending   Corporate Bonds   Equities   © 2014 Zeihan on Geopolitics

simply have no resources remaining to lend to businesses and consumers. This means that until Europe can rectify the financial imbalances the euro has caused, any growth in Europe must occur without more than middling participation from its banking sector—a sector that controls nearly all of the system's available credit.

That would be bad enough if everyone involved still agreed what the goal of a united Europe was. That, alas, is a degree of unity that no longer exists.

Problem Three: Two Drivers, No Steering Wheel

The European Union, and its predecessor, the European Economic Community, has always been a strange animal. Any organization that was formed in the early years of Bretton Woods was going to have an economic underpinning considerably different from the previous era, and in this the EU did not disappoint. But more than an economic grouping designed to take full advantage of the security and trade network the Americans had created, the EEC/EU ultimately had a political rationale.

That rationale belonged to Paris. While France had always been near the top of the European pile, it had only rarely been actually on top, and even when it was during the Napoleonic era, the other European powers ruthlessly tore it down from its perch. After Napoleon's fall from grace, France refounded itself and attempted to resume its position as the premier European power. It never made it. The British stymied the French in the wider world just as the Prussians did within Europe, and in 1871 Paris found itself not simply under German occupation but being forced to cede territory and the authority to manipulate Central European affairs to Berlin. The rest of the story includes French devastation in the world wars.

But the American-forged security arrangements of the post–World War II era provided Paris with some interesting opportunities. Austria had been split off from Germany and both had been parceled up and occupied. Italy was cast adrift. The British had gone home. The Iberians and Turks had skipped the war and were languishing under their own local authoritarian governments. The Russians loomed large, but rather than manipulate European events, they had drawn the Iron Curtain and were busy digesting Central and Eastern Europe. The only truly involved powers on the Continent were the Low Countries of the Netherlands, Belgium, and Luxembourg, a trio that could not resist French power without considerable assistance, and there was no assistance to be found.

And so the French launched the "European" integration process. I use quotes there because the initial goal very clearly was not to create a truly European system, but to band together countries that the French *could* dominate into a grouping that the French *would* dominate. The Low Countries were weak. Italy was a mess. Germany was divided, occupied (in part by France), and its opinion was neither allowed nor issued. After over a century of coming in second or worse in the European game, France finally reigned supreme. For the next two generations, German industrial profits were funneled via the EU budget to fund French national and geopolitical goals. France was able to count upon Germany to back any position Paris wanted to stake out, and the two NEP heavyweights were able to impose French desires upon the rest of the Union.

But the gravy train couldn't last forever.

In time the artificial circumstances of the Cold War ended. The Iron

Curtain collapsed and the Central European states joined the EU in the 2000s. All of them remembered what French security guarantees had meant in the run-up to World War II, and so were not willing to sign away their newfound independence to a French-dominated institution. Sweden and Finland, fiercely independent from decades of resisting the Soviets without the NATO umbrella, joined in 1995 and were not interested in being springboards for French ambition. France no longer automatically got its way, but with the Germans reflexive, silent partners, Paris could still fairly easily forge ad hoc coalitions to get whatever it wanted.

Then, in 2008, a process that had begun twenty years earlier culminated in disaster for Paris. In 1989, the Cold War ended. In 1993, Germany began the reunification process, which was completed in 2003. And then in 2008 the Germans elected a two-party coalition led by politicians unencumbered by any connection to wartime or Cold War German politics. These new German politicians still saw themselves as allied with France, but no longer beholden to it. The days of Paris telling the Germans what the German position was were over.

France and Germany are still partners, allies even, but the relationship is thinning. By far the biggest point of disagreement is on Union control. The Germans are still willing to foot the bill for a united Europe, bailouts and all—but now they want a few things in exchange for their commitment. They want reforms to be hardwired into EU treaty law and even the constitutions of the EU's members that will outlaw budget deficits. They want approval of national budgets to be the responsibility of EU institutions, institutions that are beholden to German norms. Collectively these "reforms" would lock all of the European countries into how the Germans do things, and since many of the weaker states are weaker because of geography, they would become permanently servile to German supply chains and financial might. In essence, the Germans want to use German money to solidify German control of the European system. And the Germans have the gall to insist that France is not exempt.

The French, in contrast, want to go back to how things were before 2008, back to the era of French exceptionalism and control. They want the Germans to keep paying to keep the EU afloat, but to do so without significant changes in how it operates, and certainly how France operates.

They want budgetary control to remain at the national level and for deficit restrictions to remain somewhat loose. They want to keep getting financial transfers from Germany, even though France is one of the Union's richest members. In essence, they want to reachieve what they once had: to use German money to support French control of the European system.

Until and unless the French and Germans can close ranks, everything else about the European Union degrades into near pointlessness. The EU hasn't enacted a meaningful foreign policy stance since the financial breakdown of 2007. Critical needs such as a banking union have been negotiated (due to French insistence), but not armed with the money or authority required to make them functional (due to German insistence). Bailouts have been awarded (as Berlin realizes they must), but the terms have been so constantly abrogated that the weaker countries (often due to French intervention) have been able to enjoy a revolving door of fresh credits. This furious running in place will last until the Franco-German relationship heals.

The Franco-German disconnect would be bad enough if German money were sufficient to fix the European system, but it isn't.

Problem Four: Out of Money (and Time)

There are three routes a country can take to economic growth: consumption-led, export-led, and investment-led. Germany in the 2010s is very similar to the Germany of the late nineteenth century in that it is an investment- and export-led system. Most German capital is poured into its industrial base and educational system, leaving little money in the hands of the people to spend. This was a wonderful model (for the Germans) in the 2000s: The unity of the eurozone allowed all of the Europeans—and in particular Southern Europeans—to access German credit to finance the purchase of German goods. Also, Europe, and in particular Southern Europe, had a demographic hot-wired for mass consumption.

But that was then. What is rapidly taking root in Europe is a near-perfect storm of economic challenges:

- The countries that face the most systemic financial pressure—Greece, Portugal, Spain, and Italy—are among the most rapidly

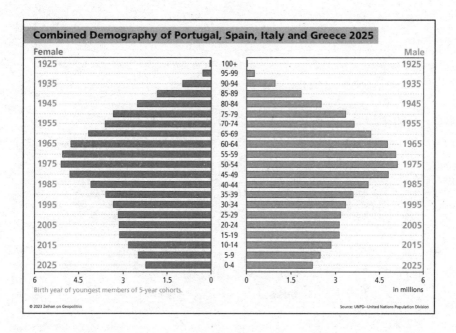

Combined Demography of Portugal, Spain, Italy and Greece 2025

Female | Male — age cohorts from 0-4 to 100+, years 1925 to 2025. Birth year of youngest members of 5-year cohorts. in millions. © 2023 Zeihan on Geopolitics. Source: UNPD—United Nations Population Division

aging European states. Of the danger states, only Spain still has a bulge in its population profile that is under forty, and even they are already in their late thirties. Consumption-led growth in Southern Europe is now largely impossible.

- For Germany and other heavily technocratic European states like Finland and the Netherlands, their development policy combined with a lack of young people means that a local-consumption-driven model hasn't been possible for twenty years. And with no replacement generation growing into adulthood, such a model cannot be returned to within the next thirty years.

- Aggressive German exports limited industrial expansion across Southern Europe, meaning fewer local jobs for the few twenty- and thirty-somethings who remained. Southern Europe was never competitive with Germany in the first place. Now, with all of Southern Europe in the eurozone, these countries cannot devalue their currencies to compete on cost. Southern Europe cannot have export-led growth.

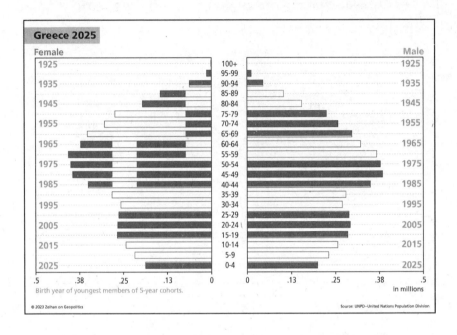

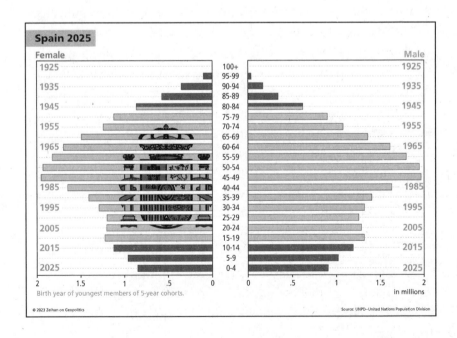

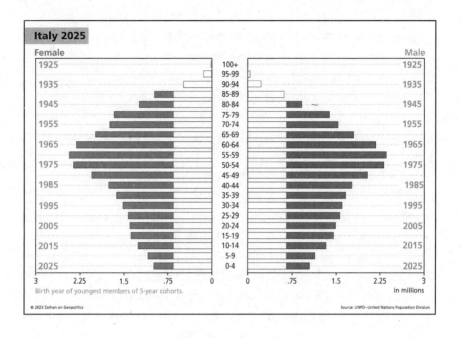

Italy 2025

Female / Male

Birth year of youngest members of 5-year cohorts.

in millions

© 2023 Zeihan on Geopolitics

Source: UNPD—United Nations Population Division

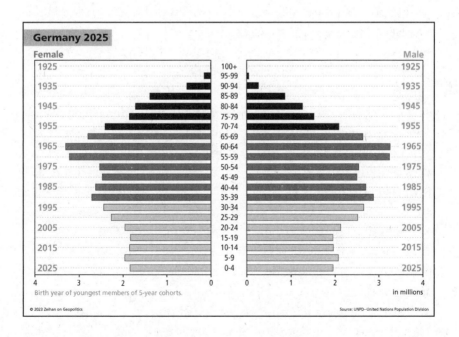

Germany 2025

Female / Male

Birth year of youngest members of 5-year cohorts.

in millions

© 2023 Zeihan on Geopolitics

Source: UNPD—United Nations Population Division

- The aging of Europe across the board has denied Germany its traditional captive market, forcing it to look beyond Europe for external markets to sustain export-led growth.
- For Southern Europe, the only remaining option is investment-led growth, but the debt crisis prevents Southern European governments from raising the necessary funds themselves. The only source of such investment is now Northern Europe, with the primary mode of financial transfer being bailout packages designed to manage Southern European debt rather than actually invest in the productivity of Southern European systems.

All of this means that these countries can only support their current systems so long as German largess continues. The Germans may be (reluctantly) willing to fund bailout after bailout to keep the Union together, but their ability to subsidize the Continent is not endless. The Germans too are aging. As of 2014, the German population bulge is in its early fifties, at the height of its technical skill and taxpaying capability. That's making German tax coffers flush with cash and allowing the German export machine to outcompete nearly everyone on not just the European but also the global stage.

Fast-forward a decade, however, and this cadre will be retiring en masse and drawing pensions. German competitiveness, German exports, and above all the German government's ability to fund the never-ending bailout of the European Union will evaporate.

The Europe of today is at the high point of a system that is now in a period of permanent shrinkage. Between banking dysfunction and aging demographics, credit will never be as accessible in Europe as it is now, and growth will never be as strong as it is now. Germany's ability to generate growth from exporting goods within the European system has ended. Even assuming that the Europeans solve all of their political and financial problems, only the Germans can afford the bill to keep Europe together economically, and they can only afford that for at most another ten years.

Even if the Europeans can save their banks and the euro, even if the French and Germans can come to an amicable (and productive) meeting of the minds on how the Union should be run, they are still staring down the maw of demographic obsolescence—and they are doing so at a time when the rest of the world still boasts a (relatively) young demography.

The Europeans can look to Japan—with its collapsing finances, hollowing-out industries, and ever-mounting debt levels—to get an idea of what the approaching financial self-immolation will feel like.

Luckily, there is one bright spot in all this. As Europe slouches into Japanese-style demographic and financial malaise, it is simultaneously retreating from the global system. Japan's banks are so insolvent that all have already withdrawn from the international system. Europe is now following suit, with European financial involvement in everything from investment in East Asia to trade finance becoming an ever less European affair. As Europe's crisis worsens and spreads, it is inadvertently fencing itself off from the international system. When the European system does finally snap, it probably won't be taking the rest of us with it.

Problem Five: Germany in Crisis

The two world wars did not so much confirm Germans' aggressiveness as it confirmed their desperation: Germany is too exposed to rivals at most points of the compass. No matter how successful the Germans may be in prosecuting a war in one direction, they simply lack the numbers to be successful in all of them. The only way Germany can compete is to be better than its neighbors: better education, faster financing, higher levels of efficiency, more productive workforce, more advanced industrial base, better infrastructure. This certainly allows them to prevail in struggles against any of their rivals, but it has never enabled them to prevail against *all* of them. Invariably, German success breeds ever larger and more powerful anti-German coalitions that eventually overpower it.

Unless, of course, someone changes the rules of the game.

That is precisely what the Americans did with Bretton Woods. The Americans granted the Germans access to all of the raw materials and markets they could ever need. The Americans also incorporated the Germans into an alliance network in which their neighbors were actually helping to defend Germany instead of threatening or resisting it. In a complete geopolitical flip, Germany's rivals-turned-alliance-partners had become economic partners as well.

But the Germans didn't stop being hyperefficient. All of their organization and energy was now wholly focused on their industrial base and export industries. Bretton Woods didn't just allow for the end of European violence and the formation of the European Union, it also created a platform from which German economic and financial power would prove unassailable. Unable to compete with a Germany that was not weighed down by egregious defense costs, countries as varied as the United Kingdom, France, Spain, and Greece saw their economies steadily hollowed out by superior German industrial output. It was a great time to be German.

And in the post–Cold War era German life got even better. NATO expanded to the former Soviet satellites, ending Germany's status as a border state. Reunification injected 16 million low-cost but still highly skilled East Germans into the West German system. That's kept a lid on labor inflation, one of the perennial bugaboos of Germany's high-skilled-labor economic model. Even the European financial crisis has helped. Lumping straggling countries like Italy, crisis countries like Ireland, and dysfunctional countries like Greece in with hyperefficient Germany has put substantial downward pressure on the euro. German exports can outcompete almost anyone, anywhere.

Well, it was fun while it lasted. Without the Americans imposing and guaranteeing Bretton Woods, there will be no NATO and no global economic trade network. The 32 percent share of German exports that requires open sea lanes and American largess represents 16 percent of German GDP, a greater relative portion than all American trade with the entire world. The remaining 68 percent of German exports—over one-third of German GDP, just shy of $1 trillion—is not immediately in danger as they are sold to countries either within the European Union or physically close neighbors such as Switzerland, Norway, Ukraine, and Russia.

But there is nothing to say that these exports will be secure or stable. Bretton Woods granted market access and physical security guarantees and made the peaceful evolution of the European Union possible. As each beneficiary has different security and economic needs, each will respond to the American withdrawal differently, particularly as a considerable list of European countries perceived the American security guarantees as guaranteeing their security *from Germany*. For nearly all EU members, the Germans are now far and away their largest source of imports. In a world in which their extra-European *exports* are suddenly in danger, this quickly escalates from a niggling political issue to a catastrophic economic one.

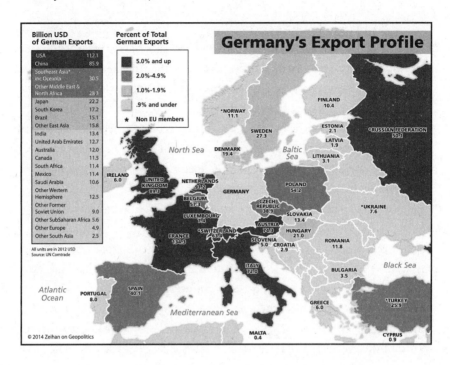

Living in a world in which German industry dominates your economic life is one thing, but waking up to discover that the Americans are no longer holding the Germans in check is quite another.

Perhaps Germany's biggest problem will be that there is no single place (or even five places) that the Germans need access to if they are to survive. Courtesy of Bretton Woods, the economic geography of early-twenty-first-century Europe is far more entangled than that of any other age of German independence. The most accessible energy production sites are nearly two thousand miles away, either in Azerbaijan or northwestern Russia, and Germany needs 2.2 million barrels of crude imports daily. As far as raw materials are concerned, everything from aluminum to iron ore is no longer even produced in Europe, which is long since mined out. German supply chains are no longer exclusively nationally held, but are instead dependent on intermediate inputs and even finishing work in Belgium, the Netherlands, Austria, Poland, and the Czech Republic.

This all makes Germany sound like a dependent has-been, doesn't it? But this is Germany, and German organizational acumen and efficiency are *not* limited to industrial policy. When sufficiently motivated, the

Germans are capable of transformations that are as startling as they are rapid. An end to Bretton Woods provides the motivation. Every country that chooses to restrict trade access will be one that the Germans will have to consider both a competitor for now-restricted supplies of raw materials and a now-denied end market. That might sound innocuous enough, but consider that such concerns were the driving rationale behind the last six wars the Germans initiated.[2] Germany may not have much of a military at the present, but neither did it in 1935, just five years before it conquered eight of the nine countries that it currently borders.

This isn't Uzbekistan or Japan where the requirements are nearby and so the path is obvious. This isn't Saudi Arabia or Iran where the threats—and so the necessary steps to counter them—are clear. Without Bretton Woods, Germany's mere existence is a threat to the very neighbors that Germany needs if it is to continue as a successful country, and under Bretton Woods the German economy has grown so much that even a deal with *all* of them still wouldn't give Germany the energy, resources, and markets it needs. Without the Americans, Germany's economic crisis quickly escalates to a European-wide strategic crisis where the paths and outcomes are clear to no one. The only certain variable is that the Germans will not lie down and die. For the fourth time in the past 150 years, they will challenge the European status quo. Only time will tell if they will shatter it.

Problem Six: Aggressive Neighbors

The Europeans have two neighbors—Turkey and Russia—who are likely to ramp up their pressure on the European periphery in the next decade. Both were discussed in the previous chapter, but there are a few Eurocentric points worthy of elaboration.

For the past decade a slowly awakening Turkey has played in the Middle Eastern sandbox, and it has discovered that the Middle East is full of intractable issues, bad blood, and, above all else, lack of economic benefit. The countries of North Africa, the Levant, and Iraq combined have a smaller combined economic footprint than Spain, a mid-sized

---

2. World War II, World War I, the Franco-Prussian War of 1870–71, the Austro-Prussian War of 1866, and the Schleswig Wars of 1848–51 and 1864.

European economy. The Middle East is not Turkey's future. Historically, the old Ottoman economic and intellectual heartland wasn't in the Middle East or even in Anatolia—it was in the Balkans. And that's where its future will be as well.

Currently, two things are holding the Turks back from this path. First, the current regime is new, having been in government for only a decade. They are still learning what works and what doesn't—and most of all why. Second, NATO and the EU dominate the Balkans, with Slovenia, Greece, Croatia, Hungary, Romania, and Bulgaria all full members of both organizations. So long as the American security umbrella remains functionally in place, and so long as the EU continues existing in its current form, the Turks face limitations in what they can do to their northwest.

Both of those barriers exist on borrowed time. The EU is likely to devolve—in the best-case scenario—into more of a glorified free trade zone, but not one with any pretensions to a common foreign or security policy. As for the Americans, their falling interest in the world writ large is something the Turks will be able to scrutinize closely. Turkey is a NATO member: Ankara will be able to detect precisely when the alliance's security guarantees devolve from relevance to mere words on a page. The only question is timing.

Russia, by contrast, faces no political or alliance constraints on its ability to pursue a strategic policy to its west. However, unlike Turkey, it does face a time pressure; Russia's demographics are so horrid that if it fails to act before 2022, it will lose the capacity to act both militarily and economically. This puts Russia on a collision course with the eight EU members on the edge of what the Russians see as their preferred border zone: Finland, Estonia, Latvia, Lithuania, Poland, Slovakia, Hungary, and Romania. It would seem that the Russian challenge to Europe's future is rather obvious.

Well, yes and no. Yes in that Russian pressure on places like Ukraine is both palpable and increasing, yes in that the emotional state of these eight European countries ranges from intense concern to panicked paranoia at the rising Russian tide, and yes in that should Russia follow a piecemeal approach it can encroach upon Europe's eastern borders without unduly provoking Western Europe's heavyweights. No in that the reactions of some of these countries to Russian encroachment may be even more injurious to the concept of European unity than the Russians themselves.

Problem Seven: Men in the Middle

As the country where the North European Plain transitions into the Eurasian Hordelands, Poland will decide Russia's success in reanchoring between the Baltic Sea and the Carpathians. The Poles realize what is at stake and have been taking steps toward a plan for several years.

Poland, as Central Europe's largest industrial power and with its largest population, sees itself as the natural leader of former Soviet satellites who joined the EU and NATO in the 1990s and 2000s. There is more than a small credence to that claim. But the crew that Poland seeks to lead is a motley one. Even after a quarter century of effort, the region's infrastructure is remarkably fractured. The Baltic states have far better links to Russia, a holdover of the Soviet era, than they do to one another or the Western European region. Romania and Bulgaria are south of the Carpathians and have but one four-lane road that links them to the rest of Europe—and only two bridges that connect them across the Danube (the second of which was only completed in 2013). Slovakia is mountainous. Hungary is linked really only to Austria, and even that connection is pinched by the Vienna Gap. Poland, somewhat ironically, has the best infrastructure linkages of the lot—but those connections are largely due to its position on the North European Plain, which in turn ties it directly to both Germany and Russia, the two powers that Warsaw is most concerned about. Making matters worse, nearly all of the former satellites are dependent upon the Russians for both oil and natural gas.

An alliance of the Intermarium—the countries between the Baltic and the Black Seas—simply isn't workable. Merely coordinating the actions of such disconnected geographies and heterogeneous cultures would be an endeavor attempted only out of sheer desperation. Without some far more powerful entity—say a rejuvenated European Union or an engaged United States—actively managing such a gangly alliance, the Russians would have a fairly easy time engaging and defeating each of the Intermarium states in sequence and in isolation.

That is, with the possible exception of Poland. Despite Poland's largely indefensible position, and despite its potential need to defend against both Germany and Russia, the Poles have a Swedish ace up their sleeve.

Since being forced into strategic neutrality at the conclusion of the

Great Northern War of 1700–1721, Sweden gradually became Europe's forgotten power. While technically a Continental power, Sweden boasts water to its south and east, mountains to its west, and taiga and tundra to its north. By most definitions, Sweden operates as a naval power rather than a land power, and as such its military and economic strategies emphasize speed and reach. But they do so in a manner somewhat different from other naval powers.

Oceanic-oriented cultures like England and Japan were made famous because they became experts harnessing the wind to cover vast distances over open seas. Their vessels were notable for their relatively small crews (the wind did most of the work) and relatively large cargo areas (lots of supplies were needed to keep the crew alive on long voyages, and lots of trade goods were needed to justify the trip in the first place). With large, manpower-light vessels the British needed to interact with the locals right on the coast. They could rarely afford to penetrate inland with the men they brought, and any such excursion would have to occur on foot. Their boats, whose propulsion was limited by the whim of the wind and the depth of the water, could not easily or reliably sail on rivers. The result was an empire built on indirect rule and coastal trading depots.

Early Sweden's approach was considerably different, because Sweden's regional geography was considerably different. The Danish island of Zealand kept the Swedish Vikings and later the Swedish Empire locked in the Baltic, a very small place compared with the oceans. There was no need for the Swedes to learn to sail when they could simply row. Instead of huge, wind-powered vessels with small crews, the Swedes used small, oar-powered vessels with large crews. The more men, the faster the vessel could go. Short trips meant less need for supplies. Where the British made landfall with small, scrawny, scurvy-ridden landing parties eager to trade, the Vikings made landfall with large, strapping warriors eager to satisfy more basic instincts. Because longboats have such shallow drafts, and because they were manned by lots of brawny Vikings, they could easily be rowed upriver and even portaged. Unique among the "naval" powers, the Swedes punched deep inland, and even showed up as far away as Constantinople from time to time.

This more…direct approach is still reflected in Swedish strategy. Its military remains remarkably amphibious and its defense industry depends upon no external power. Its economic relationships are direct and deep, seeking full ownership, in contrast to the Anglo preference of involvement via minority share purchases. But Sweden remains undeniably maritime, valuing trade and financial connections over the hardwired infrastructure and military links of land-based powers. Even now, three centuries after Sweden's grand defeat in the Great Northern War and its banishment to neutrality, the Baltic Sea remains a Swedish lake.

Much of the world has forgotten this. But not Sweden's neighbors—because they were first raiding targets, then part of the Swedish Empire, and now part of the extended Swedish family (literally). Another culture that hasn't forgotten are the Russians, whose rivers are not particularly amenable to traditional maritime transport but were perfect for the Viking expeditions of the previous age.

The issue for the Russians (and Germans) isn't that Poland wants to be the brain and muscle of an anti-Russian (and maybe anti-German) Intermarium, but that Sweden has every interest in making sure that the Poles succeed. Like Poland, the Swedes fear undue German or Russian influence regardless of the form it takes. And while Poland might have difficulty spackling together an alliance, Sweden already has one. The familial relations of Viking and Imperial Sweden do not just include the weaklings of Estonia, Latvia, and Lithuania, but also Finland, Norway, and Denmark—economically developed, culturally united, militarily robust countries that boast more than enough petroleum to supply everyone in the extended Swedish family. And Poland as well.

By any measure a Swedish-Polish alliance would be a mating of synergies. Sweden is an advanced maritime technocracy, while Poland is a modernizing land-based industrial power. Sweden has the money and the technology needed to make Poland bloom, and Poland has the market to make it worth Sweden's while. And neither are in the eurozone, so at least part of the European carnage to come will pass them by.

Numbers will still prove a problem. There are under 10 million Swedes to support fewer than 40 million Poles against over 80 million Germans and some 140 million Russians. If Poland is to be successful, it will need more than simply Swedish help. Which brings us back to the Americans.

The benefits of a Poland that can preserve its independence are undeniable: It would keep Central Europe out of either the German or Russian sphere of influence, and condemn both Germany and Russia to remain locked down in local issues. Unfortunately, Poland's case—and its Intermarium alliance—is hopeless. Keeping Poland in play would require a substantial commitment of technology, treasure, and—in the end—likely even blood. It is exactly the sort of commitment that the Americans will try to avoid in the new era.

If the Americans are to be drawn into Continental European affairs, it will be via the Swedish vector. Sweden is no pocket power. Sweden has a stable economy, a tight circle of capable allies, a top-rate military force, and—uniquely in Europe—a rock-solid financial system. The trick will be to manage and bolster Poland via Sweden so that the Americans can remain one step removed from the NEP. From the American point of view, Sweden makes Poland worth a second look.

Poland will need that second look because Warsaw dare not adopt a defensive strategy. It has no geographic barriers to hunker behind and, Swedish and American backing or not, it cannot possibly absorb and repel a German or Russian surge. For Poland to be independent, it has to somehow keep the competition *away* from its borders. The best way to do that is for the Poles to poke Ukraine as mercilessly as possible to keep the Russians off balance. Considering the Russian view of the importance of Ukraine, this is far from a low-risk operation.

Should the Americans decline, the Swedes and Poles do have a fallback. Sweden nearly did not join the Treaty on the Non-Proliferation of Nuclear Weapons when it was negotiated in the 1960s because Stockholm thought it would need nukes to dissuade Soviet expansionism. Its robust nuclear industry is both sophisticated and homegrown and could construct a crude weapon in a long weekend. In this corner of the world, deterrence may not just be for superpowers.

Scared New World: Life After Europe

Any of these factors could bring everything that matters in contemporary Europe crashing down. With such a mélange of moving parts, something will have to give. What most of the world, and certainly most of the Europeans, have forgotten is that Europe has *never* taken a united foreign policy or security stance except under the direct—some would say domineering—leadership of the United States. With American economic and security guarantees on their way out, all options will be on the table and something *will* give.

In short, Europe is going to be a mess—and not the slightly amusing, organizationally dysfunctional mess that has been on display at most EU summits this past decade, but more of the seething cauldron of dislocation and war that it was in the five centuries before 1945. What is an existential challenge to one country is barely a passing concern to others. Lithuania, Poland, and Romania are in near panic about Russian activities in Ukraine, while Portugal, Italy, and Ireland insist that the real issue is the financial crisis, and Germany and the Netherlands are primarily focused on forging new trade deals with economies beyond Europe. There is no commonality. No agreement. And from that minimal coordination, Europe is becoming overwhelmed with itself.

Within that rather dark and murky forecast there is, however, one relatively bright spot. Not everyone in Europe took full economic advantage of Bretton Woods and branched out to become an international economic power. Not everyone handed over all meaningful levers of their defense policy to Washington. Not everyone in Europe is so enmeshed in the European Union that the Union's end spells utter disaster. And not everyone in Europe forgot how to have kids around 1965. One country has stood somewhat apart, and as such will have less vulnerability and more options than the others.

Irony of ironies, that country is the one that came up with the very idea of the EU in the first place: France. It shouldn't be a surprise. Just as Bretton Woods was America's *strategic* policy for fighting the Cold War, the EU was France's *strategic* policy for taking advantage of Bretton Woods. Alone among the major powers, Washington and Paris never hitched their economic systems to what were ultimately strategic gambits.

France's economy is only half as dependent on exports as Germany's. It is among the world's foremost agricultural exporters. By European standards it has a fairly healthy demography, still benefiting from a fairly robust birth rate. It is the only country besides the United States that floats an aircraft carrier worthy of the name, even if technical problems limit it to nothing more than brief regional deployments. Its use of nuclear energy keeps it largely independent of petroleum markets. What petroleum it needs it can source from nearby Algeria, a country with which it enjoys reasonably positive relations. Its position on the western end of the NEP—and its Mediterranean shoreline—both reduces its exposure and widens its reach. Unlike Germany where needs are legion and the places that can satisfy those needs are scattered, French needs are limited and solutions to those needs are nearly all local. All of the violent chaos likely to erupt involving Sweden, Germany, Poland, Russia, Ukraine, and Turkey is on the far side of Europe. And just in case all else fails, it has nuclear weapons—not can-make-them-in-a-pinch like Sweden or South Korea, but already-has-them like the United States. Unsurprisingly, France is *the* country that the Germans take most seriously.

Between its low needs and high leverage, France has not just the greatest capacity to shape Europe, but the greatest wealth of tools with which to do so. If there is to be some remnant of united Europe that will survive Europe's chaos to come, it will be France at its head. If there is to be some power that rises from the ashes as Europe tears itself apart (again), it too will be France.

European history has been on hold since the Americans restructured the world in the 1940s. Centuries-old competitions were simply smothered under the happy blanket of American security and global trade. That era is rapidly coming to a close. In its place will be a host of states terrified of a reawakened Germany, a Germany that will have to fight for its economic well-being, a Russia desperate to harden its external boundaries, a justifiably paranoid Poland backed by a no longer neutral Sweden, and a Turkey eager to carve its own sphere of influence out of the EU's and NATO's remains.

Will all of these evolutions result in wars? Probably not. But it truly would be stunning if none of them did.

History Returns to Europe: Ten Years On

I find my forecasts regarding the demise of Europe to be far and away my most problematic. Not because I don't believe in them (I'm far more confident in their fidelity than most of the others), but because I *hate* those forecasts. I'm an American. I'm a Westerner. I view Europe as central to my cultural history, as part of the extended family of civilizations that make the human condition what it is today. The idea of Europe degenerating from the ideal of united, free, and at peace to something more similar to its long, bloody history makes me throw up in my mouth a little bit.

I've been nothing short of delighted that the Europeans have found a means, at least temporarily, to muddle through.

But first let's get the bad out of the way.

Europe as a whole is in a much deeper debt hole today than it was before the euro crisis of 2007–15. Ten years on, everyone is ten years older, and now, with the notable exceptions of Sweden, the Czech Republic, Hungary, Denmark, Ireland, and France, every EU member country has aged past the point of no return. It is now statistically impossible for all but this lucky sextet to prevent eventual national disillusionment.[3] The only question is timing. For Germany, that massively skilled workforce that makes Germany Germany? It'll be mostly retired by decade's end.

If that were not enough, the Ukraine War has (re)elevated security to the very top of the European agenda. It is worse than it sounds. Many European countries, first and foremost Germany, had been hip deep in plans to close down their militaries. After all, in the post–Cold War era, history had "ended." Needless to say, cold hard reality tends to trump ideology. The Europeans immediately became dependent upon the leadership, training, industrial base, defense industries, satellite and signals intelligence of the United States. Even worse, the Americans' return has been buttressed by the return to Europe of its staunch ally, the United Kingdom, which had splashily staggered out of the EU only a few years previous.

The EU was no longer in charge of Europe. NATO and the Group of Seven rich countries took the lead at setting Ukraine policy, underlining

---

3. The one possible addition is Poland, which might squeak by because of the scads of young Ukrainian refugees likely to settle there permanently.

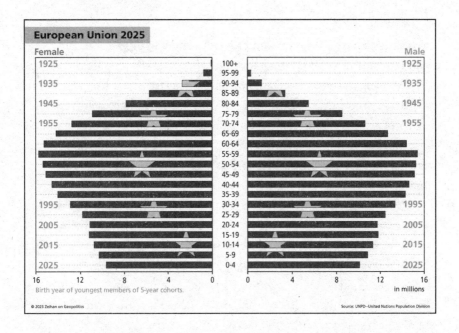

to peoples everywhere that the European Union was not even a shadow as capable as it had long claimed, and that its goals—its very existence—were impossible without a sometimes-bossy security guarantor on a different continent. It was no small mercy that the Americans under Joe Biden, and the Brits under a carousel of prime ministers, were not smug about being front and center in European policymaking.

Ego aside, the suffering is real. The suffering is deep. And the suffering has legs. Again, Germany is the best example. The German economy was based not only upon its highly skilled workforce, but also on bottomless supplies of imported Russian energy, and limitless American commitment to freedom of the seas. Within months, the Germans were shutting down not just heating in public buildings, but entire swaths of energy-intensive economic sectors that couldn't hope to function in a Europe at war. Only with the utter abandonment of the country's green ambitions, the mass expansion of lignite mining and burning, and the mortifying mass import of American shale natural gas in liquefied form have the Germans managed to keep the lights on.[4]

---

4. Lessons are being learned, but I'd argue that some will need to be learned twice. As Berlin found itself forced to cut Russia out of the German economy, the Germans doubled down in their economic relationship with that other genocidal, dictatorial power: China.

Now the good:

Ukraine has given fresh impetus not simply to NATO, but the EU as well. Explaining that requires a touch of a backstory:

No organization is free. Someone has to pay for everything, and while within a country this is always a political question, when the thing needing to be paid for is *among* countries, a whole new level of diplomatic bullshit enters into the equation. Everything about every such tax, budget, benefit, and program becomes a point of contention both within and among countries.

In the case of the EU in specific, the issue becomes one about the balance between joint responsibilities and joint commitments. The Union's wealthier countries like to talk about responsibilities; that each country should follow certain prudent principles and in doing so not unduly burden the others. The weaker countries prefer to emphasize commitments; the idea that wealth and history and unity dictate that the richer countries share what they have with their less fortunate partners.

So long as there has been an EU, Germany has been *the* wealthy country. In every phase of contemporary European history since the original formation of the EU's antecedent, the European Coal and Steel Community, the Germans have paid for the lion's share of everything. But they drew the line at the issuance of joint bonds. The idea that Europe's less stable (and responsible) countries could issue debt instruments that Germany would have to ultimately pay for was long considered a bridge too far.

That is, a bridge too far until COVID and Donald Trump. COVID shut Europe down. Trump threatened to end the trade relationship. The near-simultaneous loss of both consumption and exports was crippling. Berlin quickly, if reluctantly, deduced that unless something drastic occurred, the entire European project would collapse into an irrecoverable depression. As Germany was the European country least impacted by the debt crisis of 2007–15 (largely because of those aforementioned prudent principles), the Germans admitted it was time to put up or shut up.

In March 2020 the Germans proposed the first joint European bond, one in which they would directly benefit not at all, but they would be responsible for paying back the plurality. Working out the details took well over a year.

Just as the first bond was being issued, the Russians invaded Ukraine.

Suddenly the threat wasn't a respiratory bug or a mercurial American president, but instead the very real and present threat of Russian boots on European territory. It took *decades* to get to the first joint bond. It took mere weeks for the Europeans to activate the program to pre-purchase ammunition for the Ukrainians.

European circumstances—economically, demographically, and strategically—are far worse in 2022 than they were in 2013. Germany itself is in its final decade. The Germans are literally spending their final years of fiscal capacity to hold back the end of their world. And then? Something, somewhere—or more likely many things in many places—will break.

For now, the days-long summits over cheese policy that have marred Europe's past are gone. Europe has stared into the abyss, and there is a growing realization that, to borrow one of those infuriating American colloquialisms, if they do not hang together, then they will most assuredly hang separately. Europe will still die, and die spectacularly at that. But the Continent has at least found a way to not die *yet*.

CHAPTER 12

The Alberta Question

The United States is not very internationalized. At this point in this book that statement should not come as a major surprise. But "not very" is not the same as "not." The Americans do have—and will continue to have—foreign relations both friendly and unfriendly. With one country those relations have been so friendly for so long that they have largely been lost in the noise of American domestic politics. That country is Canada, and in the not too distant future a crisis will rock that most solid of relationships.

The Unlikelihood of Canada

Canada has many of the same features that make the United States such a rich and successful country, they're just not arranged right. Yes, the Great Lakes are in effect a series of massive waterways. The Saint Lawrence River is world-class. The natural harbors at Halifax and Vancouver are among the world's best. The Canadian Prairies are remarkably productive. But none of these things are naturally linked together in the way that the United States' geographic blessings overlap. Canada is full of natural boons, yes, but its geographic blessings are scattered "aboot," fracturing the country's economic, cultural, linguistic, and political systems. Daunting physical barriers break Canada into pieces.

Working from west to east, the first of those barriers is the Rocky Mountains. These peaks are as rugged as their American counterparts, but sufficiently far north that winter closings are common and lacking the broad open spaces of the American Rockies that might host sizable populations.

The second major internal Canadian barrier is the Canadian Shield, a creation of the many ice ages that advanced and retreated across what is now Canadian territory. When the glaciers slid southward during the waxing ice ages, they scraped the soil from the bedrock, pushing it ahead of them and depositing most of it in what is now the northern United States. Canada's shorter summers and colder winters greatly retard the process of soil formation, so now, ten millennia later, the soils are still very thin, shallow, of low fertility, and can only support conifer forests. Clearing the region generates few improvements, as the glacial weight also cracked apart the bedrock, heavily peppering the land with rock uplifts and hundreds of thousands of small lakes. The land is wholly unsuitable for agriculture and extremely difficult to build even nominal transport corridors through.

The third barrier is, somewhat ironically, a waterway. After passing by Quebec City, the Saint Lawrence River in essence becomes an ever-widening bay. While this allows oceanic traffic easy access to Quebec City, it hives off eastern Canada from the mainland.

These three barriers split Canada into five largely autonomous pieces. For all practical purposes Vancouver is a city-state perched at the westernmost edge of Western civilization. It trades more with East Asia and the American West Coast than it does with the core Canadian population centers of Toronto and Montreal. Despite being in the geographic "middle" of the country, the Prairie provinces are in many ways just as isolated: The Rockies sharply curtail contact to the west and the Canadian Shield contact to the east. Even today, there is but a single transport corridor that snakes through the twelve hundred miles of Canadian Shield between Ontario and Manitoba. As such, Canadian Railways has been forced to invest aggressively into the American railway system in order to ship the agricultural surpluses from the Prairie provinces to market, largely via the Mississippi and New Orleans. Similarly, most Albertan energy is exported south to the United States rather than west over (or around) the Rockies to the Pacific coast, or across the trackless Shield to the Ontarian core. The cost of crossing the shield is so high that very soon U.S. shale will displace Albertan natural gas as Ontario's fuel of choice.

And the shield isn't done. It also hives off Ontario from Quebec. There is only one multilane road connecting the two, the 401, which follows the shore of Lake Ontario and the Saint Lawrence River for nearly its entire length. The shield reaches down all the way to the lake and the river in several places, and dominates the northern suburbs of Toronto, Montreal, Ottawa, and Quebec City, complicating significant northward urban expansion. In fact, only Toronto is sufficiently free from the shield in other directions that it can expand in any meaningful way (mostly to the southwest along Lake Ontario). One result is that Ontarian and Quebecois cities sport some of the most expensive real estate in North America, despite being in a climate that is far from balmy. Another

Canada's Border

Legend:
△ Infrastructure of the St. Lawrence Seaway
▨ Canadian Shield
▢ Canadian populations more dense than 3 people/square mile
▢ Highlands
⋯ International border

Zeihan on Geopolitics © 2014

N ➤

is that despite being surrounded by Anglophone Canada, the Quebecois of Quebec have so few practical connections to their neighbors that they have fairly easily been able to maintain their Francophone status.

East of Francophone Canada lie the Maritime provinces, which are, well, maritime and not linked into the rest of the country much at all. From the bridge crossing at Quebec City, a single road snakes across two hundred miles of the southern extension of the Canadian Shield south of the river to the New Brunswick border. It's another 450 miles of similarly empty terrain before one finally reaches the container port of St. John's, New Brunswick, on the Atlantic Coast. Geographically, Canada just isn't a unified entity, and that's without even considering its more publicly discussed challenges such as the Anglophone-Francophone divide or the country's confederal political system, or that because of the cold climate most of the Canadian landmass is simply too inhospitable to support a large population, condemning everyone to live on the country's extreme southern fringe.

An oft-asked question in the United States—laced with no small amount of amused derision—is, why does Canada even exist? I hate to say it, but it isn't a stupid question. At best, Canada is unstable and unwieldy from a geographic and political point of view, and a series of barely connected American satellites from an economic one.

The answer is because the early Canadians, when they were still British subjects, realized their position and worked assiduously to get the Americans to see them as friends rather than British stooges. This was not a simple task. A large portion of Canadian citizens in 1800 were either of French descent or Loyalist transplants from the former American colonies who held no love for their former associates. In the War of 1812, the Canadians of American extraction were able to vent something fierce. The British used Canadian territories as their main staging ground for battering the Americans, and provided transport for Canadian marines in the (in)famous raid on Washington, D.C., that burned the capital to the ground.

And then, much to the Canadians' horror, rather than drive a stake into America's heart, the British redirected their energies to reshaping Europe in the aftermath of Napoleon's fall, leaving Canada to stand alone against the seething Americans. The Canadians, still British colonials, had an unsavory choice. They could do nothing and hope against hope that the still-mobilized Americans, who in the absence of the British fleet now held local naval superiority, would forget the enthusiastic role the Canadians had played in the war and leave them be. Or they could offer to negotiate terms. The Canadians wisely chose the latter. In the short term, this deflected American national energies west into the Ohio River valley and beyond, putting the Americans on the road to superpowerhood. In the long run, it started the process of Canada loosening the ties that bound it to the British Empire, putting it on the road first to neutrality, then friendship with the Americans, then alliance with the Americans, and finally in the contemporary period, de facto economic inclusion into the American system.

Canadian Demography: Slouching Toward Dissolution

The Canadian demographic picture is only typical in that it is very similar to that of the rest of the developed world. At some point around 1965, Canadians apparently forgot how to have kids, and their demography has been slowly hollowing out ever since. Canada's natural birth rate fell below replacement levels long ago, and only its sporting one of the highest sustained immigration rates in the world has enabled it to maintain positive population growth. On average some 250,000 people emigrate to Canada annually—nearly 1 percent of the total population. Unfortunately, while this influx certainly improves Canada's headline population figure of 35 million, it does not help repair the country's distorted demographic profile.

Unlike the United States, Canada's (non-American) would-be migrants cannot walk to Canada. That means that they have to save up for plane or boat passage, unlike Mexicans and Central Americans, who can cross the American border, quite literally, as soon as they are able to waddle. The average immigrant into Canada is thirty-two when he makes the trip, while the average Mexican immigrant into the United States is but eighteen,[1] giving would-be Americans ample time to pay into the American system before collecting pensions. In some places—the California-Mexico border outside of San Diego, for example—the concept of walking across borders is so prevalent that there are signs for it.

As such, Canada is a state in transition. It boasts a huge volume of near retirees, granting it the world's most capital-rich financial structure, and the highest tax take relative to its population in its history. Like the lopsided finances of much of the developed world, this is unfortunately

---

1. My Salvadoran sister-in-law was thirteen when she successfully completed the trip on her third try.

temporary. Between its atypical immigration patterns and its baseline demographic profile, Canada has one of the world's fastest-aging demographies, with one of the smallest replacement generations. The average Canadian is already forty-two years old, one of the oldest in the world. By 2025, Canada's demography will almost be identical to contemporary Japan's: 30 percent of the population will be sixty and older, and less than 25 percent will be in the critical twenty-to-thirty-nine band.

Canada is in for the perfect storm. Its capital structure is about to flip from one of the world's most capital-rich to one of the world's most capital-poor at the same time that the country shifts from having fairly moderate retiree needs to among the world's most massive.

As the next age unfolds, it will bring pros and cons for Canada. First, the pros. They are almost entirely geographic.

While Canadian nationalists will undoubtedly quibble with this point, far and away Canada's strongest advantage is its relationship with the United States. The most notable aspect of that is of course physical and cultural proximity. Some 80 percent of the Canadian population lives within a two-hour drive of the American border. Canada's densest population center—the Hamilton-Toronto-Montreal corridor—is on the country's only maritime system. This maritime system is not only shared with the United States, granting immediate access to major metropolitan centers like Chicago, Milwaukee, Detroit, and Buffalo, but it also empties

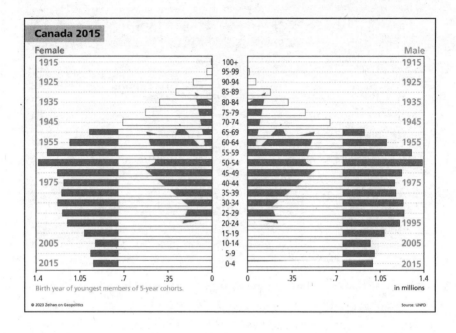

into the Atlantic just north of America's megalopolis—the home of America's densest population centers. Canada's two-century-old decision to baby-step ever closer to the Americans means that it is attached to the very center of the American trade network, no matter how the Americans choose to define the term.

Canadian state planning, consciously or not, has also been preparing the country for the new era. Canada's biggest developmental and political obstacle since the British North America Act has been a lack of physical connections among its various regions. Those connections are still middling, but they're also beside the point. Canada's rapid aging means that its consumer base isn't in Canada but rather in the United States. After 150 years of infrastructure construction, the Canadians are now fully hardwired into the American system, just in time for their own domestic consumption to plunge. Simply put, Canada does not need to sustain a large internal market or even traditional domestic financing, because for all intents and purposes Canada has already become a satellite economy of the United States. As Canadians age—and the Americans age not so much—this relationship will become more lopsided, tighter, and more essential to Canadian well-being.

There will be more to the new world for Canada than "simply" access to America's financial resources and domestic markets: On the security front the Canadians look to do very well, too. In the new world, the Americans are highly likely on occasion to waltz over into foreign lands and wreck a few things. That is not only something that the Canadians do not need to worry about affecting them directly, but they do not even have to worry about it affecting them *indirectly*. Strategically, Canada is among the Americans' firmest allies, and alone among those allies, it has no independent security threat from a third country. There simply isn't a possible evolution of international events shy of nuclear war that could potentially threaten Canadian sovereignty, and Canada's ability to avoid spending scarce resources on defense needs will reflect that. "All" the Canadians have to stomach is their status as an adjunct of the United States.

This all assumes, however, that as a country Canada can hold it together. And *that* is no longer assured.

The Quebec Question: Asked and Answered

The perennial challenge to Canadian national stability ever since its inception has been the Quebec question.

Canada's largest concern mounts not specifically from demographics or markets or finance, but from the political outcome of its fractured geography. The country's founders realized that the sort of unitary government that exists in France or Russia could never work in Canada. The citizens of Halifax simply had so few points of contact in their daily lives with the central government in Ottawa—much less Toronto, Winnipeg, or Victoria—that it made no sense to have strong centralization. The result was a confederal model of government in which most decisions not linked to defense or foreign affairs are made at the provincial rather than the national level.[2] In many ways, the Canadian government has operated in a manner similar to the United States during the Articles of Confederation. Canada is one of very few advanced countries never to have federalized

---

2. There may be some confusion here for those familiar with the Canadian political system. In Canada, "federal" actually means confederal and "unitary" means federal. There is no Canadian political term in general use for the equivalent of "unitary."

into a system where the national capital has at least as much power—if not more—than the provincial/state capitals.

Initially, the primary political logic for this setup was the French Empire in North America. The British conquered French Quebec in 1760, giving them control over a population from a rival political, cultural, economic, and linguistic system. In order to minimize the transition pains, the English authorities decided to allow Francophone Quebec largely to manage its own affairs, setting the pattern of region-center relations in what eventually became Canada. Now, 240 years after the conquest of Quebec and 140 years after the British Empire granted Canada its independence, confederalism and provincial supremacy are inseparable strands of Canadian political life. Canadian courts have ruled that Canada's provinces have full legal right to hold independence referenda.

In fact, the Canadian Supreme Court decided in favor of the legality of secession in its unanimous decision of August 20, 1998:

> A clear majority vote in Quebec on a clear question in favour of secession would confer democratic legitimacy on the secession initiative which all of the other participants in Confederation would have to recognize.... The other provinces and the federal government would have no basis to deny the right of the government of Quebec to pursue secession should a clear majority of the people of Quebec choose that goal, so long as in doing so, Quebec respects the rights of others. The negotiations that followed such a vote would address the potential act of secession as well as its possible terms should in fact secession proceed.

Should Quebec ever capitalize on this ruling and secede—the vote in the 1995 secession referendum came within a few percentage points of that happening—it would be the end of the Canadian state. Quebec controls all of the non-U.S. transport connections between Canada's most populous province, Ontario, and the Atlantic basin. To avoid destitution, the Maritime provinces would have no choice but to seek accession to the United States, and rump Canada would still be fractured into three pieces that have little to do with one another. The possibility of Quebecois separatism has long been a real and present danger to the very existence of the Canadian state.

Ottawa treated the Quebecois secession issue with the seriousness that it deserved, and in the closing decades of the twentieth century it struck upon an effective strategy for containing the threat. The Canadian national government set up a sizable fiscal transfer system that shifted money from the Ontario core to the Quebec regional government, in essence bribing Quebec to remain part of united Canada. It was an expensive solution, but manageable.

For all practical purposes, the Quebecois secession movement is now dead. Quebecois provincial mismanagement has now been entrenched for so long and the fiscal transfers from Ontario so ingrained in the system that industrial and corporate activity have vacated Quebec en masse. Should Quebec declare independence now, its currency would become soft, its finances would evaporate, and its ability to maintain its own infrastructure would devolve within a generation. It would very quickly become a Detroit without an automotive industry. Any serious Quebecois politician knows this, and over the course of the past decade Quebec's independence drive has become far less boisterous and aggressive (culminating with Bloc Quebecois' near eviction from the national parliament in the 2011 national elections). As a result, the Quebecois independence movement has now dwindled to little more than an (incredibly successful) effort to wring more transfer funds out of Ottawa.

All actions, however, have unintended consequences. Quebec couldn't simply state a number that would keep it in the Canadian system and expect to be bribed. It had to go through the motions of actually seceding. Part of this process involved not just the independence referenda, but also nudging the national government to prepare for such independence, ergo the Supreme Court ruling on the topic's constitutionality. Canada's parliament even passed a "Clarity Act" in 2000 to lay out the political process of implementing the court's decision. The mechanics of Quebec's efforts have inadvertently established just what *any* Canadian province would need to do to achieve independence.

Whether it was the result of true nationalist passions or simply a shrewd negotiating strategy, Quebec paved the road to secession, even if it has now decided that it no longer has any intention of traveling that road. So the answer may be a little awkward, but the Quebec question is answered. Quebec will not secede and so the question won't kill Canada.

But another—more deadly—question is rising rapidly to take its place.

The Alberta Question: Not Yet Asked, Already Answered

The Ontario-Quebec compact has successfully contained Quebecois separatism, but it has come at a considerable financial cost. $16.1 billion was the cost of keeping Quebec quiescent in 2013. Ontario has been able to produce this volume of money with some difficulty, but 13.5 million Ontarians paying for only 8 million Quebecois is achievable (if not enjoyable).

Or at least it was. Ontario—just like Canada on the whole—is rapidly aging. Within a few short years, masses of mature Ontarian workers—just like mature Canadian workers on the whole—will retire. That will drastically reduce the Canadian national government's ability to source compact money from Ontario. Making matters worse, Quebec's populace is actually getting older *faster* than Ontario's, so the cost of the compact is likely to increase in the years to come. Nor will the other Canadian provinces be able to bridge the gap. Quebec isn't alone in its rapid and advanced aging: Quebec-style demographics are reflected in British Columbia, Yukon, Nova Scotia, Prince Edward Island, New Brunswick, and Newfoundland. The populations of Manitoba and Saskatchewan are somewhat younger than Ontario's, but collectively they comprise only 2.2 million people— together only one-quarter that of Quebec. Their impact upon the national fiscal calculus is minimal.

Not so for Alberta. The Albertan energy boom is now well into its second decade. It has proven so successful and so deep that Alberta now enjoys the second highest income of any province anywhere in the Western world.[3] Its wealth is now so high compared to its fellow provinces

3. At $85,000 per capita (in U.S. dollars) the Albertans are richer than everyone but the Luxembourgers.

that as of 2012 it became the *only* Canadian province that is a net contributor to the national budget with a net pay-in of over $16 billion. As of 2013, that takes an average of $6,000 annually out of the pocket of every Albertan. As Canada's—and Ontario's and Quebec's—population continues to age, a far worse than disproportionate share of the compact's cost will be loaded into the Albertans' national tax bill.

And it gets worse. A lot worse. Demographically, Alberta is the anti-Canada. Largely because of the province's exploding energy sector, it is attracting masses of young people from across Canada (and the world), actually reducing the province's average age even as it raises the labor pool's skill levels. Nearly unique in the contemporary Western experience, Alberta's population is getting younger, more highly skilled, *and* better paid. As the demographic and financial disconnect between Alberta and the rest of Canada grows, these younger, more highly skilled, and better-paid Albertans will be forced to pay ever higher volumes of taxes to Ottawa to compensate for increasingly older, less skilled, and lower-income Canadians elsewhere in the country. Plagued by rafts of elderly Canadians who are no longer paying into the system but instead drawing out, the net per capita Albertan tax bill is likely to breach $20,000 by 2020.

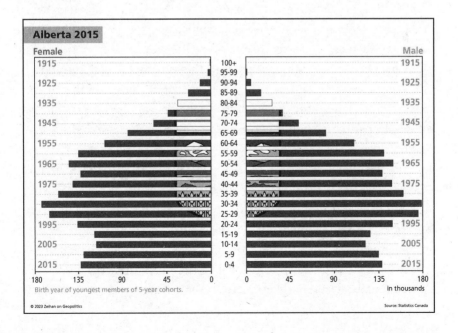

Alberta 2015

And it gets worse. As Canada ages, its currency strengthens. Mature workers—to say nothing of retirees—consume less. However, mature workers tend to be more productive than young workers. Lower consumption plus higher output results in higher exports. A sustained period of higher exports and lower consumption puts continual upward pressure on the Canadian currency. The slow and steady march higher of the Canadian dollar versus other major currencies of the past decade—from $0.65 in 2003 to $1.05 in 2013—is largely a result of the shift in Canada's current account brought about by its aging demography.

There are many pros and cons to a stronger currency, but for Alberta the impact is almost wholly negative. Like all commodities, oil, natural gas, and grains are all USD-denominated. So all of Alberta's exports are in U.S. dollars, most of its incoming investment is in U.S. dollars, but most of its expenses—and especially its tax bill—are in Canadian dollars. A strong (and strengthening) Canadian dollar squeezes not just Albertan income, but Alberta's investment plans (and from it future income) as well. In absolute terms, Albertan energy income may have increased drastically over the past decade due to rises in energy prices and increased output, but its per-barrel profit in Canadian dollars has actually dropped by over 40 percent since 2003.

And it gets worse. America's shale revolution is drastically increasing American oil output, but not in a geographically dispersed way. Nearly all of the producing shale fields are east of the Rockies and west of the Appalachians. One of the many outcomes of this geographic concentration is that there is now a sizable arbitrage between energy prices in the interior of the country and those of the coasts. In the case of oil, there is typically a $10–$15 per barrel spread between the American interior and the Gulf coast.

Yet nearly *all* Albertan oil flows via pipeline into the American Midwest, an area surrounded by major shale basins in North Dakota, Colorado, Texas, Oklahoma, Michigan, Ohio, and Pennsylvania. Put simply, Alberta is selling its energy into the United States' most saturated and most competitive market, forcing it to be sold at a discount of $20 to $40 a barrel compared to the international average. And that's the good news. Albertan natural gas—unlike American shale natural gas—is not a waste

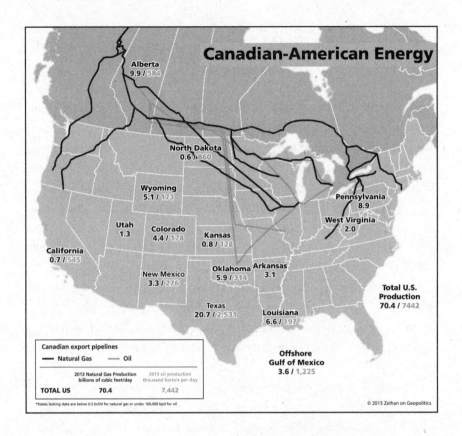

product. It is simply not price-competitive in American markets anymore and so the bulk of the subsector faces drastic drawdowns if not outright closure.

To date, landlocked Alberta's efforts to reach non-American markets have failed utterly. Its effort to participate in a pipeline project that would ship some of its crude directly to the U.S. Gulf Coast (Keystone) has become snarled in U.S. domestic politics. Its attempts to build a similar export infrastructure to the Pacific coast have proven even less successful. The political debate in British Columbia—the Canadian province through which Albertan energy would have to flow—is between those who wish to shut down the Albertan energy complex and those who would charge so much for transit rights that British Columbia would gain more income from Albertan energy production than Alberta itself.

And it isn't just Albertan energy that faces a troubled future. Alberta is also part of the Canadian grain belt. Just like oil and natural gas, wheat and barley are also USD-denominated commodities. Here transport puts Alberta in a double bind. The closest obvious market for Albertan foodstuffs is the United States, but the United States is the world's largest grain producer, making sales opportunities few and far between. Then, Alberta is landlocked and lacks access to any navigable waterways, so it must rail its grain at considerable expense either around or through the Rockies to British Columbian ports, or send it south through the United States to New Orleans. Once on the ocean, Albertan grain then has to sail all the way around the world to find a sure market. American grain tends to capture most of the South American and East Asian markets, while grain from Europe and the former Soviet Union dominates African and Middle Eastern markets. Albertan grain has to settle for South Asia, and even that market depends on whether South Asians have a good harvest. Alberta—in good times—is already the bottom feeder in international grain markets. Add in a strengthening currency, and Albertan agriculture may well cease to be economically viable. That would limit the province to an energy-only economy.

And it gets worse. Perhaps the most damning angle of the emerging Alberta Question is that, at present, Alberta doesn't get much of a say in what happens. Keystone is a purely American decision. British Columbia's extortion is a completely B.C. decision. Alberta's tax rate is a completely Ontarian and Quebecois decision: Ontarians and Quebecois together outnumber Albertans by five to one, more than enough to impose a decision on Edmonton without even preliminary consultation.

This should not come as a shock, but as of this writing there are very few issues that Edmonton and Ottawa agree on, with the two capitals regularly sparring over everything from nuclear power to carbon policy to labor regulations to health policy to pensions to tax levels. What most fail to realize—and I'm not limiting this assessment to non-Canadians—is that Alberta-Ottawa relations in 2014 are the *best* they can be expected to be for decades. Not only will Albertans become younger, more skilled, more economically dynamic, and less connected to broader Canada as the years roll by, but the current national government *is from Alberta*, up to and including Prime Minister Stephen Harper. It is the Alberta-originated Conservatives who have run the national government since 2006, working tirelessly to limit the growth of the Canadian government and its pension outlays, blunt the financial impact upon Alberta, and give Alberta as large a voice in Canadian decision making as possible. It is on the Conservatives' watch that Alberta became the only payer into the Canadian system and was put on the track to injecting exorbitant volumes into a system that they cannot influence. One can only imagine how Alberta's fiscal position will deteriorate when its chosen sons and daughters are no longer calling the shots in Ottawa.

The core issue is pretty simple. While the Quebecois—and to a slightly lesser degree the rest of Canada—now need Alberta to maintain their standard of living, the Albertans now need *not* to be a part of Canada in order to maintain theirs.

So why not just declare independence and be done with it? Well, there's a complication.

The American Option

While Alberta would do much better if it were not part of Canada, it would *not* do better as an independent country. If it were an independent entity, Alberta's currency, driven by energy exports, would skyrocket to the point that its agricultural sector would quickly lead all other nonenergy sectors to collapse. An independent Alberta would be a sort of cold-temperate Kuwait, in which the lives of all of its citizens would revolve around a single sector while everything else simply withered away, to be replaced by imports. Outright independence would also not solve any of Alberta's energy transport problems; it would still be at the mercy of American—and, God help them, infuriated Canadian—domestic politics.

That only leaves one option: union with the United States.

While it is politically easier said than done, so many of Alberta's mounting economic, financial, currency, and even political problems would not only be solved but also flipped into competitive advantages should it accede to the United States.

- Merger with the U.S. system would alleviate much of Alberta's labor shortage issues. Currently the vast rafts of un(der) skilled Canadians who relocate to Alberta have to be trained in petroleum engineering. The United States, in contrast, already boasts the world's largest petroleum complex.

- Albertan grain grown within the American system would have privileged access to the American market and transport network when compared to Canadian grains, so the Albertan agricultural sector would not go the same way as Canadian agriculture.

- Statehood would grant unrestricted and unlimited access to the world's deepest and most stable capital markets, thus guaranteeing all the investment capital Alberta could ever need.

- Infrastructure projects like the Keystone Pipeline would no longer be international agreements, but instead domestic developments.[4] Interests in other U.S. states would lose the ability to block them, giving Albertan energy the ability to reach the broader global market, likely increasing the selling price of Albertan energy by a third.

- Canadian taxes on incoming investment would simply evaporate and American investment dollars could pour into Alberta as easily as they could into North Dakota or Texas.

- While Alberta as a U.S. state would still have a higher per capita tax bill than its new conationals, it would not be an outlier as it is in Canada. There are eight U.S. states spanning across American regions that have per capita incomes of $60,000 or more.[5] Alberta would still be the richest state (and like in Canada its per capita income would be about 50 percent higher than the national average), but American tax policy would not be singling it out.

- The only people besides NAFTA members who have more open access to America's consumer market are the constituent parts of the United States itself; in a world in which market access

---

4. At the time of this writing all permits for Keystone have already been approved except for a State Department waiver, which would not be needed if Alberta were a U.S. state.

5. Maryland, Alaska, New Jersey, Connecticut, Massachusetts, New Hampshire, Virginia, and Hawaii. The next one down is Texas.

will be nearly everything, that's an advantage that is impossible to ignore.

- The biggest advantage would be full inclusion in the American currency zone. Albertan inward investment and "export" income would be in the same currency as its outward tax payments and labor costs. Agriculture wouldn't struggle to survive. Manufacturing wouldn't face impossible price competition. Alberta could even get into refining and sell products like gasoline and jet fuel—also denominated in U.S. dollars—to its former countrymen for a deliciously fat profit.

Alberta as a U.S. state would not simply be rich—the richest in the Union, in fact—but would have a vibrantly well-financed and diverse economy that would put its former (and a lot of its newfound) countrymen to shame.

The question of course is, will the Albertans jump countries? The answer will be given only after the Albertans engage in a thorough debate about who they are culturally. Canadians have long defined themselves as the not-Americans, a sentiment that has traditionally been just as strong in Alberta as it has been in Ontario. But since the energy sector started

North American GDP Per Capita (2011)

	in thousand U.S. dollars*	as a % of Canadian average	as a % of American average
Alberta (richest Canadian province)	85	154%	177%
British Columbia	51	93%	107%
Ontario	53	96%	110%
Quebec	46	84%	96%
Canada (national average)	55	100%	115%
PEI (poorest Canadian province)	40	73%	84%
Delaware (richest U.S. state)	71	129%	148%
California	51	92%	105%
New York	60	109%	125%
U.S. (national average)	48	87%	100%
Texas	51	93%	107%
Mississippi (poorest U.S. state)	33	59%	68%

© 2014 Zeihan on Geopolitics   *$1.05 USD per CAN   Sources: U.S. Census, Statistics Canada booming in the 2000s, the Albertans have begun to add not-just-any-Canadians to that identity. These stirrings are distilled into the Wildrose Alliance Party, a once-fringe political group that espouses independence that has successfully transitioned to the mainstream. In the 2012 Albertan legislative elections, Wildrose captured seventeen of eighty-seven seats and established itself as the Albertan parliament's official opposition.

As time progresses, as energy becomes ever more important to Alberta, as Alberta's economic existence has less and less to do with Canada, and as the net financial cost for maintaining Canadian citizenship rises from today's $6,000 per citizen per year to something that might be considered onerous, the question of Albertan identity will become unavoidable—and the platform of Wildrose will move to the center of the Albertan political debate.

So what will the Albertans decide? I have no clue. Identity is the heart of who we are, and deciding to cut ties with one people and merge with another isn't remotely an easy decision to make, no matter how much it might make economic, financial, and even political sense. Just please bear in mind two things.

First, this discussion *will* happen. Economic and political trends are pushing Alberta out of the Canadian mainstream just as surely as they are sucking it dry.

Second, should the rest of Canada try to force Alberta to remain, secession is a viable option from a military point of view. Canada, as a country that does not share a land border with a hostile power, has never had a large army, and what it has had has been substantially downsized as part of a lengthy post–Cold War disarmament program. It is unlikely that the Canadian army, which numbers only fifty thousand soldiers, would be able to forcibly subdue four million Albertans, and even that assumes that Ottawa would be willing to turn its guns on its own, that the Quebecois would stand for the national army being used to subdue would-be secessionists, and that the Americans would stand idly by while a civil war flared on their northern border. Add in Canada's infrastructure bottlenecks—the Prairies are largely cut off from both British Columbia and the Ontario-Quebec core, doubly so in the winter—and Alberta would have far more than a fighting chance.

Should the Albertans take the plunge and replace the Maple Leaf with the Stars and Stripes, a rapid-fire sequence of events would unfold.

First, Canada would quickly dissolve as a country. British Columbia and Yukon would be separated from the rest of the Canadian territory.[6] They would have little choice but to either declare independence themselves or follow Alberta's lead. Saskatchewan too would be forced to leave Canada. After Alberta, Saskatchewan is the youngest and richest Canadian province. If Alberta managed to escape the fiscal drain of the Canadian system, all of Canada's financial needs would have to be met by the mere 1 million Saskatchewanians. If supporting Canada would damage Alberta's economy, it would eviscerate Saskatchewan's.

In the east, things would likely get very…interesting. Quebec prides itself on standing apart from the rest of Canada, and the idea that the Quebecois were not the ones to secede would undoubtedly stick in their craw so painfully that they too would consider secession. The fact that an Albertaless Canada could not hope to fund the compact would help push consideration into outright action. At that point, all that would remain of Canada is Ontario itself—now landlocked—perhaps Manitoba, and the Maritime provinces, which are already more tightly linked into the American economic system than the Ontarian. And the two regions would be separated completely by a no-longer-Canadian Quebec. Whether the rest of the (former) Canadian provinces actually applied for U.S. statehood beyond that point is irrelevant. There simply wouldn't be a "Canada" left anymore.

Scared New World: A World Without Canada

As of 2013 the total bilateral Canadian-American trade relationship was worth about $640 billion, not only making the two countries each other's largest trading partners, but making the bilateral relationship the largest in world history.

---

6. Technically they would still be connected via the Northwest Territories, but there is no meaningful infrastructure in the Territories linking the Pacific provinces to the Ontarian core.

Folding all that into the American domestic system would do more than simply increase Canadian purchasing power, or blunt the impact of aging Canadian demography, or eradicate any hint of American energy dependence upon the outside world, or do away with the barriers between Canadian and American hockey teams. At a stroke it would reduce the United States' involvement in the global system by some 2 percent of GDP and turn the expanded United States into an energy exporter. If the Americans are broadly disinterested in the wider world now, just imagine how inward focused American politics will be then.

At that point, the *only* piece of the broader international system that would reliably attract Americans' collective attention would be the only piece that composed a similar share of its trade-sourced GDP. That is the country we turn to next.

The Alberta Question: Ten Years On

Most Americans are barely aware of their neighbor in the Great White North, but even the most oblivious of us would notice if a Canadian province seceded and applied to join the States. While I stand by all the facts and analysis in *Accidental*'s Alberta chapter, Canada remains intact. The onus is on me to explain why.

Let me lead with the punch line: I'm the most positive on all things Canadian that I have been in my entire professional career. Most of the "normal" problems remain, but the same things that have proven my initial forecast incorrect have also put a slow but steady breeze in Canada's sails.

From my point of view a few wildly variant issues are in play.

Let's begin with the Albertans themselves.

The rise of the independence-minded Wildrose Party proved so rapid that it... there's no other word here to use... *broke* Albertan provincial politics. In 2015 elections, Wildrose did so well that it split the provincial vote with the Progressive Conservatives, who had run strong majority governments in Alberta since the early 1970s. Applied to Alberta's first-past-the-post electoral system, Wildrose got their most seats ever, the Progressive Conservatives lost 80 percent of their holdings, and Albertans woke up to find the leftist(ish) New Democratic Party to be in command of Canada's most conservative province.

After a few odd... minutes of NDP leftism proving wildly inappropriate, nearly every spat between Edmonton and Ottawa picked up where it had left off, just with a different party leading the head-butting. But with the rightish parties out of power, any discussion of secession was firmly off the table.

By the 2019 elections, the Progressive Conservatives and Wildrose had agreed to join forces into the United Conservative Party, and easily swept to power. A feat repeated in May 2022. The year 2019 saw the new party and its new government relearn a great deal of institutional knowledge. Secession was once again in the air, but so too was a direct attempt to broker a better deal for Alberta. Between the NDP interruption and the UCP needing to relearn the ropes, eight years passed. Things had changed.

First, Canada. In Ottawa it had sunk in that Canada's demographic future was dark, and so policies were aggressively shifted. Initially under Conservative Stephen Harper and later under Liberal Justin Trudeau,

Canada threw open its doors to immigration, this time with express efforts targeting would-be immigrants in their twenties and thirties, rather than the forty- and fifty-somethings who had been the bulk of the previous immigrant diet. A decade on, Canada has welcomed just shy of 3 *million* new citizens to a country that at the time of my original writing only had 35 million Canucks. That doesn't end the danger to Canada's future, but Ottawa has proven that it is at least possible to *manage* the threat. Such successful management has reduced somewhat Canada's financial dependence upon all things Albertan, and so taken a bit of the sting out of the cash transfers from Alberta to Canada as a whole. Alberta is still getting screwed, but not with quite as much gusto.

Second, the United States. The issue here was, in a word: Trump. It's one thing to sign on to American statehood when it is helmed by a disinterested Barack Obama or a distracted George W. Bush. But when the leader of your maybe-new association is the somewhat—can I call him "colorful" without pissing anyone off?—Donald Trump, one tends to revisit one's base assumptions about joining Team America.

Third, the American aura shifted dramatically between 2021 and 2023. In part it was the electoral jump from Trump to a more "traditional" Joe Biden. In part, China's deepening aggressiveness, oppression, and outright genocides have made countries reevaluate their economic linkages, which almost by default means giving the United States another look. But mostly it is Russia's invasion of Ukraine that has led many Western governments to the uncomfortable conclusion that even if America's military-first foreign policy isn't the "correct" way to go, it certainly was proving its contemporary usefulness. Few countries' attitudes altered as much as Canada's. Narrowing the gap, at least in public diplomacy, between Ottawa and Washington reduced the Albertans' room to maneuver.

Finally, there's the issue of national culture. When I've spoken in Canada on the Alberta question, it should come as absolutely zero surprise that I get pushback. But I've always found the nature of the pushback somewhat odd. It isn't a "we wouldn't let them do that," or "your numbers are wrong," or "they don't have the guts," or "I'm not sure we will do that," but instead—and this sentiment holds across the country, most certainly *including* in Alberta—"that would be rude."

Canadian politeness is *not* an act.

CHAPTER 13

⬤━━━━━⬤

The North American Drug War

Canada, of course, is only half of the Americans' inner circle, and evolutions on America's southern border are even stranger than what is going on in the Great White North. Like most other countries, Mexico is under assault by the three trends that will make up the new world: shifting trade patterns, inverting demographics, and spasming energy patterns. In Mexico's case the resultant changes are almost completely positive, but there is still a dark side—and it will not be contained within Mexico's borders.

The Geography of a Failed State

Mexican geography is, well, wretched. From an economic and political point of view, the country is far more fractured than even what the Canadians have had to contend with. Mexico has no navigable rivers whatsoever. Whereas Canada is too cold, Mexico is too hot: Much of its territory is fully tropical or hard desert. Worse, nearly all of Mexico, whether temperate, jungle, or desert, is mountainous as well. Cut any way, this is a bad place to start down the road to civilization and stability.

Let's begin with Mexico's tropical nature. Jungles are the worst biome from an economic development point of view:

- The unrelenting heat and humidity of jungle territories provides an endless array of biological diversity, including an endless array of diseases and disease vectors. Some diseases, like malaria and leprosy, are only rarely fatal and simply enervate all infected, imposing chronic costs in the form of lost labor productivity. Some, like cholera, can sweep through an area with terrifying speed, infecting thousands of people a day. Some, like rotavirus and dengue fever, are so deadly to children that they can impact overall demographic profiles. Others, like yellow fever and Ebola, are lethal to anyone unlucky enough to cross paths with them. What they all have in common is that they—and the vectors, mostly insects, that transmit them—thrive in the tropics. The seasonal frosts and freezes of temperate climes not only inhibit the spreads of various pathogens, but also tend to kill off the insects that carry them. People living in the tropics have no such luck.

- High heat and humidity exacts a constant toll on infrastructure, from roads to buildings. Maintenance costs tend toward the extreme because builders must choose between having to replace everything more often, or using different (and more expensive) materials in construction. Then there is the simple fact that the basic technologies of modern road building—the use of heavy machinery and the drying of concrete—are rather hard to manage in a downpour. Asphalt softens on a hot day, and the tropics have hot to spare.

- Tropical soils are very thin and shallow, only retaining their fertility when they are part of a natural biome. That fertility comes from the constant recycling of a jungle's myriad plant species, and the process of clearing land for agriculture guts the cycle. Former jungles and rainforest lands, therefore, require constant fertilization to maintain agricultural production, even for tropical crops like bananas and yams. And if surrounding jungle lands are not cleared as well, then heavy pesticide use is a must, raising costs further even as water quality declines. Often the tropics boast higher annual production totals per acre than temperate climes because the heat and sun of the tropics frequently support more than one crop cycle a year, but that increased output comes at the cost of radically increased inputs.

So more foodstuffs, yes, but the overall production is generally among the least efficient in the world. There are very few places on earth where those farming the former jungle are not mired in poverty, and Mexico is no exception.

Counteracting the effects of its tropical climate is Mexico's first challenge. The Mexicans addressed this by going uphill. Higher elevation mitigates heat and humidity, soil fertility has higher potential, and the cooler temperatures and thinner air work against diseases and their vectors. Most of Mexico's population and all but four of its major cities are nestled in the multitude of plateaus, highland basins, and mountain valleys throughout the country's midsection, where the elevation lifts the land out of the tropics into a more temperate environment. But that simply replaces the tropical challenge with a mountain challenge, which in many ways is just as onerous.

Mountains by definition don't sport large tracts of flat land. There is no Mexican equivalent of the American Midwest that has the ability to generate scads of capital or support massive populations. Unlike other locations in North America, *not one* Mexican urban region has a hinterland. Chicago and St. Louis have the entire Midwest, New York City the Hudson valley and Long Island, Orlando all of central Florida, and the cities of the coastal Southeast can draw upon the Piedmont. But when one leaves Mexico's highland valleys, one either hits deserts or jungles or mountains or—more likely—mountainous desert or mountainous jungle. Each mountain valley is limited in size and is more or less on its own. Any infrastructure that benefits one region cannot be extended to synergize with another. It must be rebuilt in each and every region without contributing to a greater whole. Mexico isn't split into five sections like Canada, but instead dozens, most of which cannot independently generate meaningful economies of scale. By far Mexico's largest highland enclave is the greater Mexico City metropolitan area, home to one in five Mexicans and built on landfill. It isn't so much a good location as it is the best that the Mexican geography has on offer. Beyond Mexico City, only ten Mexican metro areas pass the 1 million mark,[1] and none of them break

1. The United States has fifty-five, fifty-nine if you split Dallas–Fort Worth, Minneapolis–St. Paul, and San Francisco–San Jose, and include San Juan.

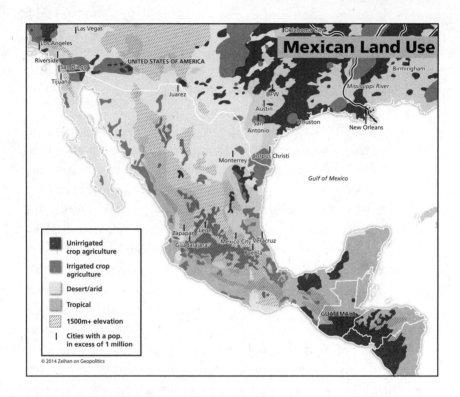

Mexican Land Use

Legend:
- Unirrigated crop agriculture
- Irrigated crop agriculture
- Desert/arid
- Tropical
- 1500m+ elevation
- Cities with a pop. in excess of 1 million

© 2014 Zeihan on Geopolitics

5 million.[2] The economies of scale, abundant capital, and ease of development that the Americans take for granted—and that make industrialization possible—are all absent in Mexico.

Transport—always the difficulty of the human condition—is more onerous in mountains than in any other terrain. Sharp elevation changes generate swift currents, meaning that not one of Mexico's rivers is navigable, naturally or otherwise. The Mexico core region of Mexico City sits at an elevation of about eight thousand feet despite being only two hundred miles inland.[3] Even when Mexico's disassociated regions manage to construct some local infrastructure, links between those regions require tackling topographic verticality that is painfully daunting not just to build but also to operate. Organic consumption growth is nearly impossible because what little capital there is must be dedicated to infrastructure.

---

2. The United States has ten.

3. In comparison, Minneapolis sits at only one-tenth the elevation despite being seven times the distance inland.

But even then basic internal distribution is nearly impossible because of the extreme operating costs. It is a recipe for disconnected poverty and fractured, ineffectual government.

Such difficult terrain skews what development that can happen into decidedly inegalitarian directions. This isn't the American riverine Midwest with low barriers to entry and cheap long-distance transport options. In Mexico, the only people who can make a serious go are those who *already* have capital to spare—those who could afford to build the expensive road/rail necessary to link a middling patch of useful land to the coast, those who could afford to pay workers for months or even years to clear and fertilize land so that it might one day support crops. Most Mexican territory requires irrigation, further increasing the gap between those with capital and those without. Even the climate works against economic liberty. Tropical plantation crops like bananas and coffee require a great deal of capital to establish, and a mammoth amount of unskilled labor throughout the crops' life cycles to tend, harvest, and ship. In comparison, temperate crops such as wheat, barley, and corn require little labor between planting and harvest, and the actual harvesting process is fairly light on labor. You can machine-harvest (or even scythe and thresh in pre-industrial times) a field of wheat in a very short period of time, but each bunch of bananas has to be harvested and carefully stored by hand.

When an oligarch uses his money to build a road and a plantation and maybe even a port, that oligarch finds himself quite literally the ruler of all he sees. He has applied his wealth to make something out of nothing, and he is well aware that no one who works for him could have possibly done the same. He has little interest in sharing his investments with anyone else, even another oligarch. To do so would dilute the absolute economic and political power that he holds in his own personal fiefdom. Perhaps Mexico's biggest tragedy is that when—against very expensive odds—someone does manage to make a portion of Mexico functional, that someone has every interest in resisting contributing to a broader regional or national effort to replicate the success. To do so would jeopardize not only control over the sunk investment but also the privileged economic and political position that comes with it. Whereas the United States was settled by the poor who became rich, Mexico was settled by the rich who commanded—and command still—the poor.

These factors—low capital generation from a lack of cheap transport, high capital demand from infrastructure, limited land due to topography, a political/economic system geared toward regional jefes and their plantations—sharply limit the ability of the country to urbanize, much less industrialize. Mexico's capital scarcity and extreme capital needs mean that much of the money that will be used for infrastructure development will have to come from foreign sources. And in a quick logic chain threading from geography to population patterns to transport needs to debt markets, you now understand how Mexico's regular bouts of debt crisis are both endemic and inevitable.

And then there is its government.

Meaningful central authority has a prerequisite: the ability to reach all portions of the territory. Not only is that far from a given in Mexico, but much of what transport infrastructure exists is beholden to the needs of the oligarchs. Its use is not automatically available to the government. Making matters worse, the oligarchs have tended to develop the most useful patches of land; in Mexico's too-dry mountainous north or its too-wet mountainous south there is little of economic interest, and thus little oligarch activity and little infrastructure. Upwards of half of Mexican territory, concentrated in the far north and far south, exists in a sort of Hobbesian limbo, where anyone who wishes to exert sufficient resources can make his will a temporary reality.

Mexico's borderlands are zones so lightly populated that local authorities cannot police them, and they have so little infrastructure that national authorities cannot reach them on a meaningful time scale. Even in periods of plenty, these areas will *always* be insufficiently patrolled and so will *always* be smuggling zones and can never be secured in the way that the Americans define the term.

In essence, Mexico lacks the geographic characteristics to be a successful state. Geography condemns it to be home to a poor, drastically unequal, underdeveloped society riven by regional and class-based cleavages that no degree of local investment or understanding can ever heal. The only other significant country in the world that was dealt as bad a geographic hand as Mexico is perhaps Afghanistan. If not for a few lucky oil discoveries around 1900, Mexico would have likely faded into oblivion long ago.

Yet Success Anyway: The Four Factors

But as wretched as Mexico seems from time to time, no serious observer would say that it is even remotely as bad as Afghanistan. The reason for that is quite simple: It is next to the United States, the global consuming superpower. Somewhat ironically, Mexico's weakness has become the key factor in ensuring its success. The sheer difference between the two countries' topographies—America's capital richness versus Mexico's capital poverty, America's ease of development versus Mexico's constant struggle—ensures that Mexican labor will always be both cheap and underutilized, making Mexican labor perennially attractive to anyone wanting to service America's nearly bottomless demand. In that differential lies the core of Mexico's economic success.

In the next couple of decades a shift of circumstances will turn Mexico from the United States' (extremely) junior partner to something significantly more. Four factors are at work:

1. Chinese Labor Costs Have Skyrocketed

No country lost out to China's emergence onto the international scene as much as Mexico. Prior to China's joining the WTO in 2001, Mexico was the primary source of textiles and low-end manufactured goods to the United States. Despite China's (many) internal weaknesses, its ability to subsidize its inputs and outputs and marry them to low-cost labor in an environment of centralized political control allowed it to undercut countries like Mexico that relied on mid-cost labor and proximity.

But those days are over. Leaving aside the issues of China's political stability (or lack thereof), ability to continue subsidizing its output (or lack thereof), and ability to manipulate the international economic system (or lack thereof), it has simply run out of cheap labor. Since 2002, Chinese labor has increased in cost by a factor of six to about $3 per hour. In relative terms Chinese labor has increased from being one-quarter as expensive as Mexican labor to one-quarter more expensive. Considering that Mexico already has far superior transport access to the United States, and that there is a decades-old tradition of collaboration between American management and Mexican oligarchs, the numbers certainly are positioned for a labor-cost-driven onshoring to Mexico.

2. American Shale Is Supercharging the Mexican Electricity System

Due to shale, the Americans have a massive glut in their natural gas system. Unlike crude oil, natural gas is, well, a gas, and the transportation of gases is difficult. There are only two means of getting it out of a supersaturated market. The first is to cool it into a liquid (about minus 260 degrees Fahrenheit) and then ship it to someone who has the infrastructure capacity to safely return it to gaseous form. This liquefied natural gas (LNG) process is the only way to ship the stuff across an ocean. However, there are also many regulatory steps involved, and as recent energy politics in the United States have amply demonstrated, gaining national approval for a transnational energy infrastructure project is somewhat difficult—not to mention that freezing natural gas into liquid form is as expensive as it sounds. While dozens of projects have applied for regulatory approval, only a small handful have achieved the necessary permits at the local, state, and national levels, and construction has only begun on one.[4] That leaves a *lot* of shale natural gas stranded in the American interior, practically begging for a market.

But one of the great open secrets of the American energy complex is that it is already legal to export natural gas, so long as it is by *pipe* and so long as it goes to *Mexico*. As of the beginning of the shale boom, there were already nine natural gas pipelines crossing the border, supplying Mexico with nearly one-quarter of its natural gas needs, about 1 billion cubic feet per day (Bcf/d). Since the shale boom, however, work has begun on three major corridors as well as expansions throughout the export system in order to marry the ultra-cheap American natural gas to the Mexican power network and labor market. Exports doubled to 2 Bcf/d between 2010 and 2013, but the real growth will come in 2016. At that point several new trunk lines will begin operation, allowing the export of U.S. energy to heretofore unreached Mexican regions up to and including the Mexico City core. Mexican imports from the United States are expected to hit *ten times* their 2010 levels.

Nearly all of that natural gas is planned to be used for electricity

---

4. Cheniere's Sabine Pass facility began construction in 2013 and is expected to begin operations in 2016.

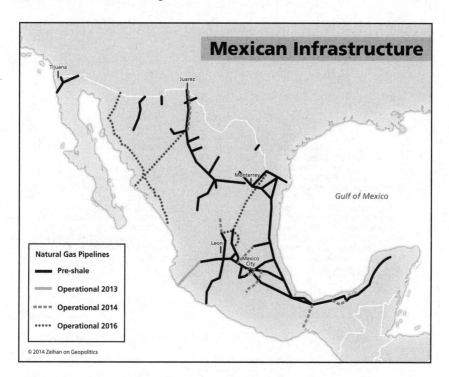

Mexican Infrastructure

Tijuana
Juarez
Monterrey
Gulf of Mexico
Leon
Mexico City

Natural Gas Pipelines
— Pre-shale
Operational 2013
Operational 2014
Operational 2016

© 2014 Zeihan on Geopolitics

generation. Chinese competition aside, the biggest hurdle that has faced Mexican industry in recent years is reliable power supplies. The surge in shale gas into Mexico has already greatly mitigated that problem, and within a (very) few short years Mexico's chronic rolling power outages will be a thing of the past. For manufacturers, whether Mexican or American, that removes one of Mexico's chronic limitations on industrial development.

3. Mexican Demography Generates a Large Market and a Larger Labor Pool

Mexico also has a young population. Normally this would be somewhat of a problem for a country at Mexico's stage of development: A capital-shy demographic combined with a capital-shy geography could forever trap Mexico in underdevelopment. In fact, that has been the trap Mexico has lived in ever since independence. But the positive aspects of a young population still apply. Mexico's young adults are hungry for goods and property. They just need paychecks. Luckily, their large number proportional to the overall population keeps their labor costs low and keeps foreign entities eager to invest in Mexico for goods production. While those investors

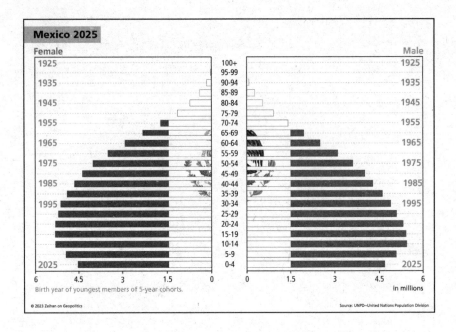

may have initially been interested in selling those goods into the American market, there is every reason to service the local population as well—doubly so since Mexico's lack of ability to self-industrialize means that internal goods supplies are so limited.[5]

If anything, Mexican demographics are even more favorable toward consumption than they look at first glance. Mexico's current demographic profile also shows a characteristic somewhat different from the normal pyramid. About twenty-five years ago, coinciding with higher labor participation rates brought upon by NAFTA, Mexican families started to shrink in size—not so much that Mexico started to undergo the demographic collapse we are seeing in Europe, or even the tightening that the

---

5. In the early years, the Americans took brutal advantage of this with the Santa Fe Trail. American manufactures were shipped to Santa Fe (a Mexican city) in order to build economic dependency upon the United States throughout the areas we now think of as the American Southwest. (At the time the Americans founded the trail, Mexico was still an imperial Spanish territory.) When the Mexican-American War occurred just thirty-five years later, most of the sparsely populated territory was so deeply within the American economic and cultural orbit that its inhabitants assisted the American war effort. The result was the capture of what is contemporary California, New Mexico, and Arizona and their transformation into American territories.

Americans are experiencing, but enough to turn the bottom portion of Mexico's population pyramid into a chimney.

Population chimneys certainly pose long-term challenges as they will in time lead to smaller (and much older) populations. But even if the rate of decline in Mexican birth rates continues unabated for another three decades, this will not be a financial problem for the Mexicans until 2050. Until then, the country has an ever larger proportion of its population in the critical twenty-to-thirty-nine-year-old age group—that's the people who are most likely to move around Mexico in order to secure work, who are most likely to attract foreign investment to generate exports for the American market, who are most likely to attract foreign investment seeking to satisfy the local market, and the cohort who are most likely to consume and so generate local growth. The mere existence of this group is sure to generate strong, sustained consumption- and foreign-direct-investment-led growth across Mexico.

The clipping of the pyramid's base, which means that Mexico has fewer children than in years past, has one other impact. It means that Mexico's young adults have greater amounts of disposable income (they are not raising as many kids), freeing up Mexico's young adults to spend just like the Europeans did during the 1990s and 2000s. However, since the inward investment reaching Mexico is foreign-directed and pouring into infra-structure and industrial plant rather than simple credit, the Mexicans will walk out on the other side of this process *being* richer and not being in debt rather than simply *feeling* richer and being in debt like the Southern Euro-peans. Collectively this makes Mexico one of only a handful of countries in an increasingly demographically inverted world that can still rely upon domestically driven growth *and* channel foreign capital in a productive manner.

4. The Drug War Has Improved Mexico's Economic Prospects

It is something of a grim irony that the drug war is perhaps the best thing that has happened to Mexico from an economic point of view. Now, *that* requires a bit of explanation.

Bear in mind that it is the differential between Mexican and Ameri-can labor costs that provides Mexico with economic opportunities that its geography would otherwise deny it. That differential is the Mexican economy's lifeblood. Nothing pushes down Mexican labor costs—increasing the differential—like a drug war raging throughout the country. In fact, the more violent the war, the lower Mexican labor costs, and so the greater the Mexican/American differential and the more attractive Mexico becomes to foreign direct investment seeking an advantage in the American market.

Obviously the war's security challenges pose any number of problems, but the drug war is not raging everywhere. Mexican drug violence is deep and endemic, but it follows the conflicts of the politics of the cartel wars. Violence is only the rule where the cartels find themselves competing for the same transport routes and choke points, such as the plazas where they can smuggle drugs across the border into the United States. Outside of those danger zones, Mexico is just another developing country, and far from being random, its dangers can be planned for and mitigated. So long as the drug war rages, the economics of integration with the American market only improve.

Taken together, this mix of local and regional geographies and local and global demographics turns Mexico from a basket case to a near-best case. Because of Mexico's proximity to the United States, it is typically one of the world's top destinations for foreign direct investment (FDI),[6] enabling Mexico to sidestep the very capital problem that will soon be gutting the vast bulk of the developing world. Put together, Mexico is poised to be the fastest-growing economy in the world for the next generation.

---

6. Portfolio investors, in contrast, find Mexico a frustrating, frightening, and even outright disgusting place to operate because the oligarchs' territoriality persists in the financial space. Oligarchs control their own banks, which finance their own projects in the regions they control. If they should find themselves willing to reach out for extra capital, they are far more likely to attempt to partner with a foreigner who would then be beholden to their political, economic, social, labor, and land connections than they would be to seek a loan from an institution run by another oligarch. As such, Mexico's stock markets are woefully underdeveloped and, in part because of the country's sharp left-right divide, overregulated. Barring changes that to date the Mexican system has proven unable to contemplate, much less initiate, the future of foreign involvement in Mexico will be the same as the past: direct investments in physical plant, infrastructure, and labor and very little involvement in Mexican stock markets, bond markets, or banks.

The Nature of the Border

Americans think of the border with Mexico as wild, untamed, lawless—
a drug-ridden, post-apocalyptic wasteland. Considering the inability
of the Mexican government to patrol, much less control, its borderland,
there is some truth to American concerns. But that image of the border
ignores the depth of the economic and cultural relationship between the
two countries. Even before one considers that Mexico is about to experience economic breakout, Mexico's proximity to the United States has not
only landed it with the status of one of the world's major economies, but is
about to make it America's *greatest ever* economic partner.

Consider the following:

- As of 2014, the United States exports to Mexico over 2 billion
  cubic feet of natural gas and nearly 1 million bpd of refined
  fuels, while Mexico ships 1 million bpd of crude north. By 2020,
  American shipments of natural gas will at least quadruple, making it the largest bilateral energy relationship in human history.
- As of 2013, some $510 billion in goods were exchanged across
  the border, making Mexico the Americans' third largest trading partner (second largest with services included). Bilateral
  trade will likely increase to $650 billion by 2020, making it
  rival U.S.-Canada trade for the largest bilateral economic relationship in human history.
- As of 2014, some 350 million *legal* border crossings were made.
  This already makes the border the most crossed border in
  human history, *before* considering illegal crossings. Projections
  indicate that legal crossings will hit a half billion annually by
  2020.
- Mexican failure leads to integration with the United States.
  Poverty, government corruption, drug-related violence, environmental catastrophe, and weak infrastructure all increase
  internal Mexican labor mobility and decrease Mexican labor
  costs. The bigger the labor cost differential with the United
  States, the more economic integration between Mexico and the
  United States.

- American success leads to integration with Mexico. Wealth, transparent government, improved local security, higher labor and health standards, and strong infrastructure all increase American consumption and American labor costs. Again, the bigger the labor cost differential with Mexico, the more economic integration between Mexico and the United States.

Acceptance of these facts changes the nature of the internal American debates about Mexico. The problem isn't so much that the Americans can't decide if they want to integrate with Mexico or not. The Americans are *already* integrated with Mexico. The issue is that they haven't decided how to manage the relationship. Side effects of that as yet unsettled relationship are an illegal immigrant community of about 7 million Mexicans and another 1.5 million Central Americans,[7] plus the tens of billions of dollars of drugs that are smuggled into the United States. With issues of this size it is worth spending a little time discussing the nature of the border, mostly because most of the mooted solutions that exist in the American political arena are at best doomed to fail, with most of them being counterproductive.

Let's leave aside the above arguments about robust economic interaction and the fact that cultural integration is already well under way with roughly one-ninth to one-sixth of U.S. citizens (it depends who is doing the math) identifying themselves as having roots in Mexico. Let's ignore all the economic arguments about how Mexican immigrants (legal or otherwise) do jobs that Americans don't want, limit inflation, and serve very real and positive roles in the American labor market. Let's ignore the moral and legal implications of expunging the United States' illegal communities. Let's focus on the border itself. I've already said that Mexico—even in the best of times—cannot secure the border.

Well, neither can the United States. The U.S.-Mexico border is roughly two thousand miles long. Two thousand miles sounds like a significant

---

7. The Central American states of Honduras, Nicaragua, El Salvador, Belize, and Costa Rica are in essence Mexico without the greater Mexico City region—city-states cursed with a territory that is impossible to develop. Panama would be the same if it were not for the canal (and drug smuggling money) providing regular financial infusions into an otherwise worthless topography.

distance. It isn't significant. It's *massive*. That is double the length of the European Cold War border—a border that could only be sealed by turning the broader region into a national security zone under military rule.

There has also been no small amount of talk of being tougher on immigration. This ignores basic human nature. The U.S. government is far more capable than Mexico's. Somewhat ironically, the American capacity to deport large volumes of people is part of the structural and organizational strength that so draws immigrants (although I think it is obvious that the specific act of deportation isn't something that would-be immigrants are all that fond of). Even stronger illegal migration penalties would not have much of an impact. Mexicans and Central Americans are fleeing not just poverty, but also the insecurity of the drug war and various Central American juntas. So unless U.S. policy is going to be to shoot people on sight in the border zone, the Departments of Immigration and Homeland Security just aren't capable of counterintimidation of anything like the environments the would-be immigrants are running from.

So if the border cannot be sealed, if the allure of the United States cannot be dampened, and if policy failures in Mexico will only enhance integration, the United States is simply stuck with a large illegal Mexican and Central American community. Considering the lack of viable options in American public discourse, what does the presence of 8.5 million illegal Hispanic immigrants mean?

The North American Drug War

Most have probably heard about the horrors of the Mexican drug wars, where kidnappings, assassinations, mass murders, public body dumpings, and beheadings are regrettably all too common. Many have heard the names of the various cartels vying for supremacy—the Zetas, the Sinaloa, the Knights Templar, and the Gulf (among others). The Mexican government's own estimate for drug-war-related deaths has now topped fifty thousand.

What is less understood is the link between illegal narcotics and illegal immigration. It is probably not what you think.

Because illegal immigrants are undocumented, they have difficulty gaining access to the basic pieces of modern society, including
identification such as driver's licenses and financial access such as bank
accounts. That has a far more damning impact than it may seem at first
blush. With limited access to the banking system, illegals operate in the
cash economy—they are far more likely to have significant quantities of
cash on their person or in their home at any given time. Since illegals fear
being discovered and deported, they often do not contact law enforcement when such inevitable attacks happen. In the modern age of credit
cards and PayPal, that makes illegals a far more lucrative target for robbers
and muggers than even rich Caucasians. There is a term for areas where
people who live outside of normal social support networks exist: ghettos.
Unique among American immigrant communities, Mexican and Central
American illegals live in ghettos. This would be a serious social problem in
need of addressing under any circumstance, but new circumstances have
pushed it from the serious to the critical.

The drug war of 2014 is considerably different from the drug war of
the twentieth century. Moving products is cheaper by water, regardless of
whether the product is legal or not. As such, most interstate trade in illegal narcotics—just like interstate trade in any other product—originally
traveled by water. In the United States, this made the port city of Miami
the premier entry point for illegal narcotics. Small fleets of vessels would
swarm from Colombia and Venezuela to Miami, and from there the drugs
would percolate throughout the country. The 1980s hit TV show *Miami
Vice* wasn't just a gripping drama, but was a little bit of geopolitics distilled into televised form: local law enforcement attempting to stem a
transcontinental smuggling effort backed by untold billions of dollars on
both ends.

As a maritime power, however, maritime interception is something
that the Americans are very good at. Once the Americans figured out what
to look for, they were able to improve everything from port security to
Coast Guard patrols, sharply limiting maritime (and airborne) shipments
first into Miami, then all of Florida, and in time all coastal approaches. By
the year 2000, maritime smuggling routes may not have been severed, but
they had become so fraught with danger that there were no longer viable

methods for transporting the bulk of the illicit narcotics the Americans so craved.[8]

But one of the quirks of narcotic economics is that addicts at the point of sale are not particularly price-sensitive. The Americans' success at blocking maritime and air routes forced the drug flows into more expensive land routes. The sonar and low-elevation radar that proved so effective at monitoring featureless water and keeping illicit shipments away from American shores proved largely useless at sealing the two-thousand-mile-long U.S.-Mexican border, and so the drug flow shifted from *Miami Vice* to something…else.

One of the (many) reasons that water transport is so much cheaper is that it is so much less complicated. There are no middlemen in the ocean. No towns to navigate. No regulatory agencies that make their homes on the waves. You leave port. You sail. You can sail around anything you don't like the look of. You enter port. And that is it. On land there are physical borders to cross. You must follow existing infrastructure. You must deal with local regulations, customs, and law enforcement at a plethora of stops along the way. But all this adds more than simply cost. It also ensures that the shippers become intimately involved in every aspect of their transport routes. And should shippers using two different routes find themselves operating at the same bottleneck—say a mountain valley where their routes merge, or an international border crossing—competition erupts.

In the case of Mexico and drugs, these features generate two results.

---

8. As of 2014, Miami is still a major point of entry for South American cocaine. Most of it comes through Venezuela and up the Lesser Antilles chain to the Dominican Republic and Haiti before making the jump to Puerto Rico (a U.S. territory) or Miami. But strong American and Cuban patrols—drug interdiction cooperation between the United States and Cuba is perhaps the highlight of the two countries' relations—prevent this flow from being more than small volumes smuggled in the holds of larger vessels or pleasure craft, resulting in much higher overhead costs and much lower volumes per shipment. This route is a faint shadow of what it used to be in its *Miami Vice* heyday. Long gone are the days when small vessels packed to the gills with cocaine could simply sail into Miami Harbor or land in or near the Everglades. Plenty of South American drugs are still shipped by water and air *toward* the United States, just not all the way *to* the United States. Most make landfall in Central America or southern Mexico before joining the cartels' land-bound supply chains.

First, they drive up the cost of the cocaine that ultimately reaches the United States. While drug smugglers aren't exactly sticklers for filing statistical data, the Department of Justice estimates that the Mexican land portion of the cocaine smuggling routes adds about $10,000 to the cost of a kilo of cocaine—about $10 a gram—as compared to 1980s seaborne routes. That is a lot of money being used to employ, corrupt, bribe, and/or heavily arm a great many people across the length and breadth of Mexico's many smuggling byways. The land-bound nature of the smuggling routes introduces so many increases to the price of cocaine that it is all but inevitable that large, well-funded organizations will arise from the trade. Best guess is that the Mexican portion of the drug supply chain has an annual turnover in excess of $60 billion, roughly 4–5 percent of Mexico's (legal) GDP. For comparison, the U.S. automotive industry comprises about 1.2 percent of U.S. GDP; the total sales of Walmart—America's largest corporation—are about 2.5 percent.

Second, it also guarantees that these well-connected, well-funded organizations have a *lot* to fight over. We know that competition as the Mexican drug war or the cartel wars. It pits the various cartels against one another, battling for control of key nodes throughout northern and southern Mexico, up to and including the major border crossings to the United States. Not just the drug war, but the very existence of the cartels themselves would have been impossible if American success in blocking maritime drug shipments had not forced the drug flows inland.

A generation after *Miami Vice*, the cartels are doing what any major corporation that controls neither the source nor destination of its product would do: diversify. First, diversify horizontally into similar "industries" in which their assets and skill sets are applicable. Things like robberies, cargo theft, and kidnappings are all now in the cartels' collective portfolio. Most notably, marijuana production and smuggling in Mexico were not part of most of the cartels' initial prerogatives. Now they are.

Second, diversify up the supply chain to take over direct control of drug production. As of 2014, the cartels already de facto control most of the cocaine gathering and production networks in Peru and Bolivia, the largest and third largest sources of raw coca in the world. The cartels are even chewing away at the Colombian supply system: In a classic case of who-do-you-cheer-for, the cartels are going head-to-head with many of

Colombia's infamous cocaine-generating entities, up to and including the FARC.

Third and most relevant to this discussion, the cartels are expanding *down* the supply chain. Long ago the cartels mastered the craft of border crossings. Now they have taken the next logical steps and are getting into retail distribution in the major American cocaine and marijuana distribution hubs. Obviously, border communities such as San Diego, El Paso, and Brownsville were the first targeted, but the cartels are also painfully active in places as far from the border as New York City. A particularly aggressive effort is even under way in British Columbia to seize control of the Canadian province's marijuana network from the Hells Angels. The cartels have also been very successful in utilizing American public lands, especially in the California state and national parks system, to grow marijuana in large quantities closer to market (not to mention on the cleared side of American customs).

Wherever the cartels go, they come into competition with local American crime networks—oftentimes inner-city gangs—for control of the local distribution systems. But while the premeditated violence of America's local inner-city gangs is no joke, it pales compared to the casual violence of the transnational drug groups that were forged in the culture of the Mexican cartel wars. Add in superior weapons, weapons training, and control over the actual supply of the narcotics, and the Mexicans are rapidly overwhelming—and in some cases co-opting—their former American sales affiliates.

Finally, there is the illegal immigration nexus. The cartels have found in each major American city one additional—critical—ingredient that has allowed them to put down roots deeper and spread faster than they could in South America or even among their own countrymen: America's Hispanic ghettos. The American method for "managing" its illegal population has created a large community in each major city that lives outside the protection of local law enforcement and financial monitoring. The cops' patrols are less effective without the illegals' active participation. The Fed has no bank data to work from. The illegals speak the same language—and often come from the same country—as the cartels' front men. It is a community setup that is perfect for the cartels to recruit from and ultimately control. As with the value of drugs, data as to the size of cartel penetration

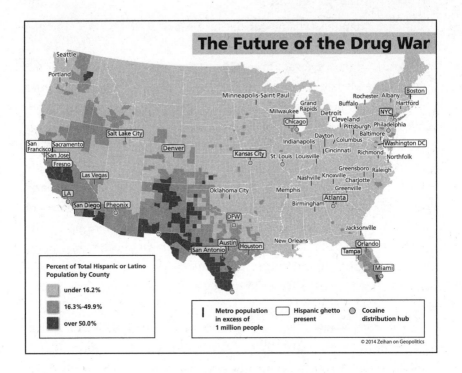

The Future of the Drug War

Percent of Total Hispanic or Latino
Population by County

- under 16.2%
- 16.3%-49.9%
- over 50.0%

Metro population in excess of 1 million people | Hispanic ghetto present | Cocaine distribution hub

© 2014 Zeihan on Geopolitics

into the United States is somewhat limited. But the Department of Justice estimates that as of 2013, the cartels are already active in over a thousand U.S. municipalities that include multitudes of communities in the greater Los Angeles, Dallas–Fort Worth, Houston, Atlanta, Kansas City, Denver, Chicago, Detroit, and Baltimore metro regions.

The cartels' expansion into the United States proper is still in its early stages, so at present their conflicts with American gangs are being swallowed up by the normal noise of gang-on-gang violence. But in the not too distant future, the cartels will have (easily) won those battles. And if the cartels are willing to go to war with each other for transport routes through Mexico, it is difficult to imagine that they'll pull punches when attempting to secure the cash cow of American demand from each other.

Scared New World: Something to Be Scared About

This is the point where I think I'm supposed to say something dramatic, like "the drug war will be with us soon," only that's not the point: The Mexican drug war has *already* expanded north of the border. It is no longer a question of prevention, but mitigation. I normally hesitate to suggest any courses of action. Geopolitical and demographic forces are so rooted in the unchangeable that political action often generates little but noise. But in this case a course of action does present itself, even if that "solution" is politically problematic.

Border security is at best a (painfully expensive) patch. The answer—I think—lies in legalization. Not of drugs,[9] but of immigration. Opening of the border with the issuance of worker and travel permits would with the speed of a printer transform America's Hispanic ghettos into areas where people have legitimate identification and store their money in banks like everyone else. Cooperation with police would no longer be perceived as a sharp negative, and the Federal Reserve's anti–money laundering tools would suddenly have data to work with. Most of all, the cartels would lose their fertile rest-and-recruitment grounds north of the border. Legalization wouldn't solve everything, but it is the single biggest step that the United States could take.

Should the Americans, however, choose to leave the border and ghettos as is, they face the dawn of the most horrible conflict they have ever fought. Unlike Vietnam or Iraq, the next chapter of the drug war will be fought at home. More than China, more than Russia, more than Iran, it is expansion of the Mexican drug war to all of North America that is emerging as the single greatest geopolitical threat to the American way of life.

---

9. What studies I've examined indicate that legalizing illegal drugs is probably a financial wash. In most studies any money saved in terms of law enforcement would most likely be lost in terms of higher health care costs and lost worker productivity. Additionally, most studies assume that a legal market for narcotics would eliminate the illegal market. Unfortunately, any legal, regulated drug distribution system will have end costs higher than the black market, all but guaranteeing the black market's parallel existence, mitigating any cost savings. For soft drugs like marijuana legalization might be a break-even proposition, but for hard drugs like cocaine legalization would cause more problems—financial and otherwise—than it would solve. As regards the cartels, legalization provides some interesting possibilities. They battle each other over supplies and transport routes, and a legal supply and transport system is simply another source of competition to be addressed with their normal brutal skill set. Colorado's and Washington's experiments with legalizing marijuana mean that they have volunteered to be case studies in a way I seriously doubt they have contemplated.

The North American Drug War: Ten Years On

In my experience Americans aren't satisfied unless they have something to stress about, which generates one of the odder sources of pushback against my work. When I tell folks they need not overly concern themselves with China or Russia or Iran or trade or energy or food or debt they often find themselves at the intersection of loss-for-words and somewhat-pissed-off.

To those folks, fear not! You can always worry about drugs.

America's illicit drug industry (if that is the right word) is probably worth upwards of $150 billion annually. In the time since *Accidental Superpower*'s writing in 2013, America has doubled down on its already horrific opioid epidemic, as well as suffering from an ever-intensifying fentanyl epidemic. Combined with COVID, America's death rate in 2020–22 reached its highest in decades, and American life expectancy has become bar none the *lowest in the entire developed world*.

I have few reasons to expect that any of these issues will get better anytime soon, and there is ample reason to not simply expect a deterioration, but to expect the drugs issue to metastasize into broader security and trade concerns with painfully real geopolitical impacts.

This requires some backstory.

Something I didn't go into the details of in *Accidental*'s first run is the kaleidoscope of Mexico's shifting cartel map. It's been a long time since the country had a singular, dominant force. Instead, it at times has had a fractious, shifting constellation of literally dozens of major drug trafficking groups. That was too much mess to address in the broad-sweep topics of *Accidental*, but in the decade since it was first published, that constellation has evolved in an extremely dangerous direction. Let's dive into some of that now.

The relevant bits begin with the specific personality of Joaquín Archivaldo Guzmán Loera, a.k.a. "El Chapo." Unlike most folks in criminal underworlds, El Chapo saw himself as a businessman. A businessman in the business of committing repeated felonies, but a businessman nonetheless. For him violence was less a goal, but instead a tool. A means to an end.

Apocryphally, his message to his underlings was pretty straightforward: You don't rob old ladies. You don't beat up the locals. You don't knock off cops (if they are not in your way). You are a *drug runner*. Running drugs is how we make money. Focus on *that*.

The pragmatism wasn't simply a successful "business" strategy, it somewhat endeared the Sinaloa to whatever communities it found itself operating in.[10] With local opposition reduced to a manageable level, Sinaloa was able not simply to more easily recruit, but also to work out a de facto partnership with the Mexican national government to target the *other* cartels. By the mid-2010s the Sinaloa had easily become the most powerful trafficking organization in Mexico. El Chapo's position as a sort of antihero was also cemented by Mexican president Andrés Manual López Obrador's decision in 2020 to flout COVID restrictions and shake hands with the kingpin's mother during a visit to Sinaloa.

There was much more to Sinaloa's rise than simply size, however. By expanding its physical footprint, the Sinaloa was able to turn much of its smuggling operations into mere transport. After all, in its expanded territories it faced no meaningful opposition from either other cartels or Mexican law enforcement. That improved the cartel's bottom line as well as its reliability. It also reduced the deaths from the Mexican drug war in Sinaloa's jurisdictions. After all, if there were no cartels within its own zones of influence and the Mexican state was focused on Sinaloa's competitors, then the security free-for-all of the Mexican drug war largely did not apply to Sinaloa territories.

Now benefiting from a free hand and *LOTS* of cash, Sinaloa expanded north across the border into the United States. It was a very different operating environment where law enforcement was most assuredly *not* interested in any sort of deal, but El Chapo's business-first approach still paid handsomely. Sinaloa went to war with America's internal drug *distribution* networks, in essence the country's inner-city gangs, in order to take over that end of the transnational drug business (something similar went down in South America on the production side).

In a bass-ackwards sort of way, Americans benefited from the Sinaloa's expansion; the Mexicans vastly reduced the indigenous American gang

---

10. A *very* strong emphasis on the word "somewhat." Think of it this way: Among drug cartels, Sinaloa is full of the most considerate murdering, extortionist smugglers you could hope to meet. Unless you are in their way.

infrastructure. Hispanic gangs were typically absorbed (and sternly informed that attacking locals was kiboshed), while many African American gangs were either cowed into weakness or eliminated. The end result was a decade-long decline in deaths from violence, largely because Sinaloa killed the people doing the killing. Since the violence rarely affected folks unaffiliated with gangs, most Americans did nothing more than notice that violence was fading. With the Americans remaining unriled, Sinaloa was able to become the largest organized crime group not simply in America, but in the world.

U.S. law enforcement was hardly blind to the shift. Sinaloa's north-of-the-border activities earned El Chapo the honor of the very top spot on the FBI's most-wanted list. It earned him a sting operation with none other than Sean Penn playing the role of unknowing bait. It got El Chapo captured. He escaped, only to be captured again, extradited, and sentenced to life plus thirty years in prison.[11] And with the jefe's disappearance from the Mexican scene, El Chapo's carefully crafted empire began to break apart.

By 2023 the Sinaloa cartel was functionally in dozens of pieces, many of which had taken up arms against one another in a reprise of its pre–El Chapo era. Many of the more violent Sinaloa members defected to join/ form a completely different cartel, known as Jalisco New Generation. Their leader, Nemesio Ruben Oseguera Cervantes, a.k.a. "El Mencho," sported a...unique worldview. Much *unlike* El Chapo, El Mencho believes that violence is "the way." The first thing the Jalisco does when it enters a new area is publicly, and *randomly*, kill a bunch of people in the general vicinity of the local police station. Jalisco has expanded aggressively and violently, picking fights with law enforcement, other cartels, and parts of civil society more or less just 'cause.

Jalisco's doctrine is brutally straightforward: Apply violence vigorously and often, for if everyone is terrified of us, not only will no one stand in our way, but the dead ones can't even think about doing so. If El Chapo's motto was "don't shit where you sleep," then El Mencho's is "the shit is

---

11. The sentencing hearing was high entertainment. El Chapo broke into a diatribe of disbelief that anyone who had bribed the Mexican government as much as he had should ever go to jail. The (American) judge was unmoved.

the point." Even before one considers the post–El Chapo fracturing of the Sinaloa alliance, as of 2023 the Jalisco has probably already become Mexico's most powerful crime group.

But Jalisco has *not* managed to cross into the United States. As one might expect from an "industry" that has become as large as drug trafficking, bulk access matters. Most Mexican-created or -transited drugs cross the border at one of the major crossing points. On the Mexican side of the border, these plazas are choice points of competition among the cartels. After all, limits on access translate directly to limits on income. As of the time of this writing, the Jalisco New Generation, as the new kids on the block, have yet to dominate a single plaza—but they are actively contesting *all* of them.

Should the Jalisco New Generation succeed in but one, they will be able to cross the border in numbers. They will then bring El Mencho's unique management style into the underbelly of American society, and *that* Americans cannot help but notice. It is one thing when the Sinaloa is liquidating the Bloods, or when Jalisco New Generation engages in demonstration hangings from overpasses en route to the Cabo airport. It is quite another when the Jalisco New Generation starts killing white chicks named Debbie in Dallas.

Mexico is *already* the most important economic partner the United States has ever had. In a post-China, post-Germany, post-globalized world, bilateral American-Mexico trade will at a minimum *double* within a decade. Mexico is *already* central to American manufacturing supply chains, the portion of the American economy in need of the greatest expansion as globalization unwinds. Should Jalisco New Generation succeed in crossing the border, Americans will think of Mexico and drugs and the border and trade *very* differently.

If you insist upon worrying about something, worry about *that*.

CHAPTER 14

The China Wars

Most people in the United States—most everyone, really—see China as the future of the world. The largest country by population, the largest exporter, and according to the conventional wisdom soon to be the largest economy and the most powerful military. The Chinese rise during the past three decades has been nothing but spectacular.

But what is almost never considered is why *now*? If China's rise is so inevitable, why is it that only now—some thirty-five hundred years after the Han Chinese first emerged as an ethnicity—is Chinese dominance so obvious and inevitable? The first warning that not all is as it seems is that the China mythos is ingrained nowhere more deeply than in the American psyche—the same psyche that was recently convinced of the "obvious and inevitable" rise of the Soviet Union and Japan.

The reality of China is considerably different from the conventional wisdom. There are many reasons to doubt the strength of the Chinese system, but let's focus on those relevant to things geographic and demographic. Individually, any of the raft of concerns I'm about to detail would be enough to derail the Chinese rise. Collectively they are more than enough to return China to the fractured, self-containing mess that it has been for most of its history.

Chinese geography is, if anything, more problematic than European geography.

The Northern Militarists

China's dominant Han ethnic group traces its roots to early cultures along the Yellow River in what is today northern China. But the Yellow is not a friendly river. It is extremely flood-prone. Seasonal rains in multiple parts of the watershed lead to large-scale flooding at various times of the year. The Yellow is also not tightly contained in a narrow valley as the Nile is, but instead flows through an extremely broad and very flat floodplain. When the river overflows its banks, it regularly inundates broad swaths of territory, far in excess of the sorts of floodings that are common—and largely constrained in reach—elsewhere in the world.

As a result, Chinese society has developed along starkly different lines than Western versions. Chinese political development manifested less out of a need to manage food surpluses and expand populations than out of a need to manage the ravages of the Yellow River. One result among many was a much tighter hold by the government on the populace. Work gangs were regularly formed to construct river levees stretching for miles, not simply to

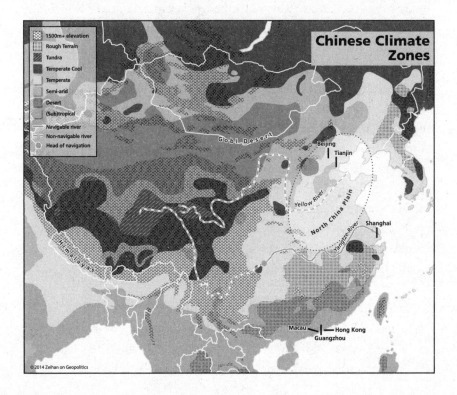

guard populated areas but agricultural fields as well. China may be better known for its Great Wall and Grand Canal, but the Han's tethering of the Yellow was the first and the greatest of their mass construction works.

As the years turned into centuries, these levees expanded to contain nearly all of the river's lower reaches, which actually compounded the problem. While all rivers carry silt, the Yellow's silt load is particularly heavy. Once the river became in essence a managed canal, it couldn't dump its silt in the floodplain. The steady accumulation of sediment resulted in the rise of the river bottom over the centuries. Successive Chinese governments had no choice but to build the river levees higher. At some time in the last millennium, the lower Yellow started defying the classification of "river" and became more of a raised aqueduct with its bottom now above the elevation of the surrounding lands. When the Yellow bursts its banks, the entirety of its flow crashes *down* into the plains that are now beneath it, unleashing heretofore unheard-of floods that dispossess Chinese in hundreds of thousands. A single flood in 1931 killed more than a million people.

The result is that a successful Chinese government *must* be *very* tightly managed. The people *must* be fashioned in such a way that they can be hurled at engineering problems. Failure to maintain such organizational control at all times means that something as innocuous as a hard rain could literally wash Chinese civilization away.

But this tendency toward unitary political systems hasn't granted a history of more unified and coherent governments. On the contrary, China is a land of failed empires and shattered hopes. Again, the reason is geographic. The Yellow River's lower watershed is the North China Plain, a wide, vast landscape completely empty of internal geographic barriers. Like its Northern European equivalent, the NCP is incredibly fertile and absolutely huge: At 158,000 square miles, it is as large as the prime agricultural lands of the U.S. states of Nebraska, Iowa, and Illinois combined.

But that is where the similarities end.

- The long, thin nature of the North European Plain resulted in multiple, competing powers, each arising from and defending its own segment of the plain, often using the NEP's many transecting rivers as defensive lines. The North China Plain, in contrast, has no "thin" dimension and is instead broad and deep, with only the Yellow River bisecting it. The wide-open space of the NCP encouraged cultural and linguistic unity, but not political unity. There are no local geographies from within which a local power could arise independently of its neighbors, and any local power that does successfully cohere is forced to use a great deal of its labor resources to tame the river. That commitment makes the "successful" power vulnerable, leaving less manpower available for defense. A rival does not even need to defeat it in battle, or even target the river works. It can simply distract the population at a critical time—such as during a hard rain—and let nature wash away the competition.

- Unlike the NEP's host of navigable rivers, the Yellow is not navigable—in part due to its heavy engineering. Northern China is as capital-poor as Northern Europe is capital-rich. Since capital has not traditionally been available in China in large volumes, and because high levels of labor concentration and control have been required to hold the river in place (and so are not available for things like technological development), China has not known the high levels of development or fast rates of technological advance that the West enjoyed once the Dark Ages ended.

- Where the NEP receives ample rainfall year round, the NCP is subject to frequent periods of heavy flooding (even without the Yellow River's particular problems) or drought. The result has been regular population booms and busts, and a bust that reduces the population is one that risks allowing the river to rage out of control in the next wet season. The only way to endure a drought is to engage in large-scale irrigation, which requires mastering the river…making you a target for everyone else. Strategically, the result is a region shattered by multiple, competing powers perfectly willing to inflict mass civilian casualties upon each other and even hurl their collective civilization down in order to gain a tactical advantage. The Chinese—quite accurately—refer to long stretches of their own history as the "warlord" era. Unifying northern China into an all-Han zone took nothing less than millennia of wars, civil conflict, and ethnic cleansing. And even once that was achieved, maintaining its unity requires a degree of oppression that is onerous by nearly anyone's standards but Beijing's own. The Chinese civil war between the forces of Mao Zedong and Chang Kai-shek, complete with its 7 million deaths, was but the most recent incarnation of this eternal pattern.

Economically, the result is a system with little trade and even less technological innovation. The northern Chinese system is instead dependent upon the application of labor—mass labor—to whatever problems arise. Even the traditional Chinese staple food fits the pattern. Wheat requires sowing, harvesting, and threshing—and the rest of a wheat farmer's time can be spent on other exploits. Not so for paddy rice. It must be prepared before planting, planted stalk by stalk in specially prepared clay beds that can hold water, flooded, fertilized, emptied, flooded again, emptied and dried, harvested stalk by stalk, threshed, threshed again, followed by a reflooding and refertilizing of the clay bed. It screams for a system in which the average person—that is, the average peasant—has no political voice whatsoever. What little time is not spent on such a labor-heavy food source is claimed by the state to achieve other aims. This can get you a Great Wall or three, but it prevents the sort of labor differentiation and capital accumulation that lets a culture even dream of industrializing.

Politically, the result is a system in which local authorities exercise autonomy so great that it risks bringing the system down. Even once a Chinese leader succeeds in rising to the top of his local heap—or even commanding the entirety of China—he then must begin the even longer and more painful slog of purging all those who have visions that clash with his own. Considering how fractured China is normally and how many power centers there are, this typically requires all of the leader's attention. That was as true for the empires of old as it was for Mao Zedong as it is for the current premier, Xi Jinping.

The good news, such as it is, is that while the wide-open nature of the NCP makes unity very difficult, it is at least possible. As such, almost every attempt to unify China into a single nation has originated in the north. Once the north is mostly on the same page, attention invariably turns to central China.

The Central Traders

Flowing through central China is the mighty Yangtze, one of the world's greatest rivers. Indeed, the Yangtze River basin boasts some nine thousand miles of the same sort of interconnected waterways that have made the United States so successful. But this does not make the Yangtze China's ticket to superpowerhood.

- The Yangtze is China's sole navigable river, so while it is impressive, it is a one-shot deal. Central China is the one part of the country that is naturally trade-focused and capital-rich, but it does not naturally link to its conationals elsewhere. The country doesn't even have a barrier island chain that might help link the Yangtze cities to the rest of the country. But the north does not see this as an argument against integration. The north needs the center's capital and so traditionally uses its superior military position to drain the center dry.

- The central Chinese would prefer to not be drained dry. Given the choice, Shanghai and the rest of its riverine region tend to look beyond northern China to more developed parts of the world, whether that means Taipei, Tokyo, London, or San Francisco. As much as union between north and center might make sense for Beijing on economic grounds, the primary reason for the north's desire to integrate is typically strategic: to keep the foreigners out.

- The Yangtze River basin isn't as nice as it seems, because it isn't actually a basin like its Mississippi or Rhine equivalent. Instead, the Yangtze cuts through a series of mountain chains and ridges on its path to the sea and along many stretches lacks a floodplain even wide enough for a footpath. Such breaks in continuity split identities rather than uniting them. This has pros and cons. On the one hand, it makes it very difficult for the central Chinese to unify themselves into a single political entity. On the other, it makes it far easier for a unified northern China to forcibly assimilate the various pieces of central China one at a time. Historically, the most reliable means of unifying northern and central China has been to alter their geography physically to give them an economic linkage: the Grand Canal. Canals offer the best and worst in terms of infrastructure. Best in that they allow for linkages between various regions that would not otherwise exist, and the operating cost on a canal is quite reasonable. Worst in that crafting and maintaining an artificial river is as difficult and expensive as it sounds. So while a short canal like the Panama or Suez makes a great deal of economic sense, a massive project like the *eleven-hundred-mile*-long Grand Canal is an exorbitant expense that exists only due to political rationale in a system where labor is, in essence, free.

- The areas that the Yangtze drains are as mountainous as its main course. The elevation means that many of the basin's "nine thousand miles of navigability" are seasonal and/or shallow. If you eliminate any Yangtze River basin waterways that lack a channel of at least nine feet of depth for nine months of the year, that figure drops to seventeen hundred, and the number of navigable tributaries drops from over one hundred to just one. While it seems huge on a map—and the Yangtze is indeed navigable sixteen hundred miles inland from the coast—the area of usable territory it empowers is less than that of the Elbe.

Is the Yangtze useful and worth having? Of course. Transport along it makes central China far and away the most capital-rich part of the country. But central China is neither integrated with the political core of the north, nor does its own fractured nature do anything but complicate northern China's always vexing problem of internal disunity.

The Southern Secessionists

Then there is the south, which is a world apart.

- South China is a riot of hills and mountains extending south from the same ranges that so hobble the Yangtze. Such rugged topography has the same impact on cultural and political unity—and wealth—as the rough terrain in Mexico or the

Balkans. Very few coherent large powers have ever arisen in the south.

- Aside from a short stretch of the Pearl River in the far south, none of the many southern Chinese rivers are navigable. Making matters worse, southern China is sufficiently far south that it has moved fully out of the temperate climate zone that dominates North America and Europe. Most of southern China is subtropical, with the southern coast being fully tropical. Just as the diseases native to the tropics of India or Brazil have hugely slowed their cultural unification, the same is true of China.

- The northern Chinese coastline is flat, shallow, and plagued by sandbars. Natural ports are few and far between, and what few exist cannot support large vessels. Even in the rare instances when northern China was unified, it only rarely engaged in maritime commerce. The south is the opposite: Its coastline is both deep and severely indented, allowing easy maritime access and egress all the way to the earliest days of Chinese history. Southern China sports the majority of the natural harbors of all of mainland East and Southeast Asia.

Mix the good port potential with a lack of rivers, a host of mountains, and the enervating impact of the tropics and you get a bizarre geopolitical mix.

While the Han of northern China have always had problems penetrating the area, maritime-based foreigners have not. Southern China's excellent harbors back directly into rugged highlands. Just as that rugged territory limits northern penetration or southern consolidation, it also limits the ability of any local southern power to look to the sea—they just can't reach the coast easily. Instead of the excellent southern harbors serving the needs of Chinese (either northern or southern), they instead serve as the perfect perches for outsiders. The area has long been a foreigners' playground, but one in which the locals welcomed the interference. Trapped in small inland pockets by their geography, the southern Chinese regularly collaborated with the foreigners to access the outside world. So yes, pirates and traders have long enriched themselves along the southern coast, but the locals often participated in empire as a sort of surrogate or sidekick, with Hong Kong being the most recognizable example. As early as the twelfth century, southern Chinese cities were importing over half their foodstuffs, largely via such collaborative links. Entrenching the sense of regional uniqueness is that the Han ethnic group just hasn't been able to scour this part of China free of non-Han as they have in the north. This is the portion of the contemporary state that is home to most of China's remaining minority and language groups.

Southern willingness to work with outsiders and the region's ethnic heterogeneity has not gone unnoticed—or unresented or unfeared—in northern halls of power.

... And the Rest

That's a lot to take in, but the real surprise of China is that the north, center, and south account for but half of China's 1.35 billion people. North, center, and south are China's lowland and coastal regions. The rest of the Chinese actually live in the interior.

That interior is a smorgasbord of geographic diversity. Sichuan sits on the Yangtze's upper reaches and so is somewhat integrated with Shanghai and the outside world. Inner Mongolia is partially barren. The mountains of interior Yunnan are packed with poor minorities. The wide-open spaces of Tibet and Xinjang, also minority-dominated regions, have resisted central control for millennia. It is difficult to find many generalities to describe such a grab bag of variation, but this one is close: Transport is an absolute nightmare, and so the interior is extremely poor compared to the coastal provinces, with per capita income roughly half that of the coast. What images the world of 2014 holds of a bustling, growing China simply don't apply to the interior. Like nearly all other interior, rugged regions of the planet, this portion of China seems stuck in another age.

Unlike the three coastal regions, the interior does not often dominate the day-to-day affairs of the Chinese nation. Geography keeps the interior populations sequestered from the coast and one another, making it difficult for them to interact, much less set China's agenda. Yet there are still some 650 million people living there. Combine such populations with such poverty, and on the rare occasions when some charismatic figure can unite the interior every part of China shakes. While Mao Zedong's effort at consolidation may have hit critical mass in the north, it was his efforts to mobilize the interior that set him on the path to leadership.

Dispelling Myths

One of the most unexpected results of this mélange of geographic factors is that the Chinese are remarkably non-naval. Northern China was largely incapable of going to the sea right up until the technologies of industrialization allowed for the brute-force fashioning of artificial ports. Southern China may have the harbors, but it is so rugged that it lacks much in the way of hinterlands to turn them into ports without extreme amounts of resources—resources that didn't exist in large enough local concentrations until industrialization could stitch the area's various population centers together. That just leaves central China, where Shanghai is a world-class city and world-class port in any era. However, the territory that Shanghai "controls" is very small: Upriver Yangtze cities are well beyond Shanghai's reach courtesy of rugged ridges, while Shanghai itself often falls prey to the power and interests of the North China Plain entities that tend to view international trade as more of a threat than an opportunity.

This tripartite system—northern China as the stable-as-glass political core, central China as the nationally disinterested economic core, and southern China as the potentially secessionist territory (and the interior being largely ignored)—holds to the present day. Even contemporary China's political system reflects it: All of the critical military branches of government are headquartered in the north, the north and central regions trade off the premiership every decade in order to balance security and trade interests, while the south is not even represented on the Politburo.

Such a geographic look at the country lays bare the greatest myth about China: that it is united. I'm not talking here about the concept of the mainland versus Taiwan (Red China versus White China), but rather the idea that the mainland itself can ever truly be a unified entity. Taking a closer look at history indicates that China's past periods of "unity" are anything but.

The Han and Tang dynasties are often held up as the exemplars of Chinese unity, but the Han were typically split among regional power centers. At times the Han bloodline held together while the actual territories it controlled shifted, while the Tang spent the first third of their era engaged in military activities to expand their empire and the last half in (failed) efforts to maintain it. The two other major "unified" periods—the Yuan and the Qing—were actually spearheaded by non-Han ethnicities that managed to achieve what the Han Chinese couldn't do for themselves,[1] which was to conquer and hold all of China.

So that's the problem. China does not naturally hold together, even within its "core" regions. Its different regions want different things and access the world on different terms, if they want access to the world at all. Making matters worse, the outside world accesses different parts of China in different ways. Guangdong and southern China are often de facto colonies. Shanghai and central China are accessed as peers. Northern China tends to be avoided—unless it is being occupied. And just as maritime powers can choose the time and place of their invasions and interactions, the Chinese have almost never been able to defend themselves from ship-based outsiders.

The outsider who has always mattered the most was very close to home.

Japan: China's Bogeyman

The Japanese islands are incredibly mountainous; 90 percent of the population lives in a series of small coastal enclaves. As soon as an enterprising Japanese figured out how to float a boat large enough to transport a few soldiers, the Japanese people unified in terms of culture, identity, and even government—very early compared to most of the world's other peoples. The islands' ruggedness also meant that Japan's maritime nature became infused into Japanese culture; boats of all sizes played the part of roads and tunnels right up until the third century of the industrial era. This mix of factors makes Japan a strategic extrovert. If your country has loads of ships as part of its basic operation, it is very easy for you to reach out and touch others. Due to proximity, Japan touched the Koreans the most, exploiting Korean resources and labor and ultimately generating a visceral

---

1. Don't be too harsh on the Chinese. The Yuan were the Mongols. Not a lot slowed them down.

enmity between the two cultures that will long outlast the present day. China was the next most touched, and understanding the Japanese impact upon China requires a bit of a diversion into the geopolitics of Japan.

By the time deepwater navigation technologies reached the Orient in the eighteenth century, the Japanese had already been pirates without peer for over two hundred years. While the East Asian coast was far harsher than the Mediterranean, there are strings of islands that roughly parallel the coastline from the southern tip of Japan all the way to contemporary Indonesia. Getting lost was hard to do. As with most naval powers, over time raiding turned into brokering and the Japanese became the trading middlemen across the East Asian rim. But when the industrial age reached Japan in the 1800s, the Japanese discovered that they brought almost nothing to the table; the home islands possessed next to nothing in terms of material resources, at best a mediocre market, and one segmented by their islands' rugged topography at that. So the Japanese used the one tool they did have—their navy—and took what they needed from their Asian neighbors, whether resources or markets. In the case of China, they took both. A *lot* of both.

The degree of Japanese action on the Chinese mainland ebbed and flowed over time, but Japanese expansionism typically marched to the drum of Japanese internal politics rather than Chinese resistance. By the early twentieth century, the Japanese had repeatedly pressed home to the Chinese—and the Koreans and the Russians[2]—just how potent a competent naval power could be. In a strategic sense, it was a purely one-way relationship. Throughout the long reach of Chinese history, Chinese culture may have wielded rich influence throughout East Asia and even in Japan, but it was almost unheard of for the land-bound Chinese to exercise physical control over their own borderlands, much less the maritime zones that dominated the entirety of the Chinese offshore, much less the wider world.

---

2. Japan conquered Korea outright in 1905, and, in the Russo-Japanese War of 1904–5, sank the entirety of Russia's Pacific and Baltic fleets in just two battles.

The China We Know

So what changed? If the concept of a unified China, much less a globally significant China, is an aberration, then something drastic must have happened to overcome the many traps of the Chinese geography.

Well, it comes back to those damned Americans. They did three things that not only preserved China, but made the contemporary colossus we currently know as modern China possible.

First, it was the Americans who removed Japan as a threat. Japan and China had been locked in a bilateral war for nearly five years before the Americans joined World War II. Historians and theorists can of course debate how the Japanese-Chinese war would have ended if not for its folding into World War II, but the simple fact remains that at the time of Pearl Harbor the Chinese had already lost the conventional war and were pouring all of their efforts into guerrilla tactics. Even when the Japanese started fighting—and losing to—the Americans in the Southeast Asian and Pacific theaters, they were still making steady progress across China where their foes represented a not yet industrialized civilization. And as the Japanese vividly demonstrated in the execution of some 250,000 Chinese in Nanking, they would not be leaving without exacting a heavy toll.

By the time the mushroom clouds rose over Hiroshima and Nagasaki, the Japanese had—for years—held every part of Chinese territory that made China economically and politically viable, including the entirety of the North China Plain, all of the lower Yangtze including Shanghai, and all of the major southern port cities across Fujian and Guangdong, including Xiapu, Xiamen, Fuzhou, Shantou, and Hong Kong. If it was worth taking, the Japanese took it. "Independent" China was left with the interior scraps, and China only regained its sovereignty because Japan's surrender to the Americans in 1945 stipulated the recall of all Japanese forces from all theaters.

Japan's subsequent folding into the growing Bretton Woods network in 1955 ended Japan's imperial interest in China. Under the Bretton Woods system, the Japanese had full access to resources and markets on a global scale, far more than the relatively piddling Chinese resources and markets that Japan had waged war to secure only two decades previously. In a stroke, the Americans had not so much ended Japanese imperialism as removed any rationale Japan might have had to be imperialist in the first place. An East Asia without Japanese aggression was one in which China could potentially unify. In the five years after World War II, China finally finished its civil war—an internal conflict that was fought alongside the Sino-Japanese War and World War II—and became truly unified.

Second, World War II's conclusion radically changed the region's naval balance of power. By war's end, the Americans had wiped the Pacific clean of Japanese forces, but that was only one piece of the puzzle. The European navies were also gone, in part due to the Japanese themselves, but mostly due to American actions in Europe. While Japan was certainly the country guiltiest of suppressing the Chinese, they were far from the only one. In the century leading up to World War II, all the Europeans had carved out pieces of the globe for their respective empires, and China was hardly exempt. Most European countries cut economic and military deals with individual Chinese cities—some willingly, some at the end of a gun—in order to access Chinese labor and markets, often integrating them into imperial supply chains. In the most infamous cases, the Europeans forced addictive narcotics onto the Chinese populations, generating robust market demand and security dependency at the same time. With good reason, the Chinese look back on the Opium Wars of the "spheres of influence" period as one of the darkest moments of their history.

What is often overlooked is what made China such an easy target for the Europeans (and Japanese and Americans): deepwater navigation and industrialization. Without their long-reach navies and advanced military technologies the Europeans would have never been able to reach China in the first place, much less subjugate it more or less at their whim. At the end of World War II, the European navies were simply gone, so any thought that the spheres-of-influence period could continue evaporated. Moreover, the Americans' imposition of Bretton Woods upon Europe meant that the Europeans no longer had an interest in even trying. For the first time in four centuries, with the notable exception of the British in Hong Kong and the Portuguese in Macau, there was no European footprint in China. The American defeat of Japan may have ended the war on the mainland, but it was the American presence in Europe that actually gave China its economy back.

Third, Bretton Woods turned out to not just be for America's Western

European allies and the defeated Axis. As part of American Cold War strategic maneuvering, the Chinese themselves were eased into the system starting in the early 1970s. Suddenly, instead of *being* the target market, China could access the global market. Instead of being raided for raw materials, China was guaranteed access to global supplies. The endless supplies of cheap labor that the Europeans and Japanese ruthlessly tapped now allowed China to generate its own goods for export, this time with the revenues flowing to the Chinese instead of overseas interests.

The American-crafted strategic environment, most notably the Bretton Woods element of it, created the best of all worlds for the Chinese. It eliminated the only significant military and economic rival in East Asia. It all but banned European influence east of India. And it provided both the strategic freedom and the economic means to attempt true Chinese unification.

Which doesn't mean it will hold. Contemporary China faces three simultaneous crises, any one of which could undo all that it has achieved since the end of its civil war in 1950.

Problem One: The Financial System

China's regions have little in common and do not naturally cohere. Getting nationalist, security-minded northerners to cooperate with the business-savvy central Chinese as well as the occupied southerners is not an easy task. And that is before you take into account that the interior is a chunky, seething morass of dissatisfaction or that the primary hub of the south is Hong Kong, until recently part of the free world.

China needs a social binding agent. It needs to be a strong adhesive and applied in huge volumes. Without it China not only spins out into its constituent fragments, but large numbers of its citizens tend to gather into large groups and go on long walks together. None of this is a surprise to the Communist Party. After all, its founders took advantage of China's many regional and socioeconomic cleavages in their rise to power in the first place. Rather than deny contemporary China's origin story, they instead have used the opportunities presented by Bretton Woods to forge a solution.

It comes down to money. The Chinese government starkly limits what its citizens can do with their savings. Rather than allowing a wealth of investment options as exists in the capital-rich American or British system, private savings are instead funneled to state goals in a manner somewhat similar to the German system. Specifically, there are very few banks in China, with some three-quarters of all deposits held in four large state-owned institutions: the Agricultural Bank of China, the Bank of China, the Construction Bank of China, and the Industrial and Commercial Bank of China.

Those four banks have very clear mandates. They are to use the citizenry's deposits to maximize bank lending to the economy as a whole. The goal of the policy is a simple one: maximum possible employment. While this is technically a lending model, it is more accurately thought of as a system of subsidization. Since Chinese citizens have so few investment options, the banks have access to their deposits at rates that are ridiculously low. Consequently, internal interest rates in China are artificially held well below global norms and are certainly far below what they would normally be in an economy at China's level of development.

Loans are available for everything. Want to launch a new product? Take out a loan to finance the development, to pay the staff, to cover marketing expenses, to build a warehouse to store output that doesn't sell as planned. Find yourself under the burden of too many loans? Take out another to cover the loan payments. The result is an ever-rising mountain of loans gone bad and ever less efficient firms, held together by nothing more than the system's bottomless supply of cheap labor and cheap credit.

The distortions this system creates are ones very familiar to all of us living in the contemporary world:

- The Chinese financial system subsidizes prices for finished outputs. This drives down the price of Chinese finished goods and allows their exports to displace most global competition. Normally such price crashes would induce producers to reduce output, but in China profits and even sales are not the driving rationale for business. Employment is. And Bretton Woods, by its very design, gives the Chinese access to a bottomless global market.

- The Chinese financial system subsidizes the consumption for inputs. In effect, the Chinese system doesn't care whether oil costs $8 a barrel or $180 a barrel. Everything is paid for with borrowed money you don't have to pay back anyway, so demand builds upon itself. Chinese demand is the primary cause for the drastic price increases of the past fifteen years in everything from oil to copper to tin to concrete. It's not just happening abroad, but at home as well. The Chinese property boom is ultimately caused by huge volumes of loans chasing a fixed supply of a product, in this case housing.

- When you don't care about prices or output or debt or quality or safety or reputation, your economic growth is truly impressive. China has achieved over 9 percent economic growth annually now for thirty years, elevating it to its current status as the world's second largest economy.

- China has expanded so much that in some sectors its demand has swallowed up all that remained of several industrial commodities in the world at large, forcing its state-owned firms to venture out and invest in projects that otherwise wouldn't have happened—LNG in Australia, copper in Zambia, soy in Brazil. Chinese overseas investments are a who's who of what is technically possible but economically ridiculous.

- Finally, as cheap and plentiful as Chinese capital is, it isn't available for everyone. Because the Chinese system is ultimately managed by the Communist Party and because the leaders of localities hold so much power versus the center, there is extreme collusion between bank management and the local Communist Party leaderships. This collusion funnels capital to local state firms affiliated with friends and family of the local governing elite, often depriving smaller—and typically more efficient—firms of the loans that they need to expand. The result is a system skewed toward larger firms that, from an employment point of view, become too large to fail. Any meaningful reform of the Chinese system will not only break the links between national and local authorities, but gut the very firms that are achieving social placidity.

So how big is this problem? Pretty big. In 2007, total Chinese lending topped 3.6 trillion RMB ($600 billion). How much is that really? Well, that's more than total lending into the U.S. economy when the U.S. subprime bubble was at its maximum inflation, and that in a year when the Chinese economy was less than *one-third* the size of the U.S. economy. As the 2007–9 global financial crisis bit, the Chinese government discovered that demand for goods was collapsing on a global scale, with Chinese goods being no exception. In other countries, the drop in demand for goods forced companies out of business along with the expected impact upon employment levels.

Not in China. Following such a normal business cycle in China would have resulted in unemployment and social unrest (or worse). Instead of the credit crunch that the rest of the world suffered, Chinese companies were encouraged to borrow ever larger volumes, allowing them to finance their way through the downturn. Overall lending not only increased, it tripled in just two years. Normally, such a credit explosion would generate massive inefficiencies, bubbles, and other distortions that would be damning to an economy—but such problems were already embedded in the Chinese system, so the change didn't really register.

Nevertheless, the Chinese government isn't actively looking for problems, and it dialed back the credit expansion…or at least it tried to. Since the banks operate just like the rest of the country—on throughput rather than profit—they needed to keep forcing money through the system. The result was a proliferation of new methods of lending, ranging from bogus insurance policies to corporate bonds. None of these programs work in China the way that they do elsewhere. For example, in most countries, firms seeking to raise money issue corporate bonds that are purchased by interested investors. In China, the large banks issue bonds to each other and use the money raised to support their own phalanx of corporate customers. It is simply another means of force-feeding capital through the system to maximize short-term economic activity.

The various means of capital profusion had become so many and so lax that the government actually lost control of its own financial network. The government knew it had to somehow rein in credit, but it wanted to find a way of doing so that wouldn't actually cause a recession, much less an economic crash and the unemployment that would go along with it. The government dared not risk changing the fundamental method of handing out credit, nor the large-scale absence of quality checks, nor the absence of due diligence. The "solution" was to issue a centrally imposed quota on bank lending every month. In most months, the quota was reached well before month's end, causing the entire financial sector to seize up when the credit suddenly dried up.

This led to two outcomes. First, the central bank had to (repeatedly) pump in emergency credit the day after the quota was reached, or else face the sort of systemic financial crash that U.S. subprime caused in late 2007. Second, banks, firms, and retail investors, appalled by the idea that the government might actually deny them credit because of something as silly as a lending quota, built their own financial network to run in parallel to the existing system. This shadow system includes everything from loan-sharking to financial products with even fewer quality controls than official bank lending (after all, they were formed expressly to *bypass* government authority). By the first quarter of 2013, China's own central bank estimated that such shadow lending was exceeding all other forms of credit combined.

That puts total financing at around $5 trillion for an economy only

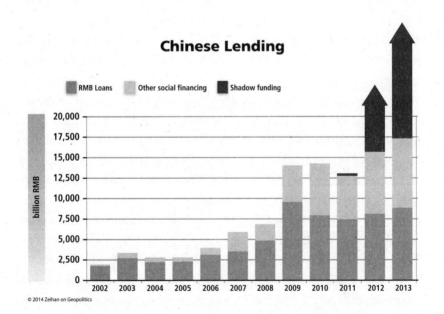

© 2014 Zeihan on Geopolitics

worth about $8 trillion. Not only is that an absolute volume of capital more than *seven times* new lending in the United States, it is the equivalent of an Obama stimulus package (that's $800 billion over two years) about every twenty-nine *days.*

Just as the United States meted out access to its market to bribe its way into the world's largest ever alliance, the Chinese used finance to bribe both its often conflicting regions and ever restive populations into quiescence and even cooperation. It is a brilliant strategy, but it has limits.

Japan followed a similar system in the 1950s through the 1980s, eventually reaching a level of overextension that brought the entire system to its knees. In the quarter century since the Japanese crash, the Japanese banking sector has retreated completely from the global system, and the Japanese economy as a whole has not grown. Such stagnation is China's best-case-scenario future. Unfortunately, it is also not a very likely one. The Japanese economy is largely domestically held and demand-driven, so while loose credit certainly helps, it is not the hedge against doomsday that it is in China. Additionally, Japan is over 98 percent ethnically Japanese, and over four-fifths of the population lives on the island of Honshu. China is considerably less unified regionally, ethnically, and spatially.

The United States even experimented with this system: the idea that growth and throughput were more important than profitability and a positive rate of return on capital. The result was a mess of graft, abuse, and unwise lending that created the failed company we knew as Enron, and the property bubble we now know as subprime. Both experiments created impressive growth for years. But such investments were geared to maximized throughput, not profits or efficiency. And so they collapsed. In essence, the *entire* Chinese system is subprime, in *every* economic sector.

Problem Two: Demography

But let's assume for a minute that China's remarkably unstable financial system holds together a bit longer. Something even worse is just around the corner. China's one-child policy is often held up as the pinnacle of what can happen when a government is willing to pair demographic concerns with a complete disregard for individual rights. In a few short years, strict enforcement slashed the birth rate, preventing an estimated 200 million to 400 million births and heading off the overpopulation problem that policy makers so feared.

Now the success of that policy means the end of the Chinese system.

There are many legitimate criticisms of one-child. Forced abortions, the ability to buy government approval to flaunt the policy, the concept that the government can choose who can reproduce when, a massive sex imbalance in a culture that prefers sons to daughters—all these and more have twisted Chinese culture in awkward and painful directions.

But the real problem with one-child is that it *worked*. During the period from 1979 to 2003 when it was strictly enforced, the birth rate dropped by half. That slashed everything from health care to education to food costs, but it gutted the most recent generation. After three decades of the policy, there has been a European-style hollowing out of the younger segments of the population.

This presents China with three unavoidable—and system-killing—problems.

First, China is aging far more quickly than it is getting rich. At the beginning of China's international resurgence in 1990, the average Chinese citizen was only 24.9 years old, and the country boasted some 350 million citizens aged fifteen to twenty-nine. It was this simple circumstance that allowed for China's massive manufacturing boom in the 1990s and 2000s: China was the world's ultimate source of cheap labor and no other developing country could compete with the Chinese on price.

Fast-forward to the present and, courtesy of one-child, the average Chinese is now 37.0, just a shade younger than Americans, who are currently 37.3 years old. The Chinese will pass the Americans in average age in 2019 and by 2030 will be 42.9 years old versus 39.6 for the Americans. The Chinese call it the 4:2:1 problem: four grandparents to two parents to one child. China is not yet wealthy enough to be able to try to afford a pension system like the advanced democracies, which places the onus of caring for the elderly on their descendants, of whom there are precious few. In terms of relative numbers, the financial cost of the one-child policy is more than double the comparative costs that the Americans face from

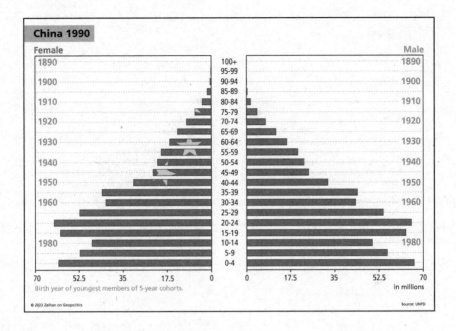

the Boomer retirement, and the Americans already have a social security system in place to absorb some of the cost. The burden of having to financially support their elderly has a catastrophic impact on young workers' professional and financial development, reducing educational opportunities, gutting consumption, and all but making savings impossible. In China's specific situation, not only will this factor alone freeze in place China's efforts to switch its economy from exports to internal consumption and stymie its efforts to move up the value-added scale, but it will also prevent the sort of savings that makes the force-fed-finance model possible in the first place.

Second, China will never be able to move away from its current export-driven model. Recall what roles each age group carries out in society from an economic point of view: Young workers do the consuming that generates economic growth. The last baby boom that China experienced was in the 1980s just as one-child was picking up, and China has suffered from an intentional baby bust ever since. Those boom babies are now aged twenty-five to twenty-nine and are very visible as a bulge in China's population pyramid. It may be only a five-year increment, but it represents about

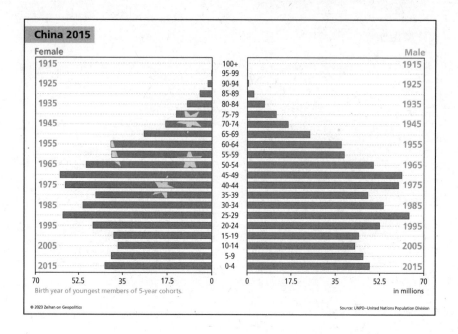

China 2015

Female / Male

Birth year of youngest members of 5-year cohorts.

in millions

© 2023 Zeihan on Geopolitics

Source: UNPD–United Nations Population Division

125 million people. This group's consumption is the primary reason why China appears to be succeeding somewhat in its current efforts to switch from an export-led to a consumption-led economy. But—again, courtesy of one-child—their successors are ever smaller population cohorts. So congratulations are due to China for having impressive consumption growth in recent years, but that consumption growth has never beat out investment/loan-driven activity, and is now nearly played out.

Third, so too is the Chinese development model. Simple aging has already reduced China's pool of young, mobile workers by over 40 million during the past decade. And because of the baby bust, that decline is about to accelerate greatly. Put simply, China has run out of surplus labor; its presence on the low-cost side of global manufacturing has run its course. This is already reflected in Chinese labor costs, which have sextupled since 2002.

Looking forward just twenty-five years, China faces a far darker financial future than Europe and a far darker demographic future than Japan.

I normally caution people I speak with about drawing forward linear trends—for example, the idea that China, or before it the Soviet Union or

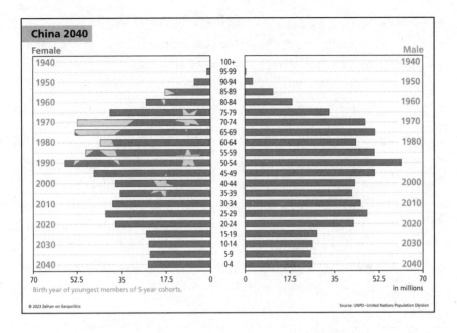

China 2040

Birth year of youngest members of 5-year cohorts.

© 2023 Zeihan on Geopolitics

Source: UNPD–United Nations Population Division

Japan, will soon rule the world. But demography is different. Young workers simply do not magically appear. They have to be born and raised. It takes twenty years to grow a twenty-year-old.[3] Changing a demography requires a broad-scale shifting of cultural and economic trends, and then holding the change for decades. Simply abolishing one-child is only one step of the process. China would then need to encourage the young workers who are crammed into apartment housing to produce multiple children while still working and taking care of their parents (and grandparents). It would have to build out an entirely new series of social services in health and child care whose absence provided the spare capital that helped make China's manufacturing boom possible.

Even if we assume that China can pull this off and an immediate abolition of the one-child policy leads to an immediate doubling of birth rates—which would be unprecedented in human history—it would still be two decades before China would begin to benefit from an expansion of the labor pool in any significant manner. That's two decades during which

---

3. Twenty years and nine months if you want to be exact.

the rest of the Chinese population would still be aging toward retirement. Two decades during which China won't have much internal consumption going on. Two decades during which the low-cost, export-led model would still not work.

Problem Three: Dependency on America

And of course, even if China could somehow survive *that*, it would still remain locked into a system whose very survival is simply beyond Beijing's control. The Bretton Woods network is what made everything about China—its unification, its existence as a modern state, its manufacturing base, its export-led economy, its military strength—possible. There are any number of reasons how the Americans backing away from Bretton Woods would be disastrous for the Chinese. Here are four:

1. As with many other countries in the Bretton Woods world, the Chinese have purposefully adjusted their system to maximize the role that exports play, so the largest and most dynamic portion of the Chinese economic system has been and remains export-driven. Roughly 10 percent of China's GDP depends upon direct exports to the United States.[4] Another 5 percent of GDP is locked up in supply chains whose ultimate destination is the American market. Should American trade access be revoked it would be as if China suffered from an equivalent of three American Great Recessions all at once. And even that "rosy" scenario assumes that all of China's other export markets remain open. All told, about one-third of Chinese economic activity is directly involved in exports, and that does not include the raft of affiliated sectors—from ports to refineries—that while technically "domestic" are largely dependent upon international links. As one would expect, the Chinese

---

4. Using any Chinese statistics is an exercise in risk. The national government regularly reforms the country's local and regional statistical reporting systems so that it too can get a more accurate picture of the Chinese system. Oftentimes such auditing efforts run afoul of the interests of local politicos to such a degree that the auditors die under somewhat suspicious circumstances.

regions with more mercantile histories—most notably the greater
Shanghai and greater Hong Kong regions—would suffer more.

2. China is now the world's largest importer of nearly everything:
iron, iron ore, aluminum, alumina, sulfur, copper, copper concentrate, nickel, plastics, wood, wood pulp, tin, glass, cotton, wool,
soybeans, rubber (both natural and synthetic). This list goes on
for a good long while. The most strategic of China's world's-largest
is of course oil. Think of the American oil neurosis of the past half
century—and that from a country that controls the global oceans,
that imports most of the oil it needs from its co–North Americans. Now think of it from China's point of view. China's oil supply lines run past a *lot* of rivals. Oil shipped in from the Middle
East or Africa must pass by India, Myanmar, Thailand, Singapore,
Vietnam, the Philippines, and Taiwan.[5] In a Bretton Woods world
in which the Americans guarantee the sea lanes for everyone, this
isn't a problem. In an Amerocentric world in which the Americans don't care—or perhaps don't care too much for China—this
is a strategic disaster. Almost all of the countries along China's oil
import route are also oil importers. All *already* have more than
enough naval power necessary to interdict supertankers that go
somewhere they don't wish them to. And China dare not risk tan-
gling with even a mid-powered navy out of range of its land-based
aircraft because it lacks meaningful blue-water capabilities.

3. Unfortunately for the Chinese, the Americans will be the least of
their worries. Ultimately, the Americans will not be worried about
China because it is a non-naval power and really not a significant
threat to American power in a post–free trade world. At the top
of the list of future Chinese concerns will be the Japanese. In a
post–Bretton Woods world, the Japanese will face many similar
constraints to the Chinese: They will need to guarantee access to
their own oil supplies, raw materials, and foreign markets. But
they will be different from China in two critical ways. First, on
average Japan's dependency on the outside world is less than half

---

5. Russian oil may face a more direct route, but the Russians are kings of using
energy dependency as strategic and political leverage.

that of the Chinese in absolute terms. Second, unlike the Chinese, the Japanese actually have a blue-water navy—the world's second most powerful, in fact—and so can go get what they need. One of the few things standing in the way of the Japanese will be anything sailing up and down the Chinese coast.

4. Even if China did have a blue-water navy, it could not use it freely. Bisecting the Chinese coastline is of course Taiwan. The biggest challenge Taiwan presents to the mainland is not its ability to make a mockery of the concept of a "united China" simply by its existence, but rather the fact that it is far cheaper to use a land-based military to threaten sea lanes than a sea-based military. Taiwanese cruise missiles and aircraft can deny Chinese shipping and even military vessels access to a wide swath of territory. And Taiwan isn't alone. Japan, Taiwan, the Philippines, Indonesia, and Singapore form a line of islands off the Chinese coast that block any possible Chinese access to the ocean blue. All of these countries

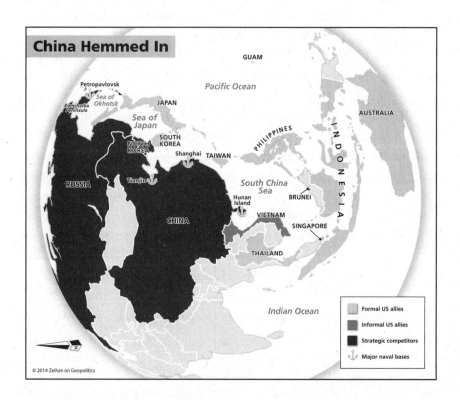

are broadly hostile to China. All of them have air forces and cruise missile assets that can threaten and in many cases destroy Chinese maritime assets that get too close. And it is likely that most if not all of them will remain allied with the United States in the future (see chapter 10).

The New/Old China

China is the country that has benefited the most from the American Cold War strategy of market access and defanging the various maritime powers, and therefore has the most to lose. In the imminent future, the Chinese face three crushing challenges. First, Japan is likely to start acting less like an NGO and more like the Japan of ages past. Second, China's geography is nearly as riven as Europe's, with the great myth of Chinese history that unity is normal soon to give way to a more complex and messier reality. Third, everything that made the Chinese economy a success, everything that has put cars on the road, roads on the map, money in the citizens' pockets, and food in their mouths, is completely dependent upon an international economic and strategic environment wholly maintained by a country that doesn't like China all that much.

China has been sliding toward disaster for some time. Two events a decade ago first revealed cracks in the Chinese juggernaut. In the first, villagers of the town of Huaxi, south of Shanghai, protesting local factory-sourced pollution overturned the buses that had brought in security personnel to quell them, in essence barricading out central authorities with their own equipment. In the second, citizens in Dongzhou, near Hong Kong, protesting the building of a power plant found themselves under fire by security personnel, resulting in at least twenty deaths. It was the first significant use of deadly force against Chinese citizens by their own government since Tiananmen Square. Since then public unrest has become nearly omnipresent, ranging from ethnic-themed clashes in places like Xinjiang and Tibet to worker disputes like the Foxconn suicides in 2010 to protests against the nearly 17 million acres of farmland that have been expropriated by various local governments. By 2011 the government was recording one hundred thousand such "mass events" annually.

The stage is most certainly already set, but how China's transition plays out will depend almost entirely upon the nature and timing of Bretton Woods' end. Considering the unpredictability of American actions, that is something I cannot forecast. A slow-motion American retreat could leave the Chinese starving for raw materials, which would trigger not just poverty in the coastal regions of Shanghai and to its south but also a contest with Japan and Taiwan that the Americans might or might not participate in. A break in the Chinese financial system would cause a national collapse in development and mass uprisings in the interior. An American panic attack could trigger an overnight revolution across the length and breadth of China as everything from markets to jobs to the power supply cuts out all at once. And that assumes that the target of America's panic attack isn't China itself. There are so many things that could trigger China's fall that mapping out the route of descent is a task best completed once free fall is already in progress.

Sketching out China's future *after* that transition, however, is actually fairly straightforward. China's ability to employ its population will end. China's ability to source the materials to modernize will end. The impacts will vary by region.

As poor as the interior is already, it is the region that will actually see the sharpest contractions in standard of living. While the coastal regions—north, center, and south—can participate in export markets, by dint of geography the interior cannot. As such, the interior is *completely* reliant upon the perilous Chinese financial system for its income and economic activity.

Interior regions dependent upon fertilizers produced elsewhere will be unable to maintain food production levels, leading to starvation in the cities. Interior regions that have partially modernized will suddenly find they need to operate without electricity, spawning mass population movements. Some of the displaced will return to the farm and so may alleviate somewhat the food production shortages. But food does not grow overnight. Even in the best-case scenario it would be months before food shortages could be meaningfully addressed. The remainder of the uprooted will move to the coast in a great exodus that Mao Zedong would find familiar. Opportunities for political demagogues not under Politburo control will abound.

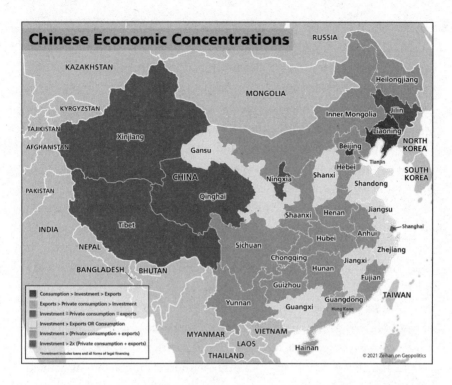

As for southern and central China—that is, southern and central *coastal* China—they will face management adjustments. Between the collapse of the Beijing-inspired financial system that has kept the southern and central Chinese happy, and the collapse of the international trade order that has made them rich, every coastal region south of the North China Plain will rebel against Beijing's control. Most will cut deals with foreign governments and corporations that can promise a degree of access to capital and markets and resources. In essence, everything from Hainan Island to Shanghai will become a series of unaffiliated city-states that hitch their wagons to American, Japanese, Taiwanese, Korean, Australian, and even Singaporean stars. Some of the outsiders might use military means to secure what they are after. Some of the coastal cities may not simply tolerate but actually suggest such moves in order to assist in their efforts to carve out a bit of wealth and security for themselves—and to keep a seething Beijing at bay.

For its part, Beijing will fail in its struggle to stay ahead of such a hydra of problems. In no particular order, Beijing will have to try to keep northern China's food production under lockdown, to make sure the North China Plain itself remains united, to maintain control of the seceding south and center, to resist the swarms of the desperate from the interior cities who have become accustomed to a lifestyle that China can no longer provide, and to stave off the Japanese who see the energy and food resources of northeastern China as a handy package. Even under good circumstances—and between food and energy shortages these will *not* be good circumstances—China would likely prove unable to handle more than one at a time, and all will hit at once.

It will come down to the unenviable task of prioritizing. Does Beijing go to war with the Japanese to keep control of its northern food- and oil-producing region? Does Beijing go to war with the belt of coastal cities from Shanghai to Hong Kong to keep China in one piece? Does Beijing attempt to intercept the foreign powers that try to fuse those cities to distant destinies? Does Beijing use a military strategy to deal with the tens of millions of would-be refugees from the interior who seek the resources that Beijing must carefully husband? Cold logic would say that China has too many people and that a "correction" of a few hundred million might actually help. Unfortunately for such a value-absent analysis, the "surplus" population lives on the farms, and so will not starve without explicitly deliberate, intentionally horrific, and cruelly and sustained action from Beijing.

Regardless of their decisions, the northern Chinese face a dark, hungry, and harsh future, and even that assumes that Beijing can hold the Chinese core together and avoid the social, economic, and political breakdowns that have plagued Chinese history for the past three and a half millennia.

Scared New World: Reverberations of a Fallen Giant

No matter how artificial, coincidental, or ill-planned China's recent rise has been, it still happened, and no multitrillion-dollar trading nation can exist in a vacuum. China's explosive rise has impacted nearly every corner of the world, but four outcomes are worthy of particular mention, because when China falls three will furiously unwind and the fourth will become the largest concentration of wealth in the world.

First, China vacuumed up much of the global market share for mid-

and especially low-skilled industries such as textiles and toys and garlic and steel and concrete. Chinese success has meant failure for countries ranging from Mexico to Morocco to India that had previous success in such industries. As China unwinds, much of this productive capacity will fall into disuse for any mix of financial, security, or trade access reasons. However, the previous homes of such industries have long since fallen into disuse and disrepair—if the infrastructure still exists in those places at all. There will be what can be described as a hiccup, although in some places a stroke might be a better analogy, as production and consumption patterns adjust to the sudden loss of supply. Finished-goods prices will have to rise. Who will be able to take China's place at that stage of the production cycle will depend upon the traditional factors: access to capital, markets, resources, and trade lanes. The biggest winners will likely be Mexico and the countries of Southeast Asia, although much of the more highly skilled industry and agricultural production is likely to relocate back to the United States itself.

Second, China's growth—and in particular its financial system that broke the link between expenditure and efficiency—resulted in unprecedented demand for every industrial commodity under the sun. Bereft of ravenous Chinese hunger, demand for industrial inputs whether they be oil or copper or zinc will plunge. Producers dependent upon the mix of Chinese-driven high prices and American-guaranteed shipping security will be those most impacted, with most output from places such as Brazil and Africa being put in extreme danger. The producers who survive will be those with lower production costs and better relations with and access to the United States: Canada, Australia, and, again, Mexico and Southeast Asia.

Third, China's rise also led to an improvement in diet for most of its 1.35 billion citizens. As with industrial commodities, much of China's food is sourced abroad. However, there will *not* be a wholesale collapse in international demand in basic foodstuffs. Most of China's food imports serviced China's coastal populations, which will still be able to somewhat access international supplies. This foreign access will be doubly important when one considers that China's financial system boosted local agricultural output right along with manufacturing. The demise of the financial system will hurt Chinese food production and may well necessitate *greater* food imports rather than the opposite. After all, the final service that any government cuts before it dies is food access. If China's failing governments cannot guarantee that, they are no longer governments.

Finally, throughout this entire process—from today until well beyond the day that a unified China is no more—U.S.-dollar-denominated assets, and especially U.S. government bonds, will become ever more popular. Many have opined how everything from America's seemingly chronic budget deficits to political deadlock to a weakening international profile demand that the days of the U.S. dollar are numbered. Even if you don't believe in the long-term strength of the American economy, the unassailable nature of the American geography, and the centrality of American decision making to how the world functions—even if you can find fault with absolutely everything presented in this book—the fact remains that there just isn't any competition to the U.S. dollar.

- Once the Europeans decided to partially fund their bailouts with insured bank accounts in 2013, the euro's candidacy for status as a global currency—much less *the* global currency—ended.
- Japan's financial system is closed to the world just as China's is; opening it would trigger heretofore unheard-of levels of capital flight.
- The remaining hard currencies of the world—the British pound, Swedish krona, and the Canadian, Australian, and Kiwi dollars—combined are but half the circulating volume of the U.S. dollar.
- Gold isn't an option either. The total value of all gold mined throughout history is about $9 trillion—shy by half of what the world would need. Half of that $9 trillion is simply unavailable for use as a currency backer, existing as it does in things like class rings, cellular phones, and Egyptian museum exhibits. Two-thirds of the remainder is held by the world's various central banks, and is unlikely to be pooled into currency that none of them would control. Various investors control the remainder, and they certainly won't be willing to part with their holdings for anything but an exorbitant price—doubly so

if those holdings are about to form the core of a new global currency regime. New gold flowing into the system is under $4 billion USD equivalent monthly. On average, China expands its money supply by forty times that rate, while global goods trade alone is worth some $18 *trillion* annually!

But don't believe me. Believe the Chinese. Specifically, believe Luo Ping, a director-general at the China Banking Regulatory Commission, the agency responsible for keeping China's banking sector functional. In 2009 he noted, "Except for U.S. Treasuries, what can you hold? Gold? You don't hold Japanese government bonds or UK bonds. U.S. Treasuries are the safe haven. For everyone, including China, it is the only option. We hate you guys. Once you start issuing $1 trillion–$2 trillion [in new debt] . . . we know the dollar is going to depreciate, so we hate you guys, but there is nothing much we can do."

If the Chinese realize that they have no options but to pour their earnings and savings into U.S. assets when their financial system is still humming along, when their demographics are still favorable, and when the global trade order still holds, just imagine the volumes that will flood toward the United States once China fails.

The China Wars: Ten Years On

Rereading the text of *Accidental Superpower* ten years later generates a never-ending spasm of memories for me. Every chapter in this, my first book, has been adapted or parsed or summarized or expanded for any number of audiences. But the chapter that has always generated the most emotion is the one on China.[6] And of course, the haters (doing what they do) gleefully point out that China isn't simply still there, but it seems far more potent on the world stage in 2023 than it was in 2013.

There's a bit more at play here than the simple issue of timing. Allow me to share a bit of geopolitical philosophy.

Countries with horrible geographies may have a moment—historically speaking—in the sun, but they will never succeed at what I call "the long game." That doesn't mean they cannot or do not participate in history, and *especially* the present, but it does mean their momentary success requires one of two things to happen.

First, they require a shift in external circumstances that ameliorates their harsh geographic reality. China has benefited from just such a shift in spades. Politically, after World War II the American-led, globalized Order sent the Europeans and Japanese who had been preying on China packing *and kept them away*. For the first time in the long pain of Chinese history, Beijing was able to achieve true national unification. Economically, the trading aspects of the Order granted China access to every raw material and end-consumer market in existence, enabling the fastest and most sustained economic growth China had ever experienced. I don't mean to wave away domestic efforts toward unification or growth, but without the American-created baseline, the China of today couldn't have even theoretically happened.

Beijing's inconvenient truth is that its sustainment is wholly dependent on American commitment to a strategic policy that Washington is increasingly disinterested in. Quick example: In the early months of 2023, Iranian naval forces detained a handful of oil tankers in protest of U.S. regional policies. The U.S. Navy issued press reports, and then took a nap.

---

6. Unless, perhaps, you are Canadian.

Beijing shit enough bricks to wall in a hippo. After all, China has *no* energy security policy independent of the U.S. Navy ensuring safety of the seas.

The second means of holding geography at bay is excellent international decision making at the top of governance. France is the country that comes to mind. I don't mean French presidents here, but rather the French institutional state, which has successfully educated, cultivated, recruited, and retained top talent in its domestic *fonctionnaires*, diplomats, military brass, and intelligence agencies. The United Kingdom, being an island with a navy, will always outmaneuver continental France on the waves. Germany often plays the part of wolf at the door. China and India are several bridges too far to shape, much less command. The sheer size of the United States regularly eclipses any French ambition. And yet and yet and yet these past seventy-five years the French have always punched above their weight.

The French focus on bureaucratic excellence ensures baseline state capacity. French leaders typically think two and three steps ahead, positioning them at every table that matters. Unlike the United States, where foreign affairs are at best the White House's mistreated stepchild, at the Élysée Palace managing France's world is an always-hands-on activity. Most often the French government is *on*. Engaged. Competent. Forward-looking. A great example of French panache and planning overwhelming geography was their forcing the postwar Germans into a subordinate position both strategically and economically as part of early European unification efforts. In essence, for a half century France's greatest historical security threat was subsidizing all things French.

But if a country can only succeed when it is *on*, should the switch flip to *off* it all goes straight to hell. Again, France is the premier example. When the European financial crisis hit in the early 2010s, the French assumed they could once again dictate that Berlin pay for everything. When Berlin issued a somewhat snarly *nein*, France not only suffered a collapse of authority within Europe, but the next decade saw the entire EU evolve from a springboard for French power to a prison with German jailers.[7]

---

7. Find this a sexy topic? I know I did. It's the core of the France chapter in my third book, *Disunited Nations*.

Chinese governance since the unfettered domestic disasters of the Cultural Revolution and Great Leap Forward feel like an *on* era, largely because of the foresight of Deng Xiaoping, the leader responsible for picking up the pieces after Mao's ideological and personal excesses wrecked the place. Deng's authority can be summed in two words: America and committees. The America bit was both membership in the Order, and a strategic policy of quiet so as to not antagonize the country ultimately responsible for China's political unity and economic dynamism. The committee part saw the establishment of a balanced decision making at the very top that incentivized China's many internal rivals—geographic, economic, ideological, personal—to work out joint governance positions. Post-Deng China was definitely a team sport.

That system is now gone.

Back in the 1980s, Deng worked out the next two *decades* of leadership secession, selecting specific men—Jiang Zemin and Hu Jintao—to represent the two most powerful Chinese political factions. Deng wasn't simply prescient in his working out of the extended cohabitation system, he was smart enough to know he wasn't smart enough to look forward *three* decades. He left it up to TeamJiang and TeamHu to select a compromise candidate to be the fourth post-Mao leader. Their joint choice was Xi Jinping, someone they felt had insufficient charisma to command a faction, insufficient creatively to rock the boat, and insufficient competence to ever rule unaided.

They were so very very very[8] wrong.

Xi spent his first five years on an "anticorruption" campaign that gutted China's regional governance of any potential threats to his national power, his second five years gutting the Jiang and Hu factions, and his time since purging the entire system of any potential successor. There's more going on here than simply Xi gathering more power unto his person than any leader in human history. Xi's consolidation campaign has exiled, imprisoned, intimidated into silence, or otherwise eliminated every capable person within the PRC. Xi's rule may be unassailable, but he's shot the messenger so often that no one will now bring him news. The biggest

---

8. *very*

change since 2013 when *The Accidental Superpower* was going to print is that contemporary China is now run by a cult of personality that penalizes governmental competence.

And so China's government is most certainly *off*.

Some rapid-fire examples of problems that should not be problems:

China's backing of Russia in the Ukraine War should have triggered Beijing to lock down energy production in Southeast Asia and the Persian Gulf in anticipation of rising energy insecurity. Instead, Xi's government opted for rote anti-Americanism and started importing Russian crude en masse. Unfortunately for China, Russia's oil infrastructure largely flows west to the Baltic and Black Seas. Russian maritime shipments to China must transit Suez before sailing by Chinese rivals in India, Australia, Indonesia, Singapore, the Philippines, and Vietnam. This is now the longest, least secure energy route on the planet, not to mention the one most vulnerable to decisions made by the world's two top naval powers: the United States and Japan. Also, India, a regional rival. Also, Vietnam, which hates all things Chinese. Also, Taiwan, which has some pointed opinion on all things Chinese. Stupid.

There's a horrible animal disease called African swine fever that is both highly contagious and always fatal to swine. China, the world's largest pork producer and consumer, was forced to cull two-thirds of its herd back in 2018–19 because of the world's worst ever epidemic. Between the end of that outbreak and the end of 2022, China did not report a single positive case even as a regional heat map of ASF showed China's border regions being on fire. Why not? Test results in China don't go directly from labs to farmers, but instead to the local Communist Party reps—reps who had not been authorized to admit to outbreaks. At the time of this writing, those unreported cases are spreading into the general swine population. A new Chinese food crisis is already in full swing. Stupid stupid.

China's economic model isn't simply the import of raw materials and the export of finished goods, but also foreign firms sourcing capital and technology for China to metabolize. Part of the China story is foreign business bigwigs having personal stakes to their China operations, but Xi's zero-COVID policies required those bigwigs to submit to *anal* swabs whenever they visit. As most titans of industry don't like it when a government gives it to them up the ass, nearly all stopped visiting. This "non-tariff barrier" persisted for three years. The average Western CEO helms his or her firm just under five years, which means most of the personal connections that enable the Chinese to dream of a better future are gone. Because of anal probes. Stupid stupid stupid!

But the best example I have is the spy balloon incident. In early 2023 a Chinese spy balloon was directed over the continental United States. Beijing insisted it was a weather balloon, but since it boasted a diameter over three hundred feet and dangled an apparatus larger than an Embraer jet, only the most poker-faced of China's own propagandists could say so with a straight face. My initial reaction was apparently the same as President Biden's: Shoot the thing down and see what we're dealing with.

I, like the U.S. president, am not an expert in...balloons. But someone within the American national security community is. The American defense and intelligence community convinced the president the balloon was no threat. The balloon was clearly going to overfly America's nuclear missile forces, but the normal state of the silos is to be closed. The balloon would not be able to garner any information that could not be gleaned from satellite. *But* every intelligence-gathering platform the Americans had—planes, helicopters, telescopes, whisper sensors, and on and on and on—was able to track the Chinese balloon for *nine days*. Messages and orders were intercepted. Networks and relays were mapped. Control nodes back in China were identified. Cryptography was recorded and cracked. And once the balloon was over the Carolina coast, it was shot down and the hardware recovered. It was the white chocolate buttercream frosting on the butterscotch cake.

Bilateral relations plummeted to the worst since the Korean War. Not because the Americans were angry, but because Xi was furious that the Americans were unwilling to help the Chinese save face in the presence of utter Chinese incompetence. We now know that Xi personally and the Chinese military in general were not even aware of the balloon before it hit global headlines. It was just some asshat in an intelligence bureau that thought he was sticking it to the Americans because that's what he thought Xi the Great wanted him to do. For the Americans, the balloon incident became the intelligence victory of the decade. It is bar none the dumbest thing I've seen any government do in the past quarter century, and if you think back on the world since 2000, there has been a *lot* of dumb.

But let's say you don't buy this line of reasoning. Let's say you don't agree with me that Xi's personality cult is generating government miscommunications and failures at every level. China is still doomed on the numbers. I'm not talking about the debt issue (although China's debt-to-GDP ratio has tripled since *The Accidental Superpower*'s initial release), or the fact that the Americans have soured in full bipartisan fashion on the issue of trade (with new export restrictions all but ending any meaningful progress in the Chinese tech sector), but instead demographics.

For nearly all countries, population statistics are a series of estimates. Educated guesses, if you will. It is only during once-a-decade censuses that the people are actually counted. China did that in 2020. Three years later the full data has not yet been released, although even the partial reports indicate that the Chinese birth rate has fallen by 40 percent *just since 2017,* and that the Chinese workforce has been shrinking in real terms for even longer. But the truly damning scuttlebutt, according to leaks out of the Shanghai Academy of Sciences, is that the Chinese have been overestimating their population in excess of 100 million people—with all of the missing millions children who would have been born since the one-child policy was adopted in the 1980s. All of the nonexistent citizens would have been under forty years old.

If this is only partially adjacent to the actual truth, the average Chinese didn't age past the average American in 2018, and India did not overtake China as the world's most populous nation in 2023. Both of those milestones occurred a decade previous. If those Shanghai Academy leaks prove true, China today is the world's fasting-aging society. And while the Chinese economy is indeed nearly four times the size it was in 2000, intensifying labor shortages mean its labor costs have gone up by a factor of thirteen. There are no longer enough Chinese citizens in their twenties and thirties to ever generate domestic, consumption-led growth again—or even produce enough children for China to even theoretically make it to the half-century mark.

Is China still there? Yep. Will anyone still think the Chinese will inherit the earth when it is time for me to take a crack at *TAS 20 Years On*?

Nope.

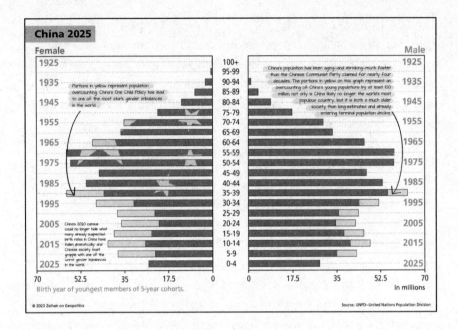

China 2025

Female

Male

China's population has been aging—and shrinking—much faster than the Chinese Communist Party claimed for nearly four decades. The portions in yellow on this graph represent an overcounting of China's young populations by at least 100 million, not only is China likely no longer the world's most populous country, but it is both a much older society than long-estimated and already entering terminal population decline.

Portions in yellow represent population overcounting China's One Child Policy has lead to one of the most stark gender imbalances in the world.

China's 2020 census could no longer hide what many already suspected: birth rates in China have fallen dramatically, and Chinese society must grapple with one of the worst gender imbalances in the world.

Birth year of youngest members of 5-year cohorts.

in millions

© 2023 Zeihan on Geopolitics

Source: UNPD–United Nations Population Division

CHAPTER 15

·◦━━━━━━━━◦·

Migration and Terrorism

In the coming age, most governments across the world are going to be suffering from problems at home that challenge their ability to cohere internally. The most dramatic changes will happen in places that are not key to U.S. security interests and yet were dependent either upon global market access and/or the security environment the Americans created. Such places will be forced to function on their own merits, most of which have precious few. Places like Greece, Lebanon, Turkmenistan, and Syria will simply die as modern states. Some that profited mightily from the global free trade network—China, South Africa, and Italy—will face pressure to simply hold themselves together. Others—with Russia and Ukraine at the top of the list—face a degree of desperation that can only come from the creeping implosion of demographic dissolution.

The Changing Nature of Immigration

What all of these groups of countries have in common is that life will get worse.

Rapidly aging populations will reduce local consumption and with that demand for locally produced goods. Consequently, employment levels will fall. Yet governments will have to increase the proportion of their spending that goes to their elderly. Lower economic activity, lower employment, and higher outlays all point to the same end result: much higher taxes. Citizens faced with an ever-increasing volume of their ever-decreasing incomes going to support governments that give them very little back will come to a hauntingly common conclusion: It is time to leave. And that's for the regions where central authority holds. In places where central government is flirting with disintegration, the decision to leave is even easier to make.

But desire will not equate to ability. Global immigration in the late twentieth and early twenty-first centuries has often had a reputation for being comprised of tired, poor, huddled masses. This is partly because tired, poor, huddled masses have been able to move relatively safely about the planet. Bretton Woods has had myriad impacts throughout the world, but it has made international transport cheap, easy, and safe compared to eras past. Everything from the EU's system of unrestricted travel among most of its members to the global airline industry is the direct outcome of Bretton Woods. Conversely, American disengagement from the global free trade network will make international travel more expensive, cumbersome, and dangerous. Between reduced travel availability and reliability and higher volumes of those wanting to relocate, the price of safe passage will inflate impressively. So while many people may try to leave home, most will only be able to reach where they can walk or drive. Immigration may be about to go big and go global, but the paths trodden will shorten to the remarkably local.

With one exception. The relatively well-off will still be able to attempt to relocate farther afield by jet or ship. People with connections who can help them through. People with marketable skills that they can peddle at their destination. People with suitcases full of cash.

Don't think it's possible? Think again. Emigration in times of economic stress is a concept as old as the hills. In the Bretton Woods era, we've just come to think of "economic stress" as synonymous with "poor countries." Roll back the clock to the 1840s and 1850s and look at America's immigrant communities. Some 1 million Germans left Europe for the United States during the political and economic upheavals surrounding the revolutions of 1848. Almost all of them were skilled labor.

Here's the global stability map from chapter 9 again, but this time with an overlay that highlights global concentrations of skilled labor. All of the countries that aren't in the "improved" or "steady state" categories are

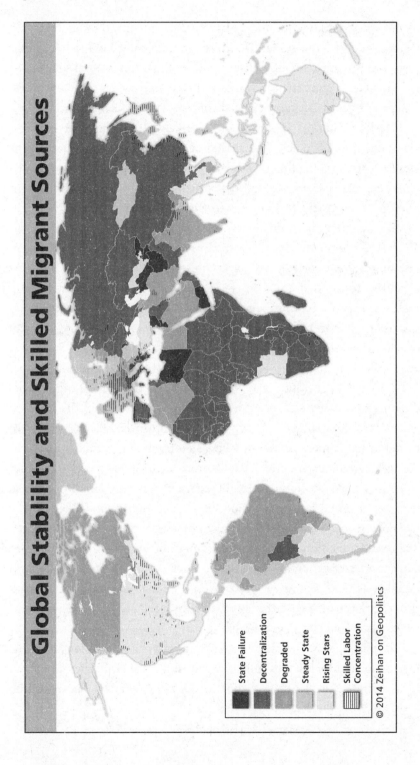

Global Stability and Skilled Migrant Sources

State Failure
Decentralization
Degraded
Steady State
Rising Stars
Skilled Labor Concentration

© 2014 Zeihan on Geopolitics

likely to generate large volumes of immigrants, but only the countries with a large proportion of skilled labor are going to contribute to long-range migration streams. The migration trends of the future are not likely to be so many Greek construction workers or Egyptian secretaries, but instead Italian architects, German financial analysts, and Chinese physicists.

The lion's share of these migrants are likely to seek entry into the same place: the United States. The reasoning is pretty straightforward. The United States is going to be somewhat above the global chaos, and its origin as a settler society makes it better able to absorb foreign populations than most countries. It will be an attractive destination from both a security and an economic point of view.

And it is more than mildly attractive to the Americans as well. Immigration is a huge societal cost saver. Raising children is one of the most expensive things that a person can do, and educating children is one of the most expensive things a government can do. Once everything from salaries to debt to busing to landscaping is factored in, the Department of Education estimates that total outlays for K-12 in the United States was $638 billion for the 2009–10 school year. That comes out to $12,750 per kid *per year*! In current dollars that means that the average high school diploma runs American society $165,000, and that's without the affiliated expenses of things like carpooling or band uniforms. Skilled labor almost by definition is more thoroughly educated than high school: a four-year college degree adds another $70,000 for a state university[1] or $160,000 for a private school. The numbers might seem a little lopsided in favor of K-12, but keep in mind that the cost of public education is embedded almost invisibly in your tax bill, while college comes directly out of your pocket. The result is the same. Each skilled immigrant who comes to the United States saves American society about a quarter million dollars in educational costs alone. But when they arrive, they don't just arrive with a useful skill set, they arrive with the ability to help fuel America's consumption-led economy and pay taxes as well.

Such labor shifts will help entrench the American position above the international disorder. Unskilled and semiskilled labor immigration from Mexico and Central America combined with skilled labor immigration

---

1. That's for in-state attendance. Out-of-state enrollment currently runs $125,000.

from the rest of the world will help limit labor costs across the board in the United States. Elsewhere in the world, however, the brain drain will lead to increases in labor inflation in every technological sector. With its role as the predominant global capital source, and now with the world's deepest and cheapest skilled labor pool, the United States should be able to maintain not just a pace of economic growth that will make it the envy of the rest of the globe, but also a pace of technological advancement that will keep it far ahead of the rest of the pack.

No one else can compete. The countries that will be sufficiently stable to theoretically still attract skilled labor fall into two categories. The first are those like Turkey or Uzbekistan that use ethnic-based nationalism as a means of mobilizing and managing their population. Outsiders are not necessarily welcome. The second are those like Australia and Canada that due to demographic factors are already *de*industrializing. They may well prove able to attract some skilled labor, but the range of careers available—and the heights of income that are likely—simply cannot compete with the United States, which is *re*industrializing, in large part because of shale.

Militancy Goes Big and Goes Global, but Terrorism Stays Home

As economies global, regional, national, and local degrade in the years ahead, there will be no end of conflicts. Some will come from government breakdown. Some will come as countries seek, whether out of opportunity or desperation, to control a resource or market or strategic spit of land held by another. In nearly all cases, there will be opposing military and political forces that will see the opposite side's civilians as legitimate targets. Militancy isn't just going to increase, it is going to become part of the landscape for upwards of one-third of the world's population.

But a distinction needs to be made between militancy and terrorism. Militancy is when groups take up arms either in opposition to or in the absence of a local government. As a rule, the weaker regional governments are, the greater the propensity for militancy to expand, both in terms of geographic reach and the number of groups involved. Militants particularly thrive when the writ of governments ends, either due to lack of resources or actual state collapse as the militants become the de facto rulers of specific territories. In war zones such militants turn to guerrilla tactics to achieve their aims.

Think of places like Afghanistan, Somalia, or Mexico's border regions where groups like the Taliban, Al-Shabaab, and the Gulf Cartel have managed to impose their own systems (or, based on your politics, challenge an occupying force) at the end of a gun. These are all classic militant groups.

Such groups thrive on disorder, and no system in world history has injected more *order* into the world than Bretton Woods. Because of the trade and alliance network the vast majority of the world is at peace and prosperous. In the absence of war and poverty, and the presence of strong, well-funded local state apparatuses, there just are not nearly as many lawless or war-torn areas as there have been by historical standards. But as the Bretton Woods system gives way this happy holiday from history will come to an end. Take a fresh look at the global stability map in chapter 9 with this in mind. Militancy will be a way of life in the failed states, a common occurrence in the decentralized states, and an irregular occurrence in many of the countries that face stability challenges.

Militants are typically not friendly folks, and they *do* tend to target civilians from time to time, up to and including with terror attacks.

A few likely examples of future guerrilla-sourced terrorism:

- Uzbek military forces will directly conquer the Tajik and Kyrgyz portions of the Fergana Valley. The region's mixed populations are obvious targets for guerrilla actions of all types.
- Angola's Ninjas are slowly but steadily eradicating the non-Mbundu populations. The effectiveness of the Mbundu's state security apparatus leaves terrorism as one of the few tools remaining for the groups slated for elimination.
- Europeans—probably French and Italians—will take command of collapsed Libya in order to secure access to oil and natural gas supplies, and will bring civilians in to operate the Libyan energy industry. The Libyans who resist will have ample targets.
- Without capital to maintain high levels of agricultural productivity, the highland Bolivians will lack enough food to survive. Their only choice will be to raid the more fertile areas of

the Bolivian lowlands. Farmers of the lowlands will be seen as prime targets.

- The failure of the European system will have a damning impact on the central governments of many states, allowing organized crime groups to exercise ever greater control over local affairs. In some places, such as Italy, expect local reigns of terror as such groups overwhelm police forces and intimidate citizens into compliance.
- Russian, Persian, and Turkish power will sweep into the Caucasus, and Persian and Turkish power into Mesopotamia. Militants—locally spawned, Saudi-planted, Iranian-funded, and/or Russian-instigated—will resist by targeting everything from imposed governments to infrastructure.
- The Chinese central government has not just smothered the cultural expressions of its minorities, it has shipped Han Chinese into their homelands in order to work a genocide by assimilation and dilution. As Chinese economic growth falters and central control cracks apart, there are a wealth of Han targets for the restless and oppressed minorities. Some of these groups, most notably the Uighurs of far western China, have little compunction about bringing the fight to the Han across the length and breadth of China.
- The current emir of Oman—Qaboos bin Said Al Said—is a brilliant man, having cobbled together a modern state out of a mutually hostile collage of communists, militants, Islamists, and various tribal groups. He is also in his mid-seventies, gay, and heirless. Upon his death, the various factions he has held together by force of personality will not just tear down everything he has built, but also open up on each other.

But terrorism is only one tool in the militant's playbook, and a rarely used one at that. When at war, militants attempt to strike when and where least expected and melt away. The whole idea is to avoid a direct slugging match with a conventional force, which will probably have aircraft and artillery. Attacking a military force, regardless of the tactics used, is by its very definition not a terror attack.

When dominating their own chunk of land, militants seek to actually *be* the government, so it matters what tools are used against the population. In both cases terrorism—the use of violence by a nonstate actor against civilians to achieve a political end—may be used, but it will not be the norm.

And most important, such tactics would "only" be used locally. Militants' concerns, motivations, resources, forces, goals, and actions are all focused on their specific geographies. They are either resisting a superior force or attempting to carve out a piece of territory for themselves. They don't have the inclination or capacity to strike out cross-border except in the narrowest sense, much less across an ocean.

This sort of "over there" terrorism is not the type that generates fear in the West. Instead it is the transnational sort that results in attacks like those of September 11, 2001. The express goal of transnational groups such as al Qaeda is to instill fear in the general population in order to shape the policies of entire governments. For transnational terrorists, the use of terror tactics is not a tool selected for a situation, but instead both the means *and* the end.

Such groups will still exist in the future, but they will face two obstacles to their operation that they currently do not. The first is a problem that transnational terror groups will find that they have in common with international migrants and multinational corporations: It will become harder to get around. Crossing international borders, much less oceans, will be a much grander undertaking than it is now. Just as economies and trade will regionalize and even localize, so too will militant activity. That leaves would-be transnational terror groups with a much-constrained definition of "transnational."

The second constraint regards the sort of home territory that transnational terror groups require to operate. If the home government is too strong, the transnational groups are hunted down and exterminated. If the home government is too weak, the transnational groups have to expend their scarce resources and personnel to carve out and maintain their own piece of territory, just as more traditional militant groups would. That would leave them with few resources with which to hurl an operation into another hemisphere. Terror groups' Goldilocks zone is a government that is on the edge—just strong enough to hold a territory together, but weak enough that it cannot actually control all of it. That's a very specific mix, and is represented by the "decentralized" layer of the global stability map.

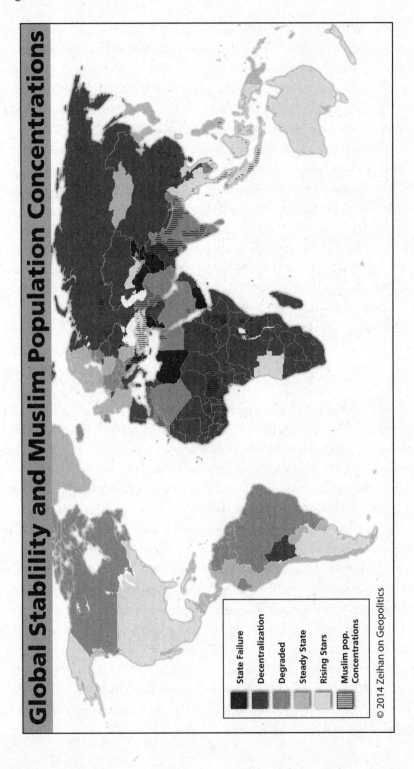

Global Stability and Muslim Population Concentrations

- State Failure
- Decentralization
- Degraded
- Steady State
- Rising Stars
- Muslim pop. Concentrations

© 2014 Zeihan on Geopolitics

I'm not going to say anything as blanket as "the United States doesn't need to worry about terrorism anymore," but the mechanics of the future are going to add an extremely thick layer of insulation to America's already impressive distance from the world at large. Take a look at the map on page 367. It is the same global stability map I've shown you before, but this time with an overlay for Muslim population concentrations.

There are a few takeaways from this map. First, not very many places in the Islamic world will have decentralized governments. Many of the locations that the West fears will become breeding grounds for terrorism—Afghanistan, Libya, Yemen, Syria—will become such security no-man's-lands that transnational groups simply will not be able to function. There will certainly be a few decentralized areas in Sub-Saharan Africa, but not only are those Muslim populations in the continental interior, they are also thoroughly engrossed in local issues rather than hellbent on launching operations in distant continents.

When I look at this map, I see two areas of concern.

The Pakistani Vise

Pakistan looms large as the most critical area.

In many ways, this was doomed to happen. As a consequence of the September 11, 2001, attacks, U.S. forces began heavy operations, first to root out al Qaeda and the Taliban from Afghanistan, and then to stabilize Afghanistan into some sort of form that could prevent al Qaeda's and the Taliban's resurgence. Considering that Afghanistan is both rugged *and* landlocked, it should come as no surprise that both tasks were difficult, with the latter proving all but impossible. At the time of this writing, the United States is attempting to negotiate the handover of authority to the local government that the Americans installed. It is highly likely that the Americans will have no more than a token presence in the country beyond 2016.

But there will certainly be debris. As part of the Afghan war effort the Americans discovered that the Afghanistan-Pakistan border region is as rugged and porous as it is densely populated. Many militant groups, most notably the Afghan and Pakistani strains of the Taliban movement, call it home. That unsavory fact introduced the Americans good and hard to Pakistan's core statehood problem.

Pakistan—in good times—is a state under siege, and it all comes down to geography. The Indus valley is the Pakistani core, and the waters of the Indus are the merger of five smaller upland rivers that all originate in the Himalayas. However, unlike the similarly sourced Ganges, the middle reaches of the Indus system receive no rainfall. All the rivers flood during the monsoons and must have their flows carefully managed to ensure regular water for the region's omnipresent irrigation works. If not for this management, the entire area, like the Nile valley, would be desert. The Indus may have been navigable at some point deep in the past, but millennia of such tight management and such seasonal input extremes mean that in the contemporary period it is only navigable to Hyderabad, just a handful of miles from the Indian Ocean. From a capital-generation and a social point of view, this puts Pakistan in a very similar basket as Egypt. A very thin crust of society manages the extremely capital-poor system and everyone else is a de facto slave.

That, however and unfortunately, is where the similarity with Egypt ends.

The middle regions of the Indus system are not only not highland, but they directly abut the Ganges region. All that separates the heavily irrigated Indus basin from the perennially fertile Ganges basin is a low saddle of land just one hundred miles deep. While this saddle is bracketed by a pair of impressive natural boundaries—the Himalayas and the Thar Desert—it is some three hundred miles wide and leads directly into the most densely populated region of the world. It is broadly indefensible. Under any circumstances, the people of the Indus valley will be heavily outnumbered by and exposed to the people of the far more populous Ganges valley, and that's before including the other Indian territories.

And that's before considering Pakistan's *other* borders. The entire western fringe of the Indus basin is mountainous, but most of it actually gets more natural rainfall than the core Pakistani lands (which have to be irrigated with waters from the Indus and its tributaries). This allows permanent populations—if far smaller than the dense footprint of the Indus itself—to exist. The Sindhi and Punjabi peoples of the Indus lowlands are somewhat traditional riverine people who have struck a political deal to run the Pakistani state. The nonriverine peoples of the highlands—a mix of Pashtuns, Kashmiris, Baluchis, and (many) more—in contrast, live

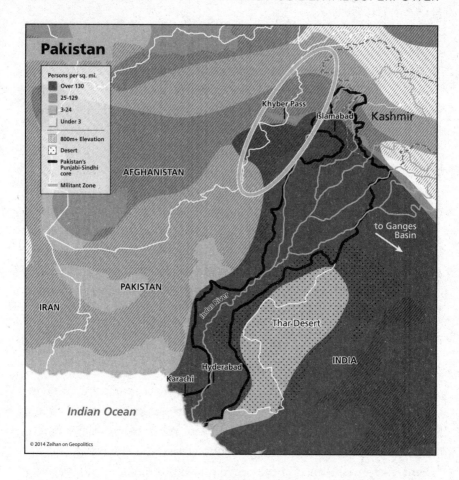

more traditionally and resent any effort by the lowlanders to assert control over them, often rebelling. The lowlanders would prefer to leave the highlanders be, but the highlanders sit upon a series of major passes—of which Kyber is the most infamous—that allow access from Central Asia and Persia into the Indus core. In times past, the Mongols used such routes. In more recent times, the Soviets threatened Pakistan via the same passes. As much as the Sindhi/Punjabi core might not want to have much to deal with the highlands, they dare not go without a military presence there.

Put all these geographic features together and you get a very ugly country. To the east is a hostile India that will be more powerful than Pakistan under almost any scenario. To the northwest are people who will always resist central power, but who must be subjugated in order to gain basic security for the core. Throughout the core Indus territories, there is a catastrophically high need for tight management and expensive irrigation to prevent desertification and starvation. Consequently, Pakistan is one of the poorest, most militarized, most corrupt, and least secure states ever created.

The problems that the Americans discovered in their Afghan adventure are a direct consequence of the Pakistanis' successful efforts to turn a negative into a positive. With the Soviet invasion of Afghanistan in 1979, the Pakistanis (reasonably) believed that they were next. They couldn't hope to stand up to the Soviets—much less the Indians combined with the Soviets—alone, and the peoples who lived in the highlands of northwest Pakistan had always been particularly unruly. The solution was to forge a new national identity based on Islam. Aggressive campaigning by the government sought to convince the mountain peoples of the border region that it was the Pakistanis' common religion that served as the glue to hold the Pakistani state together. The Soviets and Indians were portrayed as apostate foes. Instead of having to be in a state of low-grade war with their own citizens, the Pakistani core smiled as the mountain people started crossing the border to attack Soviet forces in Afghanistan or shifted into Kashmir to attack Indian forces.

Fast-forward thirty years and it is the Americans who are patrolling Afghanistan. The Pakistani Taliban—as some of the militias of the Pakistani mountain people are now known—attack the Americans just as vociferously as they attacked the Soviets.[2] They also see the Pakistani government's willingness to collaborate with the Americans in Afghanistan as a betrayal of the national "identity" at best, or as a sign of apostasy at worst. The suicide attacks that often mar Afghanistan and Kashmir now also occur within the Indus core with disturbing regularity.

The primary reason that Pakistan has proven able to survive the past decade is that the Americans needed it to. Afghanistan is landlocked and Pakistan is the route in, so for a decade the Americans bolstered Pakistan with military sales, cheap loans, and outright cash bribes that come out

---

2. There have been many concerns that Islamists within the Pakistani government have often assisted the various Afghan and Pakistani militias by sharing intelligence about the disposition of American forces. This is certainly true. However, such assistance is not given on orders of Pakistan's civilian or military leadership, but instead by Islamists within the government ranks who wish to assist the Taliban for religious or strategic reasons. In essence it is the Pakistani equivalent of Edward Snowden's leaks.

to roughly 8 percent of GDP—not to mention providing Pakistan with strategic cover versus India. Considering Pakistan's strategic vise, that could well be the difference between success and failure as a modern state.

The relationship has always been an uncomfortable one for both sides—and it is about to dissolve. The Pakistanis fear that American actions in Afghanistan have stretched their relationship with the Pakistani highlanders to the breaking point, and that when the Americans leave the lowland/highland war will resume. For their part, the Americans are far more than mildly annoyed that they ultimately found al Qaeda kingpin Osama bin Laden not just on Pakistani soil, but a short walk from the Pakistani equivalent of West Point. American largess is about to sharply end, and between the loss of resources and the newly infuriated nature of the highlanders, the Pakistani lowland's ability to manage its highlands will become sharply circumscribed. Not needing to battle for control of their own territories, the highlanders will have the magic mix of partial security, identity, ability, and incentive to strike across national borders.

Their primary target will be India, as these people have some serious bones to pick over Kashmir. They see the Indians as occupying a portion of their homeland. As Pakistan would prefer not to actually go to war with a superior India, Islamabad's efforts to rein in the highlanders make it likely that the highlanders will have on-again, off-again clashes with the Pakistani authorities in Islamabad as well. This is a problem, a *big* problem, but it is also a regionally contained problem. The Pakistani Taliban and groups like it are tied down by geography. Reaching the wider world would require first negotiating the Pakistani core, not to mention ignoring the local and compelling challenge of Kashmir. These groups certainly have the ability to strike across international borders, but there is really only one border they will care about. That's awful for India, but great for the Americans and the wider world.

The Other Russia

There is only one other location on the planet that meets the requirements for generating Muslim terrorist groups with both the interest and capacity to strike at long range. It is in Russia.

Even in times of stability, Russia is an unstable country. It isn't a normal

European country, but instead a multiethnic empire. Most of the European ethnicities rose in a zone where they were able to emerge as the dominant and even unitary group. The Hordelands hold no such ethnic uniformity. Their wide-open spaces mean that any secure people is one that has conquered all of their neighbors, and all of their neighbors' neighbors, until they can anchor themselves in geographic barriers as far removed as the Carpathians and the Altay. Any successful Hordelands government isn't a nation-state, it is a multiethnic empire. Any successful Hordelands government doesn't placate its subjects, it intimidates them into obedience.

Among the dozens of ethnicities the Russians conquered in their bid to achieve security, a people nestled on the northern slopes of the Caucasus Mountains stands out.

The Chechen Rebellion Continues

The Chechens in many ways are a relic of the deep past. Their northern lands are reliably well watered by any standard, allowing for quite productive agriculture without irrigation, while their southern lands are heavily forested, riddling their territory with redoubts and defensive positions. This combination has granted them serious staying power, enabling them to resist the multitude of invasions that have boiled out of the Hordelands every generation or three, and their national history can be traced back at least until the sixth century AD.

Most notably, the Chechens are one of the very few peoples to have survived the Mongol invasions—a period of their history that made them *very* good at guerrilla warfare. The Russians first crossed swords with them when they started their effort to conquer the Caucasus region in 1803 and did not finish their work with the Chechens until 1889. The war—or, more to the point, the Chechen guerrilla campaign—was so brutal that the Russians were forced to establish a permanent military base in Chechen territory to maintain control. The place came to be called Grozny, which roughly translates to "terrible place."

In the years since, there have been more Chechen rebellions against Russian authority than most interested parties bother to count. With the Russian near collapse at the end of the Soviet era, the rebellions turned to outright wars. While the Russians refer to the First and Second Chechen

Wars[3] as emotional landmarks of the post-Soviet era, the Chechens themselves refer to them as simply the latest campaigns in the Two Hundred Years War against the Russian occupation of their lands. The two most recent conflicts claimed at least one hundred thousand dead, a number similar to the total deaths in the first two years of the Syrian civil war, but among a population that was but one-twentieth the size.

Simply put, the Chechens have been resisting Hordelands-based forces like the Russians for at least fifteen hundred years. With the Russian decline both advanced and irreversible, it is only a matter of time before the Chechens make their next move.

Three factors argue that it will be sooner rather than later. First, there is a lack of proximity. The Russians arrived in the Caucasus in a roundabout manner. Much of the Hordelands is marginal if not outright hostile land, and some of it is nearly uninhabitable. While there is ample rainfall in the North Caucasus itself, the flatlands directly to the north are steppe, supporting hardly any population outside the tight confines of the Volga valley. There isn't a straight shot to the Caucasus from Moscow, so direct exercise of power from there is impossible. The more habitable territory arcs southwest through Ukraine before boomeranging back southeast along the Black Sea coast.

Due to this bow, the line of military, economic, and cultural projection from Moscow isn't a thousand miles, but instead sixteen hundred miles. That might not sound like a huge difference, but that's probably because you've heard the phrase "a thousand miles" so often in this book that it is losing its meaning. The additional six hundred miles is about the same as the distance between Boston and Richmond. Think of how difficult the Civil War was for the Union, and that in an era of railways with the geography of water transport to help. As for the total distance, sixteen hundred miles is a touch over the distance from Boston to Miami.

---

3. Chechen War I was 1994–96; it ended with an ignoble Russian retreat from Chechnya and de facto Russian recognition of Chechen independence. Chechen War II began in 1999, when the Russians invaded Chechnya in response to Chechen-based forces invading next-door Dagestan, another Russian republic. Formal military operations lasted until 2001, but it was nearly another decade before the Russians felt sufficiently confident that they had quelled militancy in the republic to reduce their troop deployments below fifty thousand.

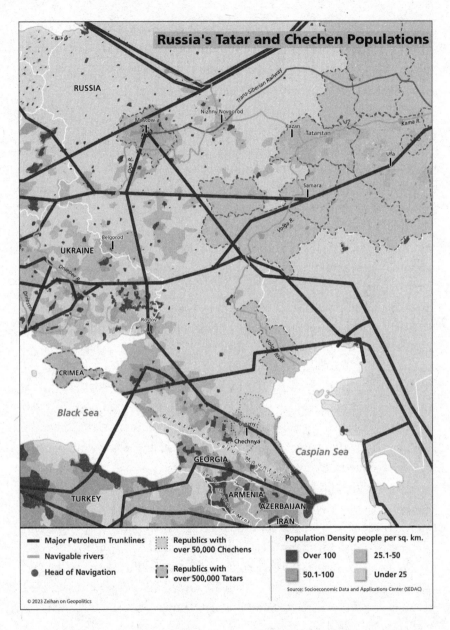

Russia's Tatar and Chechen Populations

Legend:
- **Major Petroleum Trunklines**
- **Navigable rivers**
- ● **Head of Navigation**
- ┊┊ **Republics with over 50,000 Chechens**
- ┌─┐ **Republics with over 500,000 Tatars**

Population Density people per sq. km.
- Over 100
- 50.1-100
- 25.1-50
- Under 25

Source: Socioeconomic Data and Applications Center (SEDAC)

© 2023 Zeihan on Geopolitics

Second, because of this bow in the line of approach, Russia's control of Chechnya is dependent upon its ongoing control of Ukraine, and the powers that wish to knock Russia back all see Ukraine as the weakest point in the Russian system. Romania, Poland, and Turkey in particular are all local powers that would like to loosen Russian influence over the

Ukrainian system and will certainly resist any Russian effort to control it directly. Even a modicum of failure in Ukraine would prevent the Russians from dedicating the manpower required to keep Chechnya pacified.

Third, the Chechens are *not* passive victims. As you might expect from a people who gave even the Mongols pause, they are phenomenal fighters who have integrated their social structure into their (para)military resistance strategies. In the Russian-Chechen conflicts of the past two decades, they have not hesitated to take the fight to the Russians. Some of these attacks fit the standard feel of insurgent activities, being carried out both within and beyond the confines of Chechen territory.

But the Chechens have also embraced terror tactics. In 1995, Chechen gunmen attacked the small Russian town of Budyonnovsk, taking approximately 2,000 hostages and holding them in the local hospital in a tense standoff with Russian forces that lasted five days. The Chechens are believed responsible for the infamous apartment block bombings of late 1999 in Moscow, Buynaksk, and Volgodonsk, which resulted in nearly 300 deaths and more than 650 casualties. In October 2002, Chechen gunmen invaded and laid siege to Moscow's Dubrovka Theater, capturing 850 hostages. In the ensuing raid by Russian forces three days later, all of the militants were killed, in addition to 130 of the civilian hostages. Perhaps most notorious of all was the September 2004 capture of a school in Beslan, which, after three tragic days, left almost 800 people wounded and 334 dead, including 186 schoolchildren. They have also destroyed Russian passenger jets in flight with smuggled explosives and have bombed several Russian passenger trains. The Chechen forces are highly motivated and highly capable, and very soon they will (again) be battling the Russians with every one of the many tools at their command.

What truly terrifies the Russians, however, is not that the next Chechen rebellion is coming, that it will likely be successful, or that it might even result in the full-scale ejection of Russians from their Caucasus anchor. It is that the rebellion will spread.

In the grand scheme of things the Chechens are a geographically concentrated people with some 95 percent of them in Chechnya proper and nearly all the rest in the neighboring republics of Dagestan or Ingushetia. Yes, there are small populations—Russian authorities tend to grimly call them "cells"—elsewhere, but their numbers do not raise a risk of mass upheaval. But the Chechens are not Russia's only minority, its only capable minority, or its only Muslim minority. Russia's true problem will be where its minorities cross with geographically sensitive points.

Russia has one internal waterway of note, the Volga. By North American standards it is a bit of a joke—frozen half the year, requiring a great deal of engineering to be forced to navigability, and draining into the landlocked Caspian Sea—but compared to the rest of the Hordelands it is pretty fantastic. The Russians seem to agree. The Volga's upper tributaries bracket Moscow and are part of a web of rivers and canals the Russians use aggressively in the summer months. Every major piece of infrastructure—road, rail, and pipe—that links Siberia to European Russia crosses the Volga at some point.

The thing is, the Volga really isn't traditionally a Russian river—it's a Tatar river. The Tatars are not what most would expect from a subject peoples living near the very center of the Hordelands. They are riverine—even under the brutality of Stalin, they proved to have a view of wider horizons and an interest in trade greater than nearly all other Soviet citizens, up to and including the Russians themselves. At 5.5 million strong they are the Russian Federation's largest minority group. Their cities sit on most of the aforementioned critical infrastructure. There is even a community over one hundred thousand strong on Ukraine's Crimean Peninsula. They are Muslim, but not the sort of Muslim that most Americans picture when they think of the word. They are highly educated, worldly, secular. The women wear dresses, not hijabs. Their engineers produce oil without foreign help. Their scientists design space stations.[4] And unlike the ethnic Russians, who are in a not-so-slow demographic collapse, the Tatar population is young, healthy, and growing.

Even if the Tatars never aspired to be more than a subject people, even if the Tatars did not resent Moscow, and even if the Russians did not face twilight, the Tatar rise is inevitable. And since they populate the eastern fringe of European Russia, simply a few wisps of autonomy would threaten Moscow's control over the entirety of Russia's Siberian lands—including more than three-quarters of the country's oil production.

4. Remember *Mir*? The man in charge of the entire Soviet space program was a Dr. Roald Sagdeev, an ethnic Tatar.

The Tatars have shown no sign of rebelling on the scale—or with the tactics—of the Chechens, but they have always wrested whatever autonomy they can from Moscow. As Russian rule becomes weaker and increasingly plagued by Chechen-style problems, the temptation to actively resist will rise. Moscow is right to be concerned. Because while a renewed Chechen rebellion can hurt Russia, even the mildest of Tatar rebellions would kill it.

Scared New World: Nasty, Brutish, and Short . . . or American

In the not-so-distant future economic dislocations and conflict—whether that conflict be irregular militancy or outright war—will become an unfortunate fact of life for most of the global population. The bright spot—perhaps the only bright spot—is that as trade and transport withers, the ability of this violence to directly impact countries far removed will wither as well. That's fantastic news if you are part of the inner circle of American friends and allies who will still be able to boast trade and security access sufficient to fully patrol their own territories, and very cold comfort indeed if you are anyone else.

Migration and Terrorism: Ten Years On

Shifts in immigration patterns since *Accidental*'s first publish are pretty straightforward.

Simply put, Mexico has already aged out of being a large-scale source of migrants. NAFTA negotiations began in 1990, starting Mexico down the path to mass industrialization and urbanization, the twin trends that extend life spans...at the cost of lower birth rates. Obligingly, Mexico's birth rate fell by half. Three decades later the bottom of Mexico's demographic chart has narrowed from a pyramid to a chimney and there simply are not enough Mexicans to fill all the local jobs *as well as* supply labor north of the border.

Early data for the initial version of *Accidental* suggested this factor was already in play, but since I only had few data points, I was somewhat newish to the field of demography, and past performance is not necessarily indicative of future results, I was hesitant to include the Mexican-immigration-is-already-over bombshell in a book that already boasted plenty of explosives. Now? As of 2023, net migration from Mexico to the United States has been neutral to *negative* for the past seventeen *years*.[5]

Which gives me more than sufficient confidence to say this: Not only will net migration from Mexico likely *never* again be a fixture of the American immigration story, but sharply contrary to the conventional wisdom, Central American migration is on the same path as Mexico. Just a few years after NAFTA took effect, so too did CAFTA. The Central American states have experienced a baby bust nearly identical to that of Mexico. Caution: I do not expect carbon-copy experience. Central America has not industrialized as evenly as Mexico, it started from a lower point in the development process, and all the standard regional stereotypes of legal/economic/security mayhem hold true. The slowing of migration from Central America will certainly occur in a less dramatic fashion than it did with Mexico. Americans will *always* have reasons to stress about the southern border—lawlessness, trade, and drugs are three good reasons to do so—but migration? That one is going to fade by decade's end.

---

5. In the interest of transparency, Mexico, under the blindingly incompetent leadership of López Obrador, has become a much less safe place to live. Consequently, outmigration in recent years has ticked up somewhat.

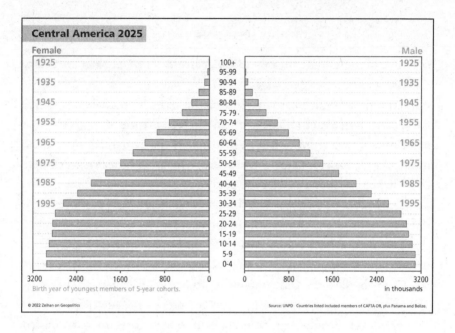

In some ways, this somewhat delayed settling of America's southern border is a negative.

Economically, we are in a rapidly graying world. Losing access to young people who *want* to work is a big step in the wrong direction. Americans might not sufficiently connect the dots in ten years' time to identify a lost opportunity, but they will acutely feel the absence of the Baby Boomers from the workforce and *allllll* the inflation pain that comes from that.

Politically, the southern border's migration pressure *has* induced the Americans to reconsider immigration laws and processes that have not seen meaningful updates for *forty* years! As the border "crisis" eases, so too will the negative incentive to continue meaningful reformation—reformation that would be hella useful in preparing for the coming waves of *skilled* migration as the world falls apart. Instead, Americans are going through one of their once-every-two-generations nativist, anti-immigration moments. This too will pass, but not likely with sufficient rapidity to make the most of this perfect moment to fish in the Chinese and European talent ponds for the best and brightest.

So that's the migration part of the "migration and terrorism" chapter. Now for the uglier part.

First and foremost, thankfully and finally, America's "Global War on Terror" is over. With the benefit of hindsight, it is easy if not altogether fair to say the whole thing was a bad idea. In going to war against a para-military tactic—Islam-inflected terrorism—as opposed to any specific group, the United States never had much of a chance of "winning." What is now equally clear, and in my opinion far fairer, is criticizing the lack of presidential leadership on the topic. George W. Bush was most certainly obliged to act after the September 11 attacks, but the orchestrator—Osama bin Laden of al Qaeda fame—was killed in Pakistan roughly ten years later. The War on Terror lasted a full additional decade.

That—the focus on the organization al Qaeda and the person of OBL—*should* have been the mission. Iraq, in contrast, was an option. The occupation and attempted reconstruction of Afghanistan was an option. Intervening in the Sahel and Mindanao in the Philippines were options. All of these options continued to be exercised by the Obama administration. And the Trump administration. Simply because the belief was that whenever U.S. troops finally left, it would be obvious it was all for naught, and none of the three presidents who presided over the war wanted to pay the political price for saying so. Joe Biden is *not* my favorite guy, but damn does the man know how to peel off a scab. His order to close down the Afghan occupation finally ended what was always a raw deal for Americans.[6]

Four hefty takeaways—and one caveat—bracket American military strategy in the aftermath of the War on Terror.

First, despite having the world's most powerful expeditionary land forces by an order of magnitude, the United States isn't going to deploy appreciable numbers of ground forces into *any* combat situation in the next decade. More likely two. Triply so for anything involving the Arab World.

Second, not engaging in mass ground force deployments is *not* the same thing as saying there will be no U.S. military action. It will just look different. The Navy will still Navy anywhere and anywhen it feels like Navying. The whole idea of an expeditionary navy is you can choose the

---

6. To say nothing of the Afghans.

time, place, and nature of a conflict, and be gone before the other side can react. That flexibility has defined U.S. strategy for over a century. We learned it from the Brits, who learned it (at high tuition) from the Spanish. It works. It will continue to work. So too will the use of special forces that combine speed, stealth, precision lethality, and, on occasion, deniability. America's Special Operations Forces have more than tripled in number since 2001. Expect more of them and more from them as they become Washington's preferred method of "direct" intervention.

Third, America's next military conflict is highly likely to be much closer to home. Americans' insatiable demand for cocaine and other Mexico-sourced and -transited drugs has ensured that what was always a somewhat rickety political, legal, and judicial system could never function well. To some parts of America's ideological spectrum, the Mexican cartels are the new terrorists and should be treated like al Qaeda and its ilk. Between that spreading identification and ever-rising deaths due to cartel-provided drugs, some degree of military intervention is unavoidable. The most likely path would be a mix of Special Operations Forces and drone monitoring and assaults throughout the border region.

To be clear, this is a prediction, *not* a recommendation. Profit, not ideology, drives cartel behavior. The cartels care nothing for political policies. True terrorists have very clear political goals in mind. Without addressing the demand side of the drug equation, even successful military operations against the cartels would only shatter them, drive up the price of drugs, and encourage more criminal elements to move into the space. If there was a place the United States could park a 500-pound bomb to end the drug war, it would have done so. *Ages* ago.

Even worse, most U.S. military activity will occur in the northern Mexican states that abut the U.S. border, simply because of deployment ranges. Not only is that well beyond the core territories of Jalisco New Generation—the cartel I personally see as the current biggest problem— but those northern states are the portions *of the planet* most integrated into U.S. manufacturing systems. Their politicians and businesspeople are among the world's most pro-American. The political damage would be incalculable. As to the economic damage, the shattering of the world's most efficient manufacturing supply chains would easily cost the average

American a few thousand dollars annually. Texas, both as America's primary Mexican partner and the leading clearing house for Mexican goods reaching the bulk of the United States, would be particularly hard hit. Houston, as the hub for all things NAFTA, would suffer worst of all. An intervention would not ameliorate the drug crisis. It. Will. Instead. Make. Everything. Worse. And I'm all but certain it will happen.

Fourth, the Ukraine War has demonstrated the weakness of the Russian state. I'm not specifically calling a Ukrainian victory here, *but* Russia's inability to overwhelm Ukraine in a matter of months is one of those things that just shouldn't have happened.[7] Russia is proving incompetent not simply at churning out materiel, but even at mobilizing its society so the country can really put its shoulder into this war. Even now with the Russians having suffered at least a quarter million casualties, the Russian defense minister remains staunchly committed to lining his own pockets rather than supplying the front. A merc group led by a former *caterer* even launched a putsch in June of 2023, as I was reviewing the copyediting for this text update, that made it to within a couple hundred miles of Moscow! I am—bit by bit—wrapping my mind around the idea that we really are at the beginning of the Russian Fall.

I make it clear in the "Players" chapter of this book that I believe I will outlive the existence of the Russian Federation, but it never occurred to me that it could occur this quickly, or that the trigger might be state…failure. Yet here we are.

The Russians see this as a battle for their Twilight. A war for their very existence. They will not stop. If ejected, they will remuster, rearm, and try again, in their own slapdash, incompetent, brutal way. *If* the Ukrainians are going to win this war, they need to do more than "merely" purge their lands of occupying forces. They need to take the battle across the border into Russia proper and smash Russia's logistical capacity to even try. That means—at a minimum—they must neutralize the cities of Belgorod and Rostov-on-Don, the cities that provide the bulk of the access points to the eastern Ukrainian city of Kharkiv, the Donbass, and above all else the Crimean Peninsula.

---

7. Most people are ecstatic when their forecasts prove true. Me? Often the opposite.

Rostov-on-Don commands more than Moscow's access to the Crimea. It also straddles the primary transport artery to the entirety of Russia's Northern Caucasus territories. Including Chechnya.

One of Russian strongman Vladimir Putin's greatest and most durable diplomatic, strategic, and political feats is his successful courting of a psychopath named Ramzan Kadyrov, a Chechen warlord who fought the Russians in the First Chechen War, a war the Russians lost. Putin flipped the Kadyrov faction to side with Russia in the Second, a war in which the Russians prevailed. In the past two decades, Ramzan Kadyrov and his forces have served Vladimir Putin in diverse capacities: political officers, agents of intimidation, assassins, and even involvement as "cleansing agents" in the Ukraine War. All Kadyrov has requested in return is the ability to rule Chechnya as he sees fit. The place was a violent cesspool before, but now? *low whistle*

The nicest thing I can say about Kadyrov is that his casual violence is as eminently predictable as his innate grasp of power balances. Even a failed Ukrainian attempt to neuter Rostov-on-Don will end Russia's ability to meaningfully influence the Caucasus. Kadyrov would turn on Moscow like a rabid dog in seconds, and a Third Chechen War would *begin* with the Russians having no troops near Chechnya, and little prospect for getting them there. I stand by everything I've said in this book and others about the nature of Russia, its coming end, and the role a newly rebellious Chechnya will play in that end. *But* the Putin-Kadyrov alliance has purchased Moscow that most precious of geopolitical resources: time. And now, with Rostov-on-Don potentially in Ukraine's sights, the end feels extremely fucking nigh.

Finally, the caveat.

Many may feel the American adventure into the Middle East in general, and Iraq in particular, was dumb. I have one foot uncomfortably in that camp. But the platinum award for stupidity in the first two decades of this century goes to the one, the only, Osama bin Laden. OBL's rationale for the 9/11 attack was that it would bait the Americans into attacking the Middle East in an attempt to hunt down the perpetrators. That wasn't the dumb part. The dumb part was his belief that the American intrusion would motivate the world's Muslim populations to overthrow their local rulers and usher in a golden age of Muslim unity under a tight theocracy.

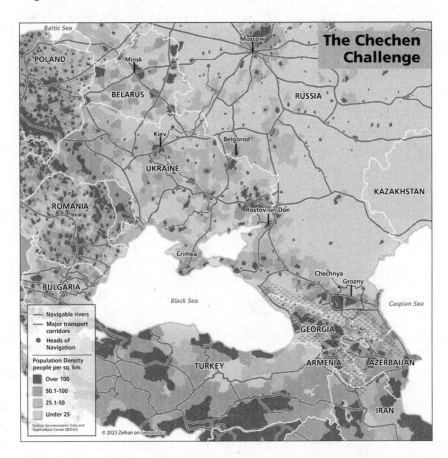

Perhaps not as dumb as what's going down in China these days, but still remarkably stupid.[8]

My point here isn't that the United States took the bait (although it did), or that OBL's foolishness was always going to cost him his life and that of his movement (although it did), but instead that there are people out there who would benefit greatly from counseling and a change to their medication regimen who nonetheless possess tools capable of impacting the American politic. Attacking the United States head-on will earn you a visit from the SEALs, an aircraft carrier battle group, or a missile carrying something fairly explosive. But, like OBL, some may still try to get a dagger between America's ribs as part of some convoluted, misadvised scheme.

---

8. You gotta have a baseline.

Black swan events are by their very nature unpredictable. I'm comforted by the fact that terrorism seeks local political change. It typically stays very close to home. The original version of this chapter still holds what I see as the biggest sources of future terror—none of which involve the United States—and events this past decade indicate I'm on the right track. But "typically" is not synonymous with "always."

The American Age

So that's…the future. Not some hazy distant future after we're all dead and gone, but the future we will all be living in for the next fifteen years of our lives.

The kicker is that this—all of this: the dissolution of the free trade order, the global demographic inversion, the collapse of Europe and China—is all just a fleeting *transition*. The period of 2015 through 2030 will be about the final washing away of the old Cold War order. It isn't the end of history. It is simply clearing the decks for what is next.

Which will be something extraordinary.

The Hobbesian period of 2015–30 will be the *least* Amerocentric portion of the twenty-first century, because by 2030 three things will have happened that will solidify the world as America's oyster.

First, everyone else in the world will have had fifteen years to rip one another apart going after the scraps of the previous system. Resource wars. Market wars. A return of naval competition. New technologies that allow countries beset by problems—especially demographic problems—to still lash out. Does anyone actually think that drones—a technology that hits hard with a minimum of manpower—will remain purely an American tool? It'll be new, exciting, terrifying. And a not insignificant portion of the world is likely to get wrecked or simply waste away. All of the powers that the Americans think of as competitors—with Russia, China, and the European Union at the top of the list—will be exposed to have feet of clay and spines of glass.

Second, most if not all of that chaos and destruction will pass the Americans by. Instead of fifteen years of struggles and pain and want, the Americans will experience fifteen years of moderate growth with stable markets and reliable energy supplies. As of 2014, the Americans are already far and away the dominant power. By 2030, they will be inordinately stronger in both absolute and relative terms while most of the rest will be struggling just to stay where they are…and most of the rest will fail. The Americans will suffer no invasions (although they might launch a couple), they will watch the shipping wars with casual disinterest (although they might capture bits of it), they'll puzzle over why everyone suddenly wants their currency again (but won't hesitate to make it available). The Americans will be able to pick and choose their fights, or not even deign to participate in the wider world.

Third, America's demographics will invert a second time. By 2030, the oldest of the Boomers will be eighty-four, but by 2040, the *youngest* will be seventy-six. The sack of bricks that started descending upon the federal government back in 2007 will be almost completely lifted. Settling daintily into the roomy space the Boomers will be vacating will be the new retiree class, Gen X—aged sixty-one to seventy-five at that point. The Boomers' children, Gen Y, will be forty to sixty. As a group the Ys' incomes will make the American system flush with cash once again. After fifteen years of ever tighter budgets, the American government's fiscal balance will heal. America's long Boomer night will be over and government finances will step back into the light…

…to find a world that is a broken wasteland. By 2040, many of the world's *developing* states will have aged into the sort of damaged demography that the Europeans had experienced only a generation before and will be starting their own crippling slide into pain and decrepitude. One notable exception to this will be China, because China will already be there. By 2040, the average Chinese will be forty-seven, versus the average American who will only be forty. By that point Americans will think of China as just as much of a has-been as they think of Japan today—assuming that China still exists as a recognizable entity. Bereft of challenges, the Americans will be able to do a lot of navel gazing.

What do the Americans have to do to make sure this comes to pass? Not a damn thing. Geography has given the Americans almost everything they could ever need. China and Europe will fall and fade without prompting. Russia will crumble on its own. Iran will scramble the Middle East like a bad omelet for its own reasons. Demographics in the United States will rebound on their own, and even determined efforts to repair the damage in other nations won't generate their first glimpses of positive results until 2035. Shale takes care of the rest. America's strengths may be accidental, but they are strengths—and durable ones at that—nonetheless.

Simply put, the world is indeed going to hell, but the Americans are going to sit this one out.

Think time will prove me wrong? Look me up in 2040 and let's discuss. I'll be sixty-six and looking forward to a much-delayed (thanks to the Boomers) retirement.

Bring a bottle of something interesting.

EPILOGUE

⟞•⟝

Ten Years After

Okay. We're done! Thanks for sticking with me. If it wasn't for your interest in our wild crazy world, I'd be a hobo. Or worse, an accountant.

One final note: I've really gotten into wine since the first edition of *The Accidental Superpower*. My definition of "interesting" has become somewhat more . . . interesting.

Appendix I   No Fear: Climate Change

I'm not nearly good enough at math or patient enough with people who love to argue endlessly to wade into the technical aspects surrounding the issue of whether or not human activity is indeed altering the Earth's climate. What I *can* do is apply the geopolitical method to the issue and highlight a few things about a future in which trade fails, populations age, *and* climates change. In what follows, I'm going to assume that climate change is real, that it is happening, and that it will trend toward some of the more dire extremes that have been predicted to date. It isn't a particularly pretty future, but once again, it is one in which the United States emerges head, shoulders, waist, knees, and ankles above most of the rest of the world.

Global warming presents three primary challenges to our future.

The first threat is that changing climate patterns will reduce the ability of various lands to serve as food production zones, leading to regional food shortages. This could hit the world fairly hard, as most grain agriculture—which is to say the agriculture that provides most of the calories that people consume—is actually monoculture, an agricultural practice where the land produces but one type of produce to which it is uniquely well suited. Change the climate and the grain in question is no longer appropriate to that geography.

The second threat is that sea levels will rise, inundating coastal regions and destroying ports and cities.

The third and final threat is from mass population movements as people flee either hunger or the advancing sea for better-supplied or drier land.

In all three cases, the United States gets a pass.

- The American agricultural heartland is the largest in the world by most measures, stretching across a wide range of longitude and latitude. A moderate shift in climate would shift the bands within which certain crops could be grown—a hotter climate would move the various crop belts north, a drier climate would move them east. Farmers might need to switch from corn to wheat or vice versa, but the vast majority of American farmland would still be usable in all but the most extreme of climatic variations, and all of it would still have the necessary infrastructure to support monoculture.
- In terms of rising sea levels, the Americans would lose New Orleans and most of Florida outright, and Manhattan would be threatened. But ports can be moved upriver, while an area as small and intensely developed as Manhattan could in theory be protected from rising sea levels with a combination of dikes and pumps. All other major American cities would remain sufficiently high and dry to continue operation, although the coastal ones would obviously require some (multibillion-dollar) infrastructure tweaking. The biggest loss to the Americans would most likely be the submersion of the barrier island chains, which would expose the Gulf and East Coasts to direct storm damage.
- In terms of refugee movements, the Americans also do well. The only two countries that they border do not have meaningful coastal populations, so no extranational refugees will be pouring in. And the United States itself has more than enough usable land under even unreasonable scenarios to resettle its own displaced Floridians.

None of this means that climate change wouldn't impact the United States. Hardly. But the impacts would be relatively moderate—minor even—and not a great deal of new infrastructure would need to be constructed to compensate for the deviations.

Elsewhere, however, climate change would be remarkably destructive.

Most of the north-south dimension of the North European Plain is narrower than the U.S. state of Arkansas, so even a mild climatic shift could destroy local monocultures in their entirety. The Argentine plains are less than half the acreage of the greater Midwest and are bracketed by mountains, desert, and tropics with very small transition zones; a mild climatic shift could obviate vast tracts of land. Similarly, the eastern half of the Russian wheat belt is a long thin strip—thinner than even the NEP—bracketed by desert to the south and the Siberian wastes to the north. A climatic shift might "just" move the belt north or south by a few dozen miles, but any such change would move it north or south into areas with no towns and no infrastructure. In all examples, the Argentines, Europeans, and Russians would also lose major cities: Buenos Aires, Rotterdam, Amsterdam, Stockholm, and Saint Petersburg would all disappear beneath the expanded sea.

Population relocations would be particularly horrifying in Northern Europe. The populations of Denmark, Sweden, and the Netherlands exist directly on top of major low-lying food-producing regions—the most densely populated portions of those three countries would for all intents and purposes cease to exist. Also joining the list of drowned countries would be Bangladesh, whose 180 million people would have nowhere to go but already impoverished India, and Egypt—where over half of the population lives on the Nile delta, which currently is just barely above sea level. Some 50 million Egyptians—including the bulk of the population of Cairo—would have to move upriver into a narrow valley that could not support one-quarter of them. Other major cities that would sink below the waves include Basra (Iraq), Bangkok, Venice, Port Harcourt (Nigeria's oil capital). Vietnam's Ho Chi Minh City and the bulk of the Mekong delta, the world's most productive rice-growing region, would also be gone. The entire northern rim of Africa could face starvation, generating a deluge of refugees who would have nowhere to go but Southern Europe, a region that will already be under extreme pressure both economically and climatically.

Somewhat less horrible threats will face populations that are fleeing hunger rather than water. Russian agricultural populations east of the Urals would be forced to abandon Siberia for European Russia. The Iberian countries would likely lose the ability to feed themselves and have

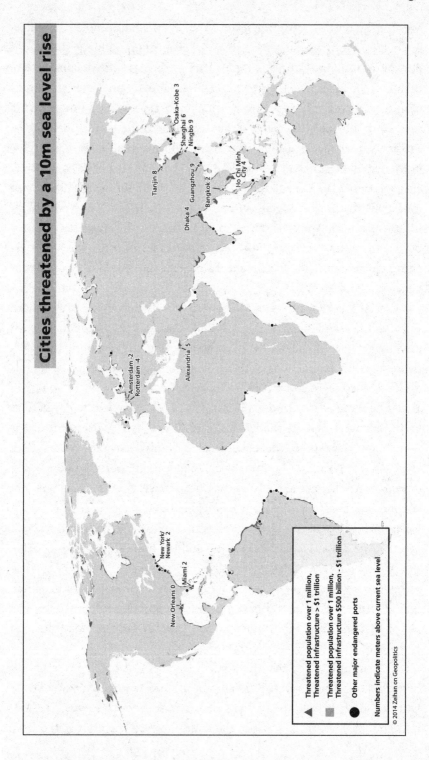

Cities threatened by a 10m sea level rise

Osaka-Kobe 3
Shanghai 6
Ningbo 9
Ho Chi Minh City 4
Tianjin 8
Guangzhou 9
Bangkok 2
Dhaka 4
Amsterdam -2
Rotterdam -4
Alexandria 5
New York/ Newark 2
Miami 2
New Orleans 0

Threatened population over 1 million,
Threatened infrastructure > $1 trillion

Threatened population over 1 million,
Threatened infrastructure $500 billion - $1 trillion

Other major endangered ports

Numbers indicate meters above current sea level

© 2014 Zeihan on Geopolitics

nowhere to go but France. Southern Italy's population would likely flee en masse north into the Po valley. Australian agriculture, most of which is located upon marginal land, could simply disappear, leaving much (more) of the continent empty. Brazil would see nearly all of its ports of significance reclaimed by the sea, forcing its small coastal populations inland and largely walling the country off from the world.

By far the biggest loser among the major players would be China. The industrialized regions of the greater Tianjin, Shanghai, and Hong Kong regions are less than sixteen feet above sea level. The agricultural belts that surround Tianjin and Shanghai are also microclimates, existing in only very tight ranges of latitude, longitude, and elevation. Even a small change in climatic variance could drastically impact the productivity of lands that exist under a fairly strict monoculture of either rice or wheat. These regions in question account for some two-thirds of Chinese export activity. And most of the 100 million Chinese who live in the threatened areas would have nowhere to go but inland into the North China Plain, an area that will already be facing extreme political and economic stress.

Appendix II Demography and Trade

Demography and Trade

	population (millions)		Median Age (years)					increase in median age from 2015 (years)			life expectancy, 2015 (years)	% of GDP from trade (2012)	
	2015	2025	2015	2020	2025	2030	2040	2025	2030	2040	2015	exports	imports
Germany	80.9	79.2	46.5	47.8	48.1	48.5	49.5	1.6	2.0	3.0	81	41	34
Japan	126.9	123.4	46.5	48.6	50.8	52.6	55.2	4.3	6.1	8.7	85	13	15
Italy	61.9	62.6	44.8	46.5	48.0	49.0	49.8	3.2	4.2	5.0	82	26	25
Spain	48.1	51.4	42.0	43.9	45.7	47.2	48.7	3.7	5.2	6.7	82	22	25
Canada	35.1	37.6	41.8	42.7	43.5	44.3	45.7	1.7	2.5	3.9	82	26	26
France	66.6	68.9	41.1	41.7	42.3	42.8	43.4	1.2	1.7	2.3	82	21	26
Korea	49.1	49.4	40.8	43.2	45.7	48.3	52.1	4.9	7.5	11.3	80	48	46
U.K.	64.1	67.2	40.4	40.6	41.1	41.9	43.1	0.7	1.5	2.7	81	20	28
Poland	38.3	37.3	39.9	42.0	44.2	46.6	50.4	4.3	6.7	10.5	77	37	39
Russia	142.4	140.1	39.1	40.3	42.0	44.0	46.6	2.9	4.9	7.5	70	26	16
Australia	22.8	25.1	38.4	39.1	39.9	40.7	42.1	1.5	2.3	3.7	82	16	16
U.S.	322.4	351.4	37.3	38.3	38.9	39.6	40.4	1.6	2.3	3.1	79	11	14
China	1362	1395	37.0	38.6	40.6	42.9	47.2	3.6	5.9	10.2	75	29	35
Thailand	68.0	69.6	36.7	39.0	41.1	42.8	46.1	4.4	6.1	9.4	74	60	65
Brazil	204.3	218.3	31.1	33.2	35.1	36.9	40.3	4.0	5.8	9.2	74	11	10
Turkey	82.5	90.5	30.0	31.8	33.5	35.2	38.5	3.5	5.2	8.5	77	19	30
Indonesia	256.0	276.7	29.6	31.1	32.7	34.4	37.8	3.1	4.8	8.2	73	22	22
Mexico	118.7	130.2	27.6	29.3	31.0	32.7	36.1	3.4	5.1	8.5	77	31	31
India	1252	1396	27.3	28.7	30.2	31.8	34.7	2.9	4.5	7.4	68	15	26

Percent of population aged 20-39						
	2010	2015	2020	2025	2030	2040
Japan	25.0	22.4	20.9	20.0	19.5	18.8
Germany	24.0	23.5	23.4	22.6	21.5	20.6
Italy	26.0	23.7	22.2	21.4	21.3	20.8
France	25.5	24.0	23.6	23.4	23.4	24.0
Canada	26.6	26.4	25.6	24.6	23.7	23.7
UK	26.4	26.3	26.2	25.3	24.6	24.9
Spain	30.0	26.3	23.4	22.2	22.3	22.4
Poland	31.4	30.4	27.4	23.7	21.7	20.8
Australia	28.6	28.0	27.7	27.0	26.2	25.5
U.S.	26.8	26.9	26.4	25.8	25.4	25.5
Russia	31.5	30.2	27.3	24.3	22.2	24.4
Korea	30.3	28.6	27.3	24.7	22.9	18.4
China	32.8	30.8	29.5	27.3	24.0	22.5
Thailand	25.1	30.9	29.0	27.1	25.5	22.3
Brazil	33.4	32.7	31.8	30.5	29.1	26.2
Turkey	33.3	32.4	31.6	30.2	29.3	27.4
Mexico	32.4	31.7	30.9	30.1	28.9	27.8
Indonesia	33.1	31.6	30.7	30.1	29.6	27.4
India	32.4	32.2	31.9	31.6	31.0	29.6

Percent of population aged 60 and up					
	2010	2015	2020	2025	2040
Japan	30.6	33.4	35.1	39.0	43.9
Germany	26.1	27.9	30.2	35.9	36.4
Italy	26.2	27.1	28.5	33.3	36.9
France	22.9	24.9	26.5	29.6	31.0
Canada	21.4	24.1	27.0	30.8	31.8
UK	22.3	23.1	24.3	27.7	28.5
Spain	22.2	23.1	24.5	29.3	35.2
Poland	19.4	22.6	25.8	28.8	34.0
Australia	19.4	21.1	22.8	25.3	27.1
U.S.	18.6	20.3	22.4	25.0	26.0
Russia	18.1	20.0	22.6	25.8	28.9
Korea	15.6	18.5	23.0	31.7	38.5
China	12.9	15.7	17.7	25.1	30.3
Thailand	12.4	14.6	17.8	24.6	30.6
Brazil	10.0	11.6	13.6	18.1	22.7
Turkey	9.3	10.6	12.2	16.3	20.9
Mexico	9.3	10.3	12.3	16.3	19.3
Indonesia	8.8	10.2	12.0	15.8	21
India	8.2	9.1	10.2	13.2	16.7

Sources: U.S. Census and World Bank

© 2014 Zeihan on Geopolitics

Acknowledgments

It took a village to raise this idiot.

Meet some of the villagers:

At the corner of Unflinching Accuracy and Dogged Persistence live the fact-checkers Matt Powers and Melissa Taylor, who have done an admirable job of preventing me from looking the fool. That classy ranch-style home is the aerie of the ever energetic researcher-goddess Athena Selim, who has seen me through this and oh-so-many other projects.

Over in the hip part of town the graphic artists are busy graffitiing up the place. Alf Pardo is the master of the all-in-one concept graphics, Adam Smith makes overlapping webworks of details absorbable at a glance, while Benjamin Sledge can turn the web into an expression of art—and even make numbers look pretty.

The sprawling campus that is part kindergarten rec room, part think tank, part *Hunger Games* death match is the private intelligence firm Stratfor, my home for twelve years. The intellectual dynamism of the place certainly helped forge many of the concepts within this book (while mercilessly incinerating many others). Never before (or again, I fear) will I be part of a bizarrely beautiful and wonderfully terrible team of savants.

Nestled in a far more respectable neighborhood resides the chain of contacts who made *The Accidental Superpower* real. Barrett Cordero at BigSpeak helped me bootstrap myself as a professional public speaker and forwarded me to Carolyn Monaco of Monaco Associates for assistance with publicity. Carolyn found me Jud Laghi of the Jud Laghi Agency to explore the idea of producing a book, and Jud linked me up with Sean Desmond at Hachette's Twelve imprint where the book took flight. So many (many) thanks to Barrett for taking the initial risk on me, Carolyn for her patience with my stratospherically impressive noncommand of all things PR-related, Jud for knowing precisely where to look, and Sean for making this whole thing actually happen.

I also owe endless thanks to you the reader, whose interest makes pretty much everything I do possible. A few of you—some more directly than others—have hinted that some of the graphics in *The Accidental Superpower* don't exactly pop in black and white. I've done what I can in this edition to re-saturate for clarity. For those where the gray-on-gray might still not make the grade, I've posted full-color versions on my site. They can be found here: http://zeihan.com/maps.

And as with most idiots, I live at the edge of town with the only person both suitably stable to talk me down and suitably odd to put up with me on a sustained basis, Wayne Watters.

Index

Page numbers in *italics* refer to maps and charts.

About the Author

Peter Zeihan has lived in the world of international affairs throughout his fifteen-year career. He launched his own firm, Zeihan on Geopolitics, in 2012 in order to specialize in customized executive briefings for his clients. Before going independent, Zeihan worked for twelve years with the geopolitical analysis firm Stratfor, where he was vice president of analysis. He is a frequent contributor in the media, and has been covered in the *New York Times*, the *Washington Post*, *Forbes*, the Associated Press, Bloomberg News, CNN, CNBC, Fox News, O'Reilly, National Public Radio, Market-Watch, and others.